Airpower for
Strategic Effect

Air University Series on
Airpower and National Security

Divining Victory
by William M. Arkin (2007)

The Quest for Relevant Air Power
by Christian F. Anrig (2011)

Airpower for Strategic Effect
by Colin S. Gray (2012)

Bomber: The Formation and Early Years
of Strategic Air Command
by Phillip S. Meilinger (forthcoming)

Airpower for Strategic Effect

Colin S. Gray

Air University Press
Air Force Research Institute
Maxwell Air Force Base, Alabama

February 2012

Library of Congress Cataloging-in-Publication Data

Gray, Colin S.
   Airpower for strategic effect / Colin S. Gray.
      p. cm.
   Includes bibliographical references and index.
   ISBN 978-1-58566-218-0
1. Air power. 2. Air power—United States. I. Title.
   UG630.G75 2011
   358.4'03--dc23

                                                            2011035404

AIR FORCE RESEARCH INSTITUTE

Air University Press
Air Force Research Institute
155 North Twining Street
Maxwell AFB, AL 36112-6026
http://aupress.au.af.mil

This book is dedicated to the memory of my father, William "Bill" Gray, who said that the proudest moment of his life was when he was awarded his "wings" in the RAF in 1943.

Contents

Foreword

The 12 years that spanned the first Persian Gulf War of 1991 and the three weeks of major combat in Operation Iraqi Freedom in 2003 were a triumphal time for American airpower. By the end of that eventful period, featuring five successful air-dominated campaigns that also included Operations Deliberate Force, Allied Force, and Enduring Freedom, America's air weapon could be fairly said to have matured in its ability to deliver repeatedly the sorts of outcome-determining results that airpower's pioneer theoreticians had foreseen generations before.

The ensuing years since that unbroken chain of successes, however, have entailed a different mode of combat and, as a result, a less-preeminent role for airpower. During the more recent period, the sorts of high-end challenges that prompted America's aerial involvements from 1991 to 2003 have been displaced, at least for the time being, by lower-intensity counterinsurgency operations in which the air input, while no less important than before as a shaper of events, has taken a secondary role to ground troops as the starring force element. In the eyes of many, this shift in the character of Washington's latest combat involvements has cast air operations in general, and the US Air Force in particular, in a decidedly subordinate role. Not only that, it has been said by some to have had the pernicious effect of inclining many younger Air Force Airmen who have been exposed to no other form of operational commitment during their relatively short time in the ranks to infer from their limited experience that their service's main purpose is to support land warfare by US Army and Marine Corps combatants. In its worst extreme, the changed nature of today's engagements and the consequent lower profile maintained by airpower in them has led more than a few to ask why the United States even needs an independent Air Force any more.

In this magisterial *tour d'horizon* of the air weapon's steady rise in effectiveness since its fledgling days, Colin Gray, a prolific strategist of long-standing scholarly achievement and international repute, has rightly taken a long view of today's pattern of regional conflict by appraising airpower in the broader context in which its operational payoff will ultimately be registered. His careful development of airpower's "strategic narrative," as he calls it, shows convincingly how the relative criticality of the air weapon in joint warfare is neither universal nor unchanging but rather is crucially dependent on the particular circumstances of a confrontation.

More to the point, viewed situationally, airpower can be everything from single-handedly decisive to largely irrelevant to a combatant commander's needs, depending on his most pressing challenges of the moment. Because its relative import, like that of all other force elements, hinges directly on how its comparative advantages relate to a commander's most immediate here-and-now concerns, airpower does not disappoint when it is not the main producer of desired outcomes. Indeed, the idea that airpower should be able to perform effectively in all forms of combat unaided by other force elements is both an absurd measure of its operational merit and a baseless arguing point that its most outspoken advocates, from Giulio Douhet and Billy Mitchell onward, have done their cause a major disservice by misguidedly espousing over many decades. Although the air weapon today may have been temporarily overshadowed by more land-centric forms of force employment, given the kinds of lower-intensity conflicts that the United States and its allies have been obliged to contend with in recent years, there will most assuredly be future times when new challenges yet to arise will again test America's air posture to the fullest extent of its deterrent and combat potential.

Professor Gray's central theme is that airpower generates strategic effect. More specifically, he maintains, airpower is a tactical equity that operates—ideally—with strategic consequences. To him, "strategic" does not inhere in the equity's physical characteristics, such as an aircraft's range or payload, but rather in what it can do by way of producing desired results. From his perspective, a strategic effect is, first and foremost, that which enables outcome-determining results. And producing such results is quintessentially the stock in trade of American airpower as it has progressively evolved since Vietnam.

Airpower for Strategic Effect offers an uncommonly thoughtful application of informed intellect to an explanation of how modern air warfare capabilities should be understood. Along the way, it puts forward a roster of observations about the air weapon that warrant careful reflection by all who would presume to find it wanting. Among the most notable of those observations are that context rules in every case and that whether airpower should be regarded as supported by or supporting of other force elements is not a question that can ever have a single answer for all time. Rather, as noted above, the answer will hinge invariably on the unique conditions of any given conflict.

It naturally follows that whenever airpower has been said to have "failed," it has only been because more was expected of it than it could deliver. *Any* tool can appear deficient if used unwisely or irresponsibly. And as both the United States and Israel have experienced in their most recent airpower applications, even the most robust and capable air weapon can never be more effective than the strategy it is intended to support.

On the strength of this teaching, perhaps the single most helpful service air warfare professionals can perform for their cause is to underpromise and overdeliver as a matter of standard practice. In this regard, Professor Gray repeatedly voices a stern reminder that a long history of overpromising on the part of airpower's most vocal proponents has needlessly sold the air weapon short for what it is actually able to deliver to joint force commanders today—and not just in high-intensity combat, but in *all* forms of operations across the conflict spectrum.

The purpose of this book is not to extol airpower but to make coherent sense of it by providing insights into it that are both timeless and policy useful. For those among its readers who are serving airmen worldwide, the greatest value that its considered appreciation of the air weapon can offer is to help them think more reflectively about their calling and, in turn, to articulate its foundational principles more effectively in the councils of war planning. For woven throughout it is a remarkably compelling explication of what modern airpower entails in its most inner strategic essence. The ultimate aim of that explication is to improve the real-world *practice* of airpower by operators at all levels most responsible for its effective use.

BENJAMIN S. LAMBETH
Senior Research Associate, RAND Corporation
Author, *The Transformation of American Air Power*

About the
Author

Colin S. Gray is a political scientist with broad interests in national security policy, strategic theory, and military history. Educated at the University of Manchester (BA, economics, 1965) and at Lincoln College, Oxford University (DPhil, international politics, 1970), he is professor of international politics and strategic studies at the University of Reading, England, and a senior fellow at the National Institute for Public Policy, Fairfax, Virginia. He holds dual UK/US citizenship.

Dr. Gray has taught at the Universities of Lancaster (UK), York (Toronto, Canada), and British Columbia (Vancouver, Canada). He served as executive secretary of the Strategic Studies Commission at the Canadian Institute of International Affairs (Toronto) and as assistant director of the International Institute for Strategic Studies (London). In 1981 he was founding president of the National Institute for Public Policy.

From 1982 until 1987 Dr. Gray served on the President's General Advisory Committee on Arms Control and Disarmament. In April 1987 he was presented the Superior Public Service Award by the US Department of the Navy. In 1997–98 he served on the Panel of Experts on the UK Strategic Defence Review.

Dr. Gray is a member of the editorial boards of *Comparative Strategy*, *Journal of Strategic Studies*, *Strategic Studies Quarterly*, *Naval War College Review*, and *Journal of Terrorism and Organised Crime* (UN). He has served on advisory panels for the Congressional Office of Technology Assessment (strategic defense initiative and space weapons), the Department of the Army (tactical nuclear weapons), the Department of the Air Force (innovations), and the US Space Command (future of space forces).

Books previously published by Dr. Gray include *Canadian Defence Priorities* (1972); *The Soviet-American Arms Race* (1976); *The MX ICBM and National Security* (1981); *Strategic Studies and Public Policy* (1982); *Strategic Studies: A Critical Assessment* (1982); *American Military Space Policy* (1983); *Nuclear Strategy and National Style* (1986); *The Geopolitics of Super Power* (1988); *War, Peace, and Victory: Strategy and Statecraft for the Next Century* (1990); *House of Cards: Why Arms Control Must Fail* (1992); *The Leverage of Sea Power: The Strategic Advantage of Navies in War* (1992); *Weapons Don't Make War: Policy, Strategy and Technology* (1993); *The Navy in the Post–Cold War World* (1994); *Explorations in Strategy* (1996); *Modern Strategy* (1999); *The Second Nuclear Age* (1999); *Strategy for Chaos: Revolutions in Military Affairs and the Evidence of History* (2002); *The Sheriff: America's Defense of the New World Order* (2004); *Another Bloody Century: Future Warfare* (2005); *Strategy and History: Essays on Theory and Practice* (2006); *War, Peace, and International Relations: An Introduction to Strategic History* (2007); *Fighting Talk: Forty Maxims on War, Peace, and Strategy* (2007); *National Security Dilemmas: Challenges and Opportunities* (2009); and his most recent major book of strategic theory, *The Strategy Bridge: Theory for Practice* (2010).

Dr. Gray has published many articles in such journals as *Foreign Affairs, Foreign Policy, Survival, Bulletin of the Atomic Scientists, Wilson Quarterly, Washington Quarterly, The National Interest*, and *International Security*. He has lectured on defense and foreign affairs in Europe and North America, as well as in China, Israel, and Australia. Dr. Gray is interested in the theory and practice of strategy, the dialogue between policy and military force, and the value of historical experience for the education of policy makers.

Preface

Airpower for Strategic Effect is intended to contribute to the understanding of airpower—what it is, what it does, why it does it, and what the consequences are. This is the plot: airpower generates strategic effect. Airpower's product is strategic effect on the course of strategic history. Everything about military airpower is instrumental to the purpose of securing strategic effect.

To adapt a familiar saying for my particular purpose, "they cannot airpower know, who only know airpower." I have attempted to explain airpower strategically, partly because that was my mission, but also because I am a strategic theorist and defense analyst and I cannot approach airpower in any other way. There is a whole library of books about airpower, some of them of high merit and with deservedly substantial reputations. When I began my research on this subject, my main anxiety was that I might find that everything worth saying had been said already. On reflection, I suspect that just about everything that needs saying has been said already, many times over. However, the strategic story of airpower and some useful distillation of that narrative in an adequate formulation of airpower theory, I found to be lacking. So, with an all too genuine humility and respect for past authors of airpower history and theory, I proceeded to attempt to provide what I believe is needed—a well enough evidenced theory of airpower.

The challenge has not been so much to explain airpower itself strategically; rather has it been to locate airpower in the contexts that must give it meaning and purpose. Given that states do not purchase airpower as an end in itself, one has to explain the benefits of airpower ownership and operation in relation to the demands placed upon it and within the framework provided by the competitive nature of strategy. My background and personal preferences, understanding of the subject, and purpose in this endeavor combined to suggest the story arc.

Summarily, this book proceeds as follows: the first three chapters establish airpower strategically in the context of the general theory of strategy, which itself has meaning strictly within a political context. These chapters also relate airpower to the variably joint story of all of the armed forces. The next block of chapters, five of them, seeks to provide a historical evidential base on airpower in strategic history. What follows is the "payoff" chapter (number 9), the one that presents the theory of airpower. The concluding chapter is terse in its offering of broad judgments on the whole subject. So the story arc moves from theory, through history, back to a more specific theory, and is rounded off with conclusions.

There may well be nothing new in this work, but the familiar is assembled in an original way. I have not striven to be different for its own sake, but neither have I shrunk from deviating from some of the more strongly held views about airpower that enjoy distinguished provenance and longevity. From the outset I decided that airpower did not require me to compose a hymn of praise; what it appeared to need was better explanation and understanding. I soon discovered that the airpower story has been and remains strategically superior to the tale that many of its more devoted advocates have managed to tell. As a result of promising too much, airpower spokespeople actually have promised too little for what they have delivered. Airpower has been undersold in good part because some among its more dedicated promoters have exaggerated what did not require exaggeration, and—most damaging of all—because they chose to advertise their product in a way that ignored or shortchanged much of what it was, did, and could do. Airpower theory has not been well enough served by its theorists. Some readers may be shocked, irritated at least, by a few of the liberties that I have taken with some hardcore airpower beliefs (for example, the items of faith that hold some airpower to be inherently strategic and the belief that airpower is naturally an offensive weapon). Aside from the demands of logic and historical evidence, I am more than modestly aware of the difficulty of explaining airpower in strategic terms to those among us who are not particularly air-minded.

Readers may discover that, possibly because I am Anglo-American (legally, if not culturally entirely both), there is more RAF in this work than is usual to see, though I believe that this fact is explained adequately simply by the historical record of airpower's first half-century and not by reference to any personal affiliation of mine. In addition, readers are certain to find here more general strategic theory than they are used to. Such an accurate appreciation is explained by my effort to situate the strategic history and theory of airpower properly in its context so that the full, though relative, merit of its contributions could be recognized properly.

Some readers will be less than happy that their favorite episodes in airpower history are either ignored or given short shrift. All I can do is apologize but explain that I have not sought to tell the airpower historical story for its own sake. Rather have I tried only to provide a sufficiency of empirical evidence, such that the theory of airpower can be derived and presented with some plausible claim to authority and credibility. Admittedly, the five strategic history chapters often fly a perilous track between, on the one hand, near anecdotal level of historical illustration and, on the other hand, full throttle historical narrative. It is possible that at times I may have veered too far toward one category of peril or the other, in which case, mea culpa! In explanation, all I can argue is that decisions for exclusion had to be made, even for a study as lengthy as this.

Finally, it is my pleasure to thank the many friends and colleagues who helped me tackle this forbidding task. I am very pleased to express my thanks to Dr. Dan Mortensen at the Air Force Research Institute, who has maintained faith in this project. His support and encouragement have been exemplary as well as essential. Next, I must state my gratitude to Col M. V. "Coyote" Smith, USAF, who helped me far above and beyond what any doctoral supervisor has a right to hope for. In addition, Dr. James Kiras of the School of Advanced Air and Space Studies (SAASS) has been outstanding in his friendship and support. When needed, Dr. John B. Sheldon, also of SAASS, has ridden rapidly and willingly to my assistance. By way of scholarly debt, I am especially grateful to Dr. Benjamin S. Lambeth of RAND, who also just happens to be one of my oldest friends, since we first met in Washington as graduate students more years ago than I care to recall.

And, penultimately but not least, I am entirely delighted to thank my long-standing, long-suffering, but blessedly good-natured manuscript preparer, Barbara Watts—who undertook a manuscript interpretation mission against long odds on success. The final note of thanks goes to my ever enduring family, Valerie and Tonia (plus pets), who flew many a hazardous sortie with me before this project was safely concluded.

COLIN S. GRAY

Chapter 1

Airpower: A Contested Narrative

Airpower is and long has been the sharpest of America's swords, as well as a highly versatile set of tools for the support of national strategy—both grand and of course military. The latter claim today is uncontested, indeed incontestable. The former, obviously, is a situational truth. Sharp swords are not always at a military premium; it is a matter of context; demands vary. More than a century on from the dawn of the air age, one might expect the inevitable and anticipatable uncertainties of technical immaturity to have been replaced by a confident consensus over at least the more significant, assuredly the more basic, issues pertaining to airpower. Alas, although the theory and practice of airpower have filled the century past with an air ocean of words, frequently strident, and a historical record crammed with deeds and arguable misdeeds, the meaning of it all as one attempts to assess it today is no simple matter to grasp and sustains a commanding grip.

The world is well stocked with people who genuinely are deeply knowledgeable about some features of airpower, but it is much less populated with those who have a plausible claim to understand airpower's strategic narrative. What has been, what is, and what is expected with some confidence to be the strategic story of airpower? It is not sufficient to offer by way of a would-be dismissive rebuttal the obvious point that the airpower story is ever on the move—it is dynamic. How much historical dynamism should suffice for theorists and historians to control this undergoverned space? It seems to this theorist that a century of airpower history and thought and their complex and contestable relationship ought to be enough. Moreover, the historical record suggests strongly that the onward and sometimes seemingly sideways, even backward, erratic march of airpower-relevant events will yield only fresh fuel for controversy, not some conclusive revelation. If this argument is deemed plausible, there is no definitive epiphany waiting in the future to cast light in places that currently are in shadow. The character of airpower's strategic narrative is always moving but not, this study suggests strongly, its nature.

The hard words offered above may appear, in fact may well be, seriously ungenerous to the efforts of hundreds, nay thousands, of people—uniformed airmen (persons), scholars, and others[1]—who have labored energetically to understand, explain, predict, and advocate for excellent reasons on the subject of airpower. This text must hasten to claim only a serious dissatisfaction with the state of the theory and historical assessment of airpower. Far from being critical of particular theorists, historians, and other commentators, this author is deeply appreciative of what has been done. Even though scholars engage in much bloodless combat, scholarship generally advances—sometimes over the wounded or slain texts of injured or newly unfashionable ideas. Rejected or at least revised ideas are necessary for the advance of understanding. Since such advance is by no means necessarily linear and progressive, it is not wholly inappropriate to borrow the notion of seasonal change to help explain the history of theory. Those especially attracted to apparent novelty can be amazed to discover just how little of great importance affecting politics, statecraft, peace, war, warfare, and strategy really changes. The nature of these enduring categories of thought and behavior is as persisting as their character is ever shifting. This is why Greek, Roman, ancient Chinese, and early nineteenth-century Prussians can still speak to us meaningfully—across time, language, and culture—in terms that we find educational and useful.[2]

The instrumental purpose of this book is to revisit the theory and practice of airpower and offer a fresh reconceptualization and historical understanding to reveal the strategic narrative of airpower—past, present, and future. The intent is to move forward with the classics and would-be classics of theory where possible and away from them when necessary. The true purpose of this work is to contribute to a better strategic understanding of airpower to improve the practice of airpower. For reasons that will be made abundantly plain, possibly beyond the point of tedium for some readers, we shall insist that strategic theory has as its sole purpose the improvement of strategic practice. Such theory is not an end in itself.

Approach

In one respect, at least, this book serves the same goal as does Carl von Clausewitz's *On War*: Both are explicitly and unashamedly educational in purpose and approach. The great man tells us that

> theory exists so that one need not start afresh each time sorting out the material and plowing through it, but will find it ready to hand and in good order. It

is meant to educate the mind of the future commander, or more accurately, to guide him in his self-education, not to accompany him to the battlefield; just as a wise teacher guides and stimulates a young man's intellectual development, but is careful not to lead him by the hand for the rest of his life.[3]

Clausewitz also advises that

the primary purpose of any theory is to classify concepts and ideas that have become, as it were, confused and entangled. Not until terms and concepts have been defined can one hope to make any progress in examining the question clearly and simply and expect the reader to share one's views. Tactics and strategy are two activities that permeate one another in time and space but are nevertheless essentially different. Their inherent laws and mutual relationship cannot be understood without a total comprehension of both.[4]

The approach adopted here, following Clausewitz in key respects, is to revisit the whole subject of airpower without fear or favor. No effort is expended in advancing particular positions on current and anticipated near-term issues. Contemporary controversies are featured only when they address issues that persist over time and reveal arguments of unusual importance. In the footsteps of the master, this theorist is concerned strictly to help people sort out those matters that need sorting, so they will be better equipped to provide right enough answers to the challenges of the day.

Similarly, these pages privilege and respect strategic theory as a guide to those who are charged with strategic practice. Basic airpower (or should it be air and space?) doctrine—even, supposedly, "basic" doctrine—is always in transition. This analysis does not seek to engage directly with current airpower doctrine, because to do so instantly dates the text, thereby guaranteeing rapid obsolescence, and inevitably would be unduly restrictive in its national focus. The United States currently is the world's leading air power, a status it has enjoyed since, plausibly, mid-to-late 1943. However, airpower and American airpower are not and have never been synonymous. While the argument here attends primarily and unapologetically to American airpower, this main thrust is never disassociated from its several contexts. Indeed, an apparently dominant military force cannot afford to be entirely disdainful of much lesser forces. Relatively minor armies, navies, and air forces—and now space and cyber forces also—may well be, by standard metrics, of scant account. But strength of motivation, cunning, and skill can enable materially inferior belligerents to compete and, in extremis, to wage warfare by asymmetric methods that can embarrass the superior party severely.[5] Moreover, different polities choose to exercise their airpower options in distinctive ways. National styles differ in the exploitation of airpower, even when proceeding from a substantially common technological base. It is all too natural for air-minded Americans to be interested overwhelmingly in American airpower. But prudence suggests that they need to be scarcely less concerned with how actual and potential rivals and enemies cast their semi-independent votes in the duel that is basic to the enduring nature and structure of politics and strategy.

The scope of this inquiry embraces four principles that command obedience to Michael Howard's demand that military history should be studied in "width, depth, and context."[6] The four are the injunctions that airpower cannot sensibly be reassessed (1) *only* as American airpower (the point made above), (2) *only* as the assets of air forces, (3) *only* as fixed- or swing-wing aircraft (and particularly as fast jets), and (4) *only* as it and its problems are manifested today. Without excuse or apology this book has the contemporary and future roles and strategic value of the US Air Force (USAF) of the early twenty-first century as the core of its interest and the focus of its educational endeavor. But that core and focus can be served adequately only if Howard's insistence upon study in width, depth, and context is taken seriously.

This study is committed to an effort to reset the theory of airpower, with much gratitude to the mighty labors of those many theorists who have provided the intellectual capital with which one can work today. Some readers are likely to be irritated, however, by my unwillingness to yield to current authority on conceptual matters. Lest the point is insufficiently clear, this book seeks to develop *theory* for the practice of airpower; it is not at all interested in debating current doctrine. The educational mission of this text is to help sharpen the ability of readers themselves to engage in such debate. Also, it must be said, there is no intention here to be different simply for the mindless purpose of being different. Much of orthodox airpower thinking in authoritative (American) air (and space) power doctrine is thoroughly praiseworthy, as we shall demonstrate.

The plan of attack for this study allows this chapter to set the scene—prepare the battlespace, as it were—by specifying the purpose and scope of the inquiry, defining key terms and concepts, and identifying challenges and explaining their significance. Chapters 2 and 3 provide the theoretical architecture needed for the narrative to proceed with discipline into the historical record of the great chain of logic and behavior which is the practice of airpower. These chapters locate airpower, first, in theory in relation to practice and, second, in geography among the five geophysically distinctive environments for warfare. Having erected the building that is theory and then identified and connected the geographies of battlespace, the narrative provides an analytical survey of the historical record of airpower in chapters 4 through 8. These vital chapters proceed, respectively, from the sands of Tripoli in 1911 to Tokyo Bay in 1945 and from that place and moment of maximum, if ominous, triumph for airpower to the undergoverned tribal area encompassing both sides of the Pakistani-Afghan border in 2010. Those who reasonably might question the necessity of revisiting familiar historical material should be reassured to learn that this theorist asked himself exactly this question. The answer is beyond serious contention. People think and argue very much by historical analogy, whether or not the analogies are apt. Attitudes and opinions on contemporary airpower issues are colored by the "lessons" that people believe we should draw from the history that they assert is relevant. At this early juncture we shall not detain the text with a critical assessment of the perils and pitfalls of argument by analogy. We accept simply that analogies are unavoidable and can matter crucially, even in current debate about the issues of today and tomorrow. It follows that this book must not even appear to shy away from airpower's past. We do insist, though, that the distinction never be lost between airpower's *past*, which is to say the actual record, and airpower's *history(ies)*, which by contrast refers to what historians of frequently conflicting persuasions claim happened.

The past record of airpower—its influence upon history, to borrow from Alfred Thayer Mahan—provides the lion's share of the candidate evidence from which theory, doctrine, and materiel decisions in the present derive most of their authority.[7] If one chooses to neglect or reject past deeds and misdeeds, by default one must lean upon anticipation, prediction, and hope duly packaged by deductive reasoning. It so happens that, far from being a well-settled zone of intellectual consensus, the past or history of airpower is exceptionally controversial in its strategic meaning. The facts are not much in dispute any longer, but judicious understanding of the relative strength of airpower's contribution to the course of strategic history from 1911 to the present is a realm of seemingly permanent controversy. For us to advance understanding, it is essential for airpower's century of activity to be examined in some width, depth, and context—an enterprise that would be truly heroic as a mission for five chapters were it not for the excellent work by historians upon which this theorist can draw gratefully.

Deploying the conceptual tools developed in chapters 2 and 3, and armed with the historical analysis provided in chapters 4 through 8, chapter 9 assembles, even compounds, the preceding analyses of conceptual, historical matters with reference to some contemporary issues and specifies an ambitious new, certainly revised, formulation of airpower theory. This theory is adapted for and to the complexities of the strategic context today and fully reflects changes in the strategic environment. No less important than change, however, is recognition of continuities, indeed of enduring truths. Finally, chapter 10 extracts from all that has gone before the key elements in the persisting strategic narrative of airpower.

This is a work of theory, but because it is about strategic theory, it must also be a work about strategic practice. The connections between theory and practice, between ideas and behavior, are much more intimate than typically is recognized.[8] Although the discussion strives to maintain a proper scholarly detachment, there can be no denying the possibly biasing influence of the author's interest in American airpower. Enculturation is beneficial for empathy and understanding but tends not to be so healthy for reliability of judgment. Since enculturation is unavoidable and scholars of strategy are concerned about a pragmatic subject in which they cannot help but have some personal stake, the possibility of bias must be admitted. Strategic theorists and historians who address contemporary topics are unable to evade the pushes and pulls that are inalienable from the role of participant-observer. Our modern historians of the Roman Empire should be unsullied by a personal stake in the struggles that they study. Alas for them, though, their feet are unmuddied by firsthand experience of their subject. They cannot even visit ancient Rome as tourists, Hollywood and escorted tours notwithstanding.

What Is Airpower? An Open Question Still

Definitions are neither true nor false. They are chosen for convenience. Moreover, choice of wording in defining an important concept is always likely to reflect a number of motives, among which clarity for ease of communication need not be dominant. Given that airpower is not a branch of philosophy, that those who theorize about it are not and have never been philosophers, and that the multidimensional stakes are high in the ongoing competition over airpower's definition, it is scarcely surprising that reason has never ruled in its regard. This is not to accuse anyone or any institution necessarily of incompetence or falsehood, though there has been plenty of both. Rather the point is that airpower is a thoroughly political subject—no less in its evolving definition—with the practical implications of that in its strategic meaning. To state the matter directly, Clausewitz rules! War and preparation for war are pervasively political—and by logical implication, peace also—including the contribution of airpower to all these weighty concerns. As the great man said, and we should never hesitate to repeat, with full understanding, "It is clear, consequently, that war is not a mere act of policy but a true political instrument, a continuation of political activity by other means."[9] By logical extension, the military instrument for war (and peace) is in a vital sense also a political instrument. Furthermore, politics is about power, and politics is about who gets what, when, how—and what they do with it. Airpower, indeed military power writ large, is not a pristine, politics-free entity or idea, no matter what myth, legend, or some occasional pure professional intention may seek to insist. For excellent and easily understandable reasons, the whole history of airpower, in all countries, has been suffused with political intentions, meaning, and consequences. To deny this is to make some reluctant and more-than-faintly distasteful admissions. To do otherwise is simply to recognize the world as it is and always has been. Although some crusaders for airpower define themselves as disciples of a true faith committed wholly to the advancement of The Truth for entirely unselfish reasons, the plain fact is that even The Truth has to be advanced by politics of both a low as well as a more respectable kind. The reason is obvious. The stakes in the ongoing, though only sometimes politically bitter, debate over airpower issues could hardly be higher. Careers, personalities, and national security play in the argument.

Airpower has always lent itself to conceptualization that was eminently challengeable on technical, geographical, political, and logical grounds; not that logic could cope at all well with the genuine complexity of the evolving subject. It is ironic that the strategic success of airpower is the core reason for the common difficulty in defining,

hence understanding, managing, and employing it. The very attrac-
tiveness of airpower itself is the principal source of the near-universal
confusion, uncertainty, and bitter arguments that have characterized
its short strategic history. A little reflection soon reveals that there are
good if not altogether persuasive reasons why most attitudes toward
airpower and its meaning, value, proper ownership, and seniority relative to other forms of military power have some merit. Decisions need
to be made as to definition, ownership, and relative strategic value,
and this text does not shy from making them, but whatever choices
one makes, it is essential to appreciate that rival positions are not beyond justification.

Lest I attract the charge of scholasticism, I must claim that the chosen definition of airpower really matters. It is not a concern for strictly
empirical, let alone deductive, and logical choice. Severe critics of
language selected primarily for the purpose of seizing and holding
contestable, certainly contested, capabilities are apt to be blind to the
fact that airpower sensibly is many things to different people with
distinctive prime concerns. Before risking confusion with identification of the complexity of our subject, we will provide a deceptively
simple definition of airpower proffered by Brig Gen William "Billy"
Mitchell: "Air power may be defined as the ability to do something in
the air. It consists of transporting all sorts of things by aircraft from
one place to another, and as air covers the whole world there is no
place that is immune from influence by aircraft."[10] A few pages later,
Mitchell drives home his central points with useful repetition: "But
what, it may be asked, is air power? Air power is the ability to do
something in or through the air, and, as the air covers the whole
world, aircraft are able to go anywhere on the planet."[11]

Mitchell's definition is not beyond criticism nor entirely satisfactory, but he is right enough. Indeed, his imperfect wording remains
by far the most useful definition of airpower that anyone has drafted
in a hundred years. Given that Mitchell was not especially gifted—let
alone original—as a theorist of airpower, his achievement in rough-
and-ready, highly inclusive definition merits much celebration. Like
Japanese operational art in World War II and some social scientific
methodologies today, the culminating point of victory in definition is
soon reached. Conceptual elaboration and the accretion of detail
have a way of achieving the opposite of what is intended. Many definitions relevant to the subject of this text have been crafted more for

imperial advantage than for clarity; all that is clear is the self-interest of the drafters.

There is a conceptual purity in the simplicity and unarguable truth in the two points of Mitchell's definition and explanation quoted above. It is unlikely that anyone could be confused by his words, but he claimed that airpower is (1) anything that flies and (2) literally global. The problem, of course, is that so marvelous an invention—a category of machines that can fly anywhere in the world over all kinds of terrain—has to be in ever greater demand. The actual and potential stakeholder communities for airpower recognized ever greater uses as its technical competence matured and assumed a wide variety of somewhat mission-specific forms. The beginning of wisdom on this important matter of definition is simply to accept that there is no "true" wording beyond the banal-seeming yet paradoxically pro-found formula provided by the colorful, energetic, and quintessentially combative General Mitchell.[12] Once one attempts to improve on Mitchell, ironically the floodgates are opened to factual and logical errors vastly more serious than the limitations chargeable to his conceptual account. I would like to try to improve on Mitchell by adding to his wording in the following way: "Air power may be defined as the ability to do something [*strategically useful*] in the air." This well-intentioned amendment has the merit of helpful focus, but by introducing two highly contestable ideas into what was an elegant if substantially rather opaque formula, it risks doing more damage than good. The strategic theorist needs to borrow and attempt to adhere to the traditional medical injunction—perhaps the prime rule of prudence in medicine—"First, do no harm."

There is no single Great Truth to be discovered about airpower. Such cannot be derived from ever more careful historical scholarship, from scrupulously faithful textual analysis of all-but-sacred manuscripts, or from philosophical discourse. Epistemology will be confounded. And as suggested already, perhaps paradoxically and ironically, the success of the airpower project (if I may express the historical effort thus) lies at the heart of the difficulty. This study subscribes to Mitchell's definition of airpower for the reasons that it is both better than the alternatives or, to be less generous, that it is less bad.

The attractions of Billy Mitchell's all-but-elemental definition of airpower—which with some justice might be freely translated as the "anything that flies" approach—glitter the more brightly in the light shed by these stellar words of Henry Kissinger: "The responsibility of statesmen . . . is to resolve complexity rather than to contemplate it."[13] Strategic theory may appear to be strategic philosophy, but its pragmatic purpose—which is to say its sole purpose—is to fuel understanding for practical benefit. Any problems with Mitchell's almost casually inclusive approach pale in comparison with its virtues. It captures the heart of the matter. His formula does not contemplate airpower and attempt to lead epistemological questions by an encyclopedic, specific inclusivity. Maxims for defense professionals include injunctions to "get the big things right (enough)" and to avoid gratuitous complication and paralysis of thought and action by efforts to accommodate needless complexity.[14] Of course, there are detailed challenges to the meaning of airpower that can be framed as theoretical issues but which have profound practical implications. However, when seeking to understand the nature of airpower, the last thing one should do is obscure what must be crystal clear with unnecessary and contentious matters—hence the glory of Mitchell's notably unphilosophical and unscholarly wording.

Regrettably, this book must register serious dissent from the oft-quoted, even somewhat celebrated and authoritatively regarded, view of David MacIsaac. MacIsaac opened his notable essay on "The Air Power Theorists" with a summary view that too many of his successor historians, and more than a few theorists, have accepted as approximating the whole truth. The time is long overdue to revisit MacIsaac critically. Excellent and stimulating though his treatment is in several respects, nonetheless this theorist finds his judgment overall to be significantly questionable at the least. MacIsaac sets his scene with these potent sentences:

> Seventy-five years have now elapsed since the advent of manned aircraft resulted in the extension of traditional forms of surface warfare into the skies above—and indeed beyond—armies and navies. Air power, the generic term widely adopted to identify this phenomenon, has nonetheless yet to find a clearly defined or unchallenged place in the history of military or strategic theory. There has been no lack of theorists, but they have had only limited influence in a field where the effects of technology and the deeds of practitioners have from the beginning played greater roles than have ideas.[15]

Alas, the words just quoted are as admirably clear and substantively engaging as they are either incorrect or misleading. To take MacIsaac's two major claims in reverse order, his charge that technology and practice have led airpower theory is, at best, seriously arguable and, at worst, thoroughly erroneous. The claim, in effect, that airpower theory largely appeared in the slipstream of machinery and deeds so therefore its principal roles were to rationalize, legitimize, and popularize material developments and behavior is not correct. This now widespread view cannot withstand careful historical assay, and it expresses, I suspect, some misunderstanding of the nature of the relationship between strategic theory and practice. Readers will have to decide whether on balance they find merit in MacIsaac's opinion.

The first of MacIsaac's major claims actually is the one more apt to mislead. He states correctly, as of his time of writing, that "air power . . . has nonetheless yet to find a clearly defined or unchallenged place in the history of military or strategic theory." He is right, but one is moved to pose the quintessential strategist's challenge: "So what?" The plain implication is one of failure. The implicit argument is that 75 years (1911–86 presumably, dating military airpower from its first employment in warfare) should have sufficed for air-minded persons to sort out the meaning of their specialty. Whether or not MacIsaac is broadly accurate in his historical claim for the poverty of definition and the uncertainty of the place of airpower, he does not recognize that his claim could be extended to refer to the definition and strategic status in relative utility of every modern military dimension. Not only did the novel military dimension of airpower alter radically by fits and starts through its first near-century (to his time of writing), but so did every other geostrategic dimension, each in itself and in relation to the others. Perhaps airpower theory and practice had never really "grown up," at least not prior to 1986, but it is a readily verifiable fact that the theory of airpower, then and now, is not notably in greater contention than is theory for land power and sea power, let alone the really new arrivals, space power and cyber power. Furthermore, since we need to accommodate the entire gamut of military instruments, the strategic value of nuclear weapons and other weapons of mass destruction (WMD) is by no means stable either. There are, and always have been, pressing and potent reasons why airpower, however defined, has comprised a historical strategic narrative so much in motion that the paint never had time to dry on a finished project. Airpower has been a work in progress ever since its military inception, arguably in 1911, and as such has contributed to the destabilization of every other facet of the strategic world. The point that needs to be emphasized is that the evolving strategic story of airpower was bound to be ever inconclusive because it was history necessarily in motion.

The paragraphs immediately above are not intended to exculpate those people and institutions apparently guilty of the neglect of theory, of inappropriate indecision, or of heinous crimes against progress as an orderly march into the future. As stated already, this text is not interested in scoring points unfairly from the commanding heights of unassailable hindsight. Its mission is only to understand airpower—both itself and in relation to its contexts—as well as can be achieved. Mistakes, great and small, have been made in the development and employment of airpower, as they have with respect to land power, sea power, space power, and now cyber power. But, so what? New military instruments will commit generically old errors in technically and tactically novel ways. Such is inevitable. However today, 100 and more years into the air age of conflict, it is appropriate, indeed necessary, to attempt to retire yesterday's beliefs, attitudes, and opinions that plainly are dysfunctional for the exploitation of airpower for national security.

Some Keys to Understanding

The domain of this book is airpower regarded from three interlocking perspectives: theory (and doctrine), historical practice, and deliberately faintly, contemporary defense issues. As a toolkit to help shape the disparate materials of ideas, deeds, and current conundrums, it is useful to provide a set of considerations and propositions that will serve as candidate keys to assist broad understanding of the more enduring themes of this analysis; seven such keys are specified. Some have been mentioned already; others have not.

Technological Dynamism

It is commonplace to observe that doctrine is doomed by its very nature always to be advice or direction for yesterday rather than today. Our narrative must make sense of a technical story that opens with a 40-yard bound and then moves on to attain the ability to function with global endurance, certainly an intercontinental reach. In short, the technological tale has been ever moving. It is not surprising that the authority of airpower theory has been apt to rest upon unstable foundations to the degree to which, unwisely, it has been fueled by particular technical assumptions.

Tactical, Operational, and Strategic Dynamism

As the technological basis of airpower has evolved, so of necessity have the prudently exploitive tactical, operational, and strategic stories. The instability of airpower progress, historically in motion, has propelled tactical, operational, and strategic innovation such that both the impression and, by and large, the reality of airpower always have been and have seemed to be in transition. Indeed, the impression of constant change is an accurate one.

Anticipation and Prediction

Airpower, as a moving target for capture by theory and doctrine—and no less by prudent defense policy, military strategy, and force posture—has been apt to confound all parties to the ever renewed debate over its relative significance and strategic meaning and value.

Context

Moreover, the technical story of airpower, even when enriched by expert tactical and operational assessment, by no means completes the domain necessary for fair assay. No technology, military or other, has entirely self-evident meaning, regardless of the context within which it is deployed. Those who would judge the relative contribution of airpower to a campaign, war, or passage of diplomacy in peacetime can make the mistake of underrating the significance of the historically specific situation. There are some enduring truths—which is to say, most-cases-valid generalizations—about airpower. But the truths about the actual historical application of airpower must be shaped by the opportunities and constraints of the particular situation. It follows that windy generalizations are ever vulnerable to embarrassing ambush by strategic circumstances wherein flying machines, at least some kinds of flying machine, in practice are only of minor supporting value to the whole project that is the conduct of a conflict.

Trial by Experience

Naturally, ideas about airpower must be tested and evaluated by experience. The strategic snapshots in time of the performances of airpower in specific events are only that: situation-specific frozen frames. Lessons of enduring worth can be drawn from history. Indeed, properly treated to merit the status of evidence, historical happenings must provide the foundation for knowledge and understanding. After all, what is the practical alternative to experience? Imagination? Speculation? Lessons about airpower will be more or less particular to the historical contexts from which they are drawn. This should be merely a banal point to make, but often airpower and sea power, inter alia, are judged to have "failed" or to have demonstrated serious limitations because too much or the wrong performance was expected of them in specific historical contexts.[16] The Luftwaffe failed to keep the Wehrmacht's encircled Sixth Army supplied adequately by air in the winter of 1942–43. This is true. But, because the Luftwaffe undoubtedly failed, does anything of general importance about the strategic value of airpower flow as a necessary conclusion that one should endorse? Of course not. Historical specificity is all important; context rules but does not entirely preprogram the course of history. To some degree context is what we make of it. There are generalizations that can and need to be made about the strategic value of airpower, but they have to be framed to accommodate the variety of historical strategic experience. Discipline and common sense are vital in the search for definition and interpretation of evidence.

Five-in-One and One-in-Five: Fission and Fusion in Warfare

Human beings can live only on the land, and they wage war in the singular, not geostrategically in the plural. Political communities do not speak of going to air war, or sea war, and so forth; rather they talk of going to war as a whole. Although warfare has become more complex as its geographical environments have increased from two (land and the surface of the sea) to five-plus (land, sea surface and subsurface, air, orbital space, and cyberspace), it retains its essential unity. These days none of the five geographies can be ignored nor their differences neglected, but some significant fungibilities do obtain. Indeed, the relations among military power tailored to each geography are so complex and dynamic that the search for simple truths is mission impossible. To focus upon the central narrative of this text, there is no simple, all-but-elemental Great Truth that can be told about airpower. Notwithstanding the many reasons that contribute to unwise military and strategic practices and to poor scholarship, there is no evading the genuine difficulty in securing a suitable grasp upon the theory and execution of airpower. Consider these complications for the dedicated pursuer after airpower Truth:

- In the grand duel of competition, conflict, war, and warfare, the military behavior in every geographical environment by ever belligerent forces makes a net contribution to a competition in strategic effect.[17] Briefings and books may tell the story of the war in the air or the war at sea, but the course of strategic history has only one course, even if many might have been possible. There was a single actual winning narrative.

- There are no great, universal, and eternal truths about the relative strategic value of airpower, or land power, or sea power, and so forth. Truth is situational; it varies with the contexts.

- Often it will not be obvious, even to truly objective assessors, just what the relative strategic value will prove to be of land power as contrasted with airpower, let alone space power, or to muddy the waters further, nuclear deterrence or even coercive nuclear employment. So complex are the factors contributing to the often erratic run of events and so fearsome can be the influence of contingency that not only is every war different, but every war is apt to change during its course.[18] Each conflict or war tends to have a "grammar" of its own, almost aside from the logic of the politics and policies that brought it to life originally.

- Airpower may be anything that flies or any capability to accomplish militarily worthwhile tasks in the air, but much of airpower's value has to lie in the importance of what it can do from, as opposed to in, the air. Is airpower actually sea power when it is deployed at sea and its tasks are either wholly naval or notably maritime? What matters about airpower, one could assert, is what it does, not what it is, technically regarded. If an AH-64 Apache helicopter is employed primarily as flying artillery for close air support missions, it can be hard to resist, at the risk of being oxymoronic, viewing the machine as flying land power. When flying machines are regarded and employed as airborne tanks, the case for their being owned by the Army would appear to make itself. The trouble is that the mind-set of the land, if not quite land-bound, warrior is apt to be locked unduly onto the noun rather than the adjective—the task rather than the "flying." And this may matter significantly. This theorist has no particular problem choosing who should own airpower, but the practical difficulties in this respect for armed forces have been, and to a degree remain, formidable. As noted before, airpower in its several forms and its maturing competencies has proven itself to be militarily and strategically so desirable that all sides want some of it for themselves. And to control securely the airpower that they need, they wish to own the capabilities in demand.

- Modern warfare inalienably is conducted as a whole, as a gestalt. The measure of true complementarity, real jointness, let alone seamless integration, always leaves more or less to be desired, but it is an undeniable fact the boundaries among the geographies of warfare are as clear geophysically as they are fuzzy and even scrambled tactically, operationally, and strategically. The B-29s of Curtis LeMay's Twentieth Air Force managed to incinerate 67 Japanese cities prior to the single-plane missions against Hiroshima and Nagasaki only because the US Navy, Marine Corps, and Army had fought their way across the Pacific and succeeded in seizing the Mariana Islands. Was the bombing of Japan from Saipan, Tinian, and Guam a triumph for US airpower, for US sea power (and land power), or both—or is the question ridiculous?

In this opening chapter it suffices merely to explain the enduring, historically conditioning complexity in airpower's connections to its strategic siblings. Different countries with distinctive strategic and military cultures, in different times and in particular characters of conflict, have answered the airpower question set in more or less unique ways. This is not to surrender mindlessly to the seductions of an undisciplined relativism. It is not the position of this theorist that "different strokes" are just fine. Local preferences granted, there are some objectively better, and worse, ways to assign shares in airpower ownership and to employ airpower. While it is true that each distinctive strategic historical project will have its distinctive airpower needs, airpower is not infinitely flexible or capable.

Assets and Capabilities

These two concepts differ critically in meaning, even though habitually confused. Whereas *assets* should refer strictly to input, to what one has, *capabilities* expresses a judgment as to what the assets should be expected to accomplish. This distinction is familiar to nearly all discussions of power, not only airpower. The problem is a careless logic, really illogic, that can have serious practical consequences. There is a host of reasons why the dueling, competitive nature of strategy tends to escape the careful attention that it merits. It is not too much of a challenge to attempt to explain that the growth in the US nuclear arsenal from 235 weapons in 1949 to its peak of 31,225 in 1967 did not mean that the United States was, wonderfully, 133 times more powerful in the mid 1960s than it had been in the late 1940s. As the saying goes, the adversary/enemy has a vote concerning a competitor's relative potency. Machines such as aircraft are vastly easier to count than the overall net fighting power of an air force. Moreover, that net fighting power will impact, positively or negatively, the fighting power of land and naval forces. By late 1944 and in 1945 Nazi Germany and imperial Japan were not starved of aircraft fit enough for combat, but increasingly they were short of pilots with the skills to fly them effectively in combat against overwhelming odds. Equipment inventories matter, but they matter far more for what they can do competitively in action or for how effective they are perceived to be rather than simply for what they are metrically. In May 1940 the French army owned more tanks than the Wehrmacht, but "So what?" Similarly, in June 1941 Soviet military aviation vastly outnumbered the Luftwaffe, a fact that translated as the juiciest of juicy targets for a Douhetian blow against airpower parked wingtip-to-wingtip on Soviet airfields.

Faith, Interest, and Fear

New arrivals have a way of presenting disturbing challenges to established ways of thought and patterns in power distribution. It would be easy to join the herd of historians and commentators who have written pejoratively about the assumptions, arguments, tactics, and strategies of airpower's advocates. There is much of which to complain. Airpower's promoters sometimes assumed the mantle of prophets; they did overpromise; they did belittle honest (as well as dishonest) arguments of which they disapproved; and they did give the appearance, overall, of people trying to sell an unproven product as a panacea for truly complex and difficult political, strategic, and tactical problems. Although most sweeping denunciations of airpower advocacy have some merit, paradoxically, they nonetheless constitute a substantially misleading indictment. To push the paradoxical claim yet further, the more insistent advocates of airpower have done net harm to an excellent broad case. However, the overstatement so characteristic of airpower's historically classic advocacy literature was all but unavoidable. Given the condition and circumstances of airpower, evolving effectively from nothing, as in zero, in 1908 to a hard-earned (US) status of coequal armed service in the new Department of Defense in 1947, it is all but inconceivable that any very different path could have been followed by its advocates.

It was never probable that those who sincerely believe that airpower could dominate warfare to the material and general human benefit would be meek by nature and in tone of argument. Unlike the nuclear age 40 years later, the air age did not erupt out of a clear blue sky, utterly unanticipated by the public, with two monstrous bangs that invited overestimation rather than polite or otherwise dismissal. Unlike airpower, nuclear weapons did not enjoy the benefits or suffer the damage in reputation of high-octane claim and counterclaim in public debate during their early technical gestation period. The historical narrative of airpower is not only technical and military-tactical; it also has sociological and cultural dimensions of more than passing significance. The point is that the strengths and limitations of airpower—both generically and in particular historical context of time, place, and circumstance—were not literally self-revealing. Airpower was not a natural product; rather, it had to be made to happen. That project could succeed only because of the efforts of particular individuals willing and able to create or exploit opportunities to help strategic history move along. Modesty, humility, and skepticism may be admirable qualities in a philosopher, but they are qualities unlikely to succeed against interests well entrenched as rivals to expansive, and expensive, visions of airpower's proper future. Early airpower theorists-advocates certainly had faith, in good part because that was all that they could have in the absence of obviously relevant strategic experience. Airpower theory has suffered in its reputation for probity and prudence as a consequence of its proclivity for peering rather too optimistically over the horizon. But, since airpower has evolved so substantially over the last 100 years, conviction resting noticeably upon anticipated prowess has been unavoidable. Also, let us not forget, the whole of our sad human strategic narrative has been moving over those years. If the strategic reality of the airpower story has changed radically, how about those of land power and sea power?

Clearly, it is quite possible for a sound idea to be so damaged by extravagant advocacy and so diminished in esteem by unreasonable expectations born of ill-educated understanding of war and warfare that merit and error become hopelessly jumbled. With some overstatement admitted, this has been the case with airpower, viewed both by a rarely attentive public and even as regarded by a supposedly expert professional defense community. Airpower nearly always has been far more valuable strategically than its strong detractors and persistent critics would allow, yet less decisive, to select a word not entirely at random, than its more impassioned promoters have claimed. The result, in war after war, has not been a happy one for the frequently lost cause of strategic reason.

One structural problem that usually could not be evaded by airpower's advocates, even when they rarely appreciated the need for such evasion, was that the sanctuaries of established military strength, viewed politically, needed to be assaulted forcefully, if not violently. Recall the non-analogy cited above of the sudden appearance of atomic bombs. Airpower is made of scarce money, factories, industrial workers, warriors, and those in and out of uniform who support them, and it is also expressed in and sustained by political influence. All too obviously, even generals and admirals who anticipated prudently some ways in which flying machines might assist in their ground- and sea-based endeavors could hardly help but harbor anxiety lest an air story capture a vulnerable civilian imagination to an imprudent degree.

Even ignoring the personal dynamics of airpower's early promotion—something difficult to do for this inalienably human subject—there is no denying these facts: (1) the technical, tactical, and strategic value of airpower, relative both to enemy airpower and to one's own land and sea power, was genuinely deeply uncertain; and (2) airpower's more strident promoters appeared to try to compensate for this uncertainty by the clarity and volume of what amounted to their (leap of) Faith. As in Thucydides' famous triptych of "fear, honor, and interest"—which enjoys paternal rights over my triptych here of faith, interest, and fear—the most vital ingredients for controversy over airpower interlock. Airpower's advocates acquired a belief system that approximated a faith in a revolutionary change in warfare.[19] This faith served their personal career designs, it must be said, as well as the interests of their nation(s) as they believed sincerely. They feared, again sincerely, that airpower was advancing on a broad, invincible front—at least it was advancing on behalf of those polities that properly anticipated modernity. As the familiar saying has it, "Those who are left behind get beaten."

Airpower is not unique in attracting a community of believers who, when confronted with the reality of a strategic future that could not be foreseen reliably—by definition, it having not yet happened—in effect, hide their true ignorance by cloaking their belief in the authority of a faith. This is neither to criticize nor to condemn; it is to note that the very process of debate itself promotes overstatement, while the tactical expedient of overpromotion triggers devaluation by prudent, somewhat skeptical opinion. Moreover, once a community is committed to an enterprise, it is not inclined to be self-critical in the face of serious opposition. Faint hearts, devotion to fair play in debate, and a readiness to acknowledge risks were not going to build a modern airpower worthy of the theory and, arguably, the strategic need and opportunity.

Disarray: Diagnosis and Prescription

Major sources of trouble for the effort to understand the strategic meaning and value of airpower have been outlined above. Since the purpose of this study is to be constructive rather than merely critical, it is important to identify the scope and depth of the overall challenge addressed here, diagnose as specifically as possible the condition that has ailed the patient—the understanding of airpower—and determine effective ways to reduce the disarray. The challenges to understanding that have been discussed or at least introduced in earlier sections of this chapter have all been—indeed, by and large, remain—serious and unavoidable. The challenge to us is to cope pragmatically with the world as it is. To do this we must attempt to make sense of the past as education for the present, and for that mission we require useful theory.

While there are many definitions of theory, the core of the better among them insists that theory is about explanation.[20] That is, what is most needed today is a plausible explanation of the meaning of airpower for the history of the past century, most especially in its strategic dimension. The past, processed as "history," is by far the best, though still admittedly unreliable, basis for the derivation of the theory that we require if we are to make sufficient sense of the opportunities and limitations of airpower today and for tomorrow. There is a place for high-flying deductive theory that knowingly transcends the prudent realistic bounds of current doctrine, but such creative theorizing should be conducted in full awareness of the fragility of its evidence in logic. As observed above, the heat of debate over matters of vital importance for national security is always likely to overcook favored arguments into the zone where the case rests mainly upon a faith that is not factually supportable. Such arguments are not necessarily wrong; indeed often they are not, but claims that are not and frequently cannot be supportable from verified experience should be noted as such. Defense planning is all about prudent, contingent prediction, which can be rephrased to say that defense planning is the practice of strategic theory. A plan—defense or anything else—is a theory that predicts the achievements of desired consequences as a result of the execution by chosen ways of purposeful actions by available military means.[21]

Superior historical scholarship is not in and of itself the answer to understanding contemporary and future airpower. Historians quite properly are dedicated to finding particular truths about particular historical contexts. The challenge to this text is to use historians' better labors as the most helpful evidential foundation for a theory of airpower that is fit for this purpose.

This book begins with the beliefs that our understanding of airpower for today and the future is hampered gratuitously by an unsound structure of theory and an unduly contested historical record. So ample and excellent are the reasons for shaky theory and disputed history that a scholar needs to be careful to resist undue empathy for those who have gone before. If I may be pardoned the familiar split infinitive, this book intends to boldly go where many have sought to go already but have found themselves fatally hindered by one of several limitations.

The principal reason for the unsatisfactory state of airpower theory, airpower history, and knowledge of how to apply airpower most effectively to contemporary security challenges is lack of contextualization. Expressed less pretentiously, and with some thanks to the late and iconic John Boyd, the challenge to those who try to comprehend the meaning of airpower is, and has always been, the difficulty of securing a workable quality of situational awareness.[22] The reality or anticipated possibility of airpower has meaning only within its ever-changing historical situation. Furthermore, no matter what the strategic and military detail of the particular airpower story is believed to be, the tale is governed by the eternal and universal general theory of strategy. That theory overlaps but is not synonymous with the theory of war.[23] The reason is because strategy functions in time of peace as well as war.

It is helpful to apply the strategist's master key—the question So what?—to the thesis just advanced. If the claim is sustainable that too much of airpower theory and history has been unduly light in situational grip, among other failings, then is there good reason to anticipate improved understanding as a consequence of paying careful attention to theoretical and historical situation or context? This book tests the proposition that the understanding of airpower historically for today, and also leaning forward toward tomorrow, can be improved to a useful degree by conscious major effort to address airpower specifics explicitly in context.

Conclusion: From Wonder to Routine

People are now so familiar with the phenomenon of flight that it can be difficult to recover the sense of wonder that it attracted late in the nineteenth century and early in the twentieth. Antulio J. Echevarria observes in his insightful study of futurological writings about war from 1880 to 1914,

> Aerial warfare was by far the most captivating of all the dimensions of modern war. The skies were humanity's last frontier, and no other realm proved quite as fertile for the imagination. Speculations ran a veritable gamut of themes: from aerial combat to airborne invasion and strategic bombing. For many, the conquest of the air was long in coming, almost too long. And, in a sense, they were right. The public grew impatient, then skeptical, so much so in fact that at first the Wright brothers' success at Kitty Hawk in December of 1903 was scarcely believed. Failure and disappointment had become so common that success, when it finally did occur, seemed incredible.[24]

One might have expected a persisting dialogue between people who, on the one hand, are captivated by the wonder of flight and approach it somewhat misty-eyed, and those, on the other hand, who are prone to accept it as just another human accomplishment—progress as usual in the modern world. Such an expectation has not been fulfilled, however. Instead of any real resemblance to such a dialogue, there have been in effect two monologues. Admittedly, this is an exaggeration but one that highlights the most enduring set of problems pertaining to airpower; simultaneously it has been overvalued and undervalued strategically (inter alia). From its earliest days until the present, the middle ground between extreme opinions has been thinly populated. The reasons for this historical phenomenon are not hard to locate; they reside in personality, perceived interest, and context. One must especially take full account of the struggle to recognize airpower's near-term and longer-term utility and translate such understanding into organization, practical ideas (doctrine), and forces. The structure of the context in question simply is the fact that the modern world entered the bloody twentieth century organized, manned, equipped, and more or less doctrinally prepared for two-dimensional warfare—on land and at sea. Airpower has been an intruder and distinctly junior for many years to the organizations that provided land and sea power. Taking the somewhat long view, no sooner had airpower delivered, or appeared to deliver, on its long-heralded promise of strategic and political decision by aerial action (in 1945 over Japan), than its status and future seemed to be challenged by the advent of new weaponry. Perhaps ironically, for a decade and a half after 1945, the dominant airpower narrative was first atomic and then thermonuclear. Somehow, unjust though it was, the adjective commanded the noun in the descriptive term of art of the period, *atomic airpower*. In the late 1940s and into the 1950s, "air-atomic" became fashionable linguistic usage.

Thus with respect to general and total war (which is to say, World Wars I, II, and the much anticipated next one), flying vehicles quite suddenly were overshadowed hugely and strategically by the self-evident revolutionary character (or nature?) of their explosive payload. To compound this fundamental challenge to the relative standing of airpower, the atomic and then thermonuclear developments were joined by a truly mighty challenge in the form of missiles, unmanned but air-breathing and, especially, ballistic. To this near breathless tempo of technical innovation and defense postural adaptation were added the wonders of earth-orbital spacecraft and the acceleration of electronic accomplishment with the cascade of inventions consequent upon emergence of the practicable computer. With the world technically, hence tactically and strategically, so rapidly in motion, it is easy to see why the airpower narrative has never had a settled character, let alone been seriously undisputed by the advocates of yet more novel wonders.

To understand contemporary airpower and be able to prescribe how best to employ it, obviously it is essential to be clear, or clear enough, in matters of definition and with regard to situation. The strategic landscape now is crowded. Five geographically distinctive environments for warfare today jostle for priority, funding, and doctrinal appreciation. One must insist that, although war and even much of warfare necessarily are joint and somewhat an integrated project, geography is not. The air environment is unique, and this uniqueness is a geophysical fact of huge significance. A major mission for this study is to unravel as much as possible, and certainly as much as necessary, of the confusion created by this complexity.

The strategic value of airpower has been limited in the past, as it is today, by the consequences of a failure on the part of polities to grasp and secure a realistic grip upon what it can and cannot accomplish for them. The debate between airpower's advocates and detractors, though inevitable, has been and continues to be harmful to understanding.

Most of the technical arguments about airpower's prowess have been answered in its favor. Indeed, most of the tactical arguments have been resolved to airpower's advantage. One hundred and a few more years on from Kitty Hawk, there is little scope for technical-tactical debate about the "what" even of (US) airpower today, let alone tomorrow. But there remains a large uncertainty over prudent generic and situationally specific answers to the strategist's question, So what? Early in the twenty-first century, the promoters of airpower have little difficulty slaying prejudiced or ignorant arguments about what airpower can and cannot do. Their challenge lies in explaining the strategic meaning of its abilities. Flight continues to be wonderful, though its familiarity is apt to dull the imagination and therefore become so routine that its military value, for strategic merit, often is underassayed.

As the strategic universe has become more complicated, the problems of satisfactory definition multiply into the severely contestable zone, even a no-man's land, wherein it is far from obvious just what is being debated as "airpower." This text is driven epistemologically to begin where it must—with theory. We need theory for the purpose of explanation, and we need clear definitions so that we can agree to use the same words to discuss the same things. If one person's attack helicopter is land power because it is a flying (seriously underarmored) tank, yet to another person it is airpower because it is an aircraft, plainly there is urgent need for theoretical, and thence doctrinal, discipline and policing. With gratitude as always to the Prussian master theorist, this book now seeks to accomplish what has been identified in this first chapter as essential and provide the theoretical armament required for better understanding. Of course, politics, ideology, personality, money, and contingency will try and probably largely succeed in contradicting the theorist's relatively neat grand design and subsequent narrative, but at least he will have done his job. This theorist does recognize that strategic theory exists only to assist strategic practice. It follows necessarily that if the structure and dynamics of the theory presented in chapters 1 and 2 have no practicable meaning or application, they must be without value.

Notes

All references appear in shortened form. For full details, see the appropriate entry in the bibliography.

1. Albeit with some sense of minor discomfort, throughout this study I shall refer to *airmen*. Of course often it would be more accurate, and certainly more politically correct, to refer to *airmen and women*, or to *air persons/people*. But such usage, though sensitive to our times, would be rather ponderous and appear stilted.

2. See Gray, *Strategy Bridge*, particularly appendix C, "Conceptual 'Hueys' at Thermopylae?"; and Hanson, *Makers of Ancient Strategy*.

3. Clausewitz, *On War*, 141.

4. Ibid., 132.

5. A recent example of this phenomenon of apparent overperformance by the militarily much weaker belligerent was the claimed "divine victory" of Hezbollah in what Israel officially has titled the Second Lebanon War (of 2006). See the analysis in Arkin, *Divining Victory*, chap. 8. For a critical Israeli view, see Siboni, "Military Campaign in Lebanon."

6. Howard, *Causes of Wars and Other Essays*, 215–16.

7. See Mahan, *Influence of Sea Power upon History, 1660–1783.*

8. Gray, *Strategy Bridge.*

9. Clausewitz, *On War*, 87.

10. Mitchell, *Winged Defence*, xiii.

11. Ibid., 3–4.

12. Waller, *Question of Loyalty*, is a recent biography of Mitchell that manages to be both empathetic and fair without sliding into capture by its charismatic subject. Waller concludes insightfully that "even [Mitchell's] friends may have been too hard on him. Great leaders, particularly those in wartime, have outsized egos. Institutional mavericks, whistle-blowers, critics who press for reforms in bureaucracies all tend to

be abrasive, outspoken, hard to get along with. Prophets by nature are opinionated and overconfident. Agents of change break china, make people uncomfortable, leave enemies in their wake." Ibid., 363–64.

13. Kissinger, *Diplomacy*, 113.

14. I seek to advance this message in my *Fighting Talk*, xiii–xvi.

15. MacIsaac, "Voices from the Central Blue," 624.

16. See Higham and Harris, *Why Air Forces Fail*.

17. Gray, *Strategy Bridge*, chap. 5, "Strategic Effect," explores and explains the meaning and practical implications of this crucial concept.

18. This claim rests upon the recognition that war has a "reciprocal, competitive nature." Porter, *Military Orientalism*, 65.

19. John Ferris hits the target in a British context with his "Catching the Wave."

20. Winton, "An Imperfect Jewel," 2–4, offers a superior understanding of the structure and functions of theory.

21. Gray, "Strategic Thoughts for Defence Planners."

22. Boyd, "Discourse on Winning and Losing."

23. I develop this important point in *Strategy Bridge*, chap. 3.

24. Echevarria, *Imagining Future War*, 81–82.

Chapter 2

Ideas for Action

How can a theorist be a practical person? Surely a theorist indulges in abstract speculation—often of a fanciful, always of a contestable kind. If the reasoning were not speculative and perhaps fanciful, then it would be fact and not theory. Since the practice of airpower in its several forms and many purposes necessarily is a pragmatic project, it is understandable that air-minded people are inclined to be impatient with, if not dismissive of, theory and theorists—at least they think they are. Given the powerful role played by theory and its flag carriers in the history of airpower, this low valuation of ideas deemed to be unduly abstract, if not actually abstruse, is in no small degree ironic.[1] We shall strive to redress the imbalance in favor of theory.

It is helpful to set the scene for this chapter by quoting what historian Frederick W. Kagan has written about the commonly disdainful attitude of military professionals toward theory:

> This dismissal of the role of theory has never been valid—theories of war have driven the planning and conduct of military operations since the mid-eighteenth century at least—but it is nowhere less valid than in the consideration of air power. From the first time a man put a bomb on a plane to drop on the enemy [1911], the planning and conduct of air operations has been a thoroughly theoretical undertaking.[2]

It is paradoxical that air forces willing and able to expend billions of dollars on technical and tactical education typically devote a trivial amount to understanding what they do or might do strategically and why they are asked to do so by their political owners.[3] Dominant theory for nearly a century has insisted that airpower must be commanded and controlled by professional airmen (if I may be permitted a nonsexist use of a gendered term).[4] The plausible thesis legitimizing this demand is that only airmen truly understand airpower and what it can and cannot do well in particular circumstances. This argument, which long has been Air Force doctrine—in effect with a capital "D"—is thoroughly plausible technically and tactically for airpower. However, it has not always been wholly true with respect to operational, strategic, and political considerations; even tactically it has been genuinely challengeable by those whose military concerns rightly have been terrestrially restricted. By no means is this to suggest that an airman's view of what airpower can contribute to warfare on the ground or at sea is inferior to the perspective of the soldier or the sailor. It is to suggest, though, that if airmen do have, or believe they can find, an air-dominant narrative for success in war, they need to be careful that they locate that air-oriented story effectively in a holistic design. Not only do airmen require a whole theory of the war for practical strategic prudence, they acutely need it to persuade their chain of higher command to license them to practice their theory in command performance as plan and then in action. Obviously self-serving strategies (theories) are identified as such in a few nano-seconds by the heavy lifters for rival strategies (theories) that lean predominantly on their particular military instrument (victory through land power, sea power, space power, cyber power, special operations cunning, nuclear menace).

Many people have difficulty understanding how, or indeed whether, the general relates to the specific. It is true that theory requires some generalization and considerable reduction in detail. Because history is always contextually specific to time, place, and situation, its executives have to be capable of providing specifically tailored solutions to unique challenges. Unfortunately for the mental comfort of many airmen—and also for the best interests of the polities that they serve, as well as their conjoint soldiers, sailors, and so forth—the specifically right-enough air story cannot be discovered, explained, accepted, and executed unless it fits into T. E. Lawrence's "whole house of war" and, as we should expand the metaphor, the whole house of strategy.[5] Neglect of this "whole house" often results in airpower being developed and employed inappropriately in some gratuitous measure, in part because its spokespeople are unable to persuade non-airpersons of the merit in their arguments. Even a seemingly parochial and self-serving strategy may be the superior option, but the more obviously it seems to reflect and express an air perspective, the greater its requirement for protection by well-constructed theory wielded by people educated to win debate with ideas. The beginning of wisdom for those who must seek pragmatically to design, acquire, and execute airpower lies in some thoughts well articulated by Britain's preeminent maritime theorist, Sir Julian S. Corbett, writing in 1906. Corbett addressed the subject of "naval strategy," but one can substitute "air" for "naval" without doing violence to his message.

> [Air] strategy does not exist as a separate branch of knowledge. It is only a section of a division of the art of war.

The study for officers is the art of war, specializing in [Air] Strategy.

The true method of procedure then is to get hold of a general theory of war, and so ascertain the exact relations of [Air] Strategy to the whole.

War is a form of political intercourse, a continuation of foreign politics which begins when force is introduced to attain our ends.[6]

Airpower is simultaneously both a general idea and a specific reality. The historically specific reality can be expressed as an absolute quantity of assets and also as a judgment of relative prowess. Thus, comment on, say, Japanese airpower after the Battle of the Philippine Sea typically would conflate well-verified claims for sharply declining effectiveness with an assessment of no less steeply diminishing inventories of useful machines and competent aircrews. Because airpower is always specific in quantity and quality, and because the airman always must endeavor to deal with the implications of physical actualities, the presence and value of theory often evade notice.

Given that airpower theory can have no strictly self-referential merit, it necessarily follows that all airpower theorists are engaged in what must be recognized as a practical pursuit. The purpose of theory is to educate, but education in and about airpower can have only one mission: to prepare people for the practice of airpower. It is sensible to concede the reality that for many aircrew, the practice of airpower—simply the act of controlling a vehicle that flies—is a joyful end in itself. But flying, controlling flight, is a pursuit that can and should serve ends above and beyond its undeniable recreational value. Even the most practical airperson—whose horizon is full and more of technical, tactical, and personal physical and even psychological challenges—functions in the air within the grasp and grip of theory. Moreover, the theory at issue here is by no means restricted to that of airpower. As Corbett insists firmly and convincingly, geographically specific military power (or in his case, naval power) makes sense only when it is approached and employed within a broader framework or context. He specified the art of war and its general theory. Such expression is correct as far as it goes, but it is not sufficient for the needs of this book.

The reformulation of airpower theory is deferred to much later in this text, to the penultimate chapter. This is to ensure that issues and evidence, ideas and history, are properly matured before they are transformed from the status of vital ingredients for the finished product, insofar as any determination of airpower theory at any time can be so described. It may be useful to emphasize that although the chief purpose of this study is to help improve the practice of airpower, the strategy by which that objective is attempted is through specification and explanation of an improved theory of airpower. My means lie in the realm of ideas for theory, but those educational means are chosen firmly with pragmatic intent.

Locating Airpower

Politics, and war as an expression of politics, is a human project with all that entails and implies.[7] The classical theorists of war and strategy tell us that war is a contest of wills, just as an abundance of historical experience supports the proposition that morale—essentially, confidence—is key to strategic performance.[8] Emphasizing the human dimension to strategy is not to discount technology but to try to ensure that the nature of the whole security enterprise, of which airpower is an integral part, is not misunderstood. Fervent, albeit honest, advocates of this or that favored military instrument and its associated strategy (should they pause to consider consequences or that much-abused concept, effect) usually succumb to the temptation to construct a helpful but unsound strategic universe that conveniently privileges the claimed strengths in their preferences. Because the stakes in relative well-being are so high, because the pressures to stray unintentionally from the straight and narrow so great, and the consequences of error potentially so unforgiving, the utmost care must be taken in building the edifice of strategic theory that accommodates airpower. An important function of theory is to sort out matters that might otherwise be confused. It is true that confusion can have its uses in debate, provided only the adversary is confused, but it is quite evident from the literature on airpower, inter alia, that much of what is confused is, alas, all too genuinely and honestly so. Notwithstanding the pervasive and critically enabling importance of technology for airpower, it is necessary not to be confused as to what airpower is all about. Airpower is about neither science and engineering nor the weapons that those linked branches of endeavor can deliver, nor even about the joy of flying. One must not collapse what airpower is with what it is about. Each element in the familiar statement of the strategic function is essential: ends, ways, and means. The connections among the three are as crucial as the merits in each regarded individually.

Because (air) strategy can be only operational and tactical, there is an obvious sense in which tactical behavior must also be strategic behavior. This logic probably will be resisted by some readers because they have been taught to use the adjective *strategic* in a different way. The study addresses this important matter explicitly and shows why much of the standard usage of *strategic* confuses what should be clear and consequently harms strategic performance properly so regarded. It is necessary to emphasize the centrality of the human dimension to all aspects of airpower, both to balance and correct for the technology focus that understandably attracts undue attention and to locate airpower properly as an inalienable part of the human activities of politics and war.

Since it is said that a picture can be worth a thousand words, figure 1 is offered as a locator for airpower in the complex terrain of ideas and behavior that it inhabits. This author is aware that diagrams can add to confusion rather than clarity. Readers are invited to use this figure in the spirit in which it is offered. Admittedly, it is somewhat idealized and much simplified; however, it is drawn that way to register with the utmost clarity a few major points that are indeed persisting, even inescapable, truths. Pathologies in behavior, confused thinking, sheer complexity, huge and small surprises, including unanticipated feedback (and "blowback"), and so forth can render historical reality very different from the relationships represented in figure 1. Nonetheless, this figure is true in the sense that it explains how things ought to be. A concern for this discussion is that much debate over airpower topics is conducted by people who, though usually honest and knowledgeable, plainly do not understand where airpower resides in the conceptual and behavioral landscape.

The following points comprise a minimal users' guide to the messages figure 1 attempts to deliver. The figure makes the following claims:

1. There is a master general theory of strategy that is authoritative for all periods, universally, and that commands all kinds of military forces in all geographies.

2. Strategy(ies) is singular and plural. *Strategy* (singular) is the general theory; *strategies* (plural) are the unique plans—which are theories—devised and sometimes attempted in execution to meet particular historical challenges.

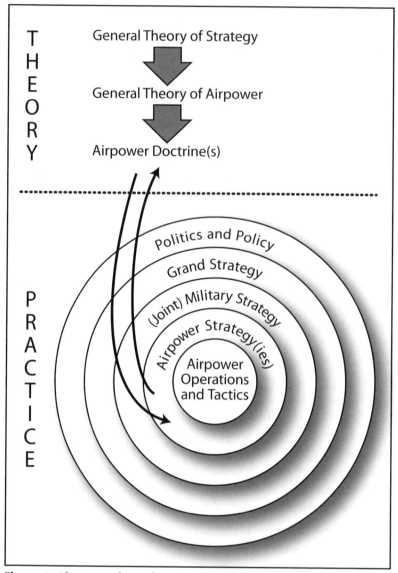

Figure 1. Airpower: from theory to practice

3. There is a general theory of airpower that is not contextually specific to time, place, situation, technology, or so forth.

4. Just as the general theory of strategy is authoritative over the general theory of airpower, so the enduring theory of airpower is a primary source of education for those who create ever-

changing doctrine for airpower that must fit dynamic contemporary conditions.

5. In the realm of practice there is, in principle at least, a very clear chain of command connecting political owners and their purpose with their military instrument acting on their behalf. Expressed visually in figure 1 as five rings—with thanks, and possibly apologies, to John Warden[9]—an aircraft, its crew, and support elements (a) behave tactically, (b) for operational purposes, (c) as a small component in execution of a joint military plan (a strategy), (d) which is a significant strand in a polity's grand strategy, (e) which is intended to advance the achievement of policy goals agreed and managed through a political process.

Key to this logic are the assertions that military threat and behavior (latent or explicit) serve the politics that make policy; airpower theory (and/or doctrine) is not synonymous with the theories of war and strategy; airpower strategy is not synonymous with military, let alone grand, strategy, because the latter almost always must be noticeably joint; and airpower itself—either on the runway (where it may function well as a threat) or in action—is and can be only tactical, in common with every other military tool in a polity's locker.

One might think that choices among alternative definitions do not much matter. After all, provided there is some approximation to consensus on what the vital words mean, surely language usage must be good enough, fit for purpose. Alas, this is not entirely so because, although it is important to communicate without unintended ambiguity, what one communicates matters as well. For the case in point, not all meanings of *strategic* were created equal. Before joining the conceptual battle, this theorist recognizes fully that the uses of *strategic* that he rejects are of long-standing, considerable authority—hence legitimacy—and have some appeal to that underused faculty, common sense. The trouble is that the familiar, the plausible, and the seemingly reasonable in the case of *strategic* tend to have dire consequences. This text argues that *strategic* does not (should not) mean long range, nuclear armed (or capable), very important, decisive, or able to impact the political level of war directly without first fighting the enemy's armed forces.[10]

Instead of any or all of the above, or any similar criteria, it is sensible to treat all armed forces as strategic in the net consequences of their behavior. All behavior chips in to the grand narrative of a conflict, from a single sortie to a massed air assault. Moreover, while it is not entirely true that what matters is strategic effect itself—a rather opaque, though alas truly vital, concept—rather than how it is achieved, still it is necessary to appreciate the fact of fungibility. There may well be several roads to Berlin, Jerusalem, or wherever. The country needs strategic effect sufficient for its political purpose; it does not need the strategic effect specifically delivered by airpower. Most emphatically, this is not to argue that there are never circumstances wherein airpower should be the leading, the dominant, or even the sole military instrument chosen to secure the desired strategic effect in support of policy.

Airpower, like land power, sea power, space power, and cyber power, is a tactical tool with strategic consequences. Thus, it has to follow that airpower "does" strategy, albeit tactically. If, instead of the clear strategic-tactical distinction preferred here, specified by no less a thinker than Carl von Clausewitz,[11] one elects to consider some weapons as inherently strategic—long-range and nuclear-armed aircraft and missiles, for the most obvious examples—then it becomes difficult to reason strategically. Is one asserting that the army and navy are not strategic instruments? Given that long-range land-based airpower, the army, and the navy should all, at the very least in concert, be contributing to a single historical narrative favorable to us, how can some of our military tools be inherently strategic while others are not? Plainly, the more sensible approach to the matter is to regard all military forces as contributors to strategic effect while recognizing that, in particular situations, the relative contributions to that overall strategic effect delivered by air, sea, and land forces will vary. When a weapon and its consequences are conflated, the result is neglect of the strategic function. It is needlessly difficult to think strategically about the value of a military force when that force is predesignated as inherently "strategic." The strategist's question "So what?" may well not be posed, let alone answered; weapons and actions themselves are defined as strategic. There is no apparent need or room for strategic effect. What the military instrument does is taken to be such effect. This historically familiar phenomenon is characterized as the tacticization of strategy.[12]

It is ironic that the bid by airpower theorists to lay a unique claim to strategic status through theoretical imperialism actually has harmed their cause. Misuse of *strategic*—disdain for Clausewitz's distinction between the *engagement* and its *use*—has had the consequences of an implicit (and much explicit) overreach in claimed ability and an immense underreach in claims for the (strategic) benefits of purportedly nonstrategic airpower. This book adheres to the rule that a weapon is more or less strategic according to how it impacts the course of strategic history, not for reasons of its range or character of armament. To understand airpower, there is no evading the requirement to understand the general theory of strategy to which it is, has been, and always must be subject.

The General Theory of Strategy

To hazard an apparent contradiction in terms, there is a specific general theory of airpower, just as there is a specific general theory of sea power. One day there will be competent and robust specific general theories of space power and cyber power, but they do not exist as of yet.[13] This hugely immature theory is a problem if one seeks essentially to fold space power and cyber power into airpower theory and doctrine, as has been the recent case in the USAF. The potential is high for serious error leading to much gratuitous strategic self-harm. Adding two theoretically ill- if not simply undigested geophysical domains to the already theoretically contested domain of airpower is obviously not wise. The connections of airpower to space power and cyber power comprise an undergoverned zone at present. Leaving aside for now detailed treatment of the issues pertaining to the multiple geophysical, let alone tactical, operational, and strategic interfaces of airpower, it is necessary to recognize fully the enduring distinctive qualities of airpower. The best way to grasp the nature of the general theory of airpower is to understand it as an explanation and a systematic, well-ordered body of knowledge that could have been written at any time, in any place, and in any strategic and technological context since the early 1900s. The assumption is that there is a truth about airpower that is as true for 1911 as for 2011 or even 2111. General theory is timeless in its imperium, whether it is the general theory of strategy, per se, or the general theory of airpower (or sea power, or land power, etc.). The key to an intelligent and constructive marriage between theory and practice is the ability to distinguish what changes from what does not. Practical people focused on the challenge of today are apt to have difficulty understanding the utility of general theory. One must sympathize with such bafflement but would sympathize more were it not that in conflict after conflict, even the most basic of theoretical precepts about strategy are ignored more often than not with well-deserved dire consequences.

Perhaps contrary to appearance, this book does not confuse theory with practice, and neither does it confuse understanding with effective execution. To comprehend one's strategic dilemmas is important, even essential, but such comprehension is no guarantee of the ability to resolve them satisfactorily. Theory itself only educates; it cannot train or specify particular solutions to historically unique problems. Nonetheless, theory is vitally important. Airmen need to know how to think about and, therefore, how to achieve effectiveness in, through, and from their domain. No less important is their requirement for a grasp of and grip upon the whole realm of strategy. A tactically superior air force can be misused, in effect wasted, if it is not directed with strategic sense. And strategies for the application of airpower in particular times and places can be devised and executed competently only by strategically well-educated, air-minded people. One might hasten to add that there is the occasional genius who has strategic sense as a gift of nature or simply by virtue of life experience.[14] There are also historical episodes wherein both friendly and enemy strategic sense plainly is missing from the action, but happily, the enemy is even more strategically illiterate than we. There are times when strategy does not much matter, so heavily loaded is the material or other iron dice in one side's favor; nonetheless, it is never prudent to discount the value of strategy.

Strategy for airpower, however it is defined, is as variable in its character as the theory behind it is stable. Confusion of general theory with the particular theories for behavior that are historical strategies has been widespread and pernicious. The geophysical truths of airpower's general theory indicate nothing, as in zero, about the wisdom or otherwise of specific strategies at specific times. Airpower has been cursed by much innocent confusion of general truth with particular practicability.

So what is the general theory of strategy to which this text insistently refers and to which it grants dominion? It is a systematically ordered body of lore—not law and arguably not even principles—that does what theory should do for its particular domain. And what is that? Several answers are plausible, but the one provided by Harold R. Winton is preferred here.[15] He stipulates that theory should "define the field of study under investigation; categorize, i.e., to break the field of study into its consistent parts; connect the field of study to other related fields in the universe; and anticipate" (to some degree, predict).[16] The general theory of strategy can be located in a few classic writings dating from ancient times to the present. Those texts of exceptional and therefore enduring value appear in different literary forms—for example as history, explicitly as policy and strategy advice to the ruler, as all-but-philosophy, and as modern, even contemporary, social science.[17] No two theorists explain strategy identically; each theorizes as his culture, situation, genius, and abilities allow. But the classic texts of general strategic theory, authored over the space of 2,500 years, all attempt to explain the same class of phenomena, that known as strategic. This theorist offers as his expression of the general theory of strategy the 21 dicta, which is to say, formal pronouncements with a status arguably short of principles, let alone laws. These dicta are presented below and discussed in detail in my *Strategy Bridge*, chapters 1–2.

The General Theory of Strategy in 21 Dicta

Nature and character of strategy

1. Grand strategy is the direction and use made of any or all of the assets of a security community, including its military instrument, for the purposes of policy as decided by politics.

2. Military strategy is the direction and use made of force and the threat of force for the purposes of policy as decided by politics.

3. Strategy is the only bridge built and held to connect policy purposefully with the military and other instruments of power and influence.

4. Strategy serves politics instrumentally by generating net strategic effect.

5. Strategy is adversarial; it functions in both peace and war, and it always seeks a measure of control over enemies (and often over allies and neutrals, as well).

6. Strategy usually requires deception, is paradoxical, and frequently is ironic.

7. Strategy is human.

8. The meaning and character of strategies are driven, though not dictated and wholly determined, by their contexts, all of which are constantly in play and can realistically be understood to constitute just one compounded super context.

9. Strategy has a permanent nature, while strategies (usually plans, formal or informal, expressing contingent operational intentions) have a variable character driven, but not mandated, by their unique and changing contexts, the needs of which are expressed in the decisions of unique individuals.

Making strategy

10. Strategy typically is made by a process of dialogue and negotiation.

11. Strategy is a value-charged zone of ideas and behavior.

12. Historically specific strategies often are driven, and always are shaped, by culture and personality, while strategy in general theory is not.

13. The strategy bridge must be held by competent strategists.

Executing strategy

14. Strategy is more difficult to devise and execute than are policy, operations, and tactics; friction of all kinds comprises phenomena inseparable from the making and conduct of strategies.

15. Strategy can be expressed in strategies that are direct or indirect, sequential or cumulative, attritional or maneuverist-annihilating, persisting or raiding (more or less expeditionary), coercive or brute force, offensive or defensive, symmetrical or asymmetrical, or a complex combination of these nominal but often false alternatives.

16. All strategies are shaped by their particular geographical contexts, but strategy itself is not.

17. Strategy is an unchanging, indeed unchangeable, human activity in thought and behavior, set in a variably dynamic technological context.

18. Unlike strategy, all strategies are temporal.

19. Strategy is logistical.

20. Strategic theory is the most fundamental source of military doctrine, while doctrine is a notable enabler of, and guide for, strategies.

Consequences of strategy

21. All military behavior is tactical in execution but must have operational and strategic effect, intended and otherwise.

If the general theory of strategy to which the air strategist or joint strategist for its air component subscribes is necessarily inclusive, that practicing strategist should be exposed to everything that he or she needs to know about strategy. Contextually unique strategies for the threat and use of airpower find relevance in each of the 21 dicta. At first glance, many of the dicta will appear elementary and beyond the point of the obvious into sheer banality. Indeed, one might argue that any competent air professional deemed promotable to positions of high responsibility should be familiar with these strategic basics. However, the history of military airpower reveals an abundance of strategic malpractice by both airmen and nonairmen. It is an attested historical fact that although the lore, the dicta, of strategy in general can be stated simply and probably even comprehended, the practice of strategy can prove all but impossibly challenging. That which is simple to grasp need not be easy to do, as Clausewitz warns wisely.[18]

The 21 dicta of general theory itemized above truly command the practice of airpower—past, present, and future. Every item has meaning for airpower (and land power and so forth) when translated for unique historical contexts. The individual points are not hard to understand; the greater challenge by far lies in execution. This is an important reason why I am not satisfied with the popular belief that while one *has* a strategy, one *does* tactics.[19] Correct though the claim is regarding the distinction between purpose and instrument, it has the unwanted harmful effect implicitly of confusing the strategist's duty too restrictively. The contrast between having and doing readily translates in actuality into a situation wherein the designated strategist merely acts as the sponsor of operational commanders, who in turn may sponsor tacticians, all of whom do the maneuvering and violence that is supposed to be the practice of strategy. All too often strategy that is more sponsored than done is frustrated because, in practice, the operational artists do only operations while the tacticians do only tactics. This is a situation wherein no one truly does strategy.[20] Practical strategic grip on operations and tactics will be lacking. The tendency for this strategically dysfunctional condition to threaten the integrity of all military enterprises lurks ready to pounce in the very structure of military projects. As Edward N. Luttwak persuasively claims, there is no natural harmony between the levels of war and warfare.[21] Politics/policy, strategy, operations, and tactics each have distinctive natures and characters that enjoy no natural unity.

The General Theory for Education

Theorists, especially civilian ones, are inclined to exaggerate the relative importance of ideas for strategic performance, while soldiers are no less prone to overemphasize the advantages of personal experience in or close to the battlespace. It is easy for both to err, but it should be no less easy for theory and practice to recognize their mutual dependence. Lest there be any misunderstanding, I hold a thoroughly pragmatic view of theory. Theory exists only for the benefit of practice, period. Notwithstanding the cultural differences between airpower theory developed for discussion in the classroom and the practice of airpower in the dangerous skies, the two are true partners. The mission of theory at every level—general theory of strategy, general theory of airpower, or strategic theory as a plan for action—is to provide the desired meaning to tactical behavior. Airmen and their aircraft should not be fighting in and from the sky simply because they are in theater as an asset and fighting is what they are available to do. While every echelon of military behavior needs to be effective at its own level, it is also an enabler for the command levels above it. Today there is misleading talk of "strategic privates" and "strategic corporals," because even the smallest unit at the working level of the military hierarchy, newly network-enabled, is deemed to enjoy an unprecedented relative importance in the conduct of irregular warfare.[22] Whether or not this claim is judged plausible, what is true beyond question is that the corporal on the ground or the aircrew of a single aircraft is the sole foundation for the whole strategic project of a belligerent. Strategy must be done tactically; it has no ethereal, alternative existence. The fact the strategy as high concepts and ideas applied in plans themselves lacks corporeality should not mislead. For example, deterrence, the master concept of the protracted Cold War stand-off, could work to the degree that it may have worked only because the military instruments whose contingent actions were intended to deter were operated tactically by people "in (and above!) the field."

Theory often has, and sometimes merits, a bad name among people obliged to function in a physically and mentally unforgiving world. Therefore, it is important for this book to state with the utmost clarity that the task of theory is to do all it can to assist the practical people who need all the help they can receive, so high are the stakes in their military profession for their own lives and the interests of their security communities. It is ironic that theory and theorists often are regarded with disdain by the people "out there, doing it," when in truth the purpose of the theory enterprise is both to reduce the risks to the warriors and to help make their efforts more useful vis-à-vis the operational goals that are set. Theory is, or at least should be, the friend of the airman, not an irrelevant distraction, let alone an enemy.

It should be clear by now that this study embraces an inclusive understanding of the theory of airpower. In addition to the general theory of strategy that is the primary focus in this chapter, general theory specifically for airpower is treated distinctively in chapter 7, while the text throughout regards the strategies of air command-ers—joint and other—as a particular class of speculative theory or contingent prediction. Let it not be understated: the entire history of aviation has been elevated and propelled by aerodynamic pre-theory (guesswork), as well as some theory proper, but pervasively and persistently by a dangerous and in large measure unavoidable process of trial and error.[23] Not unlike the frontiers of medicine, many technical solutions to aviation challenges have worked well enough, even though it has not been thoroughly understood why. To recall a thought expressed in chapter 1, our civilization has become so familiar with reliable controlled flight that the novelty of the project and the technical difficulties that have been overcome are easily overlooked or insufficiently appreciated.

It is paradoxical but unavoidable that the general theory of strategy can tell airmen simultaneously both everything they need to know about their profession and yet nothing in specifically useful detail. For the specifically useful, perhaps just relevant, airmen must now look to doctrine for guidance on best, or good enough, practice. However, since doctrine always seems to be racing to catch up with experience in and from the field, even manuals on good current practice need to be treated more or less with discretion (though this author has heard much less polite opinions from serving airmen).

General strategic theory is a tool kit for airmen—no more, but also no less. Such theory can educate, but it cannot train or instruct, advise, or direct military behavior in detail toward strategic objectives in any particular historical context. The general theory of strategy enables thinking, educable airmen to understand why they are fighting and how their fighting (or support for fighting) serves policy, but it cannot reveal the particular character of the conflict of the day. Strategic theory cannot, at least should not endeavor to, specify solutions to contemporary challenges. There is a danger of what one can term *theory creep*, arguably *doctrine creep*, whereby the frontier between theory and doctrine becomes unduly blurred and the result is an underrecognized confusion of the two. This can occur when "best practice" in one or more conflicts is confused with general theory and subsequently misapplied to a degree to conflicts where it may not even be *good* practice. Admittedly, since most military establishments tend to engage in "lessons learned" exercises sensibly and prudently, it can be difficult indeed to distinguish best practice in a past war from best practice in wars in general. For arguable examples, what is perceived to have been good doctrine for British counterinsurgency (COIN) in Malaya in the 1950s and for the United States in Vietnam in the 1960s and early 1970s is mistaken for the foundations of a valid general theory of strategy for COIN. The fact that this is done honestly and largely with irreproachable motives does not remove the danger. Some readers may have discerned the spore of the error of confusion of the general with the specific in American approaches to recent and contemporary COIN challenges in Iraq and Afghanistan. Even when it is tactically well conducted, COIN is not an effective super-hammer when the problem happens not to be a nail in need of hammering.[24]

It is precisely because every war is distinctive that each must be understood on its own terms. In the words of the master, "The first, the supreme, the most far-reaching act of judgment that the statesman and commander have to make is to establish by that test the kind of war on which they are embarking; neither mistaking it for, nor trying to turn it into, something that is alien to its nature."[25]

A vital role of strategy's general theory, and even of airpower's general theory, is to help inoculate politicians and soldiers against capture by inappropriate doctrine derived from another, possibly yesterday's, "present." General theory—of war, of strategy, as well as specifically of airpower—must be exactly that. Its function and its strength, when well crafted, lie in its distance from the present situation that cries out for applied theory in plans. Airmen need to police the frontier between theory and doctrine to ensure that even successful strands of the latter are not misjudged as belonging to the former. When this occurs—as it has and will—doctrine for today becomes general airpower theory for tomorrow, which in turn acts to inhibit the creation of doctrine tomorrow that best fits the circumstances of tomorrow.

The general theory of strategy puts airpower in its place, explains its purpose, connects it properly with everything to which it needs to be securely connected, tidies up the plethora of what could be vital if somewhat dangling undervalued (and underresourced) loose ends, and strives to help the educable airman perform better. This study lays much emphasis upon the human element. Number six among the dicta of strategy's general theory insists that "strategy is human." Undoubtedly there are many airmen who are not strategically educable. Strategy is complex, complicated, and although certainly doable, exceedingly difficult. Indeed, strategy's superior importance relative to operations and tactics is matched fully by the scale of the challenges to its satisfactory performance. It follows that although every airman performs strategically, if only innocently or ignorantly by default, only a few are fully educable as strategists for high levels of command. This is because competent strategic performance requires not only intellect but also suitable character.

Not only do outstanding strategists need to understand their strategic context and choices in a grand duel with a self-willed, albeit presumably influenceable, adversary. They must also advance mentally from adequate understanding, to judgment, to decision, and then persist through flexibly adaptable grip upon unpredictable contingent events. These are not trivial steps to specify, and it is commonplace and often necessary, if sometimes unwise, to separate the roles of strategic conceptualizer, strategic planner, and operational commander.[26] The point just made is simply that although there is theory in the practice of strategy, even a sound intellectual grasp of strategy's general theory carries no guarantee of excellence in the practice of strategy. A brilliant mind can be combined with a lack of self-confidence such that the ability to decide is weak. Similarly, an intellectually and morally admirable general may lack the personality, the necessary charisma, to command effectively in the presence of stronger, if intellectually less-gifted, personalities and possibly dispirited, skeptical, and even somewhat unwilling troops.

It is sensible to recognize that an education in general strategic theory should be valuable for all aspiring, let alone unexpectedly designated, strategists (air and other). It is also necessary to accept the human reality that people differ. Not every outstanding fighter pilot or excellent wing commander necessarily is a true strategist-in-waiting for the opportunity by promotion. To be good at doing something tactically and operationally is not necessarily a sure sign of the potential for superior comprehension of why tactical behavior and operational designs should or should not be attempted.

It would be readily understandable were any readers of this text to examine the 21 dicta listed as my take on strategy's general theory and to respond, probably with unintentional irony, with the strategist's most characteristic question, "So what?" Surely, it might be objected, the theory states the blindingly obvious. Does one need to be told that there is an enemy who has a vote in how conflicts evolve (dictum 4)? Is it necessary to specify that the strategist seeks strategic effect for political purposes (dictum 2)? Can it be an obscure revelation that strategy is a value-charged endeavor (dictum 11)? And so on and so forth. Alas, it is a matter of the plainest possible historical record, not merely opinion, that violence has been and continues to be applied, ultimately for political purposes, in the rankest practical violation of the implicit advice that the general theory of strategy seeks to convey. Strategists and aspiring strategists, including air strategists, decline or are unable to be educated by strategy's general theory with consequences that typically vary from the unfortunate to the catastrophic.

As a theorist this author somewhat reluctantly is obliged by a commitment to honesty about the rich variety of historical experience to acknowledge some limits to what is achievable by strategic competence. Clausewitz alerts us to the frighteningly ubiquitous and unpredictable phenomenon of friction.[27] He emphasizes the monumental risks and uncertainties of war.[28] Truly, as a recent US secretary of defense claimed dismissively with respect to looting in Baghdad in 2003, "Stuff happens." The best-laid schemes of well-educated strategists are apt to be thwarted or certainly hindered by an uncooperative enemy, dull-witted or unlucky subordinates, undermotivated troops, or by policy imposed by politicians who are unable or unwilling to accept the emerging verdict of nonpermissive military reality. Appropriately enough, with exceptional gratitude due to Clausewitz, the general theory of strategy strives to arm the strategist against the pragmatic assaults by appalling and specifically unanticipated strategic actualities. That said, airpower history provides convincing evidence of air strategies devised and attempted that neglected the enemy, the weather, the frailties of the human body, and the unreliability of air navigation, amidst a host of sins, major and minor. General theory cannot prevent error, but it can educate practitioners to be alert to its menace, by category, though admittedly not usually in detail.

Policy, Strategy, Tactics: What or Who Is in Charge?

Clausewitz was not confused between logical truth and truth as an often illogical, rather messy reality. His primary trinity, the core of his theory of war, postulates unstable relations among "basic hostility, the play of chance and probability . . . and the subordinating or guiding influence of purpose."[29] As noted above, he associates these fundamental trinitarian elements largely with the people, the commander and his army, and the government, respectively. Despite the political nature of war and the logical superiority of policy—which is the frequently shifting product of politics over popular feeling and the polity's military instrument—Clausewitz knew that policy was by no means always in charge of warfare. To understand the history of airpower, it is necessary to empathize with the people who made it, and that requires one to adopt a theoretical perspective as adaptable as that just cited in Clausewitz. A moment's reflection, let alone some acquaintance with the early years of airpower history, reveals with luminous clarity the fact that high policy did not bring forth airpower out of a void. The five chapters in this study devoted to airpower history demonstrate just how variable the relations have been among policy, strategy, and tactics as ends, ways, and means (the classic formula for the strategy function). Logically, one would like to insist that political purpose should guide choice of strategy, which, in turn, ought to direct the selection of the most suitable tactics. In practice, however, this logic can be reversed. The character of the available military instrument dictates what it can accomplish, the frank and prudent recognition of which should shape what strategy requires of it, while strategic feasibility limits the scope for policy choices. Thus, we have a strategy of tactics and a policy dictated by a strategy which also is driven by tactics.

The relations of influence just outlined can be characterized fairly as dysfunctional or even pathological. How can the weapon command the purpose for its employment? The world could be upside down were the sword to direct the brain that supposedly owns it. Nonetheless, it is all too obvious that the neat, logically sequenced categories of ends, ways, and means or policy, strategy, and tactics conceal almost as much as they explain. The whole house of strategy in practice may not even have robustly separate rooms called policy, strategy, and tactics. While one cannot sensibly contest Clausewitz's claim that "war is an act of policy" or that it is "a true political instrument," neither must one discount the potency of war's own grammar, the shifting details of which are unique to the peculiar nature of its means.[30] And the core of its dynamic and peculiar nature is violence. Clausewitz argues, realistically as usual, that although politics are the supreme consideration in the conduct of war, "that does not imply that the political aim is a tyrant! It must adapt itself to its chosen means, a process which can radically change it."[31] These are momentous thoughts with respect to their implications for our reading of the practice of airpower. It may be worth noting that judgments on the theory and practice of a century of airpower need to contend with the instability of a minimum of six potential drivers: theory, doctrine, policy, strategy, tactics, and technology. Should that already forbidding augmentation to the basic trinity of policy, strategy, and tactics fail to promote a prudent anxiety, one could add vision, plans, and operations as further plausible sources of the true complexity of history.

The book has no intention of suffering fatal damage from "friendly fire" imposed by any needless complication. However, it is necessary to recognize that the drivers of airpower history—past, present, and future—are indeed at least as numerous as the six, or nine, cited immediately above. It would be understandable were some readers to wish to dismiss this discussion as a mere digression, perhaps as academic self-indulgence. Would that that were so! Unfortunately, the many driving factors cited are all significant because their unstable interweaving has driven the particular course taken in the practice of airpower. The airpower literature offers contrasting theses as to whether theory drove technology, technology drove policy, and so forth. The trouble is that if one eschews the joys of vigorous debate, with its necessity for clear and simple positions, one is obliged to acknowledge that most rival arguments have more than trivial merit. The challenge then is to identify the narrative that is robustly true enough, because it cannot be wholly accurate. Theory for explanation in the social sciences satisfies by being testably true in most cases. This is to grant that there are no equivalents in strategy to the laws of physics. Social-scientific apples have been known not to drop from trees when the social scientists' equivalent to the law of gravity says that they ought. But when one endeavors to explain airpower history in the contexts of war and peace, it is important that one does not loosen one's grip on understanding how military power should relate to its directing and physically enabling drivers. One must be both ready and able to see apparently dysfunctional, certainly undesirable, relations of relative influence—tactics driving strategy, for example—and accept their inevitability, all the while holding firm to a grasp of how things should be done. Muddle and contingency may well rule and can be survived, but there is good reason why logical priorities are what they are. Clausewitz believed in the primacy of politics, in the value in military planning, in strategy—despite his full appreciation of the historical reality of friction, chance, uncertainty, and risk.

Two quotations will help to illuminate the inverted relationships discussed here. First, in a novel from a screenplay, the fictional captain of a US Navy ballistic-missile submarine utters these profoundly Clausewitzian words: "While the purpose of war is to serve a political end, the nature of war is to serve itself."[32] Second, notwithstanding the logic that should oblige tactical behavior to express strategic direction, it has been argued strongly regarding World War I that "tactics are usually derived from strategy, but in the first air war the tactics the men evolved in the air led to a greater understanding of the possible uses of air power and thus to the strategies for air war. The men doing the fighting were developing the uses for air power, while leaders like Trenchard were compiling these fragments into doctrine and strategy."[33]

Wing Cdr Robert Grattan is probably overly generous in his claim that "tactics are usually derived from strategy." Logically this should be so because one must presume that tactics ought to be developed and matured to be effective in support of a particular strategy. To quote the architectural maxim, form follows function. However, historical practice shows that what Grattan rightly finds to have been the reverse of the logical relationship in 1914–18 actually is as much, if not more, the norm than the exception. Tactics do what can be done with the military instrument of the day and of the near tomorrow, and strategy has to adapt to the tactical verdict of the dynamic battlefield. Tactical epiphanies regarding current possibilities may be turned into doctrine, formal and informal, though both doctrine and strategy are likely to be faint and only distantly pursuing contemporary military practicabilities.

The first quotation above laid emphasis upon the imperial nature of war per se, vis-à-vis its supposedly political master; the second claims that there are times wherein tactics drive strategy rather than vice versa. These apparent pathologies of servants leading masters can readily be augmented by other major examples. To quote Grattan again, "Technology was the principal driver of the development of tactics and strategy in the air war [1914–18]. Advances in engine power and aerodynamics formed the basis for the competition, and there was a constant need to improve performance to outdo, or at least match, the enemy."[34]

He concludes his useful review of the aircraft, engines, and equipment for the air war of 1914–18 with these thoughts:

> All these technological developments provided more options for the use of aircraft, which in turn demanded doctrinal, tactical and strategic thinking. The time available for analysis was limited, however, and it became a case of learning by doing and what enabled the fittest to survive was adopted, until something better came along. The men in the air did a lot of this work, but the commanders, who were closely in touch, added the refinements and tried to work out principles from the mass of detail with which they had to deal. Their development of tactics and strategy however, were often making the best of a bad situation when the equipment they had available had serious limitations.[35]

What Grattan describes is scarcely surprising, given the utter novelty of air warfare in the period. One is tempted to contrast the historical reality of the emergence of air warfare from nothing in World War I, a context that had to privilege inductive theorizing, with the situation in World War II wherein the belligerents' air forces entered combat already heavily laden with theory and theory as doctrine. It may be worth recognizing explicitly a military and strategic fact about 1914 that is so obvious that typically it escapes notice. Specifically, although it is correct and important to take account of the entire novelty of air warfare, in some ways it is even more important to appreciate that to the mature military instruments that were the armies and navies of the great powers, modern warfare among themselves was also a novelty. Yes, the almost ludicrously small, fragile, and incompetent cutting edge of military airpower in 1914 had to make it all up from scratch as it went along. Although progress was somewhat chaotic and episodic, though cumulatively revolutionary and hectic, the context of an ongoing total war certainly fast-forwarded technical, tactical, doctrinal, and strategic advance as nothing else can come close to doing. Desperate need spurs invention. Dr. Johnson was correct in his claim that the prospect of being hanged in the morning has a way of concentrating the mind. However, it is necessary to assess airpower properly, to view it in that "width, depth, and context" upon which Michael Howard insists. The military context for the all-but-nothing airpower in August–September 1914 was populated by major armies and navies that had no experience in the practice of modern warfare.[36] So, while one can empathize with the airmen of 1914–16, probably one should empathize even more with the proud commanders of mature military instruments on land and sea that were found not to be instruments of swift decision. If airmen had to learn how to conduct air warfare, soldiers and sailors first had to unlearn much that they thought they knew before they and their forces were fit to succeed in modern warfare. The burden on both sets of shoulders was awesome indeed.

Between Politics and Tactics: The Strategist's Dilemma

The air strategist, no less than his or her land and sea counterparts, holds the metaphorical bridge between the political world that generates what is known, albeit often misleadingly, as policy and the realm of military power. The chain of command and principal functions of its major connecting links are clear enough. However, the practice of (air and so forth) strategy always requires the mutual adjustment of tactical feasibility and its higher (military, strategic, political) purpose. Every conflict, probably without exception, has witnessed politicians demanding of their generals and admirals some achievements that are either infeasible or prove feasible only at such a heavy absolute or opportunity cost that they should not have been attempted at all or at least not pursued with persistence. Because every war, like every peacetime occasion for deterrence, is unique, there can be no strictly calculated metrics for threat and damage that must do the job. Every mission is different; this is why strategy is more art than science. Strategy requires judgment; strategic decision cannot be delegated to mathematical formulae. Although all forms of military power, except now for cyber, have violence at the core of their political purpose, airpower chose, probably inescapably, to hitch its main wagon to the strategic value of delivery of violence kinetically from altitude. Realistically, what other option was there that would ensure airpower's institutional survival, growth, and political success? A point to be recognized for this study is that the long-running debate over whether or not so-called strategic airpower has delivered on the promise of its doctrine should be viewed in the context of the complex relations among politics, strategy, and tactics.

Bluntly propounded, air (and other) strategists are caught between politician policy makers who are apt to demand the more or less impossible and tacticians who demonstrate bloodily that they cannot do what is demanded. The result, which all but defines the challenge of strategy, is that strategists have to identify ways that both their means can do and their political ends judge good enough. There are times when strategists are instructed by politicians to pursue military ways even though the political directors have excellent reason to anticipate military disappointment. Britain persisted with its bomber offensive against Germany in 1941–43 despite Winston Churchill's realization that it was having a far less than decisive effect upon the enemy.[37] The prime minister, and later Franklin Roosevelt also, needed the (eventually nominally "combined") bomber offensive to serve political duty as a surrogate for the still absent second front in France. On similar political grounds, in May and June 1940 Churchill reluctantly pressed the RAF to commit some of the scarce home defense Spitfire squadrons from Fighter Command to the losing, truly lost, battle in France and Belgium. Their commitment, which would have been a useless military sacrifice in a lost campaign, was believed briefly by the prime minister to be a political-moral necessity and as a consequence, only very arguably, strategic. Fortunately, the RAF, especially Fighter Command's commander in chief, Air Chief Marshal Sir Hugh Dowding, successfully resisted Churchill. The RAF already was suffering serious losses with its Advanced Air Striking Force in France and then with its heroic, though at the time greatly underappreciated, efforts to protect the evacuation of the British Expeditionary Force (BEF) and a notable fraction of French allied forces from the Dunkirk perimeter.[38] It was fortunate that the Luftwaffe believed that it was committed to destroy the BEF in a *Kesselschlacht*, or cauldron battle, rather than to prevent a wholesale evacuation. German attacks were not focused on the harbor.

Time and again this study emphasizes the importance of context. However, context is not always treated appropriately, even by scholars. Frequently, the exact definition of context—its precise characterization in time, space, and feasibility—truly is contestable. Strong proponents of a land power–, sea power–, or airpower-led (or even a nuclear weapon–led) definition of a particular strategic challenge will construct an interpretation of the context that privileges their preference. But tactical feasibility does have a way eventually of imposing discipline in choice of contextual definition. For contrasting examples of somewhat similar featured contexts, from November 1941 until the end of January 1942, the Luftwaffe proved conclusively that its leader's promise that it could logistically sustain the encircled Sixth Army in the Stalingrad *Kessel* was tactically impossible; by contrast, in 1948–49 US and British airpower demonstrated no less conclusively that it could sustain the terrestrially blockaded enclave of West Berlin. Tactical failure or success drove strategic and political choices. But it must be admitted that often, though not in the two cases just cited, there will be no way in which political prudence, reasonable operational risk, and strategic wisdom are identifiable short of the availability of tactical evidence from practice, and usually the practice of combat. Policy and strategy have to be done by troops. If the troops cannot or will not do it, then apparently sound policy and strategy, not to say theory and doctrine, will not save you from failure.

Conclusion: Scope for Discretion

There is no single right way to use airpower in all circumstances. By far the most intelligent way to answer the question, how should airpower be used? takes the form of a reply that must begin with the vital words, "It depends." As commentator after commentator has noted, the strategic value of airpower relative to the other instruments of grand strategy is situationally specific.[39] If of any consolation to especially air-minded readers, the same rule applies to land power and sea power. This is not to deny that particular security communities tend to favor a specific style in warfare that privileges land, sea, or air, basically for geographical reasons. It is understandable, actually it is strongly desirable, that a polity whose military excellence is best expressed in, say, its navy, should endeavor to identify policy goals and an implementing strategy that favor its strengths rather than its less-formidable assets. From the Peloponnesian War to the conflicts of the present, preferred ways and means in warfare are plainly identifiable. Sometimes what societies prefer as their chosen strategic style proves effective and sometimes not. It is important to recognize that airpower long has been the preferred leading edge in warfare by a technologically ascendant and casualty-sensitive America, but as a downside of the upside, this clear generic preference carries hazardous temptations, because the air environment's geophysical ubiquity encourages hopes for decisive military intervention from altitude in all terrestrial geography. Ambition is fed by geography, and geography may be destiny, to cite the long-familiar albeit somewhat controversial claim.[40]

Although context provides meaning, the context for airpower is never entirely a given. A state with an especially potent and flexible military air arm should strive to locate policy goals that plausibly ought to be achievable by the ways and means in which it is relatively superior, which is to say by its airpower. Imperial Athens had need of its army, but Pericles chose a strategy that relied most heavily upon its maritime power.[41] In 1915, during World War I, Britain's secretary of state for war, Field Marshal Herbert Lord Kitchener, stated in words of some wisdom for all time, "One makes war, not as one would like to, but as one must."[42] Because conflict, especially war itself, always entails competitors, its term of engagement must constitute a vital stake in the progress of the struggle. Admittedly, the range of discretion will be limited. For example, Nazi Germany had to be defeated first at sea and then in the air before it could be defeated on the ground; at least, that was true for the war in the west. Also, one could argue that Germany needed to be weakened massively on the ground by its cumulatively enormous losses on the eastern front before the Western Allies could exploit their victories at sea and in the air for success on land. The useful approach to context-shaping for national advantage is to seek so to structure a conflict that its battlespace, understood broadly and inclusively, maximizes the potential benefits of friendly strengths. Of course there will be practical limits to the ability to structure a conflict favorably. Nonetheless, the effort should always be made. With thanks to Sun Tzu, as well as to common sense, one should strive to undermine, perhaps evade, and thereby defeat the enemy strategically rather than tactically.[43] This advice translates as the recommendation to win the conflict rather than to win some of the fighting with strategic consequences that are politically inconclusive or irrelevant.

The analysis now turns explicitly to the crucial subject of airpower's ever-dynamic relationship to conflict as a whole and most especially to the other military instruments of grand strategy.

Notes

1. For a discussion that addresses the fallacious proposition that the evolution of airpower has been driven by technology rather than ideas, see Gray, *Understanding Airpower*, 22–27.

2. Kagan, *Finding the Target*, 125–26.

3. See Bethel et al., "Developing Air Force Strategists," and Chiabotti, "A Deeper Shade of Blue." On the subject of education in strategy more generally, see Gray, *Schools for Strategy*, and US House Armed Services Committee, *Another Crossroads?* The deficit in strategic education addressed in the references just cited is by no means a lonely American problem, as revealed in Newton, Colley, and Sharpe, "Reclaiming the Art of British Strategic Thinking."

4. Given the recent arrival of air forces, it was inevitable that some notable commanders of airpower in the first half of the twentieth century had transferred from ground-focused army careers. The leading example of this phenomenon was the highly capable General Field Marshal Albert Kesselring, who in 1940 commanded the largest of the Luftwaffe's air fleets, *Luftflotte* 2. He was an outstanding soldier and a capable air leader, but his professional association with airpower dated only from 1933, and he remained more truly land rather than air oriented. It was his misfortune to be embattled in 1940 with the ultimate of air professionals in the grim person of Air Chief Marshal Sir Hugh Dowding of the RAF's Fighter Command and his no-less-air-professional combat commander, Air Vice-Marshal Sir Keith Park. In a grand strategic duel when the two belligerent air forces have somewhat balancing strengths and weaknesses, depth and breadth of air expertise confer a significant advantage, as the course of the Battle of Britain demonstrated unmistakably. See Bungay, *Most Dangerous Enemy*, 120–27.

5. Lawrence, *Seven Pillars of Wisdom*, 191.

6. Corbett, *Some Principles of Maritime Strategy*, 307. The words quoted are from Corbett's strategy handout to students at the Royal Naval War College in 1906.

7. This claim is explained, developed, and employed in Gray, "Moral Advantage, Strategic Advantage?"

8. Following Clausewitz, *On War*, 75, it is certainly sound, indeed it is essential, to recognize the centrality of will to any strategic enterprise. That elemental point readily granted, it is still important to appreciate that the vital concept of will can be much more problematic than commonly is understood. Whose will, for the most obvious challenge in need of detailed appreciation? And how does that "will" express itself operationally? Questions such as these are usefully posed and pursued in Clodfelter, "Aiming to Break Will." He discusses the will of Nazi Germany to fight on, with reference to the people, the fighting forces, and political leaders. This not entirely

accidental match with Clausewitz's secondary trinity comprising the people, the army and its commander, and the government (*On War*, 89) fuels a productive line of inquiry. Clodfelter is convinced that kinetic airpower has a better record of coercive success against the will to resist of enemy soldiers than it does against enemy popular opinion or leaders. His argument as presented to date is far from conclusively persuasive, but it shows serious promise of bearing healthy fruit, and it highlights to military professionals and scholars the importance that they should attach to unpacking the rather slippery and assuredly "amorphous" concept of the enemy's "will." Clodfelter, "Aiming to Break Will," 403, 433.

9. John Warden and his famous five-ring grand design for aerial targeting are discussed in chap. 7.

10. For an example of error in an otherwise generally excellent study of the utility of airpower in counterinsurgency (COIN), Wg Cdr Derek Read argues that "the combination of mobility, observation and firepower through airpower has been cited as being 'decisive' in counter-insurgency and thus might be considered strategic." Read, "Airpower in COIN," 135.

11. "Tactics *teaches the use of armed forces in the engagement*; strategy, *the use of engagements for the object of war*." Clausewitz, *On War*, 128 (emphasis in the original).

12. See Handel, *Masters of War*, 353–60.

13. But for some useful pre-theory, see Oberg, *Space Power Theory*, and especially Michael Smith, "Ten Propositions Regarding Spacepower." Two books by Martin C. Libicki constitute a promising beginning for a theory of cyber power: *Conquest in Cyberspace* and *Cyberdeterrence and Cyberwar*.

14. See Gray, *Schools for Strategy*; and Kolenda, *Leadership*.

15. Winton, "An Imperfect Jewel," 2–4.

16. See Gray, *Strategy Bridge*, 264–65.

17. Examples include Thucydides, *History of the Peloponnesian War*, which is history; Sun Tzu, *Art of War*, which is all-but-PowerPoint policy, strategy, and tactical advice; Clausewitz, *On War*, which mainly is akin to philosophy; and Luttwak, *Strategy*, which principally is modern social science.

18. Clausewitz, *On War*, 178; see also Gray, *Strategy Bridge*, chap. 4.

19. See Hughes, "Strategy-Tactics Relationship," for a sophisticated analysis of the naval dimension to this key relationship.

20. For an overstatement of the case critical of the influence of the official recognition of an operational level of war, see Kelly and Brennan, *Alien*.

21. Luttwak, *Strategy*, xii.

22. For an example that I regard as somewhat overcooked in the heat of network centricity, see Schmidtchen, *Rise of the Strategic Private*.

23. It would be difficult to state more clearly the dependence of some past US airpower practice upon theory than did Maj Gen Haywood S. Hansell Jr. when he wrote, "Feasibility of effective and sustained air attack as the key to victory could not be demonstrated by past experience. Victory through airpower alone was pure theory. It had never been accomplished, and it could hardly be expected that the United States would voluntarily pin its future existence on an untried theory." Hansell, *Air Plan that Defeated Hitler*, 75.

24. See the recent debate over COIN: Jones and Smith, "Whose Hearts and Whose Minds?"; Nagl and Burton, "Thinking Globally and Acting Locally"; and

Jones and Smith, "Grammar but No Logic." Although this scholars' debate waxed perilously close to the scholastic, undeniably it has meaning for political and strategic practice.

25. Clausewitz, *On War*, 88.
26. See Gray, *Strategy Bridge*, chap. 6.
27. Clausewitz, *On War*, 119–21.
28. Ibid., 104.
29. Ibid., 89, as rephrased by Echevarria, *Clausewitz and Contemporary War*, 70.
30. Clausewitz, *On War*, 87, 605.
31. Ibid., 87.
32. Henrick, *Crimson Tide*, 97.
33. Grattan, *Origins of Air War*, 137.
34. Ibid., 85.
35. Ibid., 86.
36. This claim holds, notwithstanding the partial exception of the Russian experience of war with Japan in 1904–05 and the British wake-up call delivered in their war with the two Boer republics in South Africa from 1899 to 1902.
37. Hastings, *Finest Years*, 75, 560–61. RAF Bomber Command was seriously unfit to do damage to Germany in the early years of the war. In 1940–41 Britain bombed the Reich because there was not much else it could do to tell its own citizens and the world that it was still in the fight; while in 1942–43, the bombing was a political necessity in the context of alliance relations when the Soviet Union seemed to be, and probably was, on the edge of collapse.
38. RAF Fighter Command Spitfires, flying from England, were committed to the defense of the Dunkirk perimeter and the evacuation. Their appearance and performance were an unpleasant and unexpected surprise to the previously all-conquering Messerschmitt Bf 109s of the Luftwaffe (see the discussion in chap. 5). The Spitfires flew 706 sorties from 27 May to 2 June and suffered 48 losses. Hooton, *Phoenix Triumphant*.
39. For example, Luttwak, *Strategy*, 197–98.
40. Weigert, *Generals and Geographers*, 4.
41. Athenian fighting power at sea was the deliberate, quite sudden, and controversial creation of Themistocles in the 480s BC. The Athens whose 10,000 citizen-soldiers, with Plataean allies, beat the Persians on land at Marathon in 490 BC was not a great naval power and had no particular naval tradition. The fortuitous discovery of silver in Attica enabled erstwhile non-naval Athens to buy the combat fleet that sank the Persians and their subject allies at Salamis in 480 BC.
42. Kitchener quoted in Howard, *Continental Commitment*, 126.
43. Sun Tzu, *Art of War*, 77.

Chapter 3

Geographies of Warfare

Attempting to make strategic sense of airpower can be likened to endeavoring to provide sound yet honest advice to a person who is fundamentally healthy yet seemingly in danger of a nervous collapse due to substantially baseless anxieties. Running parallel with airpersons' recurring crises of confidence, not necessarily self-confidence, has been the paradox that remarkable technical and tactical progress has entirely failed to settle some of the more bitter controversies that characterized airpower's early decades. Experience and technology have answered many questions about what airpower can do in favorable circumstances, but some important issues are no closer to resolution today than in the 1920s and 1930s. Simply stated, three "joint" questions say it all—On the team? As the team? Off the team? Is airpower *on* the national military team? Or should airpower itself be recognized *as*, or promoted to *be*, the national military team? For a third option, should airpower be *off* the team as a semi-independent player with its constituent and variable parts owned and employed by terrestrially focused military forces?

Strategy, including air strategy, is a thoroughly human project, and human beings pursue and employ truth in a political context.[1] Since we humans are political animals, our struggles—be they personal, institutional, or beyond—entail the use of political leverage to secure more political leverage. This may sound cynical, but really it is not. We conduct all of our affairs politically, and politics is about the distribution of power. One must never forget that airpower arrived on the strategic scene just over a century ago. It has made extraordinary technical and tactical progress since it went to war in 1914 with 15-bhp engines and ground speeds as low as 30 mph in the face of a notable headwind.[2] Airpower has registered revolutionary technical and tactical advances, but—and it is a significant but—land power and sea power also have modernized technically and tactically. Airpower no longer owns the latest geography for warfare; it has been succeeded, though not superseded, by space power and cyber power; and technical and tactical revolution may not translate into strategic or political revolution. Truly, these are deep waters, as Sherlock Holmes is reported to have said.

Airpower Controversy

As is true for policy, strategy also is developed in a political process moved along by distinctive interests competing for influence over decisions. Of course, the strategy function that connects ends, ways, and means should impose discipline upon the choices advertised and advocated, but rarely are there no halfway plausible alternatives for each item in this interdependent trio. Viewed outside of a historical context that captures the *longue durée*, it is easy to rush to the mistaken judgment that airpower's relatively brief past has been characterized by inappropriately extraordinary controversy, unusual persisting parochialisms, and strategically incompetent claims and actual misbehavior of an exceptionally high order. Such heavy charges are as understandable from some interpretations of the historical record as they are substantially unjust, misleading, and plain wrong. The following are the long-persisting reasons why airpower has attracted such lively controversy:

Uncertainty I

It has been difficult to police a debate about a subject that has been constantly in technical and, soon after its birth, tactical motion. The pace of technical and tactical change has rendered consensus even on temporary apparent certainties hard to achieve, let alone sustain. The mobility of the technical and tactical stories has loaded the guns of every opinion.

Uncertainty II

From nearly its earliest days in the 1900s, the technological-tactical narrative has been moving toward the ability to function strategically as a military instrument able to achieve decisive effect in war all but independent of joint contributions from land power and sea power. However one elects to phrase this thought, the point is that strategic debate about airpower for national security long has been for and about the highest of stakes, at least since the early 1920s, with serious harbingers well in evidence in 1917 and 1918.

Vested Interests

Airpower arrived on a strategic scene that was already fully occupied institutionally. Armies and navies governed all terrestrial environments and were more, sometimes less, willing to co-opt a novel weapon to their partially combined arms baskets of assets. Initially, it may be recalled, the only officially accepted role for aircraft was reconnaissance. What followed is, as the saying goes, history. Both land power (actually ground power) and sea power had few serious ideological-doctrinal, generic objections to acquisition of some overhead augmentation to the cavalry, the observation balloon, and the scout car, and for the navies, to their frigates. Airborne cavalry and flying frigates posed some challenges to instinctively and prudently conservative military establishments. But early airpower did not appear to pose a lethal threat to the established and self-evidently rightful military order of things. The trouble was that infant airpower came to press not for a place on the army and navy teams, and then for ever larger roles, but instead to replace the old teams and become "Team Airpower," in sole strategic possession. Whatever the reasonably objective merits in the rival contemporary cases advanced in debate among the champions, it is scarcely surprising that foreign menace was distant and wispy in comparison with the threat that airpower, unchained by co-opted ownership, seemed to pose to armies and navies.

The Unforeseeable Future

Flexibility and adaptability should be key to the strategic value of an air force. However, both airpower's advocates and its detractors have sought to shape the debate over airpower's relative status and roles by pretending to a future knowledge that they did not and could not have. It is possible to be honest and admit that the future is not foreseeable and yet assert with confidence that victory can always be assured through the use of airpower. Should one feel obliged to concede that the relative strategic significance of airpower will vary with the character of a conflict, then one may be tempted to be rather more certain than the evidence allows to argue that future conflicts will provide a good fit with friendly airpower's potency. There should be no need for the generic advocates of airpower to strain against and over the bounds of evidence, because the multi-role strategic (via tactical and operational effects) utility of airpower in armed conflicts of all kinds cannot sensibly be challenged. At least this is so, provided one does not seek to insist implausibly that "victory through airpower" is a mantra that matches every strategic challenge. The golden key to begin to unravel the puzzle of how to think about and prepare for the mysteries of future conflicts is nothing more complicated than acceptance of the familiar maxim that airpower's value is highly situationally specific. Imperial claims for airpower that rest mainly upon faith and volume and frequency of assertion inflict grave self harm.

Complexity

The battlespace of warfare has always been broadly strategically competitive when rivals and belligerents have had to decide how to allocate ever-scarce resources between their land power and their sea power.[3] For security communities that did not have to balance, or purposefully materially imbalance, their efforts between land and sea, usually there have been reasons for contention as to how to balance the available options by category (more heavy, or light, infantry? more heavy, or light, cavalry? how much artillery, and of what character?). While there has been, and remains today, a fairly grand historical narrative of controversy(ies) at the master level of geographical environment—land, sea, air, space—parallel, adjunct, and sometimes more exclusive intervening narratives also have attached to the military developments specialized for each geography. Not only is it inevitable that soldiers, sailors, and airmen should contend for strategic preference in strategic planning and action, it is desirable that they should do so. Rarely is there a wholly self-evidently superior strategy for victory. More often than not even the definition of what should constitute an acceptable victory or advantage is subject to legitimate dispute. Since the stakes (ends) in war are high and the strategy (ways) contestable, it is unsurprising that the detail of human and technical assets (means) to be acquired and employed will be ever challengeable. It is through professional challenge and answer, mediated by a political process, that some approximation to functional strategic truth emerges.[4] To summarize, the context for understanding airpower, both in general and in particular historical circumstances, is almost desperately complex. There is a great deal not only over which argument can erupt, but also over which it should erupt.

The Joint Challenge

The tactical "grammar" of warfare has always tended to reward agile, and especially innovative, synergy.[5] Napoleonic warfare was a matter of tactically combining threat and action by foot, horse, and guns. Expressed functionally, both tactical and operational land warfare have ever been a matter of manipulating movement, shock, and fire. Exactly how the trio must be committed to action varies from situation to situation. However, military history is entirely unambiguous for once in recommending implicitly the benefits of appropriate synergism. Particular armies and navies are relatively stronger in some capabilities than in others, just as they vary in their competence relative to each other nationally as well as to their geographical counterparts abroad.

Airpower has always raised extraordinary difficulties for those who have sought rational yet the most militarily effective organization of armed forces. In the proverbial nutshell, there is an inescapable dilemma lurking in the facts that warfare is joint but geography is not. One might inquire why it should matter for strategy that there are at least five quite distinctive geographies/environments for warfare (land, sea surface and subsurface, air, Earth orbital space, and the electromagnetic spectrum). Surely, history and conflict in history necessarily constitute a unity. Historians may write about the air war over Vietnam, for example, but that geographically exclusive focus does not contradict the reality of a single unified course of history. America, or whoever, conducts national defense for national security; defense and security in the air can only be a subset of a whole.

A major problem has been to identify a culminating point of victory in organizational tailoring for operational reality. The essential unity of war and its warfare, as for peacetime defense preparation also, has come to be recognized in a respect for "jointness" that today typically is as mandatory as it can resemble an underexamined item in a quasireligious creed. "We believe in being joint." It is no exaggeration to claim that jointness has become a value in itself. It must be considered a quality that in and of itself is praiseworthy. This is a mixed blessing for the understanding of strategic affairs. Official belief systems tend to carry the virus of unquestionable correctness that does not tolerate prudent skepticism. Without forgetting that the subject of most interest here is airpower as a more or less joint military player, still it is necessary to begin with the basics and cast a slightly querulous eye upon the concept, practice, and frequent malpractice of jointness.

Most polities evolve and mature a strategic culture that reflects the preponderant influence of a particular dominant military culture.[6] One can slice and dice for ever-greater precision and must note the existence of other military cultures, but still no great violence is done to history by identifying many polities with a broadly continentalist or a no less broadly maritime strategic culture. Some polities have been unfortunate in that their advisable choice between the two was not always as self-evident as it might have been. The worst situation for a country is when it is either tempted into error or genuinely is obliged to pour so many scarce resources into its secondary geostrategic environment that it fails in its primary one. Imperial Germany was a continental power whose army, not navy, was the first line of national defense. But alas for imperial ambition, Berlin wasted high-quality human and material assets that it could not afford on the creation of a high seas fleet that could never compete on equal or better terms with Britain's Royal Navy. Over a much longer period than that occupied by the modern unified Germany of 1871–1945, France repeatedly from the mid-seventeenth century until late in the nineteenth failed to stabilize its power position as European hegemon. In war after war it was frustrated, ultimately quite significantly, by the economic and financial strength of a maritime Britain whose homeland its typically superior army could not reach.

The clearly identifiable continental or maritime bias in a security community's leading strategic culture is rooted in a specific national geography and the unique historical experience that that geography has bequeathed. In Britain, the Royal Navy is the senior service not merely because it was formally established prior to the Army (which notably is not called the Royal Army, for reasons that flow from England's experience of bitter civil war in the seventeenth century), but because it was England's, then Britain's, first line of defense.[7] Britain could endure defeat on land—provided it was on someone else's land or even its own colonial land abroad—but if the navy suffered defeat, the country as a whole would face defeat.[8] The British Expeditionary Force, comprising more than 350,000 men, was roundly trounced and chased off the European continent in May–June 1940, but that defeat presented the victor with a strategic problem. Without a navy remotely competitive in British waters with the Royal Navy and also without an air force capable of substituting for that absent navy, how could Germany bring Britain to terms? Would coercive force in the form of a bombing campaign or the more brutal force of invasion and military defeat on the ground at home be necessary? Theorists about airpower are wont to mislead by distinguishing between coercion and brute force, punishment versus denial or defeat.[9] In practice the two concepts tend to collapse into each other. The hurt inflicted in a campaign designed to secure military victory can be coercive. Moreover, one might choose to be coerced not only by the pain being suffered, or anticipated, but also by the growing prospect of military defeat in the field. This, for illustration, was the situation of the Confederate States of America in 1864–65.[10]

Assuming some rationality about strategic preference, communities prefer the armed forces that experience, filtered by history and legend, claims works best for them. It is only realistic to note that polities do indeed tend to excel in some military projects more than in others, among not only the army, navy, and air force of a polity but also mission areas within armed services. It is probably correct that no army can be simultaneously outstanding in the conduct of regular conventional and irregular forms of warfare. The mind-sets, skill sets, and equipment, among other factors, certainly overlap, but they are not synonymous. One might add that when an army, navy, or air force attempts to be undoubtedly superior to any and all comers in all tasks, it will find itself losing its cutting edge in more than one area. Omni-competence is achievable, but omni-superiority probably is not. Contemporary America may prove to be modern history's solitary exception, but there are reasons to doubt this. And even if it should be true, against the odds, it would be imprudent to expect it to be so.

The pressing reason for this apparent ramble through the rough terrain of geography, history, and culture is because airpower cannot be understood—yesterday, today, or tomorrow—outside of its geographical and historical contexts. Airpower in practice—as contrasted with its general theory, which must be context-free—must vie for a place on, or dare one say, sometimes all but *as* the military team in contexts of specific geography, unique historical circumstances, and established if evolving military and strategic cultures. There were a few apparently wise air-minded visionaries in the 1900s and 1910s— people whose imagination or longing, aided by some insight and lucky guesswork, enabled them to peer far over the line-of-sight time horizon. But by far the majority of people who thought about aircraft, including dirigibles, in those decades did so from the standpoint of distinctly territorial soldiers and sailors. The principal strategic challenge of the day, how to force a favorable military decision when contemporary battlefield conditions conferred apparently unshakeable systemic advantages upon the defense in land warfare—and for the greater navies, how to bring an enemy fleet to battle with favorable terms of engagement—understandably dominated strategic analysis. Most who thought about airpower in the early years of the twentieth century understandably thought as militarily encultured soldiers and sailors, in good part because they could not prudently think in any other way. Land and sea forces of all kinds had existed for millennia; military theory and practice necessarily focused exclusively upon them, and even in their seemingly simple binary case constructive, jointness was the exception rather than the rule.

Napoleon famously was ignorant of the conditioning factors for war at sea and was apt to issue commands to French admirals that were as ill judged as were many of Winston Churchill's sallies of demands upon his generals, admirals, and air marshals. Arthur Wellesley, later the Duke of Wellington, was as competent on land as he was ignorant of what the Royal Navy prudently could and could not do for his army. It is all too easy to poke fun at sea-ignorant generals and land-innocent admirals, but what history shows is that military competence and more in one geographical environment is no guarantee of a like mastery of the grammar of warfare elsewhere. When one recognizes that in many strategic cases, past and present, there will be plausible but still essentially rival theories (prospective strategies) touted as best practice to meet the challenge on hand, it becomes obvious why intelligent experts can and do differ in fairly good faith. If one introduces the inconvenient complication of an active, intelligent, and competent enemy into the puzzle, it is necessary to accommodate the unwelcome legitimacy not only of the question How would we prefer to win? but also, How would we prefer to win given the realities of war, including the need to thwart a competitive enemy?

Americans justly can be proud of their joint strategic achievement over the empire of Japan, but the history of that great project tells a story that is less than convincingly joint. By conveniently suppressing ungenerous critical thoughts, one can tell the strategic tale of how the United States, not entirely alone but still largely so, deployed a large fraction of its Army, Navy, Marine Corps, and Army Air Forces to win the transoceanic war in the Pacific. Suffice it to say for now that Japan became menaced by no fewer than three (and more) rather independent strategies, each of which, though joint in some measure, had a distinct geographical flavor. Specifically, the Japanese surrender on 2 September 1945 was the product of (1) a maritime campaign with a major degree of amphibiosity vectored from the Hawaiian Islands, eventually to the Marianas, through the Bonins, to the home islands themselves; (2) a land-oriented campaign vectored from Australia and New Zealand through the Solomons and New Guinea, through archipelagic Southeast Asia, to the Philippines; and (3) an air campaign against the Japanese homeland conducted initially from mainland China but subsequently from the recently conquered Marianas. In addition to these three strategies, only loosely coordinated to be polite, one must cite the fact that the US Navy's submarine fleet all but secured independently the isolation of Japan from its foreign holdings, especially its recent conquests in the Dutch East Indies and continental Southeast Asia.[11]

Hindsight-foresight is not helpful in the quest for understanding and empathy with those who had to deal in real time with the unforeseeability of history's future. Nonetheless, one should not hesitate to try to learn from what in retrospect were, or plausibly seem to have been, mistakes with significant strategic consequences. The enemy, contingency, and friction of all kinds mean that strategy is difficult to do well, even to do well enough.[12] This book strives to explain that to understand the past, present, and future of airpower, there is no evading the whole context within which the air element had to seek to make its way. A trouble to honest scholarship is that military cultural prejudice and the influence of personal and vested institutional interests knit together with and augment the scale of the challenge posed simply by the true difficulty of making prudent, let alone wise, decisions about the allocation of resources through grand and military strategies. Strategic debate can be motivated by interests that have little about strategy in mind, but typically this is not the case. Usually there are some largely objective grounds for strategic disagreement as well as motives of a more parochial nature. It may not be unduly cynical to observe that much sincere and objective strategic argument is subjectively determined.

Out of Joint

In practice, many inherently good ideas inadvertently license and even encourage some poor behavior. So it is with the concept of military jointness. People heavily engaged in the issues of the day, the debate of the week, the budget struggle of the season, or the strategy dispute of the most pressing current conflict can be excused a lack of perspective on their immediate and dominating problems. It is precisely because military practitioners who are practicing strategy at every level typically lack the time, energy, and compelling incentive to understand fully the structure of their practical dilemmas that theorists need to do their educational duty. Unfortunately, the unavoidable phenomenon of "presentism"—which is to say a near-total focus on the here and now, absent historical or much other context—can lead a person in the present into avoidable error. Alas, this rather abstract and, in its pejorative meaning, academic point has serious pragmatic implications for operational airpower.

Jointness, "jointery" in a disdainful view, is so much accepted as best practice today that truly it is identified in theory, doctrine, and execution as the only legitimate approach to national security, national defense, defense strategy, and military behavior. Indeed, logically, there is or should be almost no need to emphasize the desirable jointness of endeavor, because there is no halfway credible alternative. For the US or British defense establishments today to entertain a strategic and military cultural alternative to jointness is about as likely as the government of Saudi Arabia making official provision for a religion different from variants of Islam. The trouble with a great epiphany, no matter how compelling its vision, is that its practical execution is always apt to prove more challenging than the process of theoretical/theological conversion. It is one thing to grasp the near banal point that warfare, and indeed war and preparation for/prevention of war, all but invariably should be approached and conducted as a joint project. It is quite another to know just what is good enough, let alone best, practice for the unique historical situation that is actually at hand. To cite an extreme case, if the next war must be a great one, World War III between the superpowers, and the historical context is, say, 1958–61, the US Strategic Air Command (SAC) is either going to deter it or, in extremis, wage and probably win it without much help from any other military instrument, American or allied. Of course, roles in that period were found or asserted for everyone's military instrument, but had *der Tag* been triggered by the episodic Berlin crises at some point, both at the time and with some hindsight, it is difficult to discern a truly joint strategic narrative. SAC would have been our team, not only its leading player.

The admittedly extreme hypothetical case just cited is useful for our intellectual and planning discipline because it suggests that strategic history can deliver outlier, exceptional happenings. There have been rivalries and wars wherein the narrative was, at most, characterized by combined arms, not joint endeavor. A jointly waged World War III in, say, 1958 would have engaged nuclear-armed air offense, air defense, some maritime air effort, and a fragile forward continental defense of NATO-Europe that would have served as a tripwire to license SAC, if it would even have needed that. This may be an exaggeration, but it overshoots only marginally and not in a way that imperils the integrity of the big story. That story was that US, and some British, long-range nuclear-armed airpower would have waged a distinctively nonjoint war. This is to say that SAC was not, and did not need to be, joined to any other military instrument, either to prevent war through the putative deterrent effect of its obvious latent menace or to wage and in some senses probably win a war.

Although the SAC hypothetical is certainly a historical outlier, it is nonetheless important to register the category of single or all-but-single military-instrument war and warfare firmly in one's mind; all the more alert one needs to be to exceptional circumstances wherein the rule should not apply. Strategic history, with warfare at its core, has uncertainty, risk, and chance inalienably locked in its nature. Clausewitz sought to drive this claim home, and we would be wise to listen and learn.[13] Ill-conducted strategic debate can present sound ideas in a fashion that invites misrepresentation. The recurring disputes over airpower's relative importance have suffered alarmingly from competing misstatements that mislead. A basic error, which from its persistence appears to be unavoidable, is the posing of false, starkly binary alternatives. To risk preempting later discussion, debates over airpower all too often have been polarized with contending gladiators insisting that (strategic) airpower must/could deliver victory; airpower is of minor importance in warfare against irregulars; airpower is the asymmetric advantage that can be the key to victory. The history of airpower is not self-interpreting. There is need for theory designed and policed honestly as explanation, if the facts are to be permitted to speak some approximation to the truth. Let us

tackle the basics of the jointness epiphany, since truly they are fundamental to understanding airpower history.

A Joint Strategic World

To be empirically rigorous, a nonjoint, or literally disjointed, strategic context is an impossibility today. Even for Curtis LeMay's SAC
in 1957, the war he might have waged with very little help from other
US or allied military assets could have had meaning, that is to say
political purpose, only with reference to terrestrial consequences.[14]
The nuclear war most probably would not have entailed much air
warfare but rather would have comprised warfare waged largely from
the air. SAC had a terrestrial story, both in its foundation and support
and in its intended and unintended but practicably unavoidable consequences. The point that must never be forgotten about any character of warfare is that its strategic and political consequences ultimately
have to translate into consequences on land where we humans live
and have our belligerent polities. This is obvious to and beyond the
point of banality, but the preparation for and the conduct of warfare
in any environment other than the land is always somewhat menaced by
an understandable pull of environmental parochialism. And there
are usually pressing reasons why sea and air (and space and cyber?)
commanders can focus so narrowly on their perhaps desperate immediate challenges that they literally are out of joint with respect to a
strategic sense encompassing other geographies. Corrections for this
pathology of understandable geographical localism are, of course,
built into a sound chain of military, and above, command. However,
nominal recognition of the danger and formal provision of a correc-
tive process are no guarantee against dysfunctional military behavior.
Command in strategy and in tactics is inescapably human, and human performance is highly variable.

As "bomber barons" of huge importance in World War II, British
air marshal Sir Arthur Harris and, for a while his counterpart, Gen
Carl "Tooey" Spaatz differed more radically in personality than in
their opinions about how their bomber forces should best be used.
The story of the not-very-Combined Bomber Offensive cannot be
told reliably without more than a passing reference to the key personalities and their relationships.[15] The literature of strategic and
military analysis—and certainly that of strategic theory—is damag-
ingly light in its treatment of the human beings who decline, some-

times eccentrically, to think and behave fully and solely as strategically rational beings.[16]

And "Joint" Means . . .

A problem with the concept of jointness is that, like all such concepts, its essential validity is licensed only by the cogency of its logical
antithesis. One cannot be joint except in the sense of not being something else—in this case, presumably, un-joint, disjoint(ed), or separate and independent. The difficulty with this concept, perhaps with
the logic of mutually dependent opposites, is that the strategic world
is seldom intelligently viewable in such sharp binary terms. Jointness
is a spectrum, though arguably one that can have unbridged and un-
spotted gaps. Familiarity breeds an overfamiliarity that discourages
critical intelligence. What does it mean to be "joint"?

In truth, today it does not really mean anything to be joint because
we cannot possibly be disjoint. Today all kinds of US military (and
civil) power depend literally and vitally upon the use of enabling assets in orbital space and cyberspace. This claim is beyond contention.
Similarly beyond argument is the land-terrestrial connection to
everything one does at sea, in the air, in orbital space, and in cyberspace. Admittedly, the land-terrestrial connection to every other geographical domain is potentially misleading, in that inadvertently it
could serve to conceal a dominant strategic role for sea power, airpower, space power, and cyber power in particular situations, to the
arguable degree to which these noncontinental forms of military
power are sensibly distinguishable.

If jointness is a spectrum—not an identifiably stable and definite
condition clearly distinguishable from its opposite of "disjointness"—
empirically, it must embrace every state from thoroughly autonomous to entirely united. It is not unreasonable to ask whether a contemporary state of jointness is only a stage on the path to full
unification. As is well known, the United States created a single Department of Defense in 1947 in part to expedite a full divorce of the
US Army Air Forces from the US Army. A higher unity sanctioned
the disunity of military service independence. Dictionary definitions
help to educate the ignorant and police the unscrupulous, but they
also can struggle to capture reality. Armed forces can be organized to
fight jointly, but do they really fight jointly? Just how joined must they
be to be honestly characterized as joint? It is a somewhat open question

whether a master campaign plan that has ground/land, sea, air, and now space component subplans truly constitutes a single project rather than simply the stapling together of each major military stakeholder's preferred course of action.[17] And the question will be answered by argument and negotiation that is political, political-bureaucratic, strategic analytical, and human.

A Culminating Point of Jointness

Many good strategic ideas carry the seeds of being bad ideas. If some jointness is beneficial, then one might presume that more jointness must be better. Using this logic, where jointness is treated as a value in itself and its merits are assumed to have no practical limits, it would seem sensible to strive to be unified—meaning fully integrated, compounded even—and not merely joint, as in connected. The ideal American Soldier, Sailor, or Airman thus would be a military person, advantageously liberated from the parochial biases derived from specific military geographical association. This idea is as logically compelling as it continues to be impractical. Moreover, to hazard a perhaps unscholarly prediction, it is unlikely that a geographically true Universal Military Person (soldier, for convenience here) will ever be feasible. Some audiences are inclined to criticize the tribal behavior of the geographically distinctive armed forces because, in their ignorance, they do not appreciate how and why military cultures differ, let alone why those differences have strongly net-positive strategic value. Because there will usually be several grand and military strategies that are rivals for adoption, singly or in combination, competitiveness increases the likelihood that the strengths and weaknesses of some alternatives are considered in a timely fashion. The single- soldier approach to security could hardly help but risk a perilous narrowing of the funnel of military and strategic advice to the political authorities. Unity of command and singleness of strategic purpose are vital, valid principles of war, but unity of military and strategic advice most definitely is not such a principle.

The principle that a polity's military instruments, indeed all of its (grand) strategic instruments, should be employed jointly is beyond intelligent challenge. However, once one considers jointness as a spectrum of more and less rather than present or absent, the troubling thought intrudes that jointness can be taken both too far and not far enough. In fact, it becomes a compelling thought that beyond the general principle that all relevant national assets should be committed in a joint rather than disjointed manner, one has comprehended nothing much of specific situational value. The strategic logic of jointness and the technologies that increasingly enable it do not constitute a template of high strategic merit for particular contexts. Much like the idea of military transformation that was so fashionable until it was mugged by events recently, jointness has acquired a doctrinal sanctity heavily pregnant with the potential to excite its devotees unduly and mislead those susceptible to capture by dazzling visions of military advance. The problem is not with the concept of transformation but rather with the concept when it is honored as a value in itself. Regarded out of context, transformation as radical change is neither good nor bad. It is strategically meaningless.[18]

Warfare as a Military Team Event

Although it is commonplace, albeit an important truism, to note that warfare is a team activity, it is less commonplace to point out some of the pathologies that result in team misbehavior. Military jointness is more than merely a description of armed forces that are more or less joined together. The term also carries strong positive vibrations; to repeat, today it is a value. That granted and approved, though with reservations, one should not miss the paradox that although jointness is a celebration of and insistence upon the essential unity of warfare, its practice often appears more to endorse at least semi-sovereign status for the military geographies. Jointness should mean that the armed forces contribute as each is best able to a common military, strategic, and political endeavor. The logic, ideology, or faith even is unassailable. In practice, however, jointness can mean that everyone plays, everyone is entitled to play an equal role, and every service commands its own geographically specialized forces. Thus, the joint commander will have subordinate commanders for land, sea, and air components. Perhaps needless to add, each component commander does not exactly head a united military instrument but rather a set of different capabilities, each led by expert professionals probably inbred with strong views as to how their force should best be employed. Introducing the further complication of a coalition or alliance, effort that is supposed to be collective, it readily becomes apparent that jointness in theory and in practice is always liable to be different. Those who wish to examine closely the practical limits to jointness in the conduct of war are recommended to study the inter- and intra–Anglo-American-Allied debate over the most effective employment of their burgeoning and diverse airpower assets in the spring and summer of 1944.[19] For a change of scene and scale but with some instructive overlap of issues, the lessons from 1944 can be augmented profitably by a study of NATO's 78-day air war over Kosovo in 1999.[20] The continuities in strategic history, including its relatively brief airpower dimension, are impressive.

The proposition that only airmen understand airpower sufficiently to be trusted to command it is a long-standing and highly plausible belief. Nonetheless, it points toward a persisting military and strategic cultural reality that could make a mockery in practice of high-minded devotion to the unavailable principle of jointness. Specifically, as a general rule, soldiers, sailors, and airmen (and most likely spacemen and even cybermen, when their careers are permitted to mature as such) have distinctive worldviews largely derived from their geographic military affiliations. The discussion now turns to this core matter.

The Territorial Imperative

With apologies and thanks to ethnologist Robert Ardrey,[21] strategists—no matter which, if any, geography they prefer militarily—can never afford to forget the logic in the title chosen for this section. The theory and practice of airpower make sense strictly in a territorial, not merely terrestrial, context. The reason is as obvious as it is important and, therefore, bears repetition. In the enduring words of maritime historian and theorist Julian Corbett, "Since men live upon the land and not upon the sea, great issues between nations at war have always been decided—except in the rarest of cases—either by what your army can do against your enemy's territory and national life or else by the fear of what the fleet makes it possible for your army to do."[22]

The nature and evolving character of airpower requires some amendment to Corbett's potent dictum. It is not the case that airpower can have strategic effect only because of its ability to strengthen one's army. Nonetheless, when intelligently interpreted for today, Corbett does hit the target. Although there are exceptions, as there always will be, human conflicts all but invariably have important territorial definition. Enemies can inhabit only the land; their political unit is territorial; and, more often than not, the issues between territorially definable, or at least plainly associated, belligerents have some territorial control content. Corbett's strategic territorial imperative is taken a step further and made wholly explicit by J. C. Wylie, an American rear admiral.

> *The ultimate determinant in war is the man on the scene with the gun.* This man is the final power in war. He is [in] control. He determines who wins. There are those who would dispute this as an absolute, but it is my belief that while other means may critically influence war today, after what devastation and destruction may be inflicted on an enemy, if the strategist is forced to strive for final and ultimate control, he must establish, or must present as an inevitable prospect, a man on the scene with a gun.[23] (emphasis in original)

This quotation is a wonderful piece of overwriting. In these deservedly oft-quoted words, Wylie overstates, probably deliberately, a continentalist logic that is impeccable, provided one chooses to ignore the admiral's qualifications to his assertion. Should policy require absolute control over an enemy, then truly Wylie is persuasive in insisting upon the need to present him with the stark choice, preferably up close and distinctly personal, between death and constrained life by surrender. However, historical experience shows unambiguously that "final and ultimate control" is not usually the mandatory goal for strategy. Control, certainly yes, but this condition is not a single absolute state, despite its rather exclusive meaning in English. We would do better to employ the French *contróle*, meaning general supervision. In a total war between rival societies and their states, a condition that World War I began to approximate and World War II did achieve, Wylie's tight Clausewitzian formula makes sense. But for more limited contests, for contests about interests not existence, the necessary achievement is some control via influence, most prominently an influence secured by coercion, not a final literal control.

Wylie's rigor is appealing. To be certain that militarily successful warfare delivers what policy makers require, even though one knows that they might waste the advantage that should accrue from payment by blood, it would be necessary to confront the surviving enemy with the grim choice between compliance or death. In historical practice, most belligerents exercise an opportunity to comply on unfavorable terms, even with much dishonor, rather than perish in total defeat. There have been exceptions, but those unusual cases cannot sensibly be cited as convincing grounds effectively to deify a dictum that applies only rarely. It should be noted that even in the extreme case of nearly total war that was World War I by 1918, Germany chose to terminate its war effort short of utter military defeat. An armistice was recorded 11 November 1918, not unconditional surrender (unlike 8 May 1945).

The relevance of this discussion to airpower as an instrument of joint warfare should be obvious. If one takes Wylie's powerful prose and logic too literally and neglects to weigh in his significant caveat ("if the strategist is forced to strive for final and ultimate control"), then one would accept the ridiculous belief that airpower could never secure the needed control unless it imposed the control of the graveyard that would result from bombardment by air-delivered WMDs.[24] In some contexts it is probably true to argue that the quality of coercive menace useful for winning over minds, though admittedly not hearts, is achievable more reliably by ground power than by airpower in its kinetic application. However, not only should airpower not be defined strictly in kinetic regard, but often there are also pressing practical reasons why the "boots on the ground" and "loaded gun to the head" approaches to control are impracticable or undesirable. They are apt to be more certain in strategic effect, but only when they are feasible and not self-harming in their negative political effect. It should be noted that in guerrilla-style warfare waged by insurgents, alien boots, faces, and customs—up front and personal—can carry their own unique viruses unfriendly to strategic advantage. Intervening in a foreign country when the government to be assisted enjoys only a contested legitimacy runs a major risk of itself stimulating terrorism and insurgency.[25]

It is possible that the trend in this argument might seem weighted unfavorably against land power. Such an impression would be false. The primary concern here is to ensure that the land is recognized as the primary focus for strategy. Air and sea strategies matter only for their meaning for a land-oriented historical narrative. Pragmatic politics among different kinds of military power, each championed by unavoidably competing, geographically specialized military institutions, cannot help but encourage people to see airpower and the rest essentially as rivals. This is a cardinal error, and the fact that it is such an error is programmed into the near-sacred contemporary creed of military jointness. There is no denying, though, that the rivalry among the distinctive forms of military power is, in a vital sense, both natural to the political condition endemic to human relations and rational if not always reasonable in its expression of competing strategic worldviews.

For a familiar simple-minded logic, the basic geographical structure of the subject of this chapter invites misstatements of many kinds. To explain—in land warfare, high ground always has been valued (for advantage in observation, ease of defense, momentum gained from gravity in the shock through rapid descent, etc.), but suddenly, to ignore 150 years of episodic balloon experience, controlled heavier-than-air flight obliges recognition of a newly accessible, functional "high ground." The new high ground of the air happens to be global, an overhead flank to all land and sea battlespace and belligerents' societal hinterlands, while (orbital) space now is exploited as a yet higher ground, indeed a "ground" so high as literally to be all but infinitely so, though assuredly only strategically relevant at Earth-orbital altitudes. It can be a challenge to sort the strategic sense from the astrategic nonsense in all this. Strategic history does suggest that command of high ground confers military advantage; however, it does not elevate such command to the status of a golden key ensuring victory. Advancing analogously, there is good and increasingly excellent reason to see strategic advantage in control of the air, but, again, such a geographical edge does not guarantee a success that must lead to victory by plausible definition. To control the skies should make life difficult for enemies of any kind, especially of a regular conventional genus, but also for those who fight in guerrilla and even terroristic modes. Command of the overhead flank frequently is only an advantage, albeit an important one, not the ticket guaranteed to deliver strategic triumph. Why not? Because conflict, war, and warfare are complex phenomena, and that complexity includes variations in relevant terrain, in degrees of political commitment (significant for the strategic value of punishment and denial for intended coercive effect), and in a host of other dimensions to human struggle.[26] However, it so happens that airpower also is complex as well as dynamic, flexible, and adaptable, and necessarily, its strategic value is, to repeat, highly situational. The merit in this less-than-startling, let alone original, claim continues to elude many people who appear to have an absurdly monolithic concept of airpower. The fact that some airpower theorists have encouraged such misunderstanding is evidence yet again of the potency of the law of unintended consequences. The injunction to first, do no harm, which has prodigious worth for medicine, applies also to those who would theorize about and draft doctrine for airpower. Unfortunately, there is compelling evidence from both cases showing how difficult it is to avoid doing such harm. In practice, both medicine and airpower can be blunt instruments that inflict collateral damage in pursuit of decisive strategic advantage. The heart may be pure, but the blows struck often fall short of surgical, and enemies have been known to fight back and may choose to do so preemptively or preventively.

Strategy and Air Strategy

As wealth creates problems of decision and priority for those who find themselves financially privileged, so does maturing airpower beget difficulties inseparable from its technical success and tactical competence. Even primitive airpower of only marginal military importance in warfare, as in 1914 and most of 1915, presented some challenges to prudent choice, but errors could be corrected and had only modest strategic consequence. However, from 1916 to the present, the stakes in decisions about airpower's roles and character have grown from noticeable through significant to sometimes strategically determinate. The maturing of airpower necessarily has translated as a growing importance relative to, and functioning synergistically with, land power and sea power. While there is merit in regarding airpower materially and tactically as anything useful that flies, to paraphrase the ever-applicable "Mitchellism," after only a very few years what was useful is best conveyed in the French expression *un embarras de richesses*. Airpower in its ever-diversifying competent forms has offered utility for every military function of value to strategy. Well before the end of World War I, there was speculation from educated strategists that the airpower of tomorrow might become the principal military instrument in warfare among great powers. In his somewhat visionary great *Second Report*, Gen Jan Smuts offered precisely this speculation.[27] While debate over airpower as the sole or all-but-sole potential instrument of strategic decision has spluttered episodically ever since 1917—if not before—the real debate with growing and quite soon immense practical significance concerned how much of the ever-maturing technical-tactical possibilities of airpower should be acquired relative to ground power and sea power and what should be the balance among airpower's ever-expanding categories. The fact is so obvious that often it is missed: airpower has suffered in its general reputation because its near-ubiquitous utility has ensured that it would be both overused inappropriately as well as underused. Airpower theory and doctrine perennially have laid emphasis convincingly on their broad subject's militarily unique flexibility and adaptability, the natural gift of its environment, but seem never really to have grasped the scale of the ever-growing problems of choice that success had to bring.

The joint narrative for airpower inherently is more structurally complex than for land power and sea power. Armies frequently need some integral riverine, though not necessarily coastal, capability. They need to exploit rivers, lakes, and bays and cope with threats of a maritime character, which is to say from the sea. To those ends they often have preferred to provide the translittoral land-sea capability themselves. In World War II, though not subsequently, British commando formations principally were organized by the army, not the navy. Also, many countries historically allocated coastal defense duties to their army rather than their navy or some other more specialized institution. From the naval side, raiding from the sea with marine units has an ancient history traceable at least as far back as to Greece and Rome, while sea-based firepower with inland reach has expanded from perhaps a dozen miles for the heavy armament of a battleship at the beginning of the twentieth century to more than 5,000 miles with state-of-the-art submarine-launched ballistic missiles (SLBM) today. The physical geographic distinction between land and sea is not entirely beyond dispute at the margin—for example, high- or low-tide line of separation?—but even today armies do not strive to own and employ forces able to wage and win war at sea. Similarly, navies typically are content to confine their ambition to the conduct of warfare at sea and only from the sea on a modest scale and with a limited reach inland. Admittedly, modern technology, modern joint doctrine, and occasional perceived political pressure encourage land power and especially sea power to intrude invasively into each other's domain; nonetheless, each enjoys what near universally amounts to a geographically clear enough set of roles. This is not so true of airpower.

Airpower is not only the third element in a force mix (with land and sea power) that before its arrival had been issued a comprehensive license to manage and wage all terrestrial warfare, it is also a relatively new force that contributes to land and sea warfare. Institutional, reputational, budgetary, and strategic challenges are inalienable from airpower. Airpower has matured with a need to wage and win war in the air itself if it is to serve friendly land power and sea power, which initially was its sole broad function. But it was a logical step to proceed from recognition of an autonomous air war waged to enable air support for the Army and Navy to the speculative notion of waging the only warfare that really mattered strategically strictly from the air. We are habituated to honor multienvironmental jointness, and we are all too familiar with the consensus view that airpower theory, some doctrine, and painful failures in practice have reflected unrealistic, overinflated strategic ambition. Such habituation to the virtues in jointness and such widespread agreement that airpower has failed to deliver on the theory of its promise as articulated by some of its prophets have led many people astray. Indeed, it may be no exaggeration to claim that jointness not only in doctrine but as doctrine itself, viewed in the historical context of a substantial misreading of airpower history admittedly invited by overambition and overstatement, has contributed to some paralysis, at least stultification, of strategic faculties.

The challenge to those who seek to understand airpower is one of choice, or refusal of choice, of paradigm. Phrased directly, to understand the roles and relative strategic significance of airpower in war, especially in warfare, one first must settle upon authoritative understanding of the fundamental features of war and warfare. Educated by the general theory of strategy (as well as the much-less-developed general theory of war) and the specific general theory of airpower, the latter has to be interpreted for its meaning in unique historical contexts. For example, consider history's first autonomous air war, the bilateral Anglo-German event waged in the summer and early autumn of 1940. One cannot easily avoid reading history backwards, and as noted already, such use of hindsight lends an unfair and inappropriate backwards-projected foresight. But the most convincing study written today on the Battle of Britain advises that in 1940 "air power was still an unknown factor."[28] Understood in context, this is not an exaggeration. Would the defeat of the RAF lead inexorably to German victory in the war? Even if the RAF were only reduced rather than annihilated, would the bombing of civilians coerce a British surrender? And, even if one had a secure theoretical grip upon what airpower ought, or ought not, to be able to accomplish by way of strategic effect, how well would the actual Luftwaffe of July–September

1940 perform against the actual specific air defenses of Britain at that time? Strategic education can only do so much. It is able only to help prepare those who must decide and act in unique situations so that they should be adequately equipped mentally to answer testing strategic and operational questions. Even then, the people, machines, indeed the entire integrated network that produces air defense and offense, need to function well enough tactically. Theory and practice need not correlate closely.

In truth, the strategic context of the Battle of Britain was considerably more complex, especially in a multilayered way, than the paragraph above might appear to suggest. For example, even had Dowding's Fighter Command been attrited into near impotence, over southeast England at least the Germans would have faced a high likelihood of tactical, operational, and strategic failure at the hands of a Royal Navy that would have been certain to handle Germany's improvised invasion armada very roughly. It was not likely that even a Luftwaffe in command of the sky by day over the channel could have prevented the Royal Navy from inflicting catastrophic losses on the would-be invader, though on 25 May 1940 the British chiefs of staff believed that they would have been able to do so.[29]

Strategic truth is universal and eternal only at the level of strategy's general theory and for airpower specifically only for its general theory. These general theories can and should be required to light the path for the practicing strategist only insofar as they educate his or her mind by explaining the structure and dynamic working of strategy. What must not be allowed to occur is for these general theories to miseducate vulnerable minds into believing that there is a correct general theory that provides specific advice. Iraq, Afghanistan, Israel and Lebanon or Gaza, the Empire of Japan—each challenge is unique, and so must be the character of the air contribution to the joint endeavor. Airpower is not a single tool comprising a force structure beyond argument that can be applied in a single way to most conflicts in confident expectation that it will deliver victory. But increasingly through the twentieth century, airpower in control of the relevant skies has been able to offer strategic advantages that enemies unable or disabled in the air have had great difficulty offsetting, if indeed such was feasible, which often it was not.

Conclusion: *E Pluribus Unum?*

The military specialization by environment that is standard practice worldwide seems to be as unavoidably practical as unavoidably challenging for competence in generating strategic effect. Polities wage warfare of many characters in some, potentially all, among no fewer than five geophysically distinctive environments. To function in or on its particular geography, military forces are obliged to tailor themselves technically and tactically in unique ways. These unique characteristics for forces that must cope with terrain, the sea, the air, orbital space, and the electromagnetic spectrum (EMS) impose distinctive operating limitations as well as confer unique advantages. These distinctive sets of advantages and disadvantages have to be considered and then balanced for judgment as to how best the five baskets of military assets should be commanded to contribute to the common strategic enterprise for whatever the political purposes might be. To do this well enough in the face of adversaries motivated and possibly able to offer effective resistance is no mean feat. Strategy is exceedingly difficult to do well, which is why it is prudent to be willing to satisfice with a strategy that can serve simply well enough. Success can be victory enough, even if the enemy does score some points on his way to defeat.

State-of-the-art airpower has evolved into a zone where not only is it literally inseparable by intelligent definition from land power and sea power but tactically in permissive circumstances might substitute almost entirely for their more traditional contributions to strategic effect. Although airpower does have a "grammar" all its own that fundamentally is attributable to conditions set by geophysics, obviously it has to be a terrestrially dependent force. Not only does airpower derive all of its strategic and political meaning from a continental historical narrative, but also its effectiveness in and from the air always has been vitally dependent upon a more or less complex structure of support on the ground. Writing about Britain's integrated air defense system in 1940, Stephen Bungay notes tellingly that "all the fighters in the world were of little use if they could not find their enemy."[30] The ground-based elements of Dowding's Fighter Command were essential enablers of the British airpower that defeated the Luftwaffe. Although "anything that flies that is useful" can serve admirably to focus attention upon the core of what airpower has to be, it does leave something to be desired by way of holistic explanation. Billy Mitchell's definition is far superior to one that simply asserts "anything that flies," because he claimed convincingly that airpower is "the ability to do something in the air." Ground-based radar and its interpreters and air controllers did not shoot down German aircraft, but without their performance "The (not so) Few" in their Hurricanes and Spitfires certainly would have been flying crippled.

A major factor producing friction runs throughout airpower history and, necessarily, underlies the whole of this study. This factor is the potential tension and disharmonies among the unique geographies within which activities with geographically dictated unique characteristics are conducted and in the relation between the jointly, if somewhat separately, waged warfare and the strategic goals and political purposes behind the entire project. Because of politics (to repeat, the struggle to secure a favorable distribution of power),[31] personalities, friction of all kinds, and the enemy, it would be difficult even for a service de-military-cultured person to perform well as a strategist. To do well in joint strategy requires not only some ability to transcend much career conditioning to achieve breadth of strategic view, but also the skill to adapt the particular paradigms of warfare preferred by the land, sea, and air (and space and cyber) instruments to a tolerably unified definition of the mission consistent with the licensing political direction.

Historically, and not infrequently for persuasive reasons, one solution preferred to the challenge of harmonizing terrestrial and aerial efforts has simply been for land and sea forces to own and operate the airpower that they believe they need. US Navy and Marine Corps aviators traditionally have been naval officers first and aviators only second. As a tactical matter, such ownership and integrative cooption have made most kinds of sense. It is the case that modern land power and sea power cannot be understood absent their airpower components, with no specified air context to their operations. However, army aviation and naval aviation contribute to an overall strategic performance of land-air power and sea-air power, which in turn are influenced and can even be offset or strategically overwhelmed by air operations of an autonomous character. While it is true that armies and navies know what they would like airpower to do for them tactically, it is unlikely that experts in land and sea warfare would also be suitably expert in the operational and strategic potential of air operations conducted quite far away from the terrestrial battlespace occupied by land power and sea power in contact.

It is a human trait for persons' beliefs to follow and support their interests. This near-ubiquitous manifestation of human vulnerability creates persisting practical problems for joint military performance in pursuit of a single, unified strategic goal. It should be true that land power, sea power, and airpower are each better directed and commanded operationally by people who understand profoundly the tactical "grammar" of warfare in their respective geographical environments. However, along with that essential comprehension come military cultural preferences, particular military worldviews, that paradigmatically tend to privilege the contribution that the encultured expert's own military tool brings to the party. Since joint planning depends upon particular expertise, obviously the prime solution to the challenge of geostrategic parochialism needs to be a unified strategic grasp and grip upon the joint but separate tools in the military toolbox. The challenge cannot be answered sensibly and definitively by fiat, but it can be eased if the dilemmas of jointness (rather than a wholly impractical true unity) are alleviated by geographically specific theory that educates for explanation and understanding.

Notes

1. This assumption is central to my "Moral Advantage, Strategic Advantage" and *Strategy Bridge.*

2. Grattan, *Origins of Air War*, 63.

3. See Hobkirk, *Land, Sea or Air?*

4. The focus of Murray and Grimsley, "Introduction: On Strategy," was plainly, robustly stated in the book's main title, *The Making of Strategy*. Strategy is made in and by a process, and typically it is always liable to adjustment because of its need to take account of the feedback from experience. The interpretation of unfolding events should educate a strategy-making process that inalienably is more or less political.

5. Clausewitz, *On War*, 605.

6. See Sondhaus, *Strategic Culture and Ways of War*; and Johnson, Kartchner, and Larsen, *Strategic Culture and Weapons of Mass Destruction*. Porter, *Military Orientalism*, strives with some success to rain on the contemporary culturalist parade of scholars and officials.

7. See French, *British Way in Warfare.*

8. Corbett argued regarding command of the sea that "if we [Britain] have lost it completely no invasion will be necessary, since, quite apart from the threat of invasion, we must make peace on the best terms we can get." Corbett, *Some Principles of Maritime Strategy*, 239. His strategic logic may well have merit by analogy with a hypothetical defeat of the RAF in 1940.

9. See Schelling, *Arms and Influence*, chap. 1; Pape, *Bombing to Win*; Byman, Waxman, and Larson, *Air Power as a Coercive Instrument*; and Byman and Waxman, *Dynamics of Coercion*.

10. The coercive effect of military defeat and the demoralization it tends to produce is well attested for the Confederate States of America in Glatthaar, *General Lee's Army*, chap. 34.

11. From the immense library of general and specialist studies of the war against Japan, three histories stand out: Murray and Millett, *War to Be Won*; Spector, *Eagle against the Sun*; and Hastings, *Nemesis*. The first two are American authored, the third British, which provides some useful contrast in foci and judgments.

12. See Gray, *Schools for Strategy*; and Marcella, *Teaching Strategy*.

13. Clausewitz, *On War*, 85.

14. In 1957 LeMay left SAC, which he had commanded for nine years, to assume the position of deputy chief of staff of the Air Force. See Tillman, *LeMay*; and Kozak, *LeMay*.

15. Probert, *Bomber Harris*; and Davis, *Carl A. Spaatz and the Air War in Europe*, are particularly helpful. Also see Biddle, *Rhetoric and Reality in Air Warfare*, chap. 4.

16. This claim is discussed in Gray, *Strategy Bridge*.

17. Gordon and Trainor wrote of the American-led performance in Gulf War I (1991): "The campaign was 'joint' more in name than in fact. Each service fought its own war, concentrating on its own piece of the conflict with a single-minded intensity, and the commanders in Washington and Riyadh failed to fully harmonize the war plans." *Generals' War*, xiv.

18. For some healthy skepticism, see Echevarria, *Challenging Transformation's Clichés*; and Kagan, *Finding the Target*.

19. See Biddle, *Rhetoric and Reality in Air Warfare*, chap. 5.

20. Lambeth is essential as usual. See his *NATO's Air War for Kosovo*.

21. Ardrey, *Territorial Imperative*.

22. Corbett, *Some Principles of Maritime Strategy*, 16.

23. Wylie, *Military Strategy*, 72.

24. Bratton's critique of Pape, *Bombing to Win*, is highly relevant to this argument. Bratton, "A Coherent Theory of Coercion?"

25. This problem is the COIN paradox. To risk overstatement, one needs to intervene only in contexts where one is all but certain to become a serious part of an augmented problem. Respected, if not overly beloved, governing structures do not require foreign intervention to recover and stabilize their authority. The very fact of foreign intervention must damage the political legitimacy of the local government.

26. Gray, *Strategy Bridge*, chap. 3.

27. Smuts, "'Magna Carta' of British Air Power." See also, Luck, "Smuts Report."

28. Bungay, *Most Dangerous Enemy*, 32.

29. Orange, *Dowding of Fighter Command*, 220. Also see Bungay, *Most Dangerous Enemy*, 386–87.

30. Bungay, *Most Dangerous Enemy*, 60.

31. This is not to deny that politics can be about values other than power itself as a value. But it is to claim that power, inclusively understood, is essential if favored values are to flourish. Virtue tends to prosper when it is protected or advanced by well-armed guardians. This highly plausible formula runs through Kagan, *On the Origins of War and the Preservation of Peace*.

Chapter 4

Strategic History I:
Sagittarius Rising, 1903–39

The temporal domain of this first historical chapter begins on 17 December 1903 when two bicycle makers from Ohio achieved a flight lasting all of 12 seconds with a heavier-than-air craft, while the next one concludes with what must rank as a serious candidate for most awesome fly-past of all time on 2 September 1945. On that day more than 2,000 Allied aircraft circled over the scene of imperial Japan's formal surrender on the deck of the USS *Missouri* in Tokyo Bay. The 462 B-29 Superfortresses (plus some 1,500 carrier aircraft) in their display of airpower both provided obvious latent menace and served as a potent reminder of Japan's relative technological inferiority.[1] In the Pacific war, at least, airpower appeared unarguably triumphant, and American airpower played so leading a role in the victory in Asia that the United States seemed to have transformed its military strategic character with near-lightning speed from a preponderantly maritime power to an air power. Indeed, it is scarcely an exaggeration to claim that by 1945, notwithstanding the impressive scale of British and Soviet airpower, the United States plainly was the world's first air power by a wide margin in quality, quantity, and strategic effectiveness. However, it is necessary to recognize that the strategic ascendancy of long-potential American airpower was registered in demonstrated, albeit contested, achievement only in 1944–45. USAF official historian Richard P. Hallion makes what, in retrospect, is a fairly plausible claim when he asserts that "as dominant land power characterized a *Pax Romana*, and dominant sea power a *Pax Britannica*, dominant air power is the characteristic of modern America."[2] This chapter and four succeeding ones examine why and how this happened and proceed to explain how, for a while at least, the nuclear revolution paradoxically both amplified yet appeared to diminish the strategic significance of airpower.

An important function of general strategic theory is to assist people to devise contextually specific strategy. General theory offers a useful means of liberation from inadvertent capture by imprudent impulse. Acknowledgement that air warfare is subject to the same general lore—one cannot claim law—as warfare in the other environments serves as potent protection against theoretical and seemingly practical temptations that ought to be resisted. This is easy for a scholar to say today, but the human subjects of this chapter, in particular, merit no little empathy for the historical situation in which they found themselves. Airpower theory typically may have led airpower practice, contrary to the claims of some, but usually it was the handmaiden of the airpower practice that air-minded people wanted. A competent theorist can always provide the theory that legitimizes, indeed appears to mandate, the military instrument that is favored. No dishonesty is alleged here.

Understanding the pragmatic relations between continuity and change comprised the most fundamental challenge to those obliged to make strategic sense of contemporary and near-future airpower at any time in the 36 years addressed in this chapter. Generically, as polities today grope toward some comprehension of space and cyber warfare, so the first half of the twentieth century witnessed a global struggle both to make strategic sense of airpower and, of course, to express such sense as could be made in suitable behavior. The historical perspective of today aids understanding of airpower: first, because there is a century of experience on which to ponder; and second, because the augmentation of aerial battlespace with orbital space and the infosphere of cyberspace helps situate airpower strategically.[3] When airpower ascended as an overhead flank to land power and sea power, the temptation was well nigh irresistible to claim that a revolution in the nature of war was occurring. But when airpower is seen in the context of no fewer than five geographically particular military instruments and also in the company of nuclear weaponry, its status as a revolutionary tool, or toolkit, unsurprisingly is reduced. The military revolutions, if such they be, achieved subsequent to airpower's rise can hardly help but diminish its relative ability to dazzle.[4]

Unlike the pioneers of airpower theory, airpower doctrine, and air warfare, airpower theorists today have access to the experience of a century of hugely diverse and bloody airpower practice—and malpractice. It is the mission of this and the four succeeding chapters to seek to use historical knowledge to understand the strategic meaning of airpower. Paradoxical though this may read, the episodically recurring intense debates about airpower issues are vastly more heated and incompetently conducted than should be the case. The evidence of the past, as contrasted noticeably with the claims in rival histories, yields few sustainable grounds for argument today over the influence of airpower on strategic history. This judgment is exciting in its very absence of excitement. Indeed, this author was more than a little surprised when it crept up on him as an accumulating body of now adequately attested judgments that could yield no other plausible conclusion. Of course, this claim has yet to be validated in these pages at this early juncture.

The airpower history in these chapters has organic significance for today. Some major roles for airpower were identified before World War I; in very minor key they were executed in the Italian-Turkish War of 1911, in particular, and their continuity until today is beyond reasonable dispute. Despite the necessarily dominant importance of technology as an enabler for airpower, technical evolution arguably has had only a modest impact upon the terms of strategic debate. Although technology assuredly has answered many, possibly most, technical and tactical questions about airpower's efficacy, it has not stilled strategic controversy. Time after time, most recently in the late 1990s, plausible technical-tactical claims for the transformation of airpower have been less plausible at the operational level of warfare and notably contestable when examined strategically and politically. We will return to this matter in later chapters. Suffice it to say for now that the hundred-plus-years-long historical narrative of airpower is relevant in its entirety to efforts to understand airpower in the twenty-first century. These five history chapters are not "mere history" in the pejorative sense intended dismissively by narrow-minded "presentists" or "futurists."

One must hasten to note, however, that although the larger political, strategic, and some operational issues have not been resolved by cumulative technological advance, many technical and tactical and a few operational conundrums have indeed been resolved. When Benjamin S. Lambeth wrote in 2000 about what he termed the "transformation of American air power," there was an important sense in which plainly he was correct.[5] The cutting edge(s) of the American airpower of the early twenty-first century can reasonably be claimed to be a fair approximation to the character of the instrument that pioneer airpower theorists dreamt about and even anticipated. Airpower's strategic problem lies not so much in its own inadequacies—and they are increasingly modest rather than crippling—but rather in the contexts of strategy, war, and statecraft within which it must function. Airpower viewed technically and tactically now has put almost all of its own house in good enough order to meet long-standing aspirations.

But a hundred-plus years on from Kitty Hawk, there are structural difficulties constraining the strategic value of airpower that stem from the very nature of strategy, war, and politics that do not lend themselves to technical-tactical resolution.

Prelude, 1903–14

Readers will appreciate that this book is a strategic interpretation of the past and present history of airpower. It is an exercise geared to the search for a robust general theory of airpower and to development of a plausible understanding of what airpower is about and is able to achieve; answers to these challenges are provided in chapters 9 and 10. The essential evidential base of the theory and generalizations in those chapters can only derive from the historical analysis in chapters 4–8 and within the framework provided by chapters 1–3. Paradoxically, perhaps, most of the operational, tactical, and technical facts of airpower history are as uncontentious as their strategic and political meanings are a beacon for controversy. Given that the library of airpower history is vast and a great deal of its content is not controversial, I am moved to reference here only the historians' works that I have found most useful in my quest to understand strategically the earlier decades of airpower history.[6]

Trident-like, the story of the first 15 years of airpower history has three prongs: manned balloons, rigid dirigibles, and heavier-than-air craft (aircraft). Military ballooning had early modern provenance as an idea but initially was executed only in the 1780s in France. Manned unpowered (and undirected) balloons tethered to the ground made minor episodic appearance through the nineteenth century, but all too obviously, they were less than useful in the context of mobile warfare and faced difficulties from weather. Tethered balloons came into their own for observation in the static trench warfare of 1914–18, but they were so vulnerable to enemy air action, enabled by the rapid emergence of fighter aviation, that military ballooning was apt to be a career that was "nasty, brutish, and short."

The dirigible, or rigid airship, was first developed and flown successfully by Graf von Zeppelin in 1898–1900, with the first flight recorded on 2 July of the latter year; it was powered by two 16-hp engines. By 1916 the latest-model Zeppelins were propelled by six 240-hp engines and had a ceiling of 17,400 feet and a maximum speed of 60

mph. Since it was not dependent on generating lift from forward motion, it is not surprising that until the second half of World War I, the
rigid airship generally was able to outperform the latest aircraft models. It could ascend at a rate of 1,000 feet per minute, and its load-
carrying capacity was greatly superior to contemporary aircraft.
However, the competition between airships and aircraft shifted, eventually conclusively, in favor of the latter by 1917, even in Germany.
Airships were tactically impracticable in adverse weather (wind), and
though initially hard to shoot down or disable, they eventually were
opposed effectively by aircraft whose machine guns fired incendiary
bullets, contrary to the laws of war.

Aircraft won the competition with airships for nearly every military
role, with maritime surveillance and reconnaissance a partial exception. The technical narrative of airpower from 1903 to 1914 appears
modest only when compared with the pace of advance from 1914 to
1918. Understandably, war and the fear of war have a powerful fueling
effect upon technological advance in warfare machinery. Although the
science and technology applied as the engineering required for controlled powered flight were various indeed, it is appropriate to note
above all else the growth in engine power, the sine qua non of the lift
that enables flight.[7] In 1903 the Wright brothers' Flyer boasted 15 bhp,
whereas in 1918 the Rolls Royce Condor V12 (cylinders) engine produced 600 bhp. The technical progress from the Flyer's 12-second powered glide covering 40 yards in December 1903 to the ability of a Mar-
tinsyde Buzzard to attain a speed of 132.5 mph and a ceiling of 23,950
feet in 1918, only 15 years later, is remarkable by any standard.

At the beginning of the twentieth century, a modest-size popular
literature and a tiny professional military literature focused upon the
possibilities of military airpower; in no important sense did airpower
grow out of an expressed military need—that is the story of the 1910s
and after, indeed ever since. In the 1900s the rudimentary experiments that constituted the beginnings of airpower were born out of
intuitive genius, pragmatic technical skills, a lot of guesswork, and
sheer luck (trial and much dangerous error). Vision there was aplenty,
as historical scholarship reveals unmistakably.[8] But highly speculative
vision of a strategically useful, let alone decisively useful, airpower required a leap of faith that very few were able to make prior to the Great
War of 1914–18. Unarguably, the technical-tactical prowess necessary
to produce strategic effect on a potentially war-winning scale was so
far over the horizon of contemporary accomplishment as scarcely to

warrant serious thought through these early years. With the benefit of hindsight one should recognize that, plausibly, the more ambitious aspirations of the pioneer theorists of military airpower prior to 1914 were not to be met technically and tactically for nearly a hundred years. Even then, which is to say today, the story is not quite the one so long heralded. The central reason is that although technology and tactics may be revolutionized, the course of a conflict does not necessarily yield to the leverage of power from altitude. This is not a criticism of airpower, one must hasten to say. Rather is it intended as criticism of unsound expectations of airpower.

For a while, the Wrights' extraordinary achievement on 17 December 1903 did not create much public or even private excitement. However, the pace of interest and technical accomplishment picked up speed in 1905, accelerated rapidly by 1908, and never subsequently ceased to move ahead ever more speedily. What is important for this text is that by the time of the outbreak of a general war in Europe in the summer of 1914, every one of the great powers had recognized the military utility of aviation. The Italians demonstrated that aircraft could be employed for bombardment and communication, as well as observation, in their war with Turkey in North Africa in 1911. Army and naval maneuvers had shown that aircraft could supplement and, to some degree, even replace cavalry in reconnaissance though not screening security duties. It might be misleading to claim that each great power deployed some "airpower" for the contest in 1914, but it is appropriate to record that each accepted that aircraft had some limited military utility, especially for reconnaissance and for observation of fall of shot for the artillery. In addition to its somewhat feared inventory of 11 Zeppelin airships, Germany entered the war with 245 military aircraft to France's 141. Britain's Royal Flying Corps (RFC), formed in 1912, deployed just five squadrons and a reserve park to France in August 1914.[9] These were modest beginnings but a definite signpost to the future. At least, the signpost pointed clearly toward a growing strategic value, though assuredly not to a particular strategic destination.

Beginnings, 1914–18

It is hard to convey accurately a full appreciation of how rapidly the qualitative development and quantitative expansion of all dimensions of airpower occurred during World War I. To an age numbed to technical and tactical novelty by a familiarity that can almost breed indifference, the flickering films of 1914–18 showing air warfare appear to show action as primitive as it was dangerous. Historical context is necessary to grasp the scale and variety of challenges that airpower's military pioneers had to meet and surmount. Everything about aircraft was novel. Aerodynamic theory was elementary and distinctly incomplete. An aircraft industry was lacking. Institutions with careers and doctrines were barely nascent, while military organizations devoted to the execution of air warfare did not exist. Everything was in play. But, one could ask, what was the game and what role or roles should air-minded people reasonably aspire to play? Perhaps most important of all, with a view to the longer term, how important would airpower be strategically, relative to land power and sea power? The Great War provided plausible answers to these questions, though not all airmen chose to accept the verdict of experience in that conflict as constituting anything other than a launch pad for the future. Given the extreme youth of the airplane, technically and tactically, it was not unreasonable for people to draw conclusions from the combat experience of 1914–18, extensive though it had been, that were at odds with the record of actual achievement. It is the position of this study that although it is plausible to argue that World War II largely validated the lessons learned from World War I, airpower's strategic value is so highly contextual that it was entirely appropriate after 1918 for airmen to argue that different times and occasions would mean a different story.

What needs to be emphasized is how rapidly airpower advanced from all but zero as a military factor to an essential and important element in the combined arms mix and style that was to become the modern way of warfare.[10] Context always matters. Prior to August 1914, military and naval leaders had seen just enough of the potential value of aircraft in the reconnaissance role to be persuaded that aircraft had some modest utility. The future commander in chief of the British Expeditionary Force (BEF), Gen Sir Douglas Haig, was embarrassed in the British Army maneuvers in September 1912 when his corps was spotted inconveniently from the air.[11] Nonetheless, skeptics were abundant, while even those who accepted the desirability of an air instrument for reconnaissance understandably regarded it as a tool entirely auxiliary to ground power. On the evidence available, no other position was reasonable.

When war came in August 1914, the RFC deployed five squadrons to France. From fewer than 100 aircraft at the outbreak of the war, it grew prodigiously to a total of approximately 20,890 aircraft (and 291,175 men, plus possibly 25,000 noncombatant women) by 11 November 1918. British aircraft production rose from 1,680 in 1915 (4,532 for Germany; 4,489 for France) to 29,348 in 1918 (19,598 for Germany; 31,372 for France).[12] The numbers cited here, while notoriously unreliable in fine detail though not in scale, reflect the context of the Great War in which they were intended to serve. Over the course of four and a quarter years of war, the RFC suffered 16,623 dead (just under half in combat), while Germany lost 15,906.[13] These were serious losses; at least they appear so until one places them in the context of the war as a whole, wherein the British Empire suffered a total of 908,371 military fatalities to Germany's loss of 1,808,546 (though, again, one needs to beware of spurious precision). Furthermore, those 1914–18 numbers for air fatalities pale significantly in comparison with the grim statistics for 1939–45.

Airpower developed so rapidly and grew so substantially from 1914 to 1918 because the context was one of general industrialized war between coalitions of states too powerful to be defeated rapidly. This also was the political context of 1939–45. And, it must be reemphasized, military airpower was so rudimentary in 1914 that qualitative and quantitative advance was almost bound to be rapid, indeed radical. A further contextual point is that because the ground warfare proved unexpectedly to be painfully attritional yet inconclusively protracted, there was (opportunity) time and ample motive for experiments in the air. If in, say, 1912 one were seeking to identify a political and strategic context certain to promote interest in, opportunity and resources for, and experience with the acquisition of airpower, it would have been a challenge to specify any episode more likely to be fruitful than the awesomely Great War of 1914–18. Of course, military aviation was on the move prior to 1914, but the movement understandably was more hesitant and cautious than bold and accepting of risk. Unfortunately, war is by far the best school for military education and training of all kinds.[14] Although airpower grew only to fit the role of valued team player in combined arms by 1918, its combat experience and the knowledge gained about all aspects of the infrastructure on the ground essential for success in the air was, or should have been, educationally conclusive.[15] Airpower has been on the move since 1903, though at an erratic pace, but the scale of changes wrought by World War I can hardly be exaggerated. It can be claimed by some historians that American airpower, which arrived late on the scene of the crime in Europe, entered the interwar period bereft of theory and doctrine. This was true in a formal sense, but it is seriously misleading.

Prior to 1914 there had been some prescient, if mainly lucky, strategic theorizing about airpower, as we have noted already.[16] Indeed, the potent concepts of air superiority and command of the air both appeared prewar.[17] What was lacking in 1914 was a practical concept of air warfare in any useful detail. No one knew how to fight in the air. Air tactics did not exist. In fact, the very concept of air war typically invited either contempt or deep skepticism. How could the frail, unarmed aircraft of 1914 fight in the sky? Indeed, why would they want to? Furthermore, given the immensity of the sky and the uncertainties of aerial navigation, how could airmen who were motivated to fight in the sky locate their airborne enemy? These fundamental questions found no answers in August 1914. No country owned armed military airpower. Yet, it is probably no exaggeration to claim that by close of play in 1918, little of great significance about the nature of airpower and even the more enduring of its terms of engagement remained to be discovered from lessons learned in events yet to occur. Needless to say, it is infinitely easier today to identify persisting and even a few eternal truths about airpower detectable from the 1914–18 experience than it was for airmen and others soon after the event.

It is important to realize that although airpower changed radically between 1914 and 1918, its achievement was part of a whole revolution in warfare, not to constitute that revolution itself.[18] Airpower became an integral component of and an important contributing enabler for what now is recognized as the modern way in combined arms warfare. Keeping the focus on context, airpower grew rapidly and radically from nearly nothing to a significant team player in a then-modern way of warfare wherein the team leader was the artillery. No single military instrument won the land warfare of the second half of World War I, but the team leader—the key that unlocked the door of contemporary defenses—was excellence in artillery firepower. There was a revolution in the conduct of land warfare between 1914 and 1918, and it is only in that context that one should assess airpower's history.

In retrospect, there was a clear technical, tactical, and strategic logic to the overall grand narrative of the emergence of military airpower in 1914–18. This is not to dismiss the always-present potency of the contingent, but it is to argue that if the growth of airpower in those years can be characterized as mission creep, then it was a creep that had obvious tactical utility, notable operational merit, and, consequentially, strategic value. It may be true to claim that technology led tactics and strategy in the air war, though I am not convinced of the validity in this suggestion. Whether or not on balance it is true, the fact remains that air forces had the most pressing tactical need of all that science, technology, and engineering could provide: both tactics and strategy were eagerly waiting for technically better military enablers. Without forgetting the play of much technological push and the benefits and harassments of ever-powerful contingency, it is both possible and necessary to identify a great chain of military logic that goes most of the way to explain how airpower evolved from 1914 to 1918. Yes, technical discoveries were made and almost accidental findings were recorded unexpectedly from experience and were applied, but the story of airpower in 1914–18 is not one that should be understood primarily in technical terms. The cumulative technological achievement was impressive indeed, but it was technology applied for particular, most-pressing military needs. This was a case of motive propelling means to meet the demands of circumstance.

The contemporary context of the war as a whole was nearly all important. Progress in airpower was driven forward not so much by its own momentum considered in isolation as an emerging air war, though there is some merit in at least granting influence to this factor. Rather, airpower on both sides was regarded by its commanders and behind them by their commanders also, as an auxiliary supporting tool for land and sea warfare. To understand airpower in World War I, or indeed in any war, it is essential to grasp the character of the particular conflict.

Airpower was emerging in a period of desperation and, some have claimed contestably, even total war. It was evolving not on some leisurely schedule of discretionary trial and error but in a life or death competition for the highest stakes. The technical story of airpower in 1914–18 is a tale of experiment and experience as events demonstrated tactical and operational necessities.

As the most important of the arms for land warfare that eventually both sides managed to "combine" impressively in 1917 and especially in 1918, the needs of the artillery provided much of the fuel for airpower development.[19] Assessed overall, it is really incontestable that although World War I was won by a new version of combined arms tactics, nonetheless the leading edge of those more or less combined arms for both sides was the artillery.

To help the artillery be all that it could be and needed to be to unlock the fortified barrier to ground advance, aircraft were highly desirable, indeed literally essential, as an enabler of precision bombardment. In 1914 it was understood that aircraft were useful for reconnaissance and generally for observation, but the true weight of artillery's relative importance was not widely anticipated. Neither belligerent coalition anticipated a protracted, attritional, siege-like character to essentially static war on land. Consequently, the Entente Allies certainly did not have an artillery arsenal bursting at the seams with heavy guns. The true character of the land warfare was unmistakable by the end of 1915, but prior to 1918 neither side achieved the quality and quantity of combined arms, suitably guided by sound contemporary tactical doctrine, to break through the rival fortified zones. It should be added that the Allies never were able to achieve a "breakout" in conclusive strategic exploitation of first the "break-in" and then the "breakthrough." Modern scholarship, especially that produced over the past 30 years, at last has revealed how this warfare was waged tactically, both successfully and otherwise. The only reliable way to break into a trench system or fortified zone (e.g., the Siegfried Stellung, better known as the Hindenburg Line of 1917–18) was by means of highly scientific gunnery. There was no alternative in this period. Tanks, aircraft, and assault infantry (storm troopers) using infiltration tactics were all necessary, but still they were critically dependent upon artillery for suppressive and sometimes destructive fire.

Aircraft provided the platforms at altitude from which one might locate the enemy with precision, locate friendly forces (a major challenge when soldiers were engaged in combat), photograph terrain for accurate mapping (it was vital for artillery to know exactly where everyone and everything was, including itself), and transmit or drop messages to troops on the ground. Aerial observation was not the single golden key that enabled the artillery of both sides to open up enemy fortifications, but it was more than merely useful.

It should be needless to say that because "war [and warfare] is nothing but a duel on a larger scale,"[20] anything that one belligerent finds militarily valuable is certain to be contested actively by the enemy, and so it proved. Notwithstanding the typical prewar belief that war in the air was an absurd idea, it was demonstrated mutually from the outset that, absurd or not, it had to be done. The vastness of the sky and the technical limitations of current aircraft obliged war in the air (and from the ground to the air in the form of antiaircraft artillery, triple-A or AAA) to be primitive indeed. Nonetheless, air-to-air warfare proved feasible if challenging. The first victim of war in the air, a German Aviatik, fell to shots fired by a machine gun from a French Voisin, an observation aircraft, on 5 October 1914.[21] The tactical logic of the duel, great and small, was irresistible. Since observation was either important or vital to both sides, the right to do it and to deny that right had to be protected and enforced. Aerial combat was the direct and inevitable consequence of the military value of aircraft for observation, reconnaissance, and surveillance.[22] The technical problems were formidable but were solved well enough under the pressure of competitive necessity in the context of a great general war wherein belligerent societies allocated effectively an open-ended commitment of their resources to the struggle.

The step from observation protection and denial to full-scale war in the air took little more than a year. From isolated and small-scale encounters in 1914 between lone aircraft typically armed with such expedient weapons as revolvers and rifles, by the close of 1915 and especially in 1916, large-scale air-to-air warfare was an established fact. Bear in mind that at the outset of the war there were no, as in zero, armed aircraft designed for aerial combat. The pioneers of war in the air had to proceed in a hurry by trial and error because of the pressing contextual need. Aviation in 1914–18 was not propelled by scientific or any other kind of idle curiosity; rather was it driven by genuine and painful current tactical necessity. The most obvious technical problem for the would-be air warrior was how to fire a machine gun through the propeller arc. This challenge first was met successfully in practice by Anthony Fokker, working for the Germans, although the solution had been identified and offered to the RFC prior to the war. As a consequence, the Eindecker monoplane, armed with Spandau machine guns enabled by an interrupter gear to fire through the propeller blades, effected a brief but deadly "Fokker scourge" in the skies over the western front late in 1915 and into 1916.[23]

War in the air came of age in 1916. Neither side could afford to concede uncontested observation by aircraft if it hoped to be successful on the ground. As a consequence of this inexorable military and strategic logic, the first great air battles the world had seen occurred over Verdun and the Somme battlefields in 1916. The context of a great war wherein aircraft deliver potentially ever-greater tactical benefit unavoidably motivated belligerents to fight for the right to use the sky without serious enemy hindrance while precluding the enemy from doing likewise.

The initially unexpected rapid emergence of war in the air in 1915–16 triggered the creation and hasty development of practical doctrine for air warfare. Unsurprisingly, armies could not help but appreciate that they could not simply employ an air "corps" or force as they might choose for their own convenience, unimpeded by a vigorous enemy—at least they could not do so in warfare between great powers. The strategic, operational, and tactical logic of the typically unanticipated and distinctly improvised and experimental air fighting of 1914 and most of 1915 was that it was now necessary to win the war in the air if one were to exploit the air environment to assist the army and navy. It is necessary to emphasize that in all countries, prior to 1 April 1918, air "forces" unintentionally and in most other respects were more or less integral parts of their country's army and navy.

By 1917, and assuredly by early 1918, the tactical and operational "grammar," to steal yet again from Clausewitz, of military airpower was widely grasped and increasingly gripped for military effectiveness. Air observation was important as one among several enablers for the scientific gunnery that was the key to tactical success on the ground. Observation could be enforced only by the ability to protect the observing aircraft, a mission that required dedicated "pursuit," or fighter, machines.[24] The newly specialized fighter type of aircraft was needed for the demanding tasks of protecting friendly reconnaissance aircraft and attacking those of the enemy, both of which required the ability to engage in combat with the enemy's fighters.

In addition to supporting friendly artillery, fighter aircraft were found to be essential to protect the offensive style of air warfare: bombing. Aircraft specialized to carry bombs needed to be defended by dedicated fighting machines that would escort them. It was discovered, as it would have to be rediscovered in later conflicts, that success in air-to-air war was obligatory, not merely desirable, if success in air-to-ground war was to be achievable. A further dimension of the artillery connection to airpower, ironically perhaps, is that while aircraft were valuable as an enabler for the precision use of artillery, they were close to essential as a substitute for it when an army advanced or retreated so far as to disconnect its fighting edge from close artillery support. In other words, aircraft more or less well suited to the mission could function as flying artillery, more than able to keep up with the pace of advance or retreat in mobile warfare. In its most dedicated form, such close air support, including near interdiction, was provided by Germany in the organization of 38 squadrons specifically configured, trained, and employed for ground attack in direct support of what was intended to be a great war-winning offensive pushes that opened on 21 March 1918.[25]

Readers may be wondering why so little has been said thus far on the important subject of longer-range, so-called strategic bombing in World War I. The reason is because although it was conducted—especially by Germany against Britain throughout the war by Zeppelin airships and subsequently (from 1917) by dedicated Gotha long-range bombers—it was strategically the least significant of airpower's contributions to the mighty struggle. In the eyes of air-minded people, such bombing was identified early as the true strategic future of airpower, but in 1914–18 the record of strategic achievement by such bombardment was distinctly modest.

Notwithstanding the scant enthusiasm just registered for the near-term strategic consequences of long-range bombing in the war, there is no doubting the potency of its promise perceived by some airpower practitioners, theorists, and a few politician-strategists. Though ineffective strategically, the German bombing of England did trigger a political reaction in London that resulted, though not without hesitation, in the creation of the Royal Air Force (RAF) as the world's first air force independent of an army or navy on 1 April 1918. Prime Minister Lloyd George was under intense domestic political pressure in the summer and fall of 1917. The war in France was proceeding poorly, as usual, and England was being bombed, apparently at will, by German Gothas. Lloyd George passed the ball to a safe and well-trusted pair of genuinely strategic hands, those of long-lapsed Boer war hero, Gen Jan Christian Smuts, and charged him with finding a solution to the government's air defense problems. Smuts, a clever and experienced man, delivered two reports. The first dealt competently with the challenge of homeland air defense, while the second, dated 17 August 1917, ventured imprudently far, or one might claim boldly, into strategic prophecy.[26] Specifically, the characteristically wise and prudent Smuts had drafted a report that airpower historian Eugene M. Emme correctly labeled the "'Magna Carta' of British air power." In fact, with hindsight it is plausible to argue that Smuts' *Second*

Report was to assume and indeed to warrant the iconic status of being the Magna Carta for airpower in general, not merely in Britain. The former Boer general (turned imperial statesman) argued—though more truly it was an empirically unsupported assertion—that to fulfill a promise that he believed to be strategically and potentially dominant over land power and sea power, airpower should be organized and operated as an autonomous "air service" independent of military or naval command. The core justification for this radical step was the anticipated potency of long-range bombardment. This would be air warfare as the dominant strand in warfare. While there would be some need for an army and navy for the defense of national assets, the offensive or counteroffensive that could win a war would (or might) be delivered by aerial bombardment.

Although Smut's reasoning offered a dazzling vision and prospect for ambitious airmen, it was, alas for its practicality, hopelessly remote from technical, tactical, and operational feasibility in 1917–18. No less an airpower enthusiast than Hugh Trenchard was notably unfriendly to Smuts' product. Because of political wrangling and personality clashes, he was tapped to command an independent force for the long-range bombing mission. Trenchard recognized that in 1918 that mission had to take second place to the immediate need to support a potentially, episodically (from late March until July), and desperately hard-pressed BEF in the field. Close and fairly direct air support for the army was the near all-consuming Allied need in 1918.[27]

The balance of tactical and operational advantage in the air swayed back and forth from 1915 to early 1918, by which time Allied resource superiority ensured and enforced a steadily growing strategic ascendancy in the air. That granted, German airpower remained effective technically and tactically, if increasingly outnumbered, through to the armistice. Indeed, German airpower resisted more competently in the last weeks of the war than did German land power. It is doubly ironic that in the final year of both world wars, a German aircraft was technically and in key respects tactically a class ahead of its enemies—the Junkers J10 and Fokker D7 in 1918, and the jet-propelled Me 262 in 1944–45. In both cases Germany's technical superiority was expressed and exploited too little and too late in competition with enemies whose latest aircraft models were technically good enough, lent themselves to mass production, and typically were flown by tactically good-to-excellent pilots and other aircrew.

Mass as an eternal and universal principle of war was found to apply to war in and from the air. Air forces learned that tactically and for operational effect, it was highly desirable to fly in ever-larger formations. Indeed, the rules of air warfare, certainly of air fighting, specified formally and informally as early as 1916 and 1917 by German and British authors, very largely listed a common set of dicta and had long-enduring authority for decades, notwithstanding massive technical change.

It would be an exaggeration to claim that everything worth knowing about the conduct of nearly all aspects of air warfare either was learned in, has been derived from the experience of, or should have been grasped from the events of 1914–18; however, the exaggeration would have much merit. It would point accurately enough to the original circumstances that contributed a great deal of subsequent airpower thought and doctrine. Even regarded tactically and operationally, World War I provided an enduring window for those whose minds were open to education and understanding.

Promise, 1919–39

Geography may or may not be destiny, but it certainly has a lot for which to answer. The evolution of airpower in the two decades that separated the two world wars was geostrategically distinguishable from country to country.[28] Varied interpretation of the particular national experience with airpower in the Great War helped shape attitudes.[29] It is necessary to preface this analytical sketch of airpower in the interwar years with yet another warning about hindsight-foresight. Today, it is exceedingly difficult, to the point of impossibility, to review and interpret airpower developments in the 1920s, and particularly the 1930s, without exploiting a historical perspective denied to the players at the time. We have the advantage of knowing exactly how much time countries had for rearmament, as well as which among the air lessons of World War I and the Spanish Civil War (1936–39) were most important.

Although airpower had significantly shaped its whole strategic context by the second half of World War II, still it is necessary to recognize that it was only one of several strategic elements. Furthermore, the military strategic elements in their entirety by no means were the master of the course of history, even though assuredly they did perform as history's most effective executive agents. The 1920s was a postwar, not a prewar, decade, while in the first half of the 1930s it was far from obvious to most people, including politicians and soldiers, that the world was moving inexorably on a road that must end in another general war.

There was no dispute in 1919 that during the war, airpower had advanced dramatically in all respects, had proven itself useful and even essential as a vital member of a combined arms team, and had demonstrated the potential to be even more useful in the future. But in 1919 and for more than a decade thereafter, the top priorities for airmen were to retain as much as possible of the political and bureaucratic-institutional high ground already secured and to advance the airpower interest as far as it could go in a distinctly nonpermissive political context. The recently demonstrated horrors of modern war overshadowed even the possibility of serious strategic debate, and the dissatisfied among the greater powers were effectively disarmed or ill-armed (Italy, Japan, the USSR). Following precipitate military demobilization in the 1920s and early 1930s, strategic debate was dominated by initiatives for disarmament and endorsements of the marvelous promise of collective security through behavior on behalf of world order licensed and demanded by the apparently impressive, certainly novel, experiment with the League of Nations.

Whereas from 1914 to 1918 airpower was force-fed by an ever-pressing immediate strategic need, for many years after the armistice on 11 November 1918, such demand was all but entirely absent. Airpower development on all fronts did not crash and burn, but it had to be advanced on a schedule entirely different to that which had moved it from the column of fragile marginalia in 1914 to a potent military team player in 1918. Airmen, in company with military people in uniforms of every color, knew that their strategic services would be required in the future. Moreover, they believed that the future held another great war in which the relative strategic utility of airpower effectively would be unlimited. Unfortunately for the more air-minded people—at least those with geostrategically insular homelands, which is to say primarily Americans and Britons—their societies and political leaders were not interested in a next great war. This was hardly surprising, but it was to prove imprudent.

In the absence of a clear and present major security danger, airpower's defenders were obliged to be content with such consolidation of wartime gains as could be achieved, with the addition of any progress that could be gleaned from an expedient opportunism. Translated, this condition meant that Britain's RAF, only seven months old in its independence by 11 November 1918, struggled against some heavy odds to keep itself on the political gold standard of full service autonomy. For American airpower that, like the national military effort overall, had arrived in large numbers only very late in the war and unavoidably underprepared for modern warfare, the challenge was to secure such autonomy as the Army would concede, while behaving in such a way and with such a character that the gold standard of institutional independence might be achieved.

In the 1920s and early 1930s there was no plausible current menace to national or international security stemming from a great power rival, let alone a coalition of such powers.[30] As a result, the airmen of the politically satisfied great powers, which is to say of the United States and Britain, had no choice other than to press their airpower interests in terms of their own theories of airpower's role in the prevention of war, in warfare when it would recur, and as a necessary matter of precautionary modernization.[31] The "what if?" form of argument gathered political weight as undeniable perils to international security appeared and grew through the mid 1930s.

Historical context explains most that needs understanding about airpower history. Our subject is a totally new form of military power that was propelled into and through forced growth by the strategic demands of dire events between 1914 and 1918. Next, precipitately, it inhabited a historical context of 21 years' duration wherein it could demonstrate almost nothing convincingly about its contemporary or future potency. And then it was back to combat of the most intense and varied kinds imaginable for the six years from 1939 to 1945.

In 1919, airmen dared not rest their case for political respect, autonomy, and strategic importance solely on the basis of deeds done, impressive though the deeds had been by 1918 when assessed in light of the extreme modesty of the air effort possible in 1914. So, prudently if perilously, the airpower interests in the 1920s sought justification for such institutional autonomy as the political context would afford—complete but threatened, even for the RAF—with a mixture of theory building and contemporary strategic utility. As suggested above, the theory most favored by particular national air-minded military communities reflected closely their particular geostrategic contexts. Continental European airpower theorists tended to favor strongly the close support of land power as the primary duty.

Insular Britain and America tended strongly to prefer airpower as a military instrument that could wage and probably win wars in a manner largely independent of the activities of armies and navies. The fact that the most impressive of the post-1918 airpower theorists, Giulio Douhet, was Italian is easily explained geostrategically. Because of its peninsular shape and forbidding mountainous land frontiers, Italy's geostrategic context effectively was all but insular.[32] For a while in the early 1930s, the Soviet Union developed and procured the world's first large long-range bombing force, but this geostrategically eccentric episode prudently was terminated definitively by mid decade. The new Nazi Germany inherited from its Weimar predecessor the world's first theory of, and doctrine for, operational air warfare.[33] Such a focus stressed interdiction bombing in support of mobile theater-deep land operations.

Strategic experience in the 1930s reaffirmed the plainer lessons that could be learned, and were learned by some, from the airpower story of World War I. Specifically, the airpower of the day, from the 1910s through the interwar period, exercised its maximum strategic leverage by supporting land power fairly directly. This was the story both of World War I and of the Spanish Civil War. Hugh Trenchard, commander of the RFC (1915–17) and then chief of staff of the RAF in 1918 and 1919–27, conducted air warfare from 1915 to 1918 primarily as a supporting activity on behalf of the BEF. Support of the land war, however, was not the story that he judged adequate to consolidate RAF independence and to promote its political future. That story was independent, generally termed (actually mis-termed) strategic bombing.[34] For the purpose of immediate survival in the early 1970s, the RAF proposed that it should undertake imperial policing duties against recalcitrant irregulars. This use of airpower for the control of revolting tribesmen certainly saved money, which was popular in London, and it enjoyed some success.[35] But it was discovered that airpower employed coercively for punitive intent was a rather blind instrument. While 250- and 500-pound bombs did inspire some useful fear and even respect, they tended to alienate and annoy probably as much or more than they persuaded to cooperate.

Although imperial policing from the air was a helpful stopgap for an RAF that needed to demonstrate its value in the threat-light political and strategic context of the 1920s, it could not suffice as the theoretical and thence doctrinal bedrock of authority for service independence. That conceptual bedrock for insular Britain was judged to be long-range (strategic) bombing for strategic effect independent of the strategic contribution of the army and navy. Although every country's airpower community was tempted by the vision of "victory through airpower," only those in Britain and the United States succumbed decisively to the dazzling prospect.[36]

The origins, emergence, and maturing of strategic bombing theory and its translation into doctrine have been well told and do not need replaying here. The vision was rooted in a laudable desire to avoid a repetition of the attritional terrestrial warfare of World War I, a desire to be as modern as technology allowed, and of course, a wish to advance the interests of the new community of air-minded people. But also, the point needs to be registered with great emphasis that the air theorists of the 1920s and 1930s did have some persuasive, though not thoroughly compelling, reasons to believe that their favored military instrument had the potential to revolutionize warfare. It is all too easy today for scholars, reading airpower history backwards, to identify the many reasons why the vision of victory through airpower all but alone was unlikely to be realized, at least anytime in the near future. It was less clear at the time that effectively an untried mode of warfare would not, let alone could not, deliver a decisive measure of strategic success.

The strategic airpower theory, carried over from peace into war in the late 1930s, came in three major variants. First, there was the thesis of Giulio Douhet that bombardment from the air could so terrorize weak-willed civilians, who would be targeted directly, that they would compel their government to surrender. Second, there was the British thesis advanced by Hugh Trenchard that the selective bombing of "vital centers" of industrial assets would so weaken the morale of civilian workers that, as with the Douhetian thesis, they would demand national capitulation. Third, there was the American thesis that by means of unescorted (by long-range fighters) high-altitude precision daylight bombing, the key and vital nodes of an enemy's "industrial web" could be so damaged and even paralyzed that it would be unable to prosecute a war further.[37] There were variations among individual theorists and over time, but the key ideas were as just stated. To summarize, long-range bombing was believed to be potentially the war-winning military tool because either (1) uniquely among the forms of military power, it could attack and destroy directly the will of enemy society to resist; or (2) it could function uniquely as the "silver bullet" that literally would disable and disarm the enemy, again by taking direct action that would bypass the enemy's hard military shell of its army and navy. The vision was dazzling, but it was only a vision, a speculation, before the trial and error of the experience of World War II.

The conceptual reach of airpower theory did have some dynamic material basis for strategic optimism. Whereas the cutting edge of military aviation in 1918 was represented by machines capable of flying at about 120 mph (fighters), by 1939 the leading German and British fighter aircraft had top speeds approaching 350 mph. For much of the interwar period, key performance differences between specialized bomber and fighter types were only modest in favor of the fighter or tilted to privilege the bomber. This technical context helps explain why technical-tactical arguments skeptical of the strategic promise of victory through long-range bombardment were not more persuasive in the late 1920s and early 1930s. True to its reflection of the geostrategic logic of US security, American airpower theorists pinned their theoretical and then doctrinal faith on the long-range bomber from central casting, the machine that was to become the B-17 of fame and legend. Flying first in 1935 and entering service with the US Army Air Corps (USAAC, renamed in 1927 from the US Army Air Service), the B-17 enjoyed a service ceiling, nominally at least, of 38,000 feet and a top speed of 300 mph. Equipped with the air marksman–bombardier's vital aid, the excellent, but not brilliant, Norden bombsight—which worked extremely well over typically cloudless Texas—this aircraft was what the Air Corps Tactical School's (ACTS) theorists meant by airpower.[38] The B-17 would be able to deliver the high-altitude precision daylight bombing that the ACTS maintained with near-religious conviction would ensure victory. It is not a powerful criticism to argue, albeit correctly, that the ACTS's faith lacked for reliable empirical evidence. After all, only experience could provide evidence that might validate or refute the theory.

Nonetheless, there were reasons for skepticism, perhaps for a prudent caution, that ought to have been accessible to fairly open minds in the mid-to-late 1930s. Three are worthy of mention: the evidence of civilian demoralization due to aerial bombardment in World War I, though encouraging for airpower theorists, was by no means conclusive; the technical performance of specialized fighter aircraft in the 1930s climbed far above the near parity that had been the norm as late as 1930; and the discovery in 1935 of radar pointed plainly to the potential practicality of fielding an air defense system which could vector air fighting assets to bomber formations detected at some tactically useful distance. What has just been described was not reality in 1935–36, but certainly it was envisaged in Britain as a practical probability for successful homeland defense against air attack.

By 1939 the dominant theory of airpower in Britain and the United States strongly privileged long-range bombardment. In material terms, however, Britain in 1939 had a fighter-weighted air force that was in the process of being integrated into the world's first comprehensive air defense system heavily dependent upon a cordon of coastal radar stations (still under construction). In mid-decade the British government overrode RAF doctrine and decided to invest in a fighter force that might be able to demonstrate the fallaciousness of former prime minister Stanley Baldwin's oft-quoted 1932 maxim that "the bomber will always get through." On 5 March 1936 Britain boldly placed orders for 600 Hurricanes and 300 Spitfires (which were technically more challenging to manufacture). The RAF's bomber force was of the medium, not the much-desired but heretofore unafford-able as well as technically difficult heavy, four-engine category. As the early months and, alas, years of the war were to demonstrate, RAF Bomber Command was thoroughly unfit for its purpose.[39] The USAAC had a potent theory of strategic airpower, but with the United States legally and politically neutral and apparently determined to remain so, the B-17 that first entered service in 1938 was not to become even potentially strategically potent until its numbers in the tens could climb through the hundreds into the thousands. That procurement process, keyed to the necessary manpower for aircrew and to the essential ground-based infrastructure, was well over the horizon in 1939 and 1940.

German airpower was impressive by 1939, especially since the Luftwaffe was officially created only in 1935, but it was very much a shop-window air force. Its Condor Legion performed well in Spain and learned a great deal from that episode. From Spain the Germans learned that bombers needed to be protected by fighters, that interdiction and close air support generated high operational effect for strategic leverage, that the "best practice" fighter tactics proven in World War I by and large still worked in 1936–39, and overall, that air superiority was the key to the strategic value of airpower for all air warfare missions—as it had been in 1915–18.[40]

Conclusion:
Coming, Ready or Not

Major problems assail the scholar who endeavors to assess honestly the strategic performance of a particular military instrument in a particular conflict—airpower in this case. Although airpower may be appreciated and debated as a general and somewhat abstract force, potential, or even achievement, its merits and limitations are so situationally determined that it could be highly misleading to argue that it was tested in 1914–18 and again in 1939–45. Of course the airpower of the day was tested in the conditions of the day, but what can that tell us about airpower in general? The potency of even a weak weapon will be flattered when it is wielded with tactical skill under wise strategic direction against an inept enemy. It should be needless to add that the reverse must be true also. Moreover, whatever the innate strengths and weaknesses of airpower, in practice they always have unique meaning in distinctive contexts. It may seem to some readers that the point is too obvious to be worthy of explicit notice, but as a matter of integrity in historical assessment there is value in recognizing that what was ready or not for air warfare in 1930–41 could only be the airpower of the several polities in those years. Airpower is dynamic in all its aspects, save only for the general theoretical. Below the elevated conceptual level of the general theory of airpower (see chap. 9), there are no eternal or universal truths on the subject. Translated, this means that while World Wars I and II were tests of airpower, they obviously were not tests authoritative for other contexts. For an obvious example, Air Chief Marshal Sir Hugh Dowding did not prove in 1940 that air defense beats air offense. Rather, he proved only that air defense *can* defeat air offense, contrary to the teaching in much previous theory and doctrine.

The point of the substantive title of this conclusion is to emphasize that airmen generally do not determine when their military instruments will be ready to employ. The Luftwaffe that caused such anxiety in Britain in the second half of the 1930s bore no close relation to the fearsome Luftwaffe of a British public imagination. The German force was still very much a work in progress in 1939–40, a condition from which it never could quite escape.[41] Geared for a short-range continental European war by 1942, the Luftwaffe was thrown prematurely into intense attritional campaigns long before it was ready industrially and logistically, in particular. If the Luftwaffe were not ready for the air warfare it was ordered to wage in 1939, or indeed thereafter, the same was true of the RAF, the USAAC, the French Air Force, and also Soviet aviation. But it was German airmen's misfortunes to be required to wage more air warfare, more intensively, and for longer than anyone else, yet from a weaker industrial base than eventually was available to its diverse great-power enemies. As limiting as its fundamental material handicaps was the fact that the errors in strategy and operational art that marred the several collective Allied war effort(s) pale by comparison with the dysfunctional direction and management to which German airmen were hostages and victims.

The history of airpower in times of peace, crisis, and war carries potent lessons of enduring value. That granted, it is probably no less accurate to say that history carries the potential to mislead when historically local truths are lifted out of context, either ignorantly or with fell intent, and are deployed to support or allegedly confirm claimed perpetual truths. Airpower in its many national and several functional forms came to the party to fight in World War II, no matter how unready it was for strategic prime time. One truth of strategic history that truly is eternal and universal is the persisting reality of the revelatory nature of experience. Only warfare can confirm how potent or otherwise is one's airpower. However, while World War II could not help but serve as a Super Bowl trial by fire for the underprepared airpower of the early 1940s, it was only *a*, not *the* conclusive, test. In addition to a need for caution in drawing lessons from those extraordinarily busy years, it is only prudent to remember that while strategic history can have just one actual course, that unique and real past might have been very different; one cannot know. Employed and misemployed in the ways that it was in some hugely unanticipated contexts, airpower from 1939 to 1945 provided a densely rich, if more than a little chaotic, mixed story of high and low achievement. Those, like this author, who depend upon a contested historical record in the search for the evidence of experience on the basis of which theory can be constructed, have to police our investigations lest we misread the transitory for the enduring.

Now it is time and more for what must be characterized as the main event to this date of writing in the history of airpower, World War II. If the Great War of 1914–18 was, at its combined-arms heart, the great and greatest artillery war, would the airpower theorists of the 1920s and 1930s be proved correct in predicting that the next great struggle would be the Great Air War?

Notes

With gratitude I borrow the title of this chapter from Cecil Lewis' *Sagittarius Rising*. Lewis joined the Royal Flying Corps (RFC) at age 16 and one-half and miraculously survived three operational tours over the western front as well as duty in the air defense of London. Sagittarius is the ninth sign of the zodiac, the archer, governing voyages, weapons, and all swift things.

1. See the almost lyrical description of this awesome event in Budiansky, *Air Power*, 440.

2. Hallion, *Storm over Iraq*, 267. This bold claim has much to recommend it when it is endorsed with some restraint, but it is a dangerous idea to plant in the minds of those who are strategically challenged. Cohen, "Mystique of U.S. Air Power," is a valuable period piece (1994) by the director of the USAF Gulf War Air-power Survey that does retain value, as is characteristic of Cohen's typically insightful writings.

3. The concept of an infosphere is developed and tested in Lonsdale's useful study, *Clausewitzian Future: The Nature of War in the Information Age*.

4. See Murray, "Thinking about Revolutions in Military Affairs"; Knox and Murray, *Dynamics of Military Revolution*; Gray, *Strategy for Chaos*; Benbow, *Magic Bullet?*; and Gray, *National Security Dilemmas*, chap. 5.

5. Lambeth, *Transformation of American Air Power*, was a major milestone statement of enduring merit by a truly expert analyst and historian of air operations.

6. I am much indebted to the following in particular, amongst a plethora of useful studies: Hallion, *Strike from the Sky*; Kennett, *First Air War*; Paris, *Winged Warfare*; Morrow, *Great War in the Air*; Buckley, *Air Power in the Age of Total War*; Wells, *Air Power*; Biddle, *Rhetoric and Reality in Air Warfare*; Cox and Gray, *Air Power History*; Budiansky, *Air Power*; Gates, *Sky Wars*; Grattan, *Origins of Air War*; Hooton, *War over the Trenches*; Olsen, *History of Air Warfare* and *Global Air Power*. I apologize to any other authors who might believe that their scholarship merits recognition here. There is a culminating point of sufficiency in proper and fair citation.

7. See especially Grattan, *Origins of Air War*, chap. 3.

8. See Paris, *Winged Warfare*; and Wells, *Air Power*, pt. I.

9. Grattan, *Origins of Air War*, 67. Also see Kennett, *First Air War*, 21.

10. See Bailey, *First World War and the Birth of the Modern Style of Warfare*; and Hooton, *War over the Trenches*.

11. Grattan, *Origins of Air War*, 6.

12. Ibid., 33, 216.

13. Ibid., 17. The casualties caused by accidents in both world wars can come as a melancholy surprise to people who fail to appreciate that military flying is a dangerous activity, even when enemy action is not a factor.

14. For an important caveat, one must insist that although any war can provide fuel for military education, a particular war yields reliable lessons only about its own conduct. Some experienced, and by definition successful, aerial warriors of 1914–18 had nontrivial difficulty recognizing the full extent of the differences in conditions that pertained to the challenges of 1939–45. This is a recurrent general problem in military command. The commanders in a later war were junior or at least young field-grade officers in a previous, very different war. Career-long learning is a worthy and necessary aspiration in all professions, but in the military as in others it is ever likely to be imperfect.

15. I employ the word "only" strictly to indicate that airpower had much yet to achieve by way of demonstrated strategic effectiveness. I do not intend to imply that airpower was regarded as unimportant in 1918; emphatically it was not.

16. Biddle, *Rhetoric and Reality in Air Warfare*. Chaps. 1 and 3 are particularly useful.

17. See Paris, *Winged Warfare*; and Budiansky, *Air Power*, chap. 1.

18. Mason, "British Dimension," 7–8.

19. Gray, *Strategy for Chaos*, chap. 7.

20. See Zabecki, *Steel Wind*.

21. Clausewitz, *On War*, 75.

22. Morrow, *Great War in the Air*, 64–65.

23. See Buckley, *Air Power in the Age of Total War*, 50–51.

24. Grattan, *Origins of Air War*, chap. 4.

25. Hallion, *Rise of the Fighter Aircraft*.

26. Helpful commentaries and analyses include Hallion, *Strike from the Sky*, chap. 2; Muller, "Close Air Support," 145–55; and Hooton, *War over the Trenches*, chaps. 6–7.

27. See Luck, "Smuts Report."

28. Smuts, " 'Magna Carta' of British Air Power," in Emme's useful collection of foundation writings, *Impact of Air Power*.

29. Although he was a firm believer in the strategic value of long-range bombing, then–Wg Cdr John C. Slessor, speaking and writing in the early 1930s about the airpower experience of 1914–18, was in no doubt about the effectiveness of air interdiction of supplies to the enemy army in the field. Slessor, *Air Power and Armies*.

30. For example, see Grattan, *Origins of Air War*, 233–62, which reproduces the memorandum issued by British GHQ, France, February 1918, on "Fighting in the Air."

31. See Murray and Millett, *Military Innovation in the Interwar Period*; Buckley, *Air Power in the Age of Total War*; and Gat, *Fascist and Liberal Visions of War*.

32. Serious plausible threats may have been absent, but see Ferris, "Theory of a 'French Air Menace.' " Also see Malcolm Smith, *British Air Strategy between the Wars*.

33. See Douhet, *Command of the Air*; and Meilinger, "Giulio Douhet and the Origins of Airpower Theory."

34. Corum, *Luftwaffe*.

35. Trenchard, "Air Power and National Security." Also see Meilinger, "Trenchard, Slessor, and Royal Air Force Doctrine before World War II"; and Biddle, *Rhetoric and Reality in Air Warfare*, chap. 2.

36. See Omissi, *Royal Air Force, Air Power and Colonial Control*.

37. MacIsaac, "Voices from the Central Blue," is useful, as is Biddle, *Rhetoric and Reality in Air Warfare*, chaps. 2–3.

38. Faber, "Interwar US Army Aviation and the Air Corps Tactical School," is excellent, as is David Johnson, *Fast Tanks and Heavy Bombers*, especially chaps. 3, 7, and 11. Prominent among first-rate broad studies are Sherry, *Rise of American Air Power*; Buckley, *Air Power in the Age of Total War*, chaps 4–5; Biddle, *Rhetoric and Reality in Air Warfare*; and Overy, "Air Power and the Origins of Deterrence Theory before 1939," 40. Also see Finney, *History of the Air Corps Tactical School*; and Donald Miller, *Eighth Air Force*, chap. 1.

39. See Hastings, *Bomber Command*, chaps. 1–4; Biddle, *Rhetoric and Reality in Air Warfare*, chap. 4; and Jacobs, "British Strategic Air Offensive against Germany in World War II." The official history is exemplary: Webster and Frankland, *History of the Second World War*, 4 vols.

40. See Corum, *Luftwaffe*, chap. 6; and idem., "Luftwaffe and Lessons Learned in the Spanish Civil War."

41. Murray, *Luftwaffe*, is a first-rate analytical history.

Chapter 5

Strategic History II:
The Great Test, 1939–45

In retrospect one can hypothesize fancifully that World War II might have been conceived by history's planners as a comprehensive examination of the theory and practice of airpower. If World War I provided a guide to the future, and the lengthy pause of the interwar decades laid on potentially adequate time to prepare, then the course and outcome of World War II should deliver plausible if not necessarily conclusive verdicts on the major issues outstanding about the strategic value of airpower. As airpower historian Richard Overy has written with reference to the prewar context:

> Above all, the instability of air doctrine lay in the fact that air forces were compelled to make guesses about how aircraft would be used once war had actually broken out. There was little experience to draw on about the kind of air war most powers expected to fight, so that much air doctrine was an act of faith that the guesses of one particular air force were the right ones. As powers became more aware of what potential air enemies were preparing to do, the initial guesswork was often modified or abandoned. The large quantity of conflicting and uncertain doctrine contrasted sharply with the small quantity of practical experience. When the experience was widened in exercises and maneuvers to test out particular doctrines it was discovered that there had been too little preparation and too much theory. The practical capabilities of aircraft had been prone to much exaggeration.[1]

Overy registers important points about the lack of experience with modern airpower, but it would be a mistake to dwell too heavily on the novelty of the challenge. After all, with few exceptions the air commanders of World War II had extensive firsthand experience of air warfare in World War I. Although the critical technical enablers of airpower matured enormously between 1918 and 1939, they of course matured for all belligerents. Notwithstanding national differences in airpower preferences, the great powers shared a reasonably common technological menu.[2] The tactical story associated with that menu, with its operational and strategic implications, would be distinctly familiar to those who had been bloodied in the earlier conflict. As for what plainly can be characterized in hindsight as a triumph of theory and doctrine over experience, because there was no relevant experience in the 1920s and 1930s apart from that in Spain, it is a little too easy to be critical. The four and a quarter years of warfare from 1914 to 1918, though both extensive and intensive, could hardly serve as a satisfactory empirical base from which to derive a general theory of airpower. In retrospect we are able to identify with some confidence enduring tactical and strategic truths about airpower as revealed in 1914–18, but in the 1920s and 1930s one could not, at least should not, be so certain that transient realities could be distinguished from enduring ones. Moreover, the technical changes of the interwar years and their apparent tactical implications did not point with complete assurance to best practices for airpower in a future war, as Overy rightly claims. A major addition to the challenge to predict well enough the character of future air warfare lurked in the vital unanswerable questions of political and strategic context: Who would be fighting whom, about what, where, and for how long? The second of these four fundamental questions was answered with some confidence by those few willing to grant the prospects of future war a high probability. They anticipated some approximation to another "total war."[3] John Buckley may well be somewhat correct when he argues that "in many ways air war was the epitome of total war, an icon of a specific age in warfare and human civilization." While allowing necessarily for uniqueness in detail, it was expected that another great war in and for mastery over Europe would proceed slowly and by attrition, much like World War I. Because strategic thought is not created in a social-cultural and intellectual vacuum, it is scarcely surprising that the doom-laden notion of total war was popular in a 1930s decade that registered strong pessimism over the future of Western liberal values. In those years it was popular, fashionable even, to be pessimistic about the survival prospects for the civilization that then was on the back foot economically, politically, and seemingly strategically as well.[4]

The strategic and military contexts for the forced growth of airpower from 1914 to 1918 were aided by a stable continental battlefront. Notwithstanding minor forays in longer-range bombing, the dominant airpower narrative of that war was the continental one of aerial support for armies in close contact with each other.[5] Of course, the technical basis for airpower in World War I mandated missions of relatively short range, but still it is useful to remember that the long-range bombing mission truly was strategically discretionary. Given the very limited military capability even of the aircraft designed to be heavy bombers in 1917 and especially 1918, there was no strategic justification in those years for a substantial diversion of scarce air assets away from the mission of fairly direct support for the army. No one could know in advance, really know, that is, how much land warfare there would be in the next great struggle and of how long a duration it would be.

With hindsight one can explain how the course of World War II in Europe and the Pacific both helped shape and was partially shaped by the terms of engagement for and the actual conduct of air warfare. To amend the ever-prescient Clausewitz, it is essential to understand the character (he wrote "nature") of the war.[6] However, for a potent caveat, contingency rules. There was excellent reason for the Prussian soldier-theorist to privilege the role of chance, uncertainty, and risk in his general theory of war.[7]

So pervasive was the influence of airpower on the hugely complex historical experience that has been almost bowdlerized by the grotesquely terse and compounded title "World War II" that no attempt can be made here to tell the airpower story of the years 1939–45 in the form of narrative history. Instead, this discussion must be content to offer analytical sketches of principal features of the airpower contribution to the course and outcome of the global struggle. Lest the point still should be obscure, the massive and diverse experience of airpower at war from 1939 to 1945 was indeed a most authoritative audit; however, it was truly authoritative only for the historical time and strategic moment of the early 1940s.

Air War within the War

Some authors prefer to assemble and construct, while others privilege disassembly, deconstruction, and dissection. This one favors the former approach, which is why a major theme running through the text is the essential unity of war, warfare, strategy, airpower, and air warfare. A maritime historian has asserted fairly persuasively that "all the seas of the world are one,"[8] but his insight applies more exactly to the air. The father of the RAF, Hugh Trenchard, said on 12 April 1934, "I believe the air is one."[9] This geophysical fact is as obvious a global reality as it is profound in its implications. To so comprehend the structure and dynamics of strategic history that a single unitary narrative of understanding is attainable, it is essential to grasp the fact that airpower truly is a gestalt. This does not mean that a single airplane type, for example, Giulio Douhet's concept of a "battle plane," must express this unity.[10] But it does mean that a combined-arms approach is at least as authoritative a rule for best practice in air warfare as it is for warfare on land. As early as 1915, it became self-evident that pursuit (fighter) aircraft and bombers needed to be specialized for their tactical roles. The distinction made by Billy Mitchell in 1917 between "tactical" and "strategical" aviation was a conceptual confusion that was to have damaging consequences for the better part of a hundred years.[11] However, the material military necessity for a distinction was unarguable.

Two interfaces lie at the center of our concerns: one between air warfare and the warfare on land and at sea, the other among different forms of air warfare. This chapter addresses both of these interfaces by means of the primary question of the strategist, "So what?" The answers to the "So what?" question vary from war to war, indeed from theater of war to theater of war, as well as over time. However, when one discerns that the answers in most historical cases, though necessarily differing in detail, nonetheless have roughly the same strategic meaning, then one is in evidential country appropriate for theory building. It must be granted that the combatants in the two world wars strove heroically to provide a convincingly adequate foundation in experience as candidate evidence for the construction of airpower theory.

Trenchard's assertion as to the global unity of the air alerts us to the necessity for joined-up analysis. In 1944, for example, Nazi Germany waged warfare intensively on four geostrategically distinguishable fronts: the eastern, against the Soviet Union; the western continental (from 6 June 1944), against the Western allies; the Italian, also against the Western allies; and the home, in air defense against Anglo-American long-range bombing. The maritime front was conceded in May 1943 with the withdrawal of the U-boats from the Atlantic. This modestly oversimplified quadripartite division posed an acute challenge to a Germany that could make only a single war effort and whose allies were a net liability rather than a source of support. Every belligerent faced the same eternal conundrum of the defense planner: how best to distribute scarce finite resources among competing military and other demands. But from 1942 onward, Germany proved uniquely unable to match its strategic supply to its strategic demands.[12] Among the major belligerents, only the Soviet Union was committed to a single-front war. But that strategic advantage must be considered in the context of the reason for it—the overwhelming, indeed existential and absolute, character of the menace that mandated such a single-track conduct of war.[13]

The United States was obliged to conduct two largely separate, indeed strategically disconnected, struggles half a world apart. It was ultimately triumphant not only because of the tactical fighting prowess of its armed forces, but also, as a prerequisite, because of an absolute human and material strength that enabled strategic dispersion, even profligacy. That said, the US military effort so abundant in the air and at sea in 1944 and 1945 emphatically had not been so in 1942 and 1943. The price of unpreparedness for major warfare was paid by American airmen, inter alia, ordered to attempt to accomplish too much with too little while their country armed energetically at last for a war that already was well under way. It is also worth noting that the US Army was always short of high-quality manpower in its combat arms.[14] American airpower was partially responsible for the shortage, though certainly it served as some substitute for the absent boots on the ground.

In addition to the two structural interfaces cited earlier—those between air and terrestrial warfare and among different forms of air warfare—it is necessary to appreciate how the air war narrative interwove with the other geostrategic dimensions of the war to create the grand narrative of the whole conflict. Accepting some risk of oversimplification, what follows in the remainder of the chapter is an effort to connect consequentially the air warfare story to the entire story arc of the conflict.[15]

Blitzkrieg and the Battle of Britain, 1939–40

In the mid-to-late 1930s, the British RAF's theory and doctrine of deterrence by the menace of strategic bombing did not frighten the Germans, but it did frighten the British themselves.[16] This strategic "own goal" had a potent influence on the British public mood and on British policy, in 1938 in particular on the repeated occasions of the German-engineered Czech crisis of that year, nominally over the Sudetenland. "The shadow of the bomber" was contextually significant, though ultimately not decisive, of course, for British attitudes toward both the rules of war and the casus belli.[17] As 1939 unfolded, the British government was driven by events to define Nazi Germany as an enemy of the existing European order that could not be appeased on reasonable terms. Scarcely less important was the military appreciation in London late in 1938 and then in 1939 that progress in all aspects of the still maturing air defense system meant that the former axiomatic assumption that "the bomber will always get through," was no longer sound.[18] Britain and France were neither deterred by Germany nor self-deterred by fear of countercivilian terror bombing from declaring war on Germany on 3 September 1939.

The so-called blitzkrieg campaigns of 1939 and 1940, including that against Norway, were seriously joint events on the German part, but the Luftwaffe's contribution was not of such a decisive character that it was the leading, and therefore the supported, military instrument.[19] The Wehrmacht discovered from rigorous self-examination of its performance in Poland that it had a great deal yet to learn and apply by way of effective joint operations.[20] The Luftwaffe's performance against Poland and then France (and the BEF) was flattered both by the weakness of opposition in the air and by the modest level of support that the army required. German airpower did well enough over Poland and France. It gained a sufficiency of air superiority to enable its obsolescent dive-bombers and medium bomber forces to prosecute useful operational air warfare—which is to say principally interdiction—as well as some distinctly limited close air support.[21] However, contrary to Reichsmarschal Hermann Göring's promise, the Luftwaffe was not able to enforce an air blockade of the BEF and the French forces that had retreated into a perimeter around Dunkirk. The BEF escaped, albeit without its heavy equipment, despite the efforts of a Luftwaffe operating under serious logistical handicaps. The Advanced Air Striking Force of the RAF that deployed to France with the BEF suffered badly and was caught up in the general defeat that it could not avert, but flying from home airfields under the command of Fighter Command 11 Group to cover the Dunkirk evacuation, it performed well enough by any reasonable standard. In the air warfare associated with the nine days of the evacuation from Dunkirk, the balance of aircraft losses was 177 for the RAF to 240 for the Luftwaffe.[22] Despite the excellent histories available, to this day British popular mythology does not recognize the logistical realities that placed the RAF at a modest combat advantage over the Luftwaffe at Dunkirk.[23]

Blitzkrieg, or "lightning war," was a myth. It was a conceptual invention by journalists that was seized upon and deployed by politicians—not in Germany, one must add—eager to explain why the Wehrmacht had succeeded so swiftly in its campaigns in 1939–41 (until the mud arrived in Russia in the fall). Credulous or ill-informed commentators at the time, and many historians since, were persuaded that the Third Reich had discovered a new way in joint and combined-arms warfare. The truth was more prosaic. From the conquest of Poland in September 1939 until the invasion of the Soviet Union ran out of steam several times on the road to Moscow in the fall of 1941, the German armed forces succeeded for two broad reasons. First, their enemies were grossly incompetent. Second, they applied an updated variant of the modern way in warfare that they had quarried from the experience of 1916–18.[24] At least they waged that modern way to the degree that the highly dysfunctional military and political command structures of the Nazi regime would permit. The German strategic achievements of 1939–41 glittered indeed, but most definitely all that glittered was not gold. The essential hopelessness of Polish military resistance—maldeployed as the Polish army was even to thwart invasion from the west and north, let alone to counter the stab in the back from Stalin in the east—flattered German performance. The Wehrmacht had done well enough. Similarly, the apparent magic of the defeat of France and the BEF concealed German weaknesses, even from many Germans who should have known better. Germany won in the continental west in May–June 1940 primarily because its armed forces were much better trained and led than their French and British enemies.[25] Also, and as important if not more so, they confounded and defeated the Franco-British campaign plan operationally. The Germans waged modern (joint and combined-arms) warfare better than their enemies, but that was not an entirely solid achievement, as the unraveling of *der führer's* great Russian adventure was to demonstrate unmistakably in the winter of 1941–42.

Blitzkrieg was not so much a new way in warfare characterized by close tactical cooperation between armored and mechanized ground forces and supporting airpower, as rather the much improved execution of the methods already identified as best practice in 1918. But superior military technique cannot always substitute sufficiently for disadvantageous material realities—which was the strategic story overall of 1918, as it was to be in the pivotal years of 1942–43 in the return engagement. The core of the airpower narrative of 1918 was the same as in the campaign against France and the BEF in 1940. Specifically, airpower was able to serve as a potent force multiplier for air-land, or perhaps land-air, warfare only if it secured a plausible approximation to command of the air. At a minimum it was necessary to secure local air superiority for control, if not imperial air supremacy, over the most relevant terrain and sea space. With one exception, the Luftwaffe achieved air superiority over the battlefield in France and Belgium in May–June 1940 and as a consequence "was all that it could be" as an enabler of victory. The sole exception in the six-week period of the continental campaign of that year was the modest level of embarrassment that RAF Fighter Command managed to enforce in protecting the evacuation from Dunkirk. The Luftwaffe was not defeated in the air battle, but neither did it sweep the sky preclusively clear of the Spitfires (which it met for the first time in combat) and Hurricanes that Fighter Command released sparingly from home defense to help jointly (with the Royal Navy) to save the country's field army. The RAF that had been deployed forward with the BEF in France (the Advanced Air Striking Force, of optimistic title) was caught up in the general continental disaster. As the Luftwaffe was to learn to its cost, it was one thing to win air superiority against an enemy who lacked a modern air defense system; whose pilots were inexperienced and consequently employed fatally unsound, though properly official, air fighting tactics; and whose aircraft were not quite fully competitive with the frontline of the Luftwaffe in the context of a successful enemy ground offensive. But it would be another thing entirely to fight an air campaign against a truly modern, indeed more modern than Germany, enemy who need only engage in combat on terms it judged to be to its own advantage. Undoubtedly the Luftwaffe was good, very good. But by the end of June 1940, it had been tested only against Poles, who suffered from terminal strategic military operational disadvantages; against a maldeployed, mishandled, and not quite modern enough French Air Force; and against performance away from home by the RAF. From July to October 1940 the Luftwaffe was to learn to its cost the strategic meaning of home-field advantage.

Because war is a realm of chance wherein uncertainty encompasses some risks that cannot be calculated and contingency may rule, it would be incorrect to argue that German defeat in the Battle of Britain was a foregone conclusion. However, with hindsight, and even at the time because of much—unusual, for once—British foresight, the deck was stacked heavily against the Luftwaffe. Needless to add, this can be claimed with more confidence today than was possible, let alone prudent, at the time in Britain. It must also be noted that although the RAF had reason to be confident in the summer of 1940, the degree of their good fortune could not be known to them. Two basic points are significant. First, notwithstanding the intensive and extensive air warfare conducted in World War I and the notable air fighting in Spain (1936–39), Poland (1939), and France (May–June 1940), there was no historical precedent for the Battle of Britain. To that date, no countries ever had engaged in an air battle or campaign conceived as an operation completely independent of combat on the ground or at sea. Of course the Luftwaffe's mission was to prepare the way for a successful invasion, but the putative invasion was contingent upon the achievement of prior victory in and from the air. Second, the full force of the Luftwaffe playing offense had yet to meet the full force of the RAF playing defense at home. The general theory of strategy applied as always, but how it would translate into behavior and outcome was a matter for some human choices and was ripe for speculation and well-merited anxiety. The Germans were confident, indeed overconfident, because of their success in the air over France, though, as noted already, they were marginally troubled by the technical excellence of the relatively few Spitfires they encountered over Dunkirk. Most especially, Luftwaffe pilots were more than a little dismissive of RAF tactics, and with solid reason. The RAF's doctrine for aerial combat in the Battle of Britain, especially its insistence upon tight formation flying in triangular "vics," was not one of its relative strengths. Fortunately, the RAF's tactical deficiencies proved not to be fatal at the level of operational, let alone strategic, effect.

Despite the somewhat mythical aura that still surrounds the much popular and even more expert British reflection on the battle, careful scholarship reveals unmistakably that the Luftwaffe was not likely to win.[26] The fundamental reasons were that the RAF chose the strategy that was correct for its total strategic context and feasible with the material and human means available to it and executed it consistently and competently at all necessary levels of performance. Rephrased, the commander in chief of RAF Fighter Command since its creation in July 1936, Air Chief Marshal Sir Hugh Dowding, had settled upon the right aim for his military assets, those assets were managed well enough to achieve his aims, and the people in the loop everywhere were able to do their jobs satisfactorily. No part of this chain of strategic logic could be said of the Luftwaffe as a whole, though certainly little if any blame attaches to its pilots and aircrew, who typically were deficient neither in skill nor courage.

Stephen Bungay is probably correct when he claims that "the core problem for Kesselring and Sperrle [commanders of *Luftflotte* 2 in Brussels and *Luftflotte* 3 in Paris, respectively] was that they literally did not know what they were doing."[27] They understood that RAF Fighter Command employed the newly constructed radar stations for ground direction of the fighter force but had no comprehension of the systemic functioning of their enemy. The Chain Home (and Chain Home Low) radar stations were not employed, as the Luftwaffe believed, to direct squadrons in ones and twos. Rather radar data was filtered centrally at Fighter Command headquarters and passed down to enable its principal battlespace commander, the admirable Keith Park, commander of 11 Group in the southeast, to decide how to fight the battle in real time.[28] Park at Group HQ made the key tactical decisions on when, how, and with which squadrons to fight and exercised his command over seven sector stations, each of which had the responsibility of managing the actual interceptions. To do strategically decisive damage to Fighter Command, the Luftwaffe needed to understand how its enemy used its radar data and how that data, once filtered and interpreted, was transmitted. The Germans needed to appreciate how data and decisions moved from coastal radar stations to Dowding at Fighter Command HQ and then to Park at 11 Group HQ, and then how the fighter force was commanded and controlled by sector stations to squadrons at many airfields (including secondary dispersal ones). Plainly, Dowding's system was least resilient in its complete dependence upon the radar installations. These were not easy to destroy or damage, but the Germans did not persist very long in the attempt. Inland, British air defense was notably robust. The operations rooms at the seven sector stations comprised seven vital targets, but they were small and the Luftwaffe failed to recognize their key role.

One is tempted to argue, as more or less does John Ferris, that RAF Fighter Command's air defense system truly won the protracted battle that occurred from July to September 1940 long before the fighting started. That is a persuasive claim except for the vital caveat that even a sound system enabling execution of a good-enough strategy still has to be done "in the field" and "on the day" by commanders and warriors. History advises that war is very much the realm of chance. Nonetheless, it must be granted that German ignorance of the structure and working of Fighter Command met its due reward in operational and strategic failure.

RAF Fighter Command knew what it was about in the summer of 1940, while the Luftwaffe did not. The latter suffered fatally from an intelligence and hence a strategy deficit for which its relative strengths—especially in general experience and air fighting tactics in particular—could not provide sufficient compensation.[29] Considering the whole trinity of ends, ways, and means, the Luftwaffe faced a daunting strategic task. First, as to "ends," its goal of eliminating Fighter Command as a potentially deadly factor to an invasion was sound in principle, at least as one necessary step. The trouble was that even if it had succeeded, the answer to the "So what?" strategist's question may not have been sufficiently encouraging. It was still quite possible that the Royal Navy, with some assistance from a defeated Fighter Command and a Bomber Command that was still functional, if unimpressive, would be able to destroy or at least terminally disrupt a German invasion armada comprised in the main of troop delivery by scarcely seaworthy barges.[30] As for the other two items in the strategic trinity, the Luftwaffe lacked an appropriate operational strategy in the ways and was notably short of the military means plausibly necessary to win the battle.

The truth is that the Luftwaffe was short of everything except courageous airmen, good equipment for some contexts of air warfare, and effective tactics. But high human, technical, and tactical quality could not compensate for operational and strategic folly; to do so would have required quite extraordinary luck. The Luftwaffe sought to defeat RAF Fighter Command by (1) endeavoring to flush it into the air in large numbers where it could be shot down; (2) attacking it on the ground on its airfields; (3) destroying or disrupting the radar stations vital to its effectiveness; and (4) destroying or damaging and disrupting the factories that produced British fighters. The Luftwaffe achieved some success in air combat, but the odds were loaded quite heavily against it. While the Luftwaffe had just two months to prepare to defeat RAF Fighter Command in an operational context which was unanticipated, the latter had prepared most carefully for nearly five years to conduct an approximation of the battle that came its way in August–September 1940 (with the admittedly unexpected major disadvantage of German airpower based on the coast of France and Belgium). Fighter Command also modernized an air defense system that had been fundamentally sound from its inception in 1917. Not least among the Luftwaffe's constraints was its strategic need to retain the ability to defend an invasion armada and the subsequent beachhead against assault by an as yet undefeated RAF Bomber Command. If it was a truly Pyrrhic victory against Fighter Command, it probably could not adequately protect the amphibious and airborne assault. Albert Kesselring and Hugo Sperrle, commanders of the Luftwaffe's most relevant air fleets, *Luftflotten* 2 and 3, did not know how to defeat Fighter Command. They rested their hopes on the strategic value of anticipated tactical success. In truth they could not paralyze, let alone destroy, Fighter Command, save largely by accident, because they did not know how to attack it beyond shooting down Hurricanes and Spitfires. The British aircraft industry was outproducing Germany's, and Fighter Command had an adequate supply of replacement pilots (as well as aircraft). Also because the balance of relevant forces (single-seater fighters) was only on the order of 1.5:1 in Germany's favor, an attritional battle over England was never likely to end in a German victory.[31]

The Luftwaffe expected to defeat Fighter Command in four days in early August 1940. But because it did not know how to cripple its enemy at the operational level, and because Fighter Command almost always could pace itself in the scale and character of its commitment to battle and hence control its loss rate, there was no plausible way it could be eliminated as a serious concern for German invasion planners. RAF Fighter Command was large enough and fought well enough tactically with adequate or better machines to be decisive strategically and operationally. The RAF won the battle by not losing it. Its strategic task in the summer and fall of 1940 was to remain combat competitive in the skies over southeast England. It did not really matter how many German planes it shot down or even how many it lost itself. What was necessary was for the Germans, from an early euphoria born out of false confidence and appalling intelligence gaps, to be sufficiently discouraged by their unmistakable inability to drive Fighter Command out of the relevant skies. So long as Fighter Command could replace its combat losses in pilots and aircraft, the Luftwaffe could not succeed.

By the beginning of September the German failure was seriously affecting the morale of its pilots and aircrew. The Germans calculated RAF losses in the context of their erroneous beliefs about the size of the enemy's first-line fighter force and ability to replace lost pilots and planes. Unreasonably, they concluded that RAF Fighter Command had to be on its last legs. Apparent weakening in the RAF opposition toward the end of August reinforced this tentative conclusion. The

English Channel is rarely millpond-smooth; its sea state was near certain to be a definitive invasion stopper in October, regardless of predictable opposition by a fanatically determined RAF and Royal Navy. With the pressure of diminishing available time if an invasion were to be at all feasible in September—the 20th being the last date with favorable tides—which meant in 1940 altogether, the Luftwaffe changed its strategy radically for a huge assault against London on 7 September. Many influential German voices had come to believe by the first week of September that with the RAF manifestly failing—or so the assumed numbers of British losses-to-replacements showed—and the weather-dominated window of opportunity nearing closure, it was past time for the Luftwaffe to deliver the mortal blow. Not wholly without good reason, the Germans believed that the surviving rump of Dowding's fighter force would be obliged to engage in combat to near extinction in protecting the Empire's capital.

The battle changed in character somewhat as the revised German strategy was first executed in a truly enormous and unprecedented daylight attack on targets in London, especially the docks of the East End. This was not an indiscriminate effort to terrorize civilians; the principal German economic targets in London were in densely populated urban areas. Fighter Command was caught by surprise, since the enemy had trained it to anticipate assaults on its airfields, occasional raids on radar stations, and episodic attacks on aircraft manufacturing plants. Instead, on this afternoon Fighter Command abruptly found itself drawn into battle with no fewer than 965 enemy aircraft bound for London (348 bombers and 617 fighters).[32] From 7 September until the 15th—the latter came to be celebrated in Britain as "Battle of Britain Day"—London was the primary, though certainly not sole, target and focus for the air war that still was being conducted mainly in daylight. In darkness the Luftwaffe could not even aspire to bomb accurately. By 15 September the German invasion already had been postponed indefinitely, pending the forcible removal of the putative Soviet sword from Britain's hand. In that happy event, predicted with confidence by the führer as well as his military commanders, it was expected that Britain would judge itself to be strategically so disadvantaged that it would be ready to make the peace of all but submission that it stubbornly would not make in the summer of 1940. Meanwhile, a nighttime bombing campaign would weaken the British ability and will to fight as well as preserve the Luftwaffe from the decline through an unsustainable attrition that it was suffering in daytime air warfare.

The truth of the balance of air strength, whatever the claims of "kills," was revealed to an ever more shocked, even somewhat traumatized, Luftwaffe in the first half of September. German pilots and aircrew were facing not a diminishing band of desperate British (and foreign volunteer) air warriors who were short of equipment, but rather an enemy who, if anything, appeared in greater numbers to oppose them.[33] The negative impact on the morale of the German airmen was all the more severe because it so rapidly succeeded the extravagant confidence in imminent victory that had been believed sincerely by most until the end of August. The RAF's resistance to the Luftwaffe daylight assault on London on 15 September was so robust that the Germans were obliged to recognize that although they had fought the tactical fight well, they had failed operationally and strategically. RAF Fighter Command had won by not losing.

In land warfare, tactically excellent forces can be so well handled operationally that an enemy army is effectively annihilated or at least rendered operationally and probably strategically impotent. In air warfare, by contrast, provided one is not destroyed en masse by surprise attacks and one's command and control system and the real-time information vital to it are not destroyed or seriously disrupted, no operational maneuver can deliver victory. Inherently, aircraft are highly agile in their mobility, and air warfare is cumulatively attritional; gains and losses are recorded machine by machine, airman by airman. Air warfare is identical to land and sea warfare in its subordination to the general theory of strategy, but it is unique in the character that the laws of physics impose upon it.

Although the physics of aerodynamics require aircraft to be relatively fragile machines tactically, it is in the ever-changing nature as well as the changing character of air forces to be distinctively robust when they are viewed operationally. When military value is distributed extensively over hundreds or even thousands of platforms that are inherently highly agile and mobile, annihilating defeat is unlikely unless one belligerent is all but criminally incompetent or is hopelessly outclassed technically. The historical record demonstrates clearly that neither side in the Battle of Britain was hopelessly overborne technically and that German tactical competence ensured that it would hold its own, by and large, with respect to the air fighting, though its operational-level errors fatally devalued its tactical achievements. Denied rapid operational-level success, the Luftwaffe was obliged, unexpectedly, to commit to an open-ended attritional contest for which it lacked the depth of assets as well as the time to reach a victorious closure. Mention has been made already of the German air losses over Dunkirk in May–June 1940. It is necessary to recognize that a Luftwaffe unready for a long, hard war against first-class enemies who would be granted the time to mobilize their potential air strength was compelled to accept perilously weakening losses in 1939 and 1940, long before it would be tested to the uttermost and beyond in 1943–45.

In the brief Polish campaign of 1939, the Luftwaffe suffered a total of 285 aircraft lost and 279 damaged. In the generally outstanding, well-conducted joint campaign against Norway in April–May 1940, it lost 260 aircraft (to the British 169). The conquest of France in May–June 1940 cost the Luftwaffe 1,428 destroyed plus 488 damaged. An important quantitative thread to the narrative that Bungay rightly notes is the fact that between the outbreak of the war on 1 September 1939 and the opening of the main event against France and the BEF on 10 May 1940, the Luftwaffe had lost no fewer than 1,460 aircraft, with another 1,074 damaged. These bare statistics mean that the Luftwaffe "had to replace and substantially repair 88 percent of the machines operational at the outbreak of the war before the 'real' war even began." Furthermore, "over 40 percent of these losses were suffered in training."[34] The Luftwaffe more than made good these losses (plus 20 percent), but it did not build a large safety margin of reserves in trained airmen or machines. The measure of the Luftwaffe's operational and strategic failure in the Battle of Britain is reflected revealingly when the order of battle of RAF Fighter Command is compared between 1 July 1940, before the struggle commenced; 1 September, by which time the contest had been well and truly joined; and later in the year. On 6 July, Fighter Command had 640 fighters (nearly all first-line Hurricanes and Spitfires) and 1,259 pilots; on 1 September it could deploy 648 serviceable fighter aircraft and 1,142 pilots, while by 2 November the number of operationally available pilots stood at 1,796. On 13 August 1940, the overheralded "*Adler Tag*" ("Eagle Day") of the big push, the Luftwaffe's *Luftflotten* 2 and 3 could commit 871 single-seat fighters (Bf 109s) and 231 two-seat Bf 110s.[35] Since the Bf 110s scarcely counted in the air battle, except as victims, it is plain to see that the undoubted, if modest, attritional damage done to RAF Fighter Command was thoroughly offset and more by the depth of its ability to replace machines and pilots. Because the Luftwaffe did not try hard enough strategically to find an operational-level way to defeat Fighter Command, it had no choice but to attempt to win by attrition. Alas for German hopes, it could not win an air war of attrition against a Britain that was outproducing it in aircraft and airmen. From August to December 1940 the Luftwaffe suffered a drop in fighter strength of 30 percent and 25 percent in bomber strength.[36] Aircraft losses could be made good, but the attrition of experienced aircrew was a wasting disease for an air force that was nowhere near as large as it needed to be for the strategic demands made of it.

The Battle of Britain—so labeled rather early on in dramatic but prudent anticipation by Prime Minister Churchill on 18 June 1940 and waged from July through September, though (British) officially from 8 August to 31 October—was a decisive battle in several respects. The RAF victory decided that a German invasion in 1940 would be impracticable, leaving aside the question of its practicability in the face of the Royal Navy. Also, the victory kept Britain in the war because it enabled Churchill to survive politically at home, and British belligerency literally was essential if the United States was ever to be able to apply its mighty strength, once mobilized, against Germany—should Washington ever decide or be obliged to fight.[37] It is difficult to exaggerate the importance of the German defeat in the air in the summer and fall of 1940.

Airpower, Joint Warfare in the West, 1941–45

Airpower played a vital, joint role in warfare in the Mediterranean theater from 1941 to 1943 and subsequently in northwest Europe in 1944–45. In North Africa its joint significance was flattered by the relatively featureless geography of the region and by the frequent tenuousness, or worse, of warfare logistics for both sides (especially the German). By 1943, with the German defeat and surrender in Tunisia, the air balance had shifted decisively in the Allied favor, but for most of the period air control was in contention. The strenuous and persistent German (and Italian) efforts to subdue the British "fortress" island of Malta by aerial bombardment failed, though Axis airpower in combination with a theoretically potent Italian naval menace did succeed in compelling British logistical support for the war in North Africa to take the lengthy Cape route or fly across west and central

Africa rather than through the Mediterranean from Gibraltar, via Malta, to Alexandria.[38]

In a dramatic demonstration of the versatility of airpower, the Luftwaffe successfully invaded Crete by means of airborne forces. However, this proved so costly in casualties to elite troops that airborne operations on a large scale were never attempted again by the Wehrmacht. The Allies were less daunted by the Luftwaffe's paratroop and Ju 52 transport plane losses than the Germans, and, if anything, were encouraged to pursue the airborne option. Airpower in the Mediterranean was not the leading edge of the joint force story for victory and defeat—largely because it usually was a bilateral and heavily contested tale—but its operational effectiveness in sea and desert warfare was of high importance.

In the desert war—though, sad to relate for the Allies, not in the Italian campaign that followed—air support for the army was essential.[39] This took the necessary defensive form of protecting friendly troops and their fragile lines of communication against a predatory Luftwaffe as well as the offensive form of providing both airborne fire support for troops in contact and interdiction of enemy logistics. As always, the rival air forces were reacquainted by reality with the necessity to fight for air control as a prerequisite for air support. If one could not fly at will and enforce denial of that same privilege to the enemy, one could not support one's army as effectively as it might require. Aerial combat in North Africa was not waged for its own sake by the RAF and the Luftwaffe, but rather to buy the right to support their armies.

If the desert terrain of North Africa somewhat flattered the value of air support in joint warfare, the subsequent campaign in Italy demonstrated that highly complex terrain meant the opposite. Although Allied air superiority was useful in Sicily and mainland Italy, it proved entirely unable to provide a golden key that would enable the multinational ground forces to achieve a swift theater victory.

The Italian campaign may or may not have been of net strategic benefit to the Allied cause, though I am skeptical at the very least. Assuredly it was ill advised from the point of view of deriving high leverage from one's relative strengths while evading punishment for one's relative weaknesses. The Allied campaign design could hardly have been better chosen were its purpose the multiplication of the enemy's force. By electing to crawl up a narrow mountainous peninsula, the Allies invited the Germans to demonstrate their mastery in the skilled and tenacious defense of difficult terrain in often appalling weather. It is true that the Grand Alliance could better afford the Italian campaign than could Germany. Nonetheless, on balance it is plausible to argue that the always-stretched combat ground power of the Western allies would have been of greater strategic value had it been concentrated much more rigorously upon the vital cross-channel mission.

The North African and Italian campaigns provided the painful experience apparently required for truly joint warfare to be realized in practice under fire. In the Mediterranean the Allies learned from their mistakes—much as the Germans had in Poland in 1939—how airpower can and should be employed to support land power. Notwithstanding resistance by some recalcitrant, reluctant, and even unwilling elements in the Allied air forces, the D-day operation and the great campaign from Normandy to the Elbe that succeeded it were a triumph of intelligent air-ground cooperation. All aspects of air warfare contributed to the success of General Eisenhower's armies. The Luftwaffe that could have rendered impracticable the landings and subsequent exploitation out of a beachhead had already been defeated in the skies over the Reich itself. What remained of the Luftwaffe's fighter assets was committed near exclusively to the continuing, losing battle to defend Germany from air assault.[40]

In the summer of 1944 Allied airpower of all kinds ensured the Luftwaffe was scarcely in evidence over Normandy, even as an agent of only moderate harassment (on 6 June 1944, the Luftwaffe could oppose the invasion with only 466 serviceable aircraft able to operate just 189 sorties, as compared with the 12,837 aircraft available to Eisenhower);[41] provided fire support from altitude both in preparation for the initial landings and subsequently by way of close air support in real time on demand; nearly isolated the battlefield with interdiction bombing; and delivered airborne forces to protect the flanks of the five invasion beaches from being rolled up.[42] In addition, of course, the air assault on Germany at home, though somewhat enervated by the diversion of Allied air assets to direct and indirect support of the campaign in France, was weakening Germany cumulatively, both by virtual attrition and by the infliction of damage. Although it would be far from true to claim that Allied airpower won the war in the west in 1944–45, it is persuasive to argue that it contributed in so many ways to overall strategic effect that it did guarantee eventual victory on the ground.

By interdicting the lengthy German lines of communication to the fighting in Normandy, Allied airpower all but negated the strategic value of the enemy's superior operational-level and tactical skills. To illustrate, two weeks after D-day the German army in Normandy had received only five of the 17 divisions committed as counterattack formations and reinforcement.[43] With some assistance from sabotage by the French Resistance and Allied special forces teams, Allied airpower came close to shutting down German exploitation of the French railway network. Experience showed that although close air support of troops in contact with the enemy could be of tactical value, not least for morale, it had notable limitations even though the Luftwaffe was not often a constraining factor. Allied airpower discovered that tanks were neither easy to hit nor easy to kill with the technologies of 1944 vintage air-to-ground warfare. To be suspiciously precise, it has been calculated that it took 3,500 bombs or 800 rockets to kill a tank.[44] Needless to say, perhaps, thin-skinned vehicles were thoroughly at the mercy of the Allies' marauding fighter-bombers. Less happily, and to strike a familiar note about the realities of joint warfare, "friendly fire" was an inevitable persisting problem in the northwest Europe campaign, as indeed it was elsewhere. It was not only the enemy's air force that comprised a peril in the sky to troops on the ground.

As the survivors of the German defense in Normandy retreated, regrouped, somewhat recovered, and eventually staged a large-scale counterattack, ever closer to the frontiers of the Reich itself, the German army in the field was less vulnerable to logistical starvation by blockade from the air. In part this was because the terrain was complex and highly defensible, unlike that in much of France beyond the close country of the *bocage* in Normandy. However, by the winter of 1944–45 the cumulative attrition suffered by Germany on all fronts was so great that its home-field logistical advantage of fighting on its own frontiers was far more than offset by its absolute weakness. Whatever advantages Germany retained by early 1945 could not be exploited for strategic gain. Ironically, the more tactically effective the German war effort in 1944–45, the more damaging must the consequences be for itself.

For the Allies, the airpower devoted to support its land campaigns undoubtedly compensated more than adequately for the weakness in its ground-fighting power relative to an already heavily diminished German army. This is not to demean the effort and skills of Allied soldiers, but it is to say that to hold their own and more against the

German army, they needed all of the assistance, all of the enabling leverage, that their joint superior airpower could provide.[45]

The Eastern Front, 1941–45

The warfare on the eastern front between Germany and its allies and the Soviet Union was waged on so vast a territorial canvas and engaged such large numbers of soldiers and machines that airpower could play, at most, only an important but not decisive role. For the invasion of the Soviet Union on 22 June 1941, the Luftwaffe deployed 2,775 aircraft, 65 percent of its strength, and was opposed by some 10,000 Soviet aircraft (though German intelligence wrongly believed the number to be approximately 5,000).[46] The Luftwaffe destroyed 1,200 Soviet aircraft in the opening 8.5 hours of the Barbarossa campaign; 1,800 by the close of the first day; approximately 4,000 by the end of a week; and 7,500 by September. Truly the Luftwaffe had imposed a catastrophic defeat on Soviet aviation. However, the nagging strategist's question "So what?" intrudes forcefully. The Soviet air force was all but eliminated for a while as an operationally significant factor, though the large number of aircraft destroyed on their airfields meant that the loss of pilots and aircrew was far lower than the machine loss figures might seem to indicate. Nonetheless, friendly aircraft were not there to support the Soviet army in its most desperate straits. However, the unquestionably superior Luftwaffe of 1941 on the eastern front was not so potent that its control of the Russian skies enabled it to offset the several ultimately fatal weaknesses in the German campaign and war effort.

The Luftwaffe lacked the physical means, intelligence, doctrine, and training to assault Soviet aircraft production.[47] It was harassed persistently by the same logistic weaknesses that assailed the army—German warfare was never strong on supply and reserves—and the fall and winter weather, mud and then cold, accelerated its decline. Combat attrition, accidents, unserviceability of aircraft, the sheer dimensions and scale of the operational air tasks in Russia, and the competing demands from other fronts meant that air superiority became fleeting, local, and insufficient to make a decisive difference to the course of the monumental scale of the fighting on the ground.

Heroic though its performance was in Russia, the Luftwaffe was a team player in joint warfare that from late 1941 through 1944 increasingly proved insufficient for its tasking. The war in the east was the most vital theater within the war for Germany, but alas for German soldiers it was not the whole of the struggle. As the Western allies slowly developed their nominally combined day and night bomber offensive against the Reich, more and more of Germany's fighter assets had to be returned from the east to protect the homeland on its overhead flank. By late 1943, the Luftwaffe deployed 70 percent of its fighter strength for the air defense of the Reich. In terms of joint warfare this meant that when the German army was in ever greater need of help from friendly airpower, that assistance was ever less available. The story of the Luftwaffe in the east, as elsewhere, is one of too little, too late, and too dispersed. No matter how formidable the Wehrmacht was tactically, and it was superior as a killing machine to all of its enemies, eventually it was lethally disadvantaged both quantitatively and in quality of operational and strategic direction. Its many battlefield victories decided nothing conclusively. Tactical success often led to eccentrically imprudent operational opportunism, and through an unavoidable attrition, to eventual complete defeat.[48] The Luftwaffe might have made the decisive difference had it been better employed; but the "what ifs," though interesting and possibly instructive, are as nothing compared with the facts of the real, not a virtual, strategic past. The strengths and weaknesses of a society and its political system are reflected all too well in the character and performance of its armed forces. The air warfare story of the eastern front was subsumed within the grander narrative of land warfare with air support. On the Soviet side, that support grew back from its hecatomb of summer 1941 to be an important factor in the overall military endeavor, while for the Germans, the Luftwaffe was a distinctly episodic and eventually an absent source of support for the army.

Germany did not lose its war in the east because it lost control of the air, but the latter operational and strategic fact meant that the Östheer essentially could not look to the Luftwaffe to compensate jointly for adverse numbers and diminishing combat power on the ground. Although the Soviet air forces (VVS, Voenno-Vozdushnye Sily) were privileged with impressive quantity, it would be a mistake to believe that the air war in the east typically was a contest between German quality and Soviet quantity. A large fraction of the VVS destroyed in the summer of 1941 comprised obsolescent or obsolete types of machines. By mid-1943, and certainly in 1944, the VVS flew fighter aircraft, especially the Yak-3 and La-7, that were technically competitive even with the later models of the Bf 109 and Fw 190, while the sturdy Il-2 Shturmovik ground attack aircraft was the finest machine for that exceedingly dangerous mission flown by any air force in the war (40,000 were built during the war, nearly one-third of the Soviet total).[49] Due to attrition by all causes (combat, technical malfunction, weather, pilot error) and diversion to other fronts, the Luftwaffe plainly lost air superiority in 1943. However, even in late 1942 it was unable to protect and effect the air bridge that the encircled Sixth Army needed if it were to be supplied even at a minimum level. Göring's ill-judged promise to sustain von Paulus at Stalingrad cost the Luftwaffe 490 irreplaceable transport planes.[50]

It is a general truth about warfare that belligerents' tactical and operational skills tend to equalize in the course of a protracted struggle, with the eventual outcome determined primarily by the decisive strategic effect achieved by superior mass, other factors being equal.[51] Quantity wins when quality is truly competitive, while even if quality is somewhat erratic or lacking, quantity can provide adequate compensation. Facing a German enemy that was sharply in decline in operational strength in the air, an ever-improving VVS was able to contribute more than just usefully to the success of the Soviet army on the ground.

Strategic Bombing in Europe, 1940–45

This section refers to long-range aerial bombardment not closely associated with ongoing terrestrial military operations as "strategic bombing." Such misuse of the adjective "strategic" unfortunately is necessary for no better reason than that generations of practitioners and scholars have created and licensed the error so thoroughly over the course of close to 100 years that an effort here to correct the mistake would do more harm than good in the context of this chapter.

It is necessary to be extremely careful in the derivation of purportedly general lessons from unique events and episodes, and those so derived should be presented with an intellectual health warning. The intensive and extensive experience of strategic bombardment in World War II, both in Europe and in Asia-Pacific, revealed nothing new about the natures of strategy and war. Nonetheless, the war did provide potent illustration of the authority of the dicta that theorists had been collecting specifically about airpower. Because the long-range bombing campaigns in World War II have attracted an exceptional level and persistence of controversy, it is important to flag yet again the vital significance of context. When scholars seek to identify the truth about strategic bombing from 1940 to 1945, they are apt to undervalue the authority of context in two temporal aspects. First, it is difficult to avoid projecting backwards upon the people and institutions—in this case of the early 1940s—the attitudes of today. Second, the foresight that comes as a consequence of hindsight is a notable hindrance to historical understanding. From a vantage point in the twenty-first century, one can identify, admittedly contestably, the structure and plausible dynamics of World War II and construct a fairly persuasive narrative that connects the land, sea, and air stories and the somewhat interdependent consequences of the belligerents' performances in different theaters of war into a single grand strategic story arc. With unavoidable hindsight, one passes strategic judgment upon people and organizations who lacked access to this structural explanation and understanding of the course of, to them, future strategic history. It is well to remember that World War II was unique, both in its structure and dynamics and in the character of its air warfare. Indeed there were precedents from World War I and from Spain, but they were only partial and of uncertain authority, given the pace and scale of airpower development. From Clausewitz we learn that war has a grammar of its own, to which insight we must add the codicil that every war has a dynamic peculiar to itself.[52] This dynamic can be regarded appropriately as a grammar specific to a single historical context. Without an extensive grip and grasp of historical context, it is not safe to deploy the evidence from one or another episode of air warfare in support or refutation of airpower theory.

Chapter 4 explained briefly why some air forces in the interwar period adopted a variant of strategic bombing theory as doctrine and why some did not.[53] By no means were all the true believers in airpower in the 1920s and 1930s true believers in victory by strategic bombing. Although the principal strategic bombing campaigns both in Europe and Asia were conducted by air forces that had long signed up for the theory-as-doctrine of victory by strategic bombardment, the fact that they were unleashed to practice their doctrine did not mean that their governments, or even their most senior military commanders, had high confidence in it. To quote Lord Kitchener again, "One makes war, not as one would like to, but as one must."[54] Strategy is an eminently pragmatic project. The role of strategic airpower in Allied war making expressed the choices available, especially the choices prudently not available, to Britain and the United States in the years 1940–44. The Allied commitment to strategic bombing was far more the product of highly constrained strategic circumstance than of profound belief in its efficacy as a war winner.

Many and bitter have been the critiques of British and American strategic bombing theory and practice, and it must be granted that some of what was done merits serious criticism.[55] Happily, at long last a plausible, dominant explanation has emerged from the historiography concerning what was attempted, why it was attempted, and what the consequences (by way of net strategic effect) were for the course of the war and the character of the peace that followed. However, before offering summative strategic judgment, it is necessary to identify the best of what long retrospective analysis of strategic bombing theory and doctrine has to offer. In my opinion, by far the most insightful and persuasive critique of the doctrine with which the USAAF went to war has been provided by Lt Col Peter R. Faber. His nine-point indictment of the theory that largely was created, developed, codified, and subsequently executed in wartime practice by the faculty and students of the Air Corps Tactical School provides an essential tool for the forensic analysis of the Allied strategic bombing campaigns of World War II. Faber charges the American "Bomber Mafia" of the 1930s and early 1940s with the following sins against sound strategy:

1. Unescorted HAPDB [high-altitude precision daylight bombing] assumed that one could scientifically manage war. Like almost all the other American theories of airpower that followed, the ACTS theory of unescorted HAPDB was part of a cause-and-effect universe where one's external means directly impacted another's internal behaviors. Unescorted HAPDB, therefore, was too mechanistic and prescriptive for its own good. It wrongly assumed that one could impose precise positive controls over complex events.

2. The "dervishes of airpower" . . . saw technology as a panacea.

3. The theory failed to acknowledge properly that armed conflict was . . . an interactive process between at least two competing wills—not the imposition of one's own will against a passive foe.

4. Unescorted HAPDB overemphasized the offensive aspects of air warfare, like all other significant airpower theories, while minimizing the mischievous potential of defensive strategies and technologies.

5. It overstressed the psychological impact of physical destruction and merely assumed that the terrors inherent in bombardment would eventually destroy an enemy's will to resist.

6. HAPDB repeatedly (and wrongly) used metaphors to imply that modern industrial states, with their "organic essentials," were brittle and closed socioeconomic systems—not the adaptable and open systems that they were in World War II.

7. The theory wrongly assumed that opposing states were rational, unitary actors that based their political decisions on lucid cost-benefit analyses and not potentially obscure organizational, bureaucratic, or emotional factors.

8. The Bomber Mafia grossly exaggerated the frailty and manipulability of popular morale.

9. The strategic economic targeting methods formulated at ACTS ran the risk of "mirror imaging," whereby the key nodes of one's own industrial infrastructure became confused with the critical vulnerabilities of an opponent's system.[56]

Granted 6,860 heavy bombers flying 66,045 sorties in a six-month campaign, American strategic bombing theory as doctrine, as war plan, and then in execution would deliver victory through airpower—or so the theory promised in early August 1941 in the form of "Air War Plans Division-1" (AWPD-1).[57] American bombers would destroy or lethally damage the 154 targets identified as vital to Germany's continuing war effort. By no means does Faber's insightful critique bring closure to the debate about strategic bombing. What he does accomplish superbly is terse presentation of a highly plausible explanation of those intellectual roots of strategic bombing theory that were most likely to promote expectations that would not be fulfilled in military execution in the near future.[58] Furthermore, Faber specifies some assumptions and attitudes that have persisted to the present day in misshaping expectations of airpower, notwithstanding radical improvements in the precision of kinetic delivery from altitude.[59]

Victory in World War II was not the victory of airpower, but it was victory ubiquitously enabled by superior airpower. It is accurate to claim that airpower enabled Allied armies to win on the ground, but it is no less true to claim that the victory was enabled by Allied sea power. To argue thus only diminishes the airpower story if that story is believed to merit dominant status as the victory narrative for the geostrategically bifurcated global conflict.

Whatever the USAAF and RAF Bomber Command preferred doctrines asserted strategic bombing to be about, one knows for certain that it was not believed, either by its political or its military masters, to be about winning the war by aerial bombardment alone. The historical record accessible today is unambiguous. The combined bomber offensive (CBO) in Europe was the product initially of circumstance and later of much inertia but not of deep highest-level conviction, at least not of belief in aerial bombardment as an independent war-winning strategy. Very sensibly, the CBO was intended to defeat the Luftwaffe, and one must recall that early in 1943, despite Stalingrad, it remained a possibility that Germany might win in the east. Had Germany defeated the Soviet Union, the Western allies would not have been able to invade continental Europe—a strategic context with profound implications for the value of the CBO.[60] Not to mince words, from late 1940 until mid-1944, British, then Anglo-American, armies were not ready to close with the Wehrmacht in large-scale continental warfare. If truth be told, the Allied air forces were not ready either, but such is the uniformity (the oneness) of the air environment, and the Western allies were so embarrassed strategically as apparent relatively underperforming coalition contributors that they felt obliged to commit their maximum possible air effort, be it fully ready or not for combat on the largest scale.

By far the greatest contribution made by Allied airpower to victory overall was its attritional defeat of the Luftwaffe. From the very beginning of the war in Poland in 1939, Germany suffered cumulative losses of well-trained pilots and aircrew that it could not adequately replace. The Luftwaffe was never of the size, or quite of the character, or supported by the infrastructure that it required to wage the war— really the wars within the war—that came its way. Considered overall, however, just as the protracted bloodbath in the east proved fatal to the German army, so the campaign to defend the Reich from Allied strategic bombing was conclusively fatal to the Luftwaffe. Of all Germany's interlocking campaign defeats in World War II, only the failure of its U-boats to blockade the British Isles was more fundamentally important than its failure to control the air. Given that Britain in the 1940s lacked a domestic source of oil and, unlike Germany, did not have an advanced synthetic oil industry (using coal), sea control in the Atlantic was required for Allied airpower to operate from Britain. If tankers could not sail from America's Gulf ports to Britain, Allied aircraft could not fly.

Sea-delivered oil was an essential enabler for the Allied conduct of air warfare. With respect to the structural dynamics of the whole war, Allied sea power enabled Allied airpower to defeat the Luftwaffe, and that defeat was both a major enabler for Russian success on land and a literally essential enabler for the Western Allies' continental campaign in France through to Germany in 1944–45. Everything related to everything else, but there was a critical path.[61] If Allied airpower, adequately fueled or not, had failed to reduce the Luftwaffe to near destruction in 1943–44 and instead had been obliged by unsustainable losses to abandon the strategic bombing of Germany, then it is certain that D-day would not have happened, at least not in the summer of 1944, and it is possible that the Russian advance might have been halted. A truly *Festung Europa* (European fortress) in the west would have permitted Germany to swing to the east major air and land force elements previously dedicated to anti-invasion duties in the west.

Much of the scholarly and popular debate about Anglo-American strategic bombing campaign(s) in the war misses the principal relevant point. Specifically, because of the inherent unity of war, warfare, and strategy, victory over the Luftwaffe was literally essential to success in the other environments. Had Germany acquired and sustained an unbeatable Luftwaffe, it would have been highly unlikely that Russia would have triumphed on the ground, while it is certain that there would have been no amphibious invasion from the west. It is important to grasp this strategic logic if one wishes to place the still ongoing debate about strategic bombing in its proper context.

It is certainly true that the victory secured by Allied airpower was not the victory anticipated, contingently promised (if the necessary resources were committed), and attempted under great difficulty by Anglo-American "bomber barons." At least the RAF, in the minds of its commanding air marshals and generals, and the USAAF did not bomb the Reich for the purpose of enabling Allied armies in the east and the west to achieve successful military closure on the ground. Rather the dominant theories-become-doctrines of strategic bombing in Britain and the United States hold that the damage inflicted by aerial bombardment—material and psychological (morale)—would defeat Germany directly. Either Germany's will to fight on or its physical ability to do so would be lethally eroded from the sky. The latter effect was achieved by the late winter of 1944–45, certainly by the early spring, but the former was never secured with definitive strategic consequence.

Extant historical literature on the air war over Germany is so ample in argument and detail that this text may confine itself to a few summary judgments. These pertain here to World War II, of course, but they resonate all the way to strategic debate about airpower today.

Throughout the war, Allied airpower lacked an understanding of what intelligence it needed to plan its targeting efficiently in pursuit of the strategic effect that it sought. In the course of the war, intelligence and understanding inevitably improved as, markedly, did the quantity and quality of the Allied airpower instrument. Experience and events are helpful educators. Warfare is a learning project, though this is true for both sides.

Not until well into 1944 did it much matter how good Allied intelligence was on the structure and functioning of the German war economy, because the RAF and the USAAF lacked the means to do it anything even close to near-term fatal damage. The military authority of this fact was reinforced by the high quantity and quality of a still combat-competitive German air defense system. The Allied air offensive improved greatly in most respects from 1942 through late 1944, but so did the enemy's skill in resistance—though that systemic skill was undermined ever more hurtfully by attrition.[62]

There is no room for doubt that the CBO—for all its lack of true "combination" and indeed its affront to the classic "principles of war" (objective, mass, unity of command, and the rest)—made a huge but unquantifiable contribution to the strategic effect overall that defeated Germany. A historian of the USAAF's Eighth Air Force informs us that "in 1944, the German air defense system called on the services of 4.5 million workers and consumed a third of the nation's total war resources."[63] The CBO obliged Germany to divert thousands of guns to antiaircraft (AA) defense and millions of tons of chemicals to AA explosives that otherwise would have served anti-tank duty in Russia and elsewhere. Preeminently, the Luftwaffe day- and night-fighter assets, including its state-of-the-art electronic aids, were so fixed at home by late 1943 that the Grand Alliance was able to maneuver on land and amphibiously in the context of undercontested skies.

It would be an exaggeration to claim that it did not much matter what the CBO targeted, or hit (which could be rather different), because it was certain to do some damage; anyway, its primary function was to serve as bait for the air battle that was essential if the Luftwaffe were to be defeated. It is ironic, given the doctrine of unescorted

HAPDB with which the USAAF waged war until December 1943, that the Luftwaffe was defeated attritionally by the strategic fighter rather than the strategic bomber. In the words of Stephen Budiansky, "If the primary mission was to defeat the German air force, then bombing raids were less about bombing than about provoking the German fighters into aerial combat. It was the bombers that were playing the supporting role in this final showdown between Allied air forces and the Luftwaffe."[64]

The grim logic is unavoidable, but still it was necessary for the USAAF's bomber bait to menace targets that the Luftwaffe had no option other than try to defend. The Luftwaffe was destroyed by the American "strategic fighter" in 1944–45, most particularly by the P–51 Mustang and the P–47 Thunderbolt, whose range was extended radically by the seriously belated addition of fuel drop tanks.[65] Undoubtedly, major mistakes were made in target planning. Moreover, American sharpshooters with their Norden bombsights were never going to be able to paralyze the German war machine from high altitude, even under perfect weather conditions and in the absence of competent air defenses. German targets were too complex, had too much redundancy, often were ill understood, and did not function systemically as American analysts believed. In the great scheme of things, however, it seems that much of the criticism of the various painful efforts undertaken by the CBO, though well targeted in the small, generally misses the point in the large. While accepting the blanket judgment that the CBO could have done better, it is harder to be persuaded that it could have done much better in the context of the time. Furthermore, it is hard to demonstrate that doing better necessarily would have made any significant strategic difference to the course, outcome, or consequences of the war.[66]

From 1942 until June 1944 the Western allies needed a plausible facsimile of a second front (to the first, the eastern). The strategic bombing offensive, notwithstanding its deficiencies, performed well enough in this vital role, both politically and militarily. The CBO was hugely, indeed conclusively, successful in defeating the Luftwaffe, a strategic achievement that inherently had war-winning/losing meaning. Whatever the visions of victory through strategic airpower (independent of land or sea operations) held by airpower theorists, including some in high places, the CBO assuredly did contribute massively as an enabler to Allied armies and navies.

Whether or not the CBO resulted in an unwise diversion of scarce Allied manpower and materials away from land and sea duties and whether or not the balance among aircraft types was well judged, in the political and strategic context of 1942–44 the bomber offensive was unavoidable given the absence of plausible major Anglo-American alternatives. Moreover, it is questionable whether (1) the large resources devoted to the heavy-bomber forces would have been better employed in other ways; (2) viewed cost-effectively, the CBO was a gift to the Germans; and (3) alternative targeting strategies and bomber force postural choices would have secured greater strategic effect than that actually achieved.

It is a human failing not to know all of what one does not know. One thinks instantly of Donald Rumsfeld's potentially lethal "unknown unknowns." Not only does one not know all of what one does not know one needs to know, no less damaging is the human tendency, especially when under intense pressure, expediently to assume that what one believes one knows will suffice. Every variant of this somewhat convoluted logic applied to the CBO from 1942 to 1945. It is a fundamental truth about the CBO that its conceptualizers, planners, and executives did not really know how to achieve the end that they sought. Moreover, that end(s) was not exactly a clear, achievable objective. Bombing the Reich was not a problem, but what to bomb and for what purpose, how to bomb, and how much to bomb were operationally vital issues that needed to be strategy led. Initially, in 1942 and through much of 1943, it did not much matter because the military instrument was inadequate to secure only very worthwhile objectives. But when the military means improved almost beyond recognition by early 1944 and after, strategic direction did not improve to match the capabilities of ever-increasing weight of the force available.

As an instrument of Anglo-American grand strategy, the CBO made great sense. Moreover, it is important that we should attempt to recover some grasp of the 1942–43 perspective. In those years, Anglo-Americans could not be confident that Germany would not defeat the Soviet Union or at least fight to a draw. Also in those years, there was no certainty regarding the project to weaponize atomic physics. Were the German army undefeated on the eastern front, an Atlantic alliance not equipped with the atomic bomb would have been in desperate need of a CBO as its primary, perhaps only, way to carry the war to Germany.

There is little doubt today that the prime foci for the CBO in 1944 and 1945 should have been Germany's few but vast synthetic oil plants rather than its oil refining industry and heavy transportation systems of railroads and canals.[67] With the exception of the synthetic oil plants, Germany, indeed much of Western Europe, comprised a dense and highly redundant set of target arrays that could fail fairly gracefully and were not vulnerable to paralysis by the precision destruction of a few chokepoint targets of a "key node/vital center" kind. Needless to say, perhaps, this fact is more clearly perceived today than in 1942–45.

For a concluding rather unhappy reflection on the CBO, it was inconceivable that the mighty heavy-bomber forces the Allies had constructed by the close of 1944 would not continue to be employed, even if their erstwhile leading-edge role in Allied strategy had been overtaken by amphibiously propelled and airpower-enabled land power. Stated bluntly, the heavy bombers were used in Europe beyond the time their employment could be justified strategically for no better reason than they existed. Inertia can rule. All the while Allied troops were dying on the ground, it would have been hard to justify abstention from heavy aerial bombardment. The case for the continuation of the CBO into 1945 included the hopes that the German war machine finally could be paralyzed and German military and civilian morale might collapse at last. These hopes were not ill founded, but alas they did not count for much toward speeding the close of hostilities.[68]

Air Warfare in Asia-Pacific, 1941–45

The geography of the war in the Asia-Pacific region privileged airpower from the beginning to the end of the conflict. Whereas the complex structure of the war in Europe most essentially was continental, with the Soviet-German struggle as its most decisive theater, the war in Asia, geopolitically and geostrategically, was quintessentially maritime in the inclusive meaning of the adjective.[69] The rival navies by no means fully anticipated the emerging strategic fact, but airpower was far more a supported than a supporting capability in Asia.[70] However, airpower on both sides certainly was enabled by sea power. Viewed with the understanding of hindsight, the strategic history of the war in Asia-Pacific plainly comprised a lengthy attritional struggle for control of the sea-air approaches to the Japanese home islands. When we examine the course of the war with respect for the historical process, it would be accurate to say that it eventually came to focus upon the aerial bombardment of Japan. One can craft interpretation of the war's narrative drive so that it all favored such a focal point, purposefully pursued, but to do so could mislead the unwary. There was never any serious doubt that the war was going to conclude with action over or on Japan, but quite how that would occur was a somewhat open matter. The course of a war has its own dynamics and cannot be planned and executed mechanistically, according to plan, on a preset, sequential, critical path of strategic achievement. As always with war, this particular struggle did not have to take the course that it did, though it is difficult to imagine it having any result other than complete defeat for Japan. Even had Germany managed to defend its *Festung Europa* and compel a negotiated draw in its war, it is unlikely that the United States would have been willing to settle for anything short of total victory over Japan. American long-range airpower assuredly was the sword that struck the final blows that brought the empire of Japan to the point of surrender—but how did that happen?[71]

Japan's continental ambitions, necessarily focused on China, required a military effort that needed material resources owned and controlled by foreign powers. Aside from the general logic of balance-of-power politics among great powers,[72] Japan's ambition to dominate China ensured the hostility of the United States, and that antagonism mandated that Japan be competitive in armaments. By the late 1930s, unless Japan were willing to reverse its long-standing policy of intervention to dominate China, which it was not, active conflict with the United States was very likely.

The political and strategic situation of 1940–41 seemed to many in Japan to provide an opportunity for major gain. Germany was triumphant nearly everywhere, the continental European colonial empires were defeated at home, and Britain was massively preoccupied with survival at home and defense of Egypt and the Suez Canal in the Middle East. These circumstances, apparently favorable for Japan's strategic context, coincided with an acute worsening of US-Japanese relations, focused on China. The imposition of stringent economic sanctions by Washington (bearing in particular on such crucial matters as credit availability to fund trade, iron ore, scrap metal, and oil) triggered the Japanese decision to endeavor to liberate itself strategically by war.[73]

Strictly speaking, the Japanese decision to strike at the United States—at Pearl Harbor and in the Philippines—was discretionary. Japan decided to strike south for the resources of Southeast Asia rather than north for revenge upon the Soviet Union for the defeat it inflicted on the Japanese army in Manchuria in 1939 and to support its German ally's thus-far successful adventure in the East. Japanese official opinion was divided on the crucial question of whether or not to break its five-year neutrality treaty with the Soviet Union (signed on 13 April 1941) and rush to the aid of the apparent German victor. Although correctly divining that its German ally was not quite the certain victor as yet, Tokyo elected incorrectly to strike south. The sense in this decision seemed vindicated by the fact that the Pearl Harbor assault happened to coincide almost exactly with the near rout of the German army in front of Moscow. Tokyo reasoned fatally that it needed to disable the only strategic force in the Asia-Pacific region that might prevent the conquest and consolidation of Southeast Asia. That force was the US Navy, whose principal combat power was based quite far forward at Pearl Harbor. The forward deployment from the US West Coast had been intended as a deterrent to Japanese military adventure. In practice the move was more of a provocation, a motive, and an opportunity for aggression.

The attack on Pearl Harbor was a considerable tactical success, an operational-level failure, a strategic mistake, and a political disaster. The tactical success achieved by the temporary near elimination of the US Navy's surface battle line had the necessary result of promoting the tactical and operational value of its carrier aviation assets, modest though they were in 1941–42.[74]

The grand strategic narrative of the war in Asia-Pacific was a combination of fairly distinctive campaigns which, notwithstanding their geostrategic diversity, secured so severe a cumulative attrition of Japan's most relevant military assets that the ultimately fatal blows could be struck with concentrated force. In the last resort, which is to say by the summer of 1945, all strategic roads, seaways, and airways led to Tokyo.

Japan was defeated because it was unable to defend its homeland against a lethal quantity of air bombardment. That failure was the result of the warfare it waged from late spring to mid-summer 1945, wherein it suffered irreplaceable losses. To oversimply, Japan was beaten by the efforts of the US Twentieth Air Force flying its B-29s from the Mariana Islands in the summer of 1945. But in strategic truth Japan was beaten because its forces that might have defeated that air force, indeed have prevented it from reaching the Japanese home islands, had been expended, often profligately, in the battles of 1942–44. The battles of the Coral Sea, Midway, Guadalcanal, Rabaul, Saipan, and the rest had cumulatively eroded a Japanese combat power that had always lacked depth.

Hard as it is to admit, given the suffering in the other battles and campaigns, the only campaign that ultimately mattered was the Twentieth Air Force's burning and then atomic bombing of urban Japan. To say this is, however, to mislead. The strategic story of the war against Japan is one of reduction of an essentially maritime empire by maritime siege and amphibious assault. The leading edge of that sea power–enabled amphibiosity was airpower. The Japanese sea- and land-based airpower that resisted the American-led drive toward Tokyo had to be eliminated by attritional warfare in several subtheater campaigns. Although the warfare was attritional in historical perspective, nonetheless the core of elite Japanese combat airpower was concentrated on only a handful of major platforms. The imperial Japanese navy lost four fleet carriers and all of the aviators from those vessels in a matter of a few hours, even a few minutes, at Midway in June 1942.

Essentially, the march toward Tokyo was mutually enabled by sea power and airpower. The reconquest of the Solomons, the Dutch East Indies, Peleliu in the Palaus, the Philippines, and even Okinawa did not count by way of geostrategic gain. But those bloody campaigns, not excluding even the long British campaign in Burma, did count cumulatively for attrition of the Japanese military assets that might have been able to oppose the US Navy–led drive to the Marianas and thence, most essentially by air, the drive that could coerce Japan to the point of surrender. This is an intricately joint and combined-arms tale.

The B-29s that Curtis LeMay wielded as the sword of strategic and moral justice comprised initially a technically, tactically, and operationally untested and more than a little unready force.[75] LeMay inherited a command by relieving a commander who had been a leading light for the doctrine of unescorted HAPDB, Hayward Hansell. Under Hansell, the mighty Twentieth with its revolutionary new aircraft appeared to be failing in its mission. High-altitude bombing at high speed proved deadly for accuracy, while daylight operations flattered the effectiveness of what should have been unimpressive Japanese air defenses. LeMay effected a radical shift in operational concept and tactics, committing the Twentieth to the relatively low-altitude area fire-bombing of Japanese cities at night. The destructive results were as spectacular as the style in air warfare was a rank, or brilliant, expedient doctrinal heresy.

The B-29s, with their 20,000-lb. bomb load, burned out 67 Japanese cities and were running out of plausible urban target-victims by August of 1945. It can be argued with some justice that the US Navy's submarine force, once it had armed its boats with torpedoes that worked, all but won the war independently with its blockade of Japanese sea communications. Also, it can be claimed, accurately enough, that the B-29s' coastal mining operations went far toward paralysis of Japan's war-making capacity. To those thoughts one can add the valid points that Japan was defeated conclusively on land in Burma by British imperial land and air forces and, at the 11th, 12th, and beyond hours, by Soviet land power and airpower in Manchuria. All those and a few other similar, distinctive defeats for Japan do not serve adequately to cancel out or even notably detract from the significance of the USAAF's achievement in bombing Tokyo to the point of surrender. The bombing campaign of course was severally enabled by sea power and land power, but that does not alter the reality of the potency of a long-range airpower wielded with utter ruthlessness against an already militarily depleted and socially demoralized enemy. Without demeaning the vital enabling roles played by other military instruments, whatever else it was, victory over Japan was a triumph for the coercive effect of aerial bombardment.

Conclusion: Slessor Was Mainly Correct

It is no longer a matter of the soldier making his plan for battle on the ground and then turning to see how the air can help him. Land and air operations must be deliberately planned to get the best out of each other; and the plan of campaign on the ground, whether in attack or defense, may be profoundly influenced by the air factor.

—Wg Cdr John Slessor, RAF (1936)

Slessor believed that airpower was of most assistance to land power in its demonstrated ability to "isolate the area attacked from reinforcement and supply; and thus to ensure that the impetus of the attack on the ground is not checked by enemy reserves rushed to the threatened point by rail."[76] His analysis rested upon the experience of the Great War, especially in 1918. Slessor's exemplary commitment to joint air-land campaign planning proved thoroughly sound for World War II, and his sage words were to prove as relevant to the warfare in Korea, Vietnam, and Iraq as they had for the western front. Although the main thrust of his prescient 1936 work was to argue for the potency of air interdiction on behalf of ground forces, he was by no means a skeptic of long-range bombing.[77] However, for the air weapons of the time, at least, he was more than merely skeptical of what he deemed to be the wildly unrealistic promises made by some leading airpower theorists. He summed up his thoughts with the following judgment:

> In the more limited sphere to which this book has been confined [airpower and armies] there is one *general conclusion* of paramount significance, to which all others seem to point. No attitude could be more vain or irritating in its effects than to claim that the next great war—if and when it comes—will be decided in the air, and in the air alone.[78] (emphasis added)

In the main, Slessor was correct. He was substantially right on air interdiction regarding the warfare that occurred in the typically open desert terrain of North Africa in 1941–43; he was somewhat correct with reference to the eastern front; and he was most emphatically right with regard to much of the campaigning in northwest Europe in 1944–45. By way of inductive theory, Slessor in 1936 offered valuable education for those willing to listen and able to apply what he sought to teach. Nonetheless, as the history and analysis in this chapter show, even though air support of armies by interdiction may be the most potent effect of airpower upon modern warfare, the right to impose such effect had to be earned through trial by battle for air superiority. German armies were semiparalyzed by the destruction and damage wrought by Allied airpower only because the Luftwaffe could no longer provide top cover of any kind. The air battle over Germany that began at a near-trivial level in 1941 and 1942 and eventually escalated to a scale that escaped strategically intelligent purpose, let alone political control, achieved the strategic demise of enemy airpower by bloody attrition. This fact enabled Allied airpower to be all that it could be without much hindrance from the second half of 1944 until close of play on 8 May 1945. This is not to say that the Luftwaffe ceased to be able to fly. Even the Allied air dominance of 1945 did not equate to a totally preclusive blockade of German access to the air.

It is sad to note that by and large the strong advocates of airpower in the interwar years were proved correct, but that the more extreme among their views have given airpower theory an undeservedly bad name for exaggeration. Airpower did win World War II, but it did not win it alone. Richard Overy is plausible when he claims that "air power did not win the war on its own, but it proved to be the critical weakness on the Axis side and the greatest single advantage enjoyed by the Allies."[79] Billy Mitchell was on the side of the angels when he advised for all time that "air power is the ability to do something in the air." When one amends his definition to read "something strategically useful in the air,"[80] the gate to an appropriately inclusive understanding is thereby unlocked.

I owe readers an apology for not devoting additional space in this already overloaded chapter to aspects of airpower beyond the kinetic. Airpower in most forms for most purposes was amply vindicated as to its tactical, operational, and consequential strategic value in World War II. Airpower truly came of age—for transportation of most kinds, communications, reconnaissance, medical and other emergency evacuation, and weather observation. The generic transportation category included significant airborne troop assault movement (paratroops and glider-borne troops). Most of what was done, or at least attempted, from the air had some history in 1914–18 and 1936–39 (Spain). But this global conflict, actually conflicts, was an air war, inter alia, on a scale and diversity for which there had been no close precedent.

The Battle of Britain and the CBO virtually chose themselves to be the twin centerpieces of this chapter. The former deserves its prominent place in good part because its defensive outcome was decisive as the key enabler that shaped the course of the war that followed. Furthermore, it was an air battle, really a phased campaign that yields an incomparable treasure trove of evidence for the sound understanding of airpower. The CBO—notwithstanding its cost, devotion, and ferocity—proved scarcely less strategically decisive than the victory secured by RAF Fighter Command in 1940, because it was key to the definitive defeat of the Luftwaffe. The truly big story about airpower in World War II was that it enabled the two wars within the global conflict to be won. The hugely different ways in which airpower contributed to the total strategic effect needed for victories in Europe and Asia highlighted for all time the controlling importance of context. Long-range airpower, as the supported military instrument, was enabled by the context of the war in Asia to conclude hostilities. This had not been possible in Europe.

It will not have escaped the notice of alert readers that this text thus far has been silent on the subject of missiles, both air-breathing and ballistic, notwithstanding their employment by Germany in 1944–45. In addition, no less obviously, nothing noteworthy has been said in this chapter about the atomic bomb and its implications for airpower. It is to these and related matters of high strategic significance that this discussion now must turn.

Notes

1. Overy, *Air War, 1939–1945*, 62.

2. The military technological context of the 1920s and 1930s and its tactical and strategic issues and challenges are treated admirably and generally in a comparative way in Millett and Murray, *Military Effectiveness*, vol. 3; Murray and Millett, *Calculations*; Murray and Millett, *Military Innovation in the Interwar Period*; Winton and Mets, *Challenge of Change*; Chickering and Förster, *Shadows of Total War*; and, notwithstanding its explicitly US focus, Mahnken, *Uncovering Ways of War*.

3. Buckley, *Air Power in the Age of Total War*, 13. It should be noted that the concept of total war is rather more problematic than some histories recognize. See Chickering, "Total War," and Howard, "Total War," for reflective words of wisdom on the concept. Howard's essay concludes a five-book series of major historical studies literally organized around the theme of total war. Probably it is fair to say that today the idea is "walking wounded," somewhat unfashionable, but still employed and quite useful. The utility, however, is a net metric since the concept undoubtedly strays into overreach.

4. See Overy, *Morbid Age*, for a fairly convincing intellectual portrait of the interwar decades. Chapter 5, "Why War?," is especially pertinent. Burleigh, *Moral Combat*, 37, also writes pointedly about the "irrational terror" that the dread of bombing induced in the 1930s.

5. See Slessor, *Air Power and Armies*.

6. Clausewitz, *On War*, 88.

7. Krepinevich distinguishes risk from uncertainty as follows: "*Risk* is randomness with knowable probabilities; that is, we have some sense of what the probabilities might be (for example, low, medium, high). *Uncertainty* is randomness with unknowable probabilities." *7 Deadly Scenarios*, 286. This distinction is intellectually attractive, but in practice I suspect strongly that it conceals more than it helps clarify.

8. Parry, *Discovery of the Sea*, x.

9. Quoted in Meilinger, "Trenchard, Slessor, and Royal Air Force Doctrine," 47.

10. Douhet, *Command of the Air*, 117–20.

11. See Clodfelter, "Molding Airpower Convictions," 84–85.

12. Overy, *Why the Allies Won*; and Tooze, *Wages of Destruction*, are especially enlightening.

13. The Soviet war effort is treated empathetically, yet realistically, in such recent studies as Overy, *Russia's War*; Mawdsley, *Thunder in the East*; and Bellamy, *Absolute War*.

14. The combat power of the US Army in World War II is discussed and assessed fairly in Murray and Millett, *War to Be Won*; Doubler, *Closing with the Enemy*; and Mansoor, *GI Offensive in Europe*.

15. Overy, "Air Power in the Second World War," is a useful compressed overview of its subject within an excellent edited work in Boog, *Conduct of the Air War in the Second World War*, while his *Air War, 1939-1945*, has stood the test of three decades of further scholarship remarkably well.

16. Overy, "Air Power and the Origins of Deterrence Theory before 1939."

17. Bialer, *Shadow of the Bomber*.

18. Britain's then prime minister, Stanley Baldwin, uttered these dangerous words in 1934.

19. For essential background, see Citino, *German Way of War*, while the German triumph over France in 1940 is stripped of much of its magic in Frieser, *Blitzkrieg Legend*, a study that may stand for many years as a template for persuasive revisionist history.

20. Murray, *German Military Effectiveness*, 140–91, 229–43.

21. Ibid., 99–140.

22. Murray, *Luftwaffe*, 42. The Luftwaffe figure covered operations in the entire western theater. As always for air operations of war, alternative statistics are not in short supply. In that regard, there is much to recommend the numbers for comparative loss rates over Dunkirk presented in Hooton, *Phoenix Triumphant*, 260, table 26. As usual, the discrepancies in statistics are all but insignificant in comparison with the broad agreement among good historians over their meaning.

23. Myths, unlike legends, are utterly beyond careful audit or assay. They are endorsed as a matter of faith, by definition out of the reach of reason.

24. See Corum, *Roots of Blitzkrieg*.

25. Murray, "May 1940," is outstanding.

26. Today, 70 years on, the literature on the Battle of Britain is truly vast, is greatly repetitive, and in quite large measure in its more popular forms continues to be strategically misleading. In truth, British preparation for historical prime time in the summer of 1940 began seriously in 1917 and generally was gripped in safe enough hands for the next 23 years (and beyond, to this date of writing). In broad terms, July–October 1940 was the threat context for which RAF Fighter Command had been created in 1936—created more as an improvement on a sound structure rather than as a revolutionary change. One author, historian John R. Ferris, dominates the scholarship on the origins, creation, and preparation of Fighter Command prior to the test that began in July 1940. The following comprises the indispensable Ferris canon on RAF preparation for 1940: "Theory of a 'French Air Menace'"; "Airbandit"; "Air Force Brats' View of History"; "Fighter Defence before Fighter Command"; "Achieving Air Ascendancy"; and "Catching the Wave." In addition, see Ferris, *Men, Money and Diplomacy*. Two scholars dominate on the British side of the Battle of Britain itself: Bungay, whose *Most Dangerous Enemy* is the finest study to date of the battle, and Richard Overy, who has contributed many studies, all of high quality. From a long list of superior writings, see in particular Overy, *Battle of Britain*, which

is a miracle of compression without superficiality. Overy's most relevant writings that have a wider domain of attention than British air defense in 1940, include *Air War,* "Air Power in the Second World War," *Why the Allies Won,* and "Air War in Europe."

27. Bungay, *Most Dangerous Enemy,* 236.

28. See Zimmerman, *Britain's Shield;* Beyerchen, "From Radio to Radar"; and, for the whole story, Budieri, *Invention That Changed the World;* and Brown, *Technical and Military Imperatives.*

29. On the Luftwaffe, the following works are especially useful: Murray, *Luftwaffe;* Hooton, *Phoenix Triumphant;* Hooton, *Eagle in Flames;* and Boog, "Higher Command and Leadership in the Luftwaffe."

30. Robinson, *Invasion, 1940,* is a lively statement of the thesis that the Royal Navy would have made short work of a German invasion armada, regardless of the state of play in the aerial battle.

31. Bungay, *Most Dangerous Enemy,* provides a thoroughly persuasive tactical, operational, and strategic analysis of the Battle of Britain.

32. Ibid., 309.

33. Ibid., 300–1.

34. Ibid., 105.

35. Ibid., especially chap. 7, "Strength for Battle"; and Overy, *Battle of Britain,* 145–48. In common with baseball, air warfare invites an extreme granularity of data and a huge scope for rigorous and overrigorous statistical analysis. Numbers usually abound in military analysis, but never more so than for the air domain. Typically, numerical precision is both spurious and, up to a point, relatively unimportant. But, for good or ill, or both, just about every feature of air warfare seems to lend itself to metric treatment. Whether or not the data thus extracted from and about air activity is information that promotes strategically valuable understanding is, of course, another matter entirely. Lest I be misunderstood, I must rush to explain that I am critical only of deeply granular numerical data that is not meaningful until it is subjected to strategic evaluation. Numbers for their own sake are only numbers. Airpower is practiced for its output in strategic effect, not for the merit of its input in effort expended.

36. Bungay, *Most Dangerous Enemy,* 97, 368.

37. Ibid., chap. 30, and Overy, *Battle of Britain,* offer convincing and strongly complementary strategic assessments of the importance of the battle to the course of the war. Even had the Royal Navy been able to thwart an invasion, most likely it would not have been given the chance to do so because a new government in London would have been seeking an armistice. Of course, this is all speculation. Those commentators who argue that because of the Royal Navy the Battle of Britain was not critical, however, need to be reminded that their preferred scenario of a victory at sea in the channel is thoroughly hypothetical and significantly contestable.

38. See Schreiber, Stegemann, and Vogel, *Germany and the Second World War,* vol. 3; and Boog et al., *Germany and the Second World War,* vol. 6, pt. 5.

39. Holland, *Fortress Malta,* is lively and well done; Kitchen, *Rommel's Desert War,* is useful; while Murray, *Luftwaffe,* 75–80, 154–62, also is reliable.

40. See Boog et al., *Germany and the Second World War,* vol. 6, pt. 4; and Boog, Krebs, and Vogel, *Germany and the Second World War,* vol. 7, pts. 1–2. For the whole Gibbonesque saga, see Irving, *Rise and Fall of the Luftwaffe;* Cooper, *German Air*

Force, 1922–1945; Air Ministry, *Rise and Fall of the German Air Force, 1933–1945*; Murray, *Luftwaffe*; Price, *Last Year of the Luftwaffe*; Hooton, *Eagle in Flames*; and Corum, "Defeat of the Luftwaffe, 1935–1945," which though brief is outstanding.

41. Overy, *Air War*, 223–24; and Murray, *Luftwaffe*, 265. On the whole of D-day, the Allies operated close to 14,000 aircraft sorties, compared with a German number that was under 300, counting all kinds of missions relating to the invasion. This was air supremacy.

42. See Hallion, *Strike from the Sky*, chap. 14; Thomas Hughes, *Overlord*; and Gooderson, *Air Power at the Battlefront*. In addition, the evolution of Anglo-American air-land cooperation is treated well in Orange et al., "Getting Together."

43. Budiansky, *Air Power*, 304–5.

44. Ibid., 305.

45. See Creveld, *Fighting Power*; Overy, *Why the Allies Won*; Murray and Millett, *War to Be Won*; and Hastings, *Armageddon*, for views on the relative combat effectiveness of the Wehrmacht in its years of decline and fall.

46. As usual, metrics abound, nearly all of them suspect. On the air dimension to the war on the eastern front, see Boog et al., *Germany and the Second World War*, vol. 4, 326–76, 765–832; Overy, *Air War, 1939–1945*, 142–78; Murray, *Luftwaffe*; Muller, *German Air War in Russia*; Hayward, *Stopped at Stalingrad*; and Whiting, "Soviet Air Power in World War II."

47. The Luftwaffe assaulted Soviet war-supporting industry only very briefly and belatedly in June 1943. Whiting, "Soviet Air Power in World War II," 104.

48. A bold, even reckless, operational opportunism was a persisting feature of the German way of war. See Citino, *German Way of War*.

49. Whiting, "Soviet Air Power in World War II," 101.

50. Ibid., 99; and Hayward, *Stopped at Stalingrad*.

51. The qualification is added because quality and quantity of fighting power can be trumped politically if one side to a conflict suffers a collapse in domestic political support. A materially and even tactically challenged belligerent may succeed strategically if it is able to employ time as a grand strategic weapon to promote political success despite military disadvantage.

52. Clausewitz, *On War*, 605.

53. Meilinger, *Paths of Heaven*, is essential, as is Buckley, *Air Power in the Age of Total War*, chaps. 4–5. Also see Biddle, *Rhetoric and Reality in Air Warfare*, chaps. 2–3, and articles by Meilinger, Venesson, Corum, and Biddle in Gooch, *Airpower*.

54. Kitchener quoted in Howard, *Continental Commitment*, 126.

55. There is no shortage of sources for the scholar. Those in search of evidence for argument need to begin with the official histories. These are first-rate for what they are but leave a great deal of room for controversy. See Webster and Frankland, *History of the Second World War*, and Craven and Cate, *Army Air Forces in World War II*, and the small library of reports produced by the US Strategic Bombing Survey (USSBS), for which USSBS, *Summary Reports*, provides an instructive flavor, as does Frankland, *Bombing Offensive against Germany*, for the British dimension. A lively discussion of the merits and otherwise in the USSBS in comparison with the USAF's Gulf War Air Power Survey (GWAPS) of the early 1990s is offered in Gentile, *How Effective Is Strategic Bombing?* The operational narrative is well covered in Middlebrook and Everitt, *Bomber Command War Diaries*, and Davis, *Bombing the Euro-*

pean Axis Powers. Helpful and somewhat contrasting British and American perspectives and analyses include Overy, *Air War*; Overy, "World War II"; Hastings, *Bomber Command*; Levine, *Strategic Bombing of Germany*; Crane, *Bombs, Cities, and Civilians*; Pape, *Bombing to Win*, chap. 8; Probert, *Bomber Harris*; Tami Biddle, *Rhetoric and Reality in Air Warfare*; Grayling, *Among the Dead Cities*; and Donald Miller, *Eighth Air Force.* These high-quality works comprise only a distinctly short list of possible references.

56. Faber, "Interwar US Army Aviation and the Air Corps Tactical School," 220–21.

57. Ibid., 224; and Overy, *Air War*, 310.

58. See McFarland, *America's Pursuit of Precision for Bombing*; and Park, "'Precision' and 'Area' Bombing."

59. Rip and Hasik, *Precision Revolution*, brings the technical story into the twenty-first century, while Mahnken, *Technology and the American Way of War since 1945*, provides valuable contextualization.

60. See Overy, *Air War*, 212–18.

61. Barnett, *Engage the Enemy More Closely*, explains magnificently how each of land power, sea power, and airpower enabled the others.

62. See Murray, *Luftwaffe*; Price, *Last Year of the Luftwaffe*; and Hooton, *Eagle in Flames.*

63. Miller, *Eighth Air Force*, 481.

64. Budiansky, *Air Power*, 326.

65. See McFarland and Newton, *To Command the Sky.*

66. Compare Overy, *Air War*, chap. 5, with Biddle, *Rhetoric and Reality in Air Warfare*, chap. 5 and conclusion.

67. Miller, *Eighth Air Force*, chap. 15, is excellent on the continuation of the CBO until the final demise of the Reich.

68. Mierzejewski, *Collapse of the German War Economy*, is a potent reminder that German industry ran on coal, not oil, and that coal was moved mainly by rail (and barge).

69. "By maritime strategy we mean the principles which govern a war in which the sea is a substantial factor. Naval strategy is but that part of it which determines the movements of the fleet when maritime strategy has determined what part the fleet must play in relation to the action of land forces; for it scarcely needs saying that it is almost impossible that a war can be decided by naval action alone." Corbett, *Some Principles of Maritime Strategy*, 15. Corbett wrote these words in 1911. If, sensibly, we amend his reference to "land forces" to read instead "land-based forces," the vital US-AAF dimension to the Asia-Pacific war is immediately recognizable, which is not in any way to diminish the high significance, the strategic effect, of naval aviation.

70. Important contextual studies include Reynolds, *Fast Carriers*; Edward Miller, *War Plan Orange*; Millett, "Assault from the Sea"; Till, "Adopting the Aircraft Carrier"; Evans and Peattie, *Kaigun*; Murray and Millett, *War to Be Won*, chaps. 7–9, 13, 17–18; Mahnken, *Uncovering Ways of War*, chap. 3; and Pierce, *Warfighting and Disruptive Technologies*, chaps. 9–10. In addition, Harkavy, *Strategic Basing and the Great Powers*, chap. 5, is rewarding. Scholars who focus on strategic ideas have been known to underprivilege logistics.

71. Useful sources include Overy, *Air War*, chap. 4; Sherry, *Rise of American Air Power*; Werrell, *Blankets of Fire*; Murray, *War in the Air*, chap. 4; Gentile, *How Effec-*

tive Is Strategic Bombing?, chaps 4–50; and Tami Biddle, *Rhetoric and Reality in Air Warfare*, 261–70. I should point out that although I agree on some points with the more severe critics of USAAF (and RAF) bombing strategy and tactics, on balance I find them unhistorically, insufficiently empathetic to the attitudes and practicable choices of the period in question. See my discussion of strategy and morality in "Moral Advantage, Strategic Advantage?"

72. See Mearsheimer, *Tragedy of Great-Power Politics*.

73. See Barnhart, *Japan Prepares for Total War*; Iriye, *Origins of the Second World War in Asia and the Pacific*; and for a fairly brisk overview, Gray, *War, Peace and International Relations*, chap. 12.

74. See Reynolds, *Fast Carriers*.

75. See Werrell, *Blankets of Fire*; Gorman, *Endgame in the Pacific*; Murray and Millett, *War to Be Won*, 503–8; Hastings, *Nemesis*, chap. 12; Tillman, *LeMay*, chaps. 4–5; and Kozak, *LeMay*, chaps 7–9.

76. Slessor, *Air Power and Armies*, 212.

77. See Orange, *Slessor*.

78. Slessor, *Air Power and Armies*, 214.

79. Overy, *Why the Allies Won*, 323.

80. Mitchell, *Winged Defense*, xiii.

Chapter 6

Strategic History III:
Troubled Triumph, 1945–89

In the global strategic history of the past 100 years, airpower probably has been the greatest success story. However, the readily verified quantity and quality of this success sits somewhat uneasily, perhaps even paradoxically, in company with controversy over airpower's achievements, both anticipated and actual. What should be regarded as a nearly always useful, increasingly necessary, and sometimes essential strategic effect of airpower as a threat and in action persistently has been the subject of controversy. Air forces are assessed to have failed, which in a sense has been true, but any particular military instrument can fail if it is misused or ill suited to the tasks it is assigned.[1] Part of airpower's troubled history has been self-inflicted by advocates whose enthusiasm exceeded their understanding. Because airpower, as autonomous air forces, persistently has feared for its institutional existence, its banner carriers frequently have overreached in seeking strategic justification for organizational independence. The sad fact is that the unarguable strategic triumph of airpower inevitably fuels antagonistic rivalries with land power and sea power, despite the common sense as well as the near ideology of "jointness." Most of the strategic narrative of airpower is as unchanging in its elements as it is ever shifting in historical detail. This chapter advances the strategic story from Hiroshima and Nagasaki through the close of the Cold War in 1989. There would be some sense in telling the story of airpower teleologically, as a stuttering but nonetheless ever more impressive progress toward a semblance of technical-tactical perfection. But such a plausible and positive technical tale could not be matched by a narrative of maturing and progressive strategic dominance. This fact is resisted by those who are undereducated by the general theory of strategy. To cite just one aspect in support of my claims, Clausewitzian "friction" cannot be eliminated by technical progress. Barry D. Watts' theoretical and historical studies are exceptionally persuasive on this subject.[2]

Airpower and Nuclear Weapons

Despite some doubts expressed over the cost-effectiveness of the strategic bombing of Germany and the moral issues pertaining to the necessarily more or less indiscriminate devastation of the largely civilian urban enemy, in August 1945 air-minded people had much to celebrate.[3] Just about every modest prewar claim for the strategic utility of airpower had been massively vindicated by recent experience, while even some immodest aspirations arguably had been realized. By 1941, every belligerent appreciated and was obliged to recognize the military reality that land and sea operations were unlikely to succeed in the absence of friendly air superiority, be it only local and temporary. Whereas airpower in 1917–18 had been increasingly useful to armies in particular, as well as to navies, as of 1941 strategically useful airpower had advanced its status credibly to strategically essential. As long as the enemy ruled the sky, we were not going to rule the land or the surface of the sea. This was a revolutionary ascent in the strategic value of air forces, which were not quite coequal with armies and navies but plainly well on their way to becoming so, at least in the United States and Britain. But what airpower had not demonstrated beyond reasonable argument was the strategic ability to win a great war, either entirely or substantially unaided by the army and navy. At least, such was the case prior to the use of atomic bombs on Hiroshima and Nagasaki.

It was paradoxical and ironic that the very character of the triumph of long-range airpower in the bombing of Japan in 1945 proved to be something of a poisoned chalice for the USAAF (USAF in 1947). Although the Japanese surrender appeared to be a direct consequence of aerial bombardment, even more plausibly it seemed to have been triggered by the shocking and awesome events at Hiroshima and Nagasaki. So, was the Japanese surrender a triumph for airpower or for atomic-airpower, to employ a favored hyphenation of the period? LeMay's B-29s had burned the hearts out of 67 Japanese cities prior to Hiroshima.[4] Furthermore, if the surrender of Japan in 1945 truly were a triumph for airpower—a highly plausible contention—then no less contentiously, it must be assessed as a victory for indiscriminate area bombardment. The atomic bomb certainly lacked discrimination in its lethal effects, but then so had the low-altitude (7,000-ft.) fire-bombing assaults that preceded its employment by five months. Technological advances enabling precision aircraft navigation and weapons targeting eventually allowed the USAF to return to its doctrinal core beliefs, but not until the 1990s—though the targeting-accuracy revolution was first manifested in the closing years of the war in Vietnam.[5]

With hindsight it is plausible to claim that while deterrence was the dominant concept for the leading edge of airpower in the Cold War decades, for the post–Cold War years the most relevant idea has been coercion, followed by denial (or, rephrased, brute force). However, such a neat three-pronged insight risks promoting serious misunderstanding. As so often is the case, there is a curse that accompanies hindsight-foresight. Simply as a matter of the strategic historical record, defense communities in the early Cold War decades had to learn about "the bomb," and indeed the apparent facts about it changed radically from 1945 to, say, 1960.[6] Although the novelty of the dramatically revealed weaponized atomic fact was grasped, its operational, strategic, and political meanings were less readily mastered. In truth, those meanings altered as A-bomb arsenals morphed into hydrogen bomb arsenals after 1952–53 and as the American nuclear monopoly was transformed into a nuclear duopoly and then more (as first Britain, then France, China, and Israel joined the nuclear club—to which India, Pakistan, South Africa [briefly] and North Korea would compel membership).

It is well to remember that the historical context from which the atomic bomb was produced was one of a very great, contestably "total," war. The atomic and therefore utterly indiscriminate demolition of Hiroshima and Nagasaki was a terrible episode in the eternal tale of human beastliness. However, it should be recognized that 334 of LeMay's B-29s bombing from only 5,000 feet killed and injured more people and wreaked more damage upon greater Tokyo on 9 March 1945 than resulted from either of the atomic bombs. In the general's trademark robust language, "We knew we were going to kill a lot of women and kids when we burned that town [Tokyo]. Had to be done."[7] Approximately 100,000 Japanese civilians died in the assault, and 15.8 urban square miles were immolated. Contrary to appearances, perhaps, I am not seeking to criticize LeMay. Rather is it my intention to claim that the putative horrors of nuclear warfare had been seriously presaged by the deeds already done if not overdone in World War II. The world's leading air power in 1945 and long after had an abiding affection for, and aspiration to achieve, expert marksmanship in targeting from any altitude—the Minuteman tradition.[8] But the reality was one of de facto pragmatic acceptance of the unavoidable necessity for less-than-discriminate bombardment. In practice, US long-range airpower was obliged to bomb areas precisely.[9]

Today there is a long tradition of nuclear nonuse, but in 1945 and the years that closely followed, the tradition was entirely different. If there was a tradition in strategic bombing, it was a very recent one of intensive use. In the early postwar years, the prudent strategic meaning of nuclear weapons was nowhere near as obvious as it was to become by the early to mid 1950s. In the late 1940s there were few atomic bombs in the arsenal, few vehicles to deliver them, and an almost extraordinary lack of logistical infrastructure to enable a sustained atomic campaign, and it was by no means certain that the USAF would be permitted by the president to employ the bomb in a future war.[10] As a material matter, until the atomic arsenal grew mightily in scale, which did not occur until the 1950s, long-range atomic bombardment would have been only a phase in a general war, not the whole war itself. It is necessary to remember that the men who commanded American, and later British, nuclear-armed airpower from the 1940s into the 1960s had been forged strategically by the fire of strategic bombardment in World War II. Although the atomic bomb had revolutionary strategic implications for the less than reliably foreseeable future, in the late 1940s it could be regarded reasonably as just another weapon. The atomic arsenal of 1948–49 vintage was strategically valuable if released for military use, but it did not have the characteristics of a swiftly decisive capability. Until the mid to late 1950s, the more expert of strategic analysts anticipated a World War III that would witness an increasingly bilateral nuclear campaign(s) succeeded by a phase of "broken-backed warfare."[11] Not until the late 1950s was the nuclear revolution, judged by most sensible people, effectively to have consumed its subject, war—were it ever to be expressed in anger. Realization that the role of the nuclear weapon was overwhelmingly one of war prevention by deterrence rather than war winning by coercion or brute force was a veritable epiphany for the bomber barons. They had been educated by the experience of real-world war with massive bombardment of urban-industrial areas and by an atomic context that was for many years evolutionary rather than revolutionary in its most plausible military meaning.

Certainly one can detect in the history of American airpower since 1990 a grateful and sincere practicable return to the spirit and purpose of the theory and doctrine developed at the Air Corps Tactical

School in the 1920s and 1930s. But one can detect, no less persuasively, yet another continuity in American airmen's attitudes and approaches. Specifically the challenges posed by atomic, then thermonuclear, armament were met in a way distinctly familiar from the area bombing by veritable aerial armadas of B-17s, B-24s, and B-29s in 1945, notwithstanding the claims for precise targeting. Again one must hasten to add that this text is not necessarily criticism of US nuclear war planning in the 1950s.[12] The point is that the generalship that masterminded and commanded the execution of long-range bombardment from 1942 to 1945 was little altered in the postwar atomic era. To risk banality, to Curtis LeMay and his cohort of battle-hardened air warriors, strategic airpower was strategic airpower and war was war. The atomic bomb did a more effective job than its conventional brothers, but either or both ways, warfare was a massively violent project.[13] To the generation that waged World War II and forced a victory over Japan that apparently was secured ultimately by the atomic bomb, the prospect of a World War III waged in part with atomic bombs was entirely realistic, if not thoroughly reasonable. After all, the twentieth century had witnessed two world wars already, atomic bombs already had been used to obviously significant strategic effect, and there was an all-too-plausible enemy self-cast to step into Germany's shoes as the next villain.[14]

The decades of the Cold War of course had a strong nuclear flavor to their dominant strategic narrative, hence the eponymous weapon branding of the era. Nonetheless, people today are apt to forget just how prominent airpower was in the 1950s and early 1960s. Through the late 1950s, aircraft were the only means of long-range nuclear delivery. The US Army began to acquire short-range tactical nuclear weapons after mid decade in the 1950s, while the US Navy acquired the means for nuclear strikes over medium distances. However, the crown jewels of national defense in those years comprised the striking power of the Strategic Air Command (SAC). This weapon was the direct descendant of the mighty Eighth, Fifteenth, and Twentieth Air Forces of World War II and, as noted already, was commanded by men whose military culture had been created out of the experience of total war from 1941 to 1945. It is well worth noting that modest though the postwar numbers were for SAC when compared with the vast air fleets of B-17s and B-24s, SAC's posture, its order of battle, nonetheless was impressive in the 1950s and 1960s. It was especially impressive when one remembers that the aircraft in question were matched, and more, by an ever growing, eventually abundant, arsenal of atomic, then hydrogen, weapons. From 1950 to 1960, the US nuclear stockpile allegedly climbed from 369 to 20,434; the Soviets' from possibly 5 to 1,605.[15] SAC's first all-jet bomber, the medium-range B-47, was procured to a quantity of 1,150 aircraft; the final B-47E was delivered on 15 February 1957.[16] Its successor, the seemingly immortal B-52, appeared ultimately as 744 aircraft in 14 wings.

Despite the accurate equation of atomic with airpower, an equation expressed explicitly by the terms of art of the day as "atomic-airpower," the marriage of adjective and noun, though necessary at the time, was not entirely a happy one for the USAF or the country it served. The 1950s indeed was the airpower decade without compare, at least if one asks which if any form of military power was strategically the leading edge in those years. But the undoubted dominance of a nuclear-armed SAC was a strategic supremacy recorded in war prevention by deterrence, not in the waging of war. Although the concept of nuclear airpower asserted more of a surgical grafting than a marriage of convenience, it could not conceal the fact that the strategic convenience might only be temporarily expedient. The nuclear element in the nuclear airpower concept and military reality was the more potent partner. Long-range airpower enabled a latent nuclear menace to deter. Airpower supported the nuclear threat, not the other way around. The truth in this point emerged threateningly for SAC in the late 1950s, when its all-important mission of nuclear deterrence came under generic challenge from the arrival of long-range ballistic missiles. It is inappropriate to argue simplistically that long-range airpower was relegated to a supporting role, first by the nuclear character of its payload and then by the intercontinental ballistic missile (ICBM). Such relegation might appear natural, more modern, and hence more desirable to those who either were motivated by their interests to press for a comprehensive move to missiles for long-range delivery of nuclear weapons or were just so ill educated in military realities that they adopted an unduly linear and teleological view of strategic history. To many people, missiles appeared to be a more advanced form of airpower, actually its logical technical successor, certainly for nuclear delivery. In later decades this attitude encouraged the scientifically strange belief that space power was a lesser but included component of airpower.

It can be difficult to impress a due appreciation for historical chronology upon those who look back at the 45 years of the Cold

War as a complete as well as a completed strategic episode. The true dynamism as well as complexity that produces an ever-shifting master context for events can be recognized easily enough as an abstract truth, but its moving contemporary reality is hard to grip with an empathetic understanding. In particular, it can be difficult to grasp the real implications of the eternal fact that, to quote the insightfully blunt Don Rumsfeld yet again, "stuff happens." The Cold War was neither planned nor plannable with a whole story arc from start to benign conclusion. Furthermore, notwithstanding some apparent evidence to the contrary, the massive and diversely structured rival nuclear-armed forces with which it was waged also were not long planned. Both superpowers discovered that it was prudent to deploy a strategic forces triad comprised of land-based ICBMs, submarine-launched ballistic missiles, and long-range manned bombers. These triads emerged step by step in the late 1950s and early 1960s as the ballistic missile revolution matured.[17] This revolution was heralded and anticipated for most of the 1950s before it became a military reality. If one had to specify a date when the missile age assumed strategic actuality, 1960 would be a highly plausible year to select. However, the arrival of token numbers of ICBMs and SLBMs (US) in the Soviet (1959) and US (1960) strategic force postures did not mean that long-range nuclear-armed airpower was either obsolescent or obsolete, as air-minded people feared and as many others with rival interests hoped.

Although the deployment of second-generation ICBMs and SLBMs in the 1960s and beyond certainly diluted somewhat the prestige of SAC's bomber fleet and inhibited progress in long-range airpower, it did not result in the retirement of the nuclear bomber forces of East and West. Both sides rediscovered the virtues in combined arms, combined nuclear arms in this case. Just as land, sea, and air bring different strengths as well as limitations to the strategic feast for desirable synergistic effect, so each among manned bombers, ICBMs, and SLBMs contributed to a strategic whole much stronger than a posture restricted to one or two "legs." Most especially, triadic deployment and operation contributed substantially to survivability in the face of first-strike peril. Barring the far-outlier nightmare of a supremely cunning, elegantly executed, and possibly lucky political and military command decapitation strike, it was calculated to be literally impossible for either side to disarm the other with a counterforce blow. The distinctive basing and operating modes for land- and sea-based missiles and for manned bombers meant that no briefing, no matter how clever, could guarantee a truly knockout strike—meaning either zero or trivial retaliation (though bear in mind the nuclear context).[18]

The long-range manned bomber both survived the functional threat posed by the arrival of the missile age and found itself employed in a role in limited warfare in Vietnam and later for which it had not been designed or intended.[19] But survive it did. Whereas the B-52 follow-on of the late 1950s, the B-70 Valkyrie, was cancelled, long-delayed B-1 and B-2 follow-ons were acquired and operated from the 1980s until today. While the many hundreds of B-47s and B-52s were committed to turning the Soviet Union into a smoking, irradiated ruin in a matter of hours, the 21 B-2s of the 1990s and beyond were tasked initially with hunting for Soviet mobile ICBMs and later for stealthy precision delivery of nonnuclear weapons.[20] Notwithstanding a fairly similar menu of accessible technological choices, the Cold War decades reveal, perhaps unremarkably, that while the United States had become and chose to remain predominantly an air power, the Soviet Union did not betray its strategic heritage as a land power. To Russians, ICBMs essentially were artillery, with long-range bombers and SLBMs functioning in important supporting roles.[21] For Americans, despite the arrival of the ballistic missile and its procurement on a large scale, the manned bomber remained of major, albeit no longer sole or even prime, strategic importance in the nuclear posture. Moreover, when technology allowed for high accuracy by the 1970s, American strategic culture intervened to attempt to shift US nuclear war plans along the path of "key nodes" that had been doctrinally dominant at the ACTS in the 1930s.[22]

In the nuclear context of the protracted Cold War and subsequently, the missile age added a nonexclusive layer to the air age; it did not succeed it. Elementary technological determinism does not work reliably to predict the course of strategic history. Ballistic and cruise missiles have not replaced aircraft comprehensively, and—to hazard a speculative view—remotely piloted aircraft (RPA) will not replace manned aircraft completely. The missile revolution has assumed some of what otherwise would still be airpower's duties, but there are attributes inherent in manned aircraft that are not likely to be replicable in RPAs, at least not for a long time to come.

Nuclear-armed airpower itself was The Great Deterrent until the 1960s, while thereafter it shared duty with land- and sea-based ballistic missiles. Throughout the Cold War, SAC claimed without conscious irony that "Peace Is Our Profession," albeit because fitness for war is our business, as I always wanted to add respectfully. But it emerged quite early that the nuclear-armed airpower one may presume could and did deter whatever needed deterring in those years was less than useful for the mission of strategic coercion.[23] In other words, nuclear airpower was awesomely dissuasive as a threat in nonuse but was frustratingly useless for immediate coercion.[24] And the United States in the 1950s and 1960s found itself, certainly chose to place itself, in strategic contexts where it had grave need of coercive leverage.

Airpower in Korea

Although SAC may well have generated a hugely robust general deterrent effect on behalf of a tolerable international order in the 1950s and 1960s, manifestly it was less relevant to the realms of immediate deterrence and of coercion when warfare erupted.[25] The United States, with some allies, waged two major if limited wars in those decades. The good news was that World War III did not occur, a happy condition to which nuclear-armed airpower may have contributed mightily. It was not so good news that Americans and some allies chose to wage two fairly protracted land wars in Asia, wars that had a large and influential air dimension. By way of historical judgment that would fit most examples of the genre, US defense planning prior to the commitments to warfare in Korea (1950–53) and Vietnam (1965–73) proved notably lacking in strategic prescience. One may recall yet again with profit Clausewitz's insistence upon understanding the nature of the particular war upon which one embarks.[26] American political and military leaders in the late 1940s and the mid 1960s were neither stupid nor villainous, but they opted to wage wars that they did not, perhaps could not, understand in advance. Self-evidently, neither war was anticipated, let alone anticipated in tolerably accurate strategic, operational, and tactical detail. Absent a high-quality crystal ball, the only surrogate to provide genuinely useful insights for professional defense planners is a historical rearview mirror.[27] The airpower dimensions to the wars in Korea and Vietnam were unique in much of the detail and, at the outset of the former, certainly in the strategic context of a temporary US atomic monopoly. The Soviet Union had tested a bomb but was not atomic armed in any militarily meaningful sense in 1950, a condition that was eroding, of course. However, the air stories of these two conflicts were shaped by themes and terms of engagement distinctly familiar to those who are educated in the history of airpower prior to 25 June 1950.

Nuclear deterrence could not have been irrelevant as a strategic contextual constraint upon China and the Soviet Union over Korea, that is, once they belatedly grasped the fact that the United States would fight to resist the invasion of the South. Plainly, the latent dissuasive potency exercised by US-led military power was not sufficient to discourage the invasion. Also, US atomic-airpower proved inadequate as a background menace to persuade North Korean, Chinese, or Soviet leaders to cut their losses and make a hasty compromise peace, at least not until the summer of 1953. It may be necessary to remind readers that prior to Korea there was no experience of war waged by an atomic-armed state (Hiroshima and Nagasaki were strategically capstone events in a conflict already long in the tooth). The literature on "limited war in the nuclear age" that seemed to make sense of its subject, of which there was but a single case to date, postdated the war in Korea.[28] The awesome possibilities of a soon to be plausible bilateral war with nuclear weapons certainly were grasped, but exactly how great powers could wage contemporary limited war was a learning experience in real time. Unsurprisingly, one should add, much of the limited-war theory which rested unduly upon the solitary historical episode extant, Korea, proved worse than unhelpful in the 1960s when the Kennedy and Johnson administrations were obliged to seek strategic answers effective for the distinctive challenges of that decade. It may be worth noting that the particular conflict du jour rarely can serve as a sound basis upon which to theorize and plan for the future.

The airpower story of Korea was the familiar one of mixed achievement and disappointment.[29] Regarded overall, though, United Nations Command (UNC) airpower was a resounding success in support of UN ground forces; UNC airpower was obliged to substitute for allied deficiencies in combat power on land. Hugh Trenchard's 1934 maxim that "the air is one" was demonstrated to be true yet again.[30] UNC airpower provided close air support to ground forces, supply interdiction away from the battlefield, coercive as well as brute-force strategic bombing, troop and supply airlift, reconnaissance, and medical evacuation. Each of these missions was enabled and enforced by a war-long campaign to secure and maintain air superiority. The fight for air superiority—the right to use the air for any and every purpose—was never concluded beyond substantial challenge. Furthermore, communist ground-based air defenses took an enduring heavy toll on UNC aircraft. UN aircraft losses in the war totaled 1,041 (accountable to enemy action), of which no fewer than 816 were downed by enemy air defenses from the ground.[31] It is worth noting that of the 1,040,708 sorties flown by UNC airpower during the war, 69.3 percent (720,980) were flown by the USAF, 16.1 percent by the US Navy, 10.3 percent by the US Marine Corps, and 4.3 percent by land-based allied air forces.

When one poses the strategist's "So what?" question to the airpower dimension to the Korean War, the answers are not hard to provide with considerable confidence. UNC airpower fairly consistently enforced its control of the air at the satisfactory level of air superiority, though not of air supremacy. North Korean—then overwhelmingly Chinese and Russian (manned, at least)—fighters, though not victorious in concert with ground-based air defenses, were always able to impose losses on UNC air forces. UNC "ownership" of the skies over the peninsula was paid for in American and allied blood on a continuing basis from June 1950 until the armistice in July 1953. In fact, UNC air forces imposed the highest monthly loss rate of war on enemy airpower in June 1953—77 Mig-15s were downed (claimed, at least).[32]

UNC air control enabled direct and indirect kinetic support for all UNC ground forces and occasionally made the difference between survival and disaster. UNC airpower enabled the Pusan perimeter to be held in the summer of 1950 and subsequently provided literally a life-or-death quality of assistance, kinetic and other, to the ground forces that were in more or less headlong retreat on both the east and the west sides of Korea in November–December of that year following the surprise offensive ambushes by the Chinese People's Liberation Army (PLA).

UNC airpower failed as brute force and as a coercive instrument for strategic bombing. An intended "air pressure" campaign was conducted in 1952–53, but it is not obvious that the enemy in Korea could be coerced from the air, at least not if the bombing campaign fell well short of an assault that would menace civilian life on a massive scale. A campaign conducted in the free spirit of LeMay's uninhibited fire bombing of Japan in 1945 was never licensed by political guidance. This is not to deny that the bombing campaign did begin to menace the food supply in the North through limited attacks in April–May 1953 on the dams that were vital for the water supply for the North Korean rice crop. However, such a potentially devastating attack predictably fueled an international storm of moral, at least moralizing, indignation. Overall, North Korea had little that could be bombed that was economically vital, short of the dams, and it had actual as well as potential support from its Chinese and Soviet neighbors across borders that the UNC allowed to define a strategic sanctuary.

Although UNC airpower functioned jointly as a critically necessary equalizer for the struggle on the ground, the character of the terrain, the weather, the enemy, and the warfare all combined to deny it anything more than equalizing strategic value. PLA logistic needs were modest, particularly if the fighting was positional and only episodically intensive. As the Allies had discovered in Italy in 1943–45, air superiority, even air supremacy, need not confer a strategically decisive advantage upon its owner when the enemy is competent or better and can defend complex and difficult terrain.

The character of airpower that might have yielded decisive advantage, that of an atomic-armed kind, was not unleashed by a US president who was determined that this strange war in the Far East should remain limited. The war in Korea was regarded as a sideshow, even for a while in 1951 as a possible Stalinist plot to divert the West from an intended Soviet attack in Europe. President Truman did not want to expand the war in Korea at the risk of triggering thereby a war that the West would lose on the ground in Europe. In 1950 and 1951, the United States and its newfound allies in NATO were not at all ready for a wider war with Russia (than they were fighting already in Korea).[33] They had agreed upon the basic military alliance command structure for NATO only as late as December 1950 and were at least several years away from being ready to defend peninsular Europe. That potential condition was, of course, preempted strategically in 1953 by the United States' formal adoption of a master strategy of nuclear deterrence.

Although the technologies of airpower had matured significantly since 1945, the airpower dimension to the Korean War essentially was unchanged from that of 1939–45. When one considers the many and large contextual differences between the two conflicts, notwithstanding their close temporal proximity, it is hard not to be impressed, even possibly overimpressed, by some key continuities. Specifically, one should cite in particular the essential unity of air warfare: the primacy of air control as the vital enabler of activity of all kinds. Also, it would be difficult to exaggerate the scale of critical dependence of airpower's effectiveness upon the whole strategic context of the struggle to which it is committed. To clarify the last claim, airpower has a way of failing to secure, or even enable, decisive strategic advantage when policy and overall military strategy are poor. Not to mince words, airpower will fail to achieve the strategically impossible, and the same can be said of land power and sea power. However, it is necessary to add the codicil that whenever airpower, land power (or ground power), or sea power fails to achieve what is required of it by policy and strategy, the failure is always historically specific rather than generic and abstract. Airpower, as a reified great abstraction, does not fail; rather, for example, German airpower fails to subdue RAF Fighter Command in 1940 and to sustain the Sixth Army at Stalingrad in 1942–43. This distinction between the general and the historically particular is as crucial as it can be misused by careless or ill-willed people in debate.

The war in Korea from 1950 to 1953 underscored yet again some of the limitations of airpower. The eternal verity that war is a duel and not an exercise in the application of force against an inert, unresponding victim was highlighted for the benefit of those who seek to make sense of the strategic meaning of airpower. The strategic value of UNC air superiority was much reduced by the character of the warfare that China was able to adopt. Like belligerents disadvantaged in the air in World War II, the North Korean army and the Chinese PLA suffered severely when exposed by movement en masse in daylight. So, as intelligent soldiers, the commanders of the PLA endeavored to confine large-scale movement of troops and supplies to the hours of darkness. They employed terrain for natural defense against UNC firepower. They fielded potent mobile ground-based antiaircraft artillery (AAA) and only rarely waged such intensive and extensive combat that their logistical constraints became critical. The political context was unusually controlling of the dynamics of the warfare, in that neither side was motivated to press to the uttermost for victory on land in the peninsular, at least not after they had surged back, forth, then back again, and fairly forth yet again from June to December 1950. The United States was unwilling to take the war coercively across the Yalu River into China with atomic-airpower, in good part for fear of triggering a wider war than need be. But UNC land power was unable to defeat and rout the PLA, as it had all but eliminated the

North Korean invaders. For its part China was content for its PLA to hold its own on the ground close to the 38th parallel. Neither side was satisfied with the stalemate, but such a condition was preferred to the perceived risks and costs that might result from a far more energetic and ambitious strategy. It followed necessarily that the airpower of both belligerents was committed, perhaps condemned, to the conduct of attritional combat that could neither be decisive in the air nor enable decisive maneuver on the ground. Even had UNC airpower been more successful in securing control of the air—especially had it been licensed to strike across the Yalu at the infrastructure of Chinese airpower in Manchuria—UN/US policy and strategy for the war would not have exploited the military leverage gained in the air.

The strategic story of Korea, which is a mixture of success and frustration, both military and political, all but dazzles by comparison with the strategic story of the United States in Vietnam. At least for the Korean case it is plausible to argue that the United States was wise in choosing to resist the North Korean invasion, in deciding not to expand the warfare across the Yalu frontier into China, and in tolerating a protracted and indecisive conflict on the ground and in the air. UNC land, sea, and air forces performed well—as, one must add, also did the Chinese PLA—but not well enough to win in a classic military sense. But a strong statement had been registered that communist countries would not be permitted to conquer their neighbors, and that statement was written in the blood and effort of generally competent, often much better, military performance by largely American armed forces. In the 1950s and early 1960s advanced civilian strategic thinkers theorized that Korea was a model, a template—actually it was the sole model/template then extant—for the conduct of limited war in the nuclear age. But alas, strategic history brewed one of its characteristically challenging surprises for the theorists in Vietnam.

A US defense establishment that had been expanded exponentially for twin-foci global war from 1941 to 1945 and then demobilized precipitously was caught notably undercooked for strategic prime time when President Truman blew the trumpet in June 1950 over Korea. The United States and all other powers were still adjusting to the new jet age of airpower, the atomic era was only nominally bilateral in 1950, and the US nuclear arsenal was still unduly modest in scale when compared to the political demand for its strategic services. It should be recognized that in the early 1950s, although the Cold War politically was more than five years old, its military manifestation on the part of NATO members was far from mature. The line in Europe was being held principally by the growing air-atomic power of a not yet impressively long-legged SAC, and the seriously unanticipated war in Korea was a most unwelcome sideshow and potential diversion from the main event, which was security in Europe. Unfortunately, the US armed forces sought to dismiss the unsatisfactory Korean War experience and what should have been its potent lessons at least as rapidly as they were to do for the next unwelcome experience of warfare in Vietnam. It is easy to be wise long after the event, but still it is hard to resist the temptation to be critical of a military air leadership that was so nuclear tunnel-visional in the 1950s. The point is not that they were wrong to emphasize nuclear-armed, long-range airpower. Rather is the charge that they knowingly neglected the kinds of airpower that unquestionably had delivered high strategic leverage in World War II and Korea.[34]

Airpower in Vietnam

By the early 1960s the superpowers had learned some necessary valuable lessons about survival in the nuclear age. In particular they had grasped the reality that such survival was ever more mutual a benign condition. For understandable, if not wholly prudent, reasons, the rival armed forces of East and West were focused almost exclusively on the general war that might erupt out of a crisis in Central Europe. In retrospect the good news that strategic history did not deliver the World War III that seemed so imminent in the late 1950s and early 1960s was modestly offset by the ambush that it executed for the United States in Southeast Asia. Airpower, especially American airpower, unsurprisingly had been developed in the 1950s for the prime military purpose of conducting a nuclear war with the utmost violence. But in the 1960s, the war that American airpower was required to wage, rather than prevent by deterrence, was one for which it was substantially ill equipped and trained. The tactical, operational, and strategic thought for a country's air force tends to concentrate on matters pertaining to its contemporary tasks. An air force dominated by the mission to maintain a nuclear-commanded deterrence delivered by long-range bomber assets and led by airmen encultured by a service that had won its spurs in World War II, particularly in the great bomber offensive, was not a service likely to be friendly to serious preparation for limited nonnuclear war, let alone irregular warfare against an enemy whose primary combat mode was guerrilla. To summarize, US airpower in the early 1960s probably was ready enough to wage a brief theater and then truly global nuclear war, but it was less than optimal for the warfare that unwelcome policy and strategy sent its way after 1964.[35]

The scale of the USAF's unpreparedness for warfare in Vietnam may be gauged from the fact that it was obliged, with some embarrassment, to acquire aircraft developed for and deployed by the US Navy (especially the F-4 Phantom). Although the American war in Vietnam can be dated with precision to the introduction of ground forces in 1965, initially to protect air bases, US commitment to some active participation in the conflict plausibly can be rewound to 1961.[36] Some US commitment to the political integrity of the new state of South Vietnam is traceable to 1954, by which time the United States already had spent heavily in subsidizing the French effort to hold what were still its imperial colonies, known collectively as Indochina. Despite this lengthy period of substantial US backing for local clients in Southeast Asia, American airpower, particularly that owned by the USAF, could hardly have been less prepared to wage the war that came its way in 1965. It was paradoxical and ironic that US airpower capable of deterring the Soviet superpower—indeed, of consigning it to political, military, and physical oblivion—proved incapable of delivering strategically decisive effect in Vietnam. This judgment pertains to airpower employed in the direct support of ground power, in the less-direct support of ground power by supply interdiction, and as an autonomous instrument of strategic coercion. The broad meaning of the air warfare dimension to the Vietnam War for airpower theory and doctrine for effective prudent practice could hardly be more important.

Five broad claims help shed light on airpower history at most times and places and assist in the identification of airpower theory. The claims presented here are singularly appropriate to the airpower dimension of the war in Vietnam. It is all too easy to lose the plot of a war, in this case of the strategic effectiveness of airpower in a war, unless one applies a theory, which is to say a tool kit, to help explain the myriad of detail. To quote Hayek again, "without a theory the facts are silent."[37] The history of the Vietnam War is still hotly contested among scholars. I have no intention of using this text to join a fray that will reach no point of closure. My purpose here is neither to retell, however briefly, the airpower story of the war, nor to argue a case for one or another explanation of its course and outcome. Instead, what follows is a terse endeavor to explain the meaning of airpower for the war. The claims and arguments that follow serve as keys to explanation; they provide much of the needed structure of theory.

First, war and its warfare are always a "come as you are" enterprise. Even when a country can exercise discretion over the timing of its commitment to fight—which is to say, the enemy does not attack first, as on 7 December 1941—the warfare that one's airpower, inter alia, is ready to wage may not be the warfare that the enemy unexpectedly proves able to dictate. The definitional fact that war is a duel translates into a strong likelihood that even a war initiator's armed forces will prove less than optimal for the warfare that their own government may have chosen to begin.

No air force can be perfectly suited to future contexts that inherently are unique historical episodes that unfold by their own complex dynamics, greatly influenced by contingency. It is a necessary truth that tactical effectiveness is a highly mobile story. The paradoxical nature of war means that the tactics that work well enough today may, as a result, so impress an alert and agile enemy that it is able to ensure that those tactics will not work well tomorrow.[38] Poor tactics have been abundant in the relatively short history of air warfare, just as they have been in the long histories of land and sea warfare. Prominent examples include RAF Fighter Command's official doctrine for combat tactics in 1940 (the deadly "vic") and the predictable routing of the B-52 raids in Linebacker II in December 1972.[39] Of course, some poor tactical choices are obligatory when the operational tasking, available equipment, and temporal constraints allow no real discretion and all available options are unattractive. The point here is that poor tactics—whether avoidably or knowingly but unavoidably so—are not necessarily strategically and therefore politically fatal. They are highly undesirable, but that is a coat of an entirely different color. It is possible, frequently necessary, to fight handicapped yet still win.

Second, poor policy produced by lethal politics is an ever-possible challenge that a defense establishment may not be able to meet successfully. Because war is a duel fraught with friction and uncertainty, defense planners should respect the potential of both enemies and their policy makers to stage unwelcome surprises.[40] The Wehrmacht was led to anticipate a series of wars in the mid to late 1940s, not the general war that grew exponentially and contingently out of the initial aggression against Poland. Prudent defense planning can hardly afford to focus primarily upon a single category or focus of threat.[41] When this sin against strategic prudence is committed, the result is strategic failure or, at best, strategic success earned at unnecessary cost for real-time education. It is well worth noting that airpower theorists have always boasted, somewhat credibly, about the unique flexibility and agility of their military instrument. This enduring plausible claim can encourage a false self-confidence. Even air forces have a history of entering wars with equipment ill suited or worse to the nature of the conflict.

Third, even when airpower is fit for its purpose, both tactically and operationally, but high policy is fundamentally flawed, airmen will perform in vain, no matter how magnificently they do so. When the strategic challenge is poisoned in the ends that it must secure with appropriate means employed by effective ways, the whole project will collapse.[42] This was the story of France in Indochina and Algeria. It may have been the case for the United States in Vietnam, although I am not entirely convinced that defeat was unavoidable.[43]

It is persuasive to argue that even excellent airpower cannot compensate adequately for unwise policy. However, it is by no means certain that the American mission in Vietnam was as fundamentally flawed politically as seems obvious to those who choose to read history almost exclusively with the benefit of hindsight and with little respect for the potency of contingency. For France in Indochina and Algeria, the political context plainly foreclosed upon strategic success. For the United States in Vietnam, a similar judgment is plausible but not thoroughly so. It is ironic that the US failure in the Vietnam War contrasts sharply with the almost bizarre fact that the political and strategic consequences of the lost war transpired to be hugely positive for America in Asia-Pacific. Overall, it is not unreasonable to argue that the Vietnam War was a conflict that US airpower could not shape for sufficient friendly advantage, let alone conclude victoriously. However, I am unwilling to claim that US policy was fatally flawed. Such lethality is not implausible, but it remains unduly contestable for truly confident judgment. I suspect quite strongly that the overarching US weakness in Vietnam was with strategy, which is the next subject of special note here.

Fourth, just as unsound policy (politics) is fatal, so also is flawed strategy, as just recognized. Intelligent political objectives and competent armed forces between them cannot usually salvage a venture that is poorly directed strategically. Worthy policy choices do not triumph because of their innate merit, and armed forces do not win wars because they fight well. The imperial German army and its Nazi successor fought very well indeed, but both lost their wars. Similarly, the US armed forces always fought hard and typically fought well in Vietnam, but they too served strategy and arguably policy that failed.

It is worth mentioning that the now-orthodox and dominant strategic narrative of America's war in Vietnam, while convincing, is by no means beyond reasonable challenge. The authorized story, widely accepted today, holds that the United States waged the wrong kind of warfare from 1965 until mid 1968—a kind that favored, though rarely achieved, big-unit engagement. Then, after the embarrassment of the Tet offensive, even though the Vietcong suffered tactical and operational defeat, Military Assistance Command, Vietnam (MACV), under the new leadership provided by GEN Creighton Abrams, adopted a good-enough strategy built on classic COIN principles, and the war in the South effectively was more or less won by 1971.[44] However, American patience with the war expired politically before the job was completed.

Leaving aside the question of whether or not the war was winnable, a matter that will never be settled by scholars, I find the current orthodox view unduly simple and far too dependent upon hindsight; the syncopation of "Westmoreland-bad, Abrams-good" is too elementary. The Vietnam strategic context in 1965–67 differed markedly from that of 1968–71, then again from that of 1972–73. Vietnam was not simply a war waged by insurgents using guerilla methods. When it suited him, the enemy resorted to big-unit, fairly regular combat. These comments are not intended to exonerate General Westmoreland or the Joint Chiefs of Staff. They are designed to suggest to readers that they do need to be sure to attempt to contextualize Westmoreland's big war/small war dilemmas of balance of effort. Also, it is not entirely self-evident that even a much better general than Westmoreland could have achieved decisive strategic success in the early years of the US commitment on the ground. The case has been made that the COIN mission was not prosecuted with the necessary understanding by MACV under Westmoreland.[45] This was a complex war with which he was wholly unfamiliar and for which he was seriously underprepared. However, the Vietcong and the North Vietnamese Army (NVA) more or less compounded to comprise an adaptive enemy, and one should not assume that pursuit of a radically different strategy by MACV would have succeeded. These comments on the overall strategic narrative of the war, actual and hypothetical, are necessary because the assessment of airpower's achievements and failures in the struggle cannot be divorced from understanding of, and debate over, the whole strategic context.

A claim for poverty in US military strategy overall, and specifically for the exploitation of airpower, is much easier to maintain than the argument for a fatal political disability. Air warfare in Vietnam provides close to a textbook case for the demonstration of avoidable errors. The activities conducted with little strategic effect were by no means well chosen, but they also were thwarted by a cunning and competent enemy. However, the principal source of US airpower's lack of strategic effectiveness was self-inflicted damage. US airpower was extraordinarily successful tactically and even operationally but not in aid of a strategy that was likely to deliver the necessary strategic advantage for a political victory. For reasons of politics, terrain, and the grammar of this particular case of evolving irregular-regular warfare, tactical achievement and operational enablement could not produce a lasting political success. One cannot know whether or not a six-day blitz against the magical 94 most vital targets in North Vietnam would have coerced Hanoi into a settlement of surrender. It seems unlikely that LeMay's (and the other chiefs') "shock and awe" bombing preference in 1964–65 would have enabled the United States to nail the Vietcong and North Vietnamese coonskin to the wall. One cannot prove the negative. What is known is that the political context for the warfare (e.g., escalation anxieties, sensitivity to liberal opinion), the light logistical burden of the warfare waged by the Vietcong, and the Third World character of North Vietnam all conspired to frustrate aspirations for strategic victory through the coercive use of airpower. Airpower applied successfully to tasks that do not generate the strategic effect necessary to overcome the enemy physically or dominate it mentally will be airpower misapplied and therefore wasted. Strategy rules!

States have been known to blunder to victory, but such was not America's good fortune in Vietnam.[46] Strictly speaking, decisive strategic effect may be achieved in the absence of a coherent plan, a strategy worthy of the title, but this was not the American story in Vietnam. US and South Vietnamese airpower in its many forms waged warfare tactically that met all reasonable expectations and more; however, that tactical performance was not conducted in the service of coherent strategy, grand or military. The sheer intensity and scale of the warfare obscured the truth that the US military establishment did not have a feasible plan, a strategy, for victory. Generically, though fortunately only generically, the US performance in Vietnam is sadly somewhat reminiscent of Germany's performance after the defeat at Kursk in early July 1943. Both countries continued to fight and generally fight well, but neither could relate the fighting purposefully to a successful political outcome. The void that should have been filled by strategy fatally undermined the broad-gauged potential of US and Allied airpower to deliver strategic effect. Both as a force multiplier for the effort on the ground and as an all-but-independent instrument of coercion, airpower—even tactically excellent airpower—could not substitute and compensate for missing strategy. At least in the historical episode of the war in Vietnam, airpower could not do so.

I must hasten to add that I am not implying that the United States could have found and executed a strategy for Vietnam that would have secured a tolerably advantageous political outcome. The claim made here simply is that no such strategy was found and pursued. There were large operational successes, most especially after the military defeat of the Vietcong's Tet offensive in January–February 1968 and then of North Vietnam's regular-style Easter offensive in March–April 1972,[47] but neither proved to be exploitable for decisive strategic advantage as the enabler of a political settlement acceptable to the United States. After 1968, victory for the United States in Vietnam meant a strategic exit sufficiently graceful that the superpowers could disengage with some political dignity intact.

Fifth and finally in this short litany of fundamentals, poor tactics are always costly, but unlike flawed policy and poor or absent strategy, they frequently are survivable and can be corrected. Of course, tactics can be improved only over time. Armies, air forces, and navies cannot be retrained overnight. Also, the combat losses that they suffer in part as a consequence of initial tactical incompetence take some time to make up, if indeed that is even possible. Each war is a duel, as we must keep insisting; it is a mutual learning experience; and it is unforeseeable in detail and course. Nonetheless, US airpower was far less prepared to wage a substantially irregular conventional war than it should have been. Vietnam was not a lesser-but-included case for an airpower shaped to wage and dominate an extremely nuclear World War III. Leaving aside questions of policy and strategy wisdom, US airpower was not well equipped either to conduct conventional bombing effectively or to secure and maintain control of the air in the face of competent, complex, multilayered, and dense air defenses. Furthermore, US airpower lacked ready access to tactical and operational doctrine appropriate to the warfare it was committed to wage in Southeast Asia.

The heavy F-105 fighter bombers that conducted more than 75 percent of the Rolling Thunder coercive air campaign against North Vietnam from 1965 to 1968 were insufficiently agile for their role, while the F-4 Phantoms that bore the greatest load of escort duty were notably ill armed for the dog-fighting role forced upon them.[48] But because of the sheer scale of its air arsenal and the diversity of its assets, US airpower did by and large find adequate compensation for the manifestly suboptimal equipment mix through numbers, pilot skill, and some necessary technical fixes and tactical course correction. Overall, the directors of US airpower in the early-to-mid 1960s were guilty of an imprudent overspecialization in preparation for nuclear war. However, it is not plausible to argue that any one or even several of airpower's limitations in practice in the Vietnam War literally were critical to the course and outcome of the struggle.

It is exceptionally challenging to attempt to give suitable tactical credit to an airpower effort that was perhaps fatally disabled politically and assuredly misguided strategically and operationally. The errors at those levels all but necessarily meant that no airpower effort could deliver, or jointly enable the delivery of, the quality and quantity of strategic effect for advantage that might have been translated into political success. One must qualify any confidence expressed in the political benefits of strategic advantage, since politicians are more than capable of squandering what could and should be the fruits of military success.

Perhaps the most appropriate comment to make about the application of airpower in Vietnam is that it was ubiquitous and pervasive. The coercive bombing campaign against North Vietnam has been analyzed exhaustively and convincingly by scholars.[49] There is consensus that the Rolling Thunder campaign was ill conceived and poorly directed. It was ill conceived in that it sought to achieve the unachievable, which cannot be sound strategy. The dominant purpose was to inflict so much hurt upon North Vietnam that its leaders would agree to be coerced into a negotiated peace. In addition, and sometimes as an alternative to coercion, it was hoped that the bombing of key industrial and infrastructural assets in North Vietnam would, by the damage wrought by brute force, so disable the enemy that it would be unable to sustain support for the war in the South. Both the intense nature of Hanoi's commitment to the struggle and the low combat consumables character of the warfare it helped sustain translated into mission impossible for Rolling Thunder, or even for a concentrated "instant thunder" for shock and awe.

By extension, air interdiction of North Vietnamese Army logistics, let alone of NVA forces en masse, could be operationally decisive only if the enemy engaged in both intensive and open warfare in a regular manner. When that occurred—as it did only episodically, most especially in 1968 and 1972—the NVA was eviscerated by US and Allied airpower. This is a familiar phenomenon. The details varied, but dominant airpower wrought significant-to-lethal damage upon enemy forces in 1918, 1944–45, and 1950.[50] It is scarcely remarkable that the pattern continued into the 1960s and beyond.

It is ironic that although the Rolling Thunder (1965–68) and Linebacker I and II (1972) bombing campaigns against the North seem to have been the prime focus of airpower commentary in the war, the dominant airpower phenomenon in the struggle was the full-service operational arrival of the helicopter. One would be challenged to overstate the extent to which Vietnam was "the helicopter war." Helicopters had been a subject for experimentation in the 1930s, very limited realization in World War II, extensive employment in Korea for emergency medical evacuation (medevac), and a growing number of light troop and supply airlift tasks, some communications duties, and occasional fire support in Malaya and Algeria. But when powered by a gas turbine engine, the helicopter came of age in the 1960s.[51] The only aspect of the rotary-wing story more remarkable than the speed of its full-service arrival and subsequent technical and tactical refinement is the absence of a perceptive strategic literature keyed to its enabling qualities. Libraries bulge with books, reports, and studies on airpower in general, so-called strategic airpower in particular, and on the particular technical virtues and sins of individual aircraft types and models. But where is the literature on the "strategic helicopter"? Modern warfare conducted by the regular armed forces, including somewhat irregular special operations forces (SOF) "regulars," is thoroughly dependent upon rotary-wing aviation. Armies regard helicopters as an integral part of contemporary land power, just as navies view them as integral to sea power. Such an attitude is entirely appropriate.

Simply viewing the helicopter as integral to land power and sea power can be misleading. When third-dimensional mobility and agility are added to existing land power as a new supporting element, historically there has always been the risk that innovation prompts tactical advantage when it should promote a quest after operational and strategic gain. The airlift story—of which the helicopter is only one, albeit hugely important, component—was a major enabler for land power in World War II and has grown in significance ever since. The air mobility that can shift troops and supplies over increasingly long distances also is an airlift that can deliver and briefly sustain airborne assault.[52] Paratroops were strictly a conceptual novelty to forward thinkers in 1918; they were a reality in Soviet and, much later, German capabilities in the 1930s; and they dramatically erupted on the scene of active strategic history in May 1940.

Airborne soldiers were then, and remain today, elite volunteers. The high quality of airborne soldiers has been mandated not only because of the unusual physical hazards of delivery into combat by air—by parachute, glider, or aircraft directly (fixed and rotary wing)—but also because the very virtues of air insertion carry military risks of proportionate or more weight. The physics of air mobility dictate that only a modest weight and bulk of equipment can be carried or subsequently air-transported to troops once delivered, while the operational attractions of air mobility may tempt the bold commander into recklessness. More than one body of air-inserted troops has been obliged by the circumstances of its isolation behind enemy lines to behave like true heroes, with all that implies by way of casualties.[53]

To armies, airborne soldiers are still soldiers; they are ground power that happens to fly into combat from time to time. They and their flying steeds are simply another maneuver element for land power. Air mobility came of age on 28 June 1965, when the US Army stood up the 1st Cavalry Division (Airmobile) following years of technical advance, tactical experimentation, and some, though in my view with the wisdom of hindsight, insufficient operational preparation. The Air Cavalry deployed to Vietnam on 1 July 1965 with 428 helicopters, in contrast to the fewer than 100 then standard for infantry divisions in the US Army.[54] Some statistics can serve well to convey the ubiquity of rotary-wing airpower in the Vietnam War.

- More than 36,125,000 total helicopter sorties were flown.
- 7,447 air assault sorties were flown.
- 3,932,000 attack sorties were flown.
- More than 21,000,000 C3 and other sorties were flown.
- 5,042 helicopters were lost in the war.
- 4,463 helicopters were lost by US Army aviation.
- More than 6,000 helicopters were damaged and repaired.
- 1,074 helicopter pilots were killed.
- 2,809 helicopter aircrew were killed over 10 years in the war.[55]

Just about everything that the United States did or attempted in the ground war in Vietnam was enabled by rotary-wing aviation. The Bell HU-1 ("Huey") Iroquois* in many versions, including dedicated gunships, will forever be the dominant military equipment icon of the war. Self-evidently from the strategic story of the war, the enormous tactical success of the helicopter in every mission to which it was committed was not translated into the operational advantage that could promote a favorable strategic decision.

Airpower waged an intensive, extensive, and therefore bloody war in Vietnam. Its every facet was demonstrated. It is compelling to argue that tactically, American and South Vietnamese airpower performed magnificently, given the equipment available and the context for its application. However, one must recognize that there was much that it could not do, either by way of operationally independent coercion from altitude or as a direct and indirect enabler of ground power. Airpower certainly was misused in a would-be coercive and brute-force bombing campaign that made little strategic or political sense. Many airmen were convinced that their campaign of coercion could have succeeded, "If only . . ." This lament is familiar and not wholly without merit. Nonetheless, to reiterate the main point of this part of the discussion, airpower in Vietnam, though tactically as effective as it could be, was comprehensively unable to compensate by its tactical performance for an unduly nonpermissive strategic and political context.

---

*Designation changed from HU-1 to UH-1 in 1962.

Conclusion: Promise Unfulfilled

The strategic history of the Cold War decades reveals an airpower that was as ubiquitous and essential as, unarguably, it was not decisive in the sense meant by theorists in the 1930s. Airpower certainly was dominant in the hierarchy of potential violence from the 1940s to the mid 1960s; for nearly all of those years it was the only military instrument that could deliver atomic, then thermonuclear, Armageddon. Through the agency of deterrent effect, nuclear-armed airpower may have driven politicians to decide that a World War III would not occur if they were allowed any discretion over the matter. Necessarily, conclusive evidence in support of this hypothesis must always be lacking. From the 1960s to the present day, nuclear-armed, long-range airpower has been required to share the burden of responsibility for keeping the peace in the direst of menacing circumstances with land- and sea-based forces. The mission of nuclear deterrence for war prevention assuredly was essential and permanent, but it was not especially glorious in the public imagination and reckoning. Episodically, there were some causes for concern, if not necessarily alarm, over survivability in the face of an evolving Soviet threat, but the success of SAC in war prevention was not quite the victory through airpower once envisaged by Giulio Douhet, Billy Mitchell, and the theorists at the ACTS in the 1930s.

The strategic experience of airpower in Korea and Vietnam was a light year removed from the practice of nuclear-armed airpower in its deterrence mission. Airpower was dominant and decisive in its long-range nuclear role, if anything could be so described vis-à-vis war prevention. However, it was shown to lack the power of decision in nonnuclear warfare, at least in the contexts of Korea and Vietnam, and the qualifying phrase is vitally significant. The inability of airpower to compel a favorable outcome, either by its own independent action or as a force-multiplying enabler for land or sea power, should not obscure the truth that it was literally essential to the achievement of such success as friendly arms overall were able to achieve.

Regarded, as it were, from Mount Olympus and with hindsight, it is empirically safe to claim that airpower succeeded in enabling South Korea to be defended, enabling a military effort in Vietnam that delayed a communist takeover for 10 years, a consequence that had incalculably positive consequences for Southeast Asia, though not for erstwhile South Vietnam of course,[56] and bearing the heaviest load for maintaining what became, from one perspective, the "long peace" of the politically and strategically overarching Cold War.[57] These are not trivial accomplishments, even though they did not quite amount to the strategically dominant future that early theorists had predicted with much hope and confidence. The political, strategic, and budgetary dominance of nuclear-armed, long-range airpower was secured more by the terrifying nature of its payload than by the potency of its delivery vehicles. LeMay's fleet of B-47s and B-52s owed most of its political and strategic significance to the nuclear weapons it could carry. This situation was beneficial for the prevention of a very great war, but perhaps paradoxically, it was not propitious for the health of airpower as an instrument for strategic effect. Thermonuclear weapons in the megaton range did not demand the precision delivery that had been the hallmark of ACTS airpower theory and the elusive North Star for the effects sought by the "Mighty Eighth" in World War II.

As humans, the land has to matter most to us, strategically as in all other ways. But just because every conflict must have territorial referents to some extent, it does not follow that land power and the strategic perspective of the soldier should dominate strategy in all cases. There were limits to what airpower in its several forms could accomplish in the contexts of Korea and Vietnam. However, it was apparent in Korea, and even more so in Vietnam, that superior American airpower was not employed as effectively as it might have been, but only in part because it was unduly hostage to a poor strategy dominated by narrow considerations focused on the ground war. One suspects that in the circumstances of Korea and Vietnam, there was little politically acceptable scope for a more operational-level approach to the utility of airpower. Nonetheless, one is struck by the contrast between immense effort and sacrifice as input and modest strategic reward for output.

It has long been commonplace for scholars to find fault with an airpower theory and practice that promised so much yet appeared to deliver so little. The analysis here agrees with some of the criticism of classic airpower theory but finds that the critics frequently are undisciplined in their critiques. It is a triumph neither for good history nor for theoretical rigor to leap from denunciation of the thesis that airpower will always deliver victory to the antithesis that airpower can never deliver victory. Moreover, if one intelligently addresses the meaning of *victory*, indeed of *decision*, then it becomes evident that there is, certainly can be, far more merit in the claim that airpower can be a more strategically decisive force than critics generally allow.

It is quite clear, though, that airpower in any and all its manifestations typically could not serve as a panacea, let alone as the silver bullet, that would deliver strategic victory unilaterally. Having said that, it is still necessary to grant one exception of great political and strategic historical significance: the Berlin airlift of 1948–49. Stalin's ill-judged attempt to blockade the city of Berlin in an effort to arrest and reverse the process of recovery in the Western holdings in occupied Germany was thwarted by American and British airpower (principally), both military and commercial.

In 1994 Carl Builder of the RAND Corporation wrote a powerfully worded book that was a period piece lamenting the decline and eventual near absence of airpower theory.[58] He argued strongly that airpower had lost its way in the Cold War and asserted that airmen had focused on their beloved vehicles, actual and potential, rather than the strategic mission of those vehicles. He also argued that nuclear weapons were permitted to have the effect of demoting the relevance once allowed to theory. Where was the need for precision bombing when SAC could destroy the evil empire all but literally? This text chooses not to pursue questions of nuclear strategy, though this author has devoted much effort to the subject over many years.[59] The dominance of the nuclear deterrent mission and the dazzle of the new jet-age technologies did, as Builder claims, serve to depress creative thought about the uses of airpower for tactical- and operational-level effect in conventional warfare, both regular and irregular, in pursuit of the true coin of the realm, strategic effect.

Airpower was hopelessly enthralled to its Faustian pact with nuclear weapons, and it was condemned by context to play only a supporting, enabling, though essential role in Korea and Vietnam. But could and should it have been assigned more of a role than simply supporting NATO's ground forces for the defense of Western Europe during the Cold War? The theory and practice of operational air warfare in the context of ongoing land warfare was born out of the experience of World War I and was a feature of some theater warfare in World War II, but in the 1970s and 1980s, operational artistry for airpower in conventional regular warfare was notable for its absence. The sound proposition that armies should be supported by airpower translated in contemporary practice into an attitude skeptical of, if not explicitly hostile to, the idea that airpower could have an operational-level role of high strategic significance. Such skepticism may or may not have been well founded for NATO in the later decades of the Cold

War. Fortunately we shall never know. What we do know is that by the 1980s, airpower theory had long ceased to fly high and, in its strategic meaning for nonnuclear conflicts, it was in danger of being a great deal less than it could be. Given the technological advances of the 1970s and 1980s, by the end of the Cold War in 1989 the theory and practice of airpower was more than ready for intellectual refueling and operational retasking.

Notes

1. Higham and Harris, *Why Air Forces Fail*. This is an excellent book. I cite it only to make the important point that if approached and read out of strategic historical context, it may appear to singularize airpower as a defective military instrument.

2. Watts, *Foundations of US Air Doctrine*, and *Clausewitzian Friction and Future War*.

3. Superior treatment of the moral dimension to the Allied long-range bombing campaigns in Europe and Asia-Pacific is offered in Burleigh, *Moral Combat*, chaps. 19–20. A potent example of the moral indictment literature is Grayling, *Among the Dead Cities*. In addition, Schaffer, *Wings of Judgment*, strives hard to be fair, as does Harman in his well-focused and closely argued brief analysis, *"Are We Beasts?"*— while Garrett, *Ethics and Airpower in World War II*, is honest but scholarly in finding moral fault. It should be needless to say that further research and reflection will not reveal some accessible truth over the question of whether or not Allied bombing policy, strategy, and tactics constituted war crimes. It was, is, and will forever remain a matter of judgment, moral and strategic.

4. See Crane, *Bombs, Cities, and Civilians*, chap. 9; Werrell, *Blankets of Fire*; and Tami Biddle, *Rhetoric and Reality in Air Warfare*, 261–70.

5. See Rip and Hasik, *Precision Revolution*.

6. See Freedman, *Evolution of Nuclear Strategy*; and Craig and Radchenko, *Atomic Bomb and the Origins of the Cold War*.

7. LeMay quoted in Budiansky, *Air Power*, 338.

8. Carl Norden's all but magical, certainly iconic, and highly classified bombsight was adopted as the key to (unescorted) high-altitude precision bombing. Ibid., 172–76. Budiansky's intelligent observation that "a bomber was no better than its bombsight" is not to be trusted because it risks confusion of a tactical matter, bombs near or on target, with a strategic one, the (strategic) effect of the bombs delivered. Also see McFarland, *America's Pursuit of Precision Bombing*, chap. 4. MacKenzie, *Inventing Accuracy*, brings the theme forward through the Cold War.

9. See Donald Miller, *Eighth Air Force*, chap. 16.

10. See Borowski, *Hollow Threat*; and Borgiasz, *Strategic Air Command*.

11. The seriously unpleasant metaphor of "broken-backed war" was deployed in the British Defence white paper of 1954. It was discussed informatively in Brodie's 1959 minor classic, *Strategy in the Missile Age*, 160–65.

12. Anyone who should doubt this would profit from reading Rosenberg, "Smoking Radiating Ruin at the End of Two Hours," which reveals what LeMay intended SAC to do to the Soviet Union in 1954–55.

13. See Rosenberg, "Origins of Overkill."

14. On the political context, see Gray, "Mission Improbable, Fear, Culture, and Interest."

15. Norris and Kristensen, "Global Nuclear Stockpiles, 1945-2010," 81. One should be especially suspicious of precise unrounded numbers. Nonetheless, the orders of magnitude and the sharp upward trend are at least reliable. Schwartz, *Atomic Audit*, is a uniquely valuable study. The US nuclear arsenal peaked in 1967 at 31,225 warheads; the figure as of May 2010 was 5,113, with "several thousand" in reserve. Philips, "Countdown to Disarmament."

16. See Gray, "Defence Policy of the Eisenhower Administrations, 1953-1961," 215.

17. See Beard, *Developing the ICBM*; and Podvig, *Russian Strategic Nuclear Forces*—and note the title to Brodie's 1959 book, *Strategy in the Missile Age*.

18. The potential vulnerability of US long-range, nuclear-armed forces to surprise Soviet attack was the subject of scientific, and not so scientific, analysis for approximately 35 years. It all began with Wohlstetter et al., *Selection and Use of Strategic Air Bases* (declassified from Top Secret in 1954), of which SAC approved, and moved on to Wohlstetter et al., *Protecting U.S. Power to Strike Back in the 1950s and 1960s* (declassified from Top Secret in 1956), which SAC did not like. See Quade, "Selection and Use of Strategic Air Bases"; and with caution, Abella, *Soldiers of Reason*, 79-87, which needs to be balanced, not quite offset, by Marshall, Martin, and Rowen, *On Not Confusing Ourselves*, particularly the essays by Digby and Martin (3-16) and Digby (17-28).

19. See Head, *War from above the Clouds*.

20. The original size of the B-2 force was intended to be 132 (not 21!). Needless to say, when the many became the very few, the sound principle of economies of scale is flouted, with awesome consequences for individual platform fly-away cost.

21. See Zaloga, *Kremlin's Nuclear Sword*.

22. Ball and Richelson, *Strategic Nuclear Targeting*, was a useful publication in that, notwithstanding the necessary constraints imposed by official secrecy, at least it did oblige scholars to "think about the unthinkable" (with thanks to Kahn, *Thinking about the Unthinkable*) beyond standard platitudes on stable prewar deterrence. In addition see Ball and Toth, "Revising the SIOP." See my efforts to explain the structure of the challenge of nuclear strategy to Americans and Russians in my books, *Strategic Studies and Public Policy*; *Nuclear Strategy and National Style*; *Modern Strategy*, chaps. 11-12; and *Strategy for Chaos*, chap. 8.

23. See Schelling, *Arms and Influence*; Betts, *Soldiers, Statesmen, and Cold War Crises*; Betts, *Nuclear Blackmail and Nuclear Balance*; and Pape, *Bombing to Win*, 35-38.

24. See Brodie, *War and Politics*, chap. 9.

25. The conceptual distinction between immediate and general deterrence is explained in Morgan, *Deterrence*, chap. 2. Although the distinction is clear, its real-world relevance is nearly always highly problematic.

26. Clausewitz, *On War*, 88-89.

27. I employ this proposition in my article, "Strategic Thoughts for Defence Planners." For a full broadside of argument and candidate evidence, see Murray and Sinnreich, *Past as Prologue*.

28. Osgood, *Limited War* (1957) and *Limited War Revisited* (1979); and Halperin, *Limited War in the Nuclear Age* (1963), were exemplary as superior period pieces. Rosen, "Vietnam and the American Theory of Limited War," was a fairly brutal retrospective critique of what can happen when speculative strategic theory meets strategic historical reality.

29. The most useful sources are Futrell, *United States Air Force in Korea*; Crane, *American Airpower Strategy in Korea*; and Stephens, "Air War in Korea, 1950–1953." Other sources include Stewart, *Airpower*; Momyer, *Air Power in Three Wars*; and Mark, *Aerial Interdiction in Three Wars*, chaps. 8–9.

30. Trenchard quoted in Meilinger, "Trenchard, Slessor, and Royal Air Force Doctrine before World War II," 47.

31. Futrell, *United States Air Force in Korea*, 692.

32. Stephens, "Air War in Korea," 24.

33. The scale of Western military risk in Europe is emphasized in Gray, "Harry S. Truman and the Forming of American Grand Strategy in the Cold War." Also see Ross, *American War Plans, 1945–1950*; and Cornish, *British Military Planning for the Defence of Germany, 1945–1950*.

34. Suitably negative comment on the US military's reaction to their trial by fire in Korea is offered in Budiansky, *Air Power*, 369–75.

35. For reasons identified and developed in detail and with some passion in ibid., 389–97; Clodfelter, *Limits of Air Power*; Tillman, *Whirlwind*; Pape, *Bombing to Win*, chap. 6; and Wayne Thompson, "Operations over North Vietnam, 1965–1973."

36. The most persuasive study to date is McMaster, *Dereliction of Duty*; see also the vigorous argument in Moyar, *Triumph Forsaken*.

37. Hayek quoted in Keegan, *History of Warfare*, 6.

38. See Luttwak, *Strategy*, chap. 6.

39. Wayne Thompson, "Operations over North Vietnam," 125; John T. Smith seeks to tell the whole story in some context in his *Linebacker Raids*.

40. Politics is what it always is and politicians are apt to be what they typically are, which is to say people attracted to near-term expedient decisions. The challenge to the military is to cope with the often grim realities of their highly political policy context, all the while maintaining moral integrity and an attitude of strategic prudence. As McMaster shows in *Dereliction of Duty*, the senior US military has not always had the courage of its not entirely private strategic convictions.

41. I seek to stress this vital principle in "Strategic Thoughts for Defence Planners."

42. This is the core message in Yarger, *Strategy and the National Security Professional*; and Gray, *Strategy Bridge*.

43. For contrasting opinions, on the positive side see Woodruff, *Unheralded Victory*; Walton, *Myth of Inevitable US Defeat in Vietnam*; and Moyar, *Triumph Forsaken*. The now long conventionally negative assessment of the possibility of meaningful victory is reflected in a small library of retrospectives, for which Record's well-argued *Wrong War* can stand duty. This debate most probably will never end. The writing of hypothetical future history is a heroically futile enterprise. Such were and remain the passions aroused by the American war in Vietnam that no scholar's judgment can be regarded as safe in a scholarly sense; a great deal more historical perspective is required—in other words, time. These comments apply to the following general historical narratives, even though one can recommend them as useful:

Karnow, *Vietnam*; Davidson, *Vietnam at War*; Kaiser, *American Tragedy*; Wiest, *Rolling Thunder in a Gentle Land*; and Prados, *Vietnam*.

44. For this narrative see Sorley, *Better War*; while a skeptical view pervades Gentile, "Strategy of Tactics." It is worth noting that Gentile's robust critique of "population-centric COIN," while certainly worthy, needs to be regarded in the perspective of the typical thesis and antithesis that is the template for healthy strategic conceptual debate. One would like to claim that intellectual combat between thesis and antithesis results in a wise synthesis, but in practice this is rarely so. If and when it appears, the synthesis may well not be wise and quite often it does not appear at all.

45. See the damning story told in Krepinevich, *Army and Vietnam*.

46. See Connelly, *Blundering to Glory*; but also see Esdaile, "De-Constructing the French Wars," for an argument privileging strategy, the alleged absence of which is claimed to have been a significant reason for Napoleon's decline and ultimate fall.

47. See Lavalle, *Airpower and the 1972 Spring Invasion*.

48. Budiansky, *Air Power*, 389–94; and Wayne Thompson, "Operations over North Vietnam."

49. For the full story of Rolling Thunder, see James Thompson, *Rolling Thunder*; John Smith, *Rolling Thunder*; and Wayne Thompson, *To Hanoi and Back*. It is interesting to note that James Thompson's 1980 book, *Rolling Thunder*, has B-52s on its cover, which is almost wholly inappropriate and misleading.

50. See Slessor, *Air Power and Armies*; Mark, *Aerial Interdiction in Three Wars*; Meilinger, "John C. Slessor and the Genesis of Air Interdiction"; and Nalty, *War against Trucks*.

51. See Gates, *Sky Wars*, 88–89, 118–20; and Budiansky, *Air Power*, 306–7, 386–89.

52. See Galvin, *Air Assault*; and Stanton, *1st Cav in Vietnam*. For a gripping personal narrative of the helicopter at war in Vietnam, it would be difficult to improve upon Robert Mason, *Chickenhawk*.

53. The multinational array of actual and near disasters for air-inserted troops includes Crete 1941 (Germany), Arnhem 1944 (Britain), Dien Bien Phu 1954 (France), la Drang 1965 (US), and Khe Sanh 1968 (US). This shortest of short lists is restricted to relatively large-scale actions. The number of small-scale mishaps is legion.

54. Budiansky, *Air Power*, 388.

55. I am grateful to Ian Passingham for these details, provided in his lecture, "Helicopters in Vietnam," at the Royal United Services Institute, London, 24 July 2009.

56. See Lind, *Vietnam*.

57. See Gaddis, *Long Peace*, chap. 8, but also see Gaddis, "On Starting All over Again," 32–33, where he rejects his own concept, though not for the right reason. The long peace label is perilous to understanding because it asserts an imperial sway over an episode in international politics that policy makers at the time never dared to characterize thus. The concept is descriptively accurate in retrospect, but fuels a lack of historical empathy.

58. Builder, *Icarus Syndrome*.

59. For a few examples among many possible of my writings on nuclear strategy, see *Future of Land-Based Missile Forces*; "Nuclear Strategy"; *MX ICBM and National Security*; "Targeting Problems for Central War"; and *Second Nuclear Age*.

Chapter 7

Strategic History IV:
Strategic Moment, 1990–99

Airpower flies in a historical context that is ever shifting. That granted, there is no denying that there are periods, sometimes brief, when history appears to speed up. One might even be moved, perhaps unwisely, to judge that the course of history is punctuated and accelerated by occasional "strategic moments." Although it would be accurate to hold that each historical moment (of uncertain duration) has some strategic weight related to other moments, it is certain that the tempo of history does seem to move at variable speed. Conditions may change slowly, cumulatively, and then suddenly go critical and demand resolution. There is need for caution lest contingency and human choice are demoted unduly in comparison with the apparent compulsion imposed by great impersonal forces. Clearly it is a cardinal error to endorse a deterministic, teleological view of history. The meaning of this line of reasoning is more than mildly challenging. Post–Cold War airpower consists of both huge continuities from the past but also of swift change. A point, perhaps a temporal zone, is reached where the cumulative change produces what is to be regarded as a change of state; a breakpoint is reached. This phenomenon of apparent nonlinearity applies to the political, the military-strategic, and the technological contexts for airpower over the past 20 years.

First, the end of the Cold War as a consequence of the political demise of the Soviet polity and its empire in East-Central Europe radically altered the international order, effecting a momentous shift in the distribution of power in favor of the United States and its allies.[1]

Second, the retirement and substantial decay in erstwhile Soviet military power from much engagement with international conflict translated as a noticeable liberation for Western policy and strategy. With only modest caveats necessary, the United States was hoisted all but by default as the only super state left standing, to the agreeable but strategically challenging role of global hegemon.[2] In the early 1990s, the United States' strategic context suddenly and unexpectedly was a distinctly permissive one, but a notable trouble with such an environment is that one enjoys the discretion to make mistakes. There had been no prudent possibility of a basic change in course for

US national security policy for more than 40 years, though there were always issues over detail, of course. More missiles or fewer missiles, this ballistic missile defense (BMD) scheme or some other, or none at all, and the like, were debated vigorously. However, the whole framework for world order and the elements that did or might contribute harmfully to a perilous disorder were unchanging in their enduring foundations. The master military-strategic narrative of the Cold War conflict altered almost beyond technical and other recognition over 40-plus years, yet the geopolitical and geostrategic realities altered scarcely at all. Contrary to the logic of the modern theory of arms control, as well as to the rather less-modern theory of disarmament, the military balance in the 1990s between East and West rapidly ceased to have relevance for international security.[3] Politics rules. In the immortal words of Winston Churchill, uttered in 1934, "It is the greatest possible mistake to mix up disarmament with peace. When you have peace you will have disarmament." And so it proved, yet again, in the 1990s. Once again, the course of strategic history was striving to demonstrate the authority of the ancient truth that polities arm because they fear, at least they anticipate, that they may need to fight and not vice versa.

Third, just as political peace broke out in super- and great-power relations as the 1980s met the 1990s, so, accidentally, the tactical competence of airpower rose to unprecedented heights. The technical-tactical, or perhaps tactical-technical, narrative of advanced airpower characterized by a significantly new combat potency announced its arrival as the political context that had given it birth faded, collapsed, and died. Truly this appeared to be a classic case illustrating the familiar lament, "just when we found the answer, they changed the question." This ironic feature of history captures a central dilemma for defense planners who abruptly were deprived of their principal legitimizing and organizing threat. After 1990, America's dominant airpower was to be challenged not so much by the country's cunning and dangerous enemies, but rather by their undeniable absence, at least until 11 September 2001. One is reminded of the German black humor of 1945, which advised, "Enjoy the war, because the peace will be terrible." Democracies repeatedly have shown that eventually they wage war more effectively than they cope with peace. British and American airpower had difficult times postwar after 1918, 1945, and 1990. The United States (and Britain) has shown a distressing inability to cope strategically with prudence in contexts wherein the national strategic compass lacks clear political guidance. As the United States entered the 1990s, its airpower was tactically-technically ever more ready for strategic prime time. But the master narrative of history for the United States, albeit a United States enjoying a "unipolar moment," had so changed the schedule of programmed challenges that prime time was missing from the agenda. At least that seemed to be the case, following airpower's triumphant performance against Iraq early in 1991.

The subjects of this chapter and the next comprise two decades with sharply distinctive political and strategic profiles. The no-name post–Cold War decade of the 1990s emerged and matured as a period that permitted airpower and its related technologies almost to try to make its own future, with scant reference to the purpose of the project or to the eternal wisdom, including warnings, in the general theory of strategy. Yes, airpower appeared to be triumphant. Perhaps Billy Mitchell was vindicated at last, and so forth. But so what? What could a transforming airpower do that the United States, or indeed others, needed done strategically? By way of sharp contrast, after 9/11 that question seemed to have been answered by a grim event that provided an obvious major strategic challenge. Unfortunately, the unarguable fact of the challenge made manifest in 2001 was not matched by any like incontestability regarding strategy and tactics. High policy for national and international security in the 2000s was all too easy to devise, but strategy was not. And if airpower was America's most favored military tool in the 1990s, for reasons explored and explained below, the same would not prove to be so in the 2000s, despite indications to the contrary early in the decade, as the next chapter will explain.

As this analytical strategic history of airpower approaches and enters the most recent decades, it is especially important to ensure that the historical roots of substantial discontinuities in experience are accorded due recognition. Also, by attending carefully to the historical context of this post-1990 period, one should be able to encourage respect for the essential unity within the rapid change that has characterized the strategic history of airpower. With these desiderata very much in mind, the next section risks some apparent repetition of subject matter as it endeavors to explain whence the strategic narrative of airpower in the post–Cold War era arrived. Following this historical contextualization, the chapter proceeds to explain the strategically distinctive 1990s.

Recap: From the Past to the Brink of the Present

Radical changes in political and strategic context from one decade to the next have been almost routine over the past century. It is a challenge not to understate the contextual differences that succeeded each other so swiftly. The course of world events through the strategic history of every decade of the past 100 years demonstrated fairly distinctive master narratives. Unsurprisingly, the detail of the airpower story tracks closely with its strategic contexts. Brief as the history of airpower most certainly is relative to land power and sea power, it is now long enough even for radical shifts from one decade to another to be seen mainly as oscillations along a persisting path. It would be easy to allow technology an unduly leading explanatory role in airpower history, when really the strategic context as a whole offers more keys to understanding. While there is a vital story of technical advance to be told, that tale is hugely incomplete, indeed apt to be seriously misleading if told autonomously, as if it happened with scant reference to its strategic purpose.

Strategic contexts, including their distinctive conflicts with their characteristic form of warfare, shape and even dictate which technologies are pursued as well as the ways in which they are employed. Of course one fights with what one has, as noted earlier: necessarily, wars begin as come-as-you-are happenings. If a war is protracted, the belligerents will learn how best they can fight at an advantage, and they will have some time to learn what is best current practice for them (sound doctrine for now). They will discover how extant equipment can best be employed, and they may have the time to adapt and improve existing technologies.

The point to be emphasized here is that although the airpower story of the most recent decades certainly has had a massively influential technological dimension—as had been true throughout the brief course of airpower history—one must be careful not to be misled in strategic judgment by that fact. The argument in need of recognition is that although airpower helped shape strategic history for decade after decade, actually it was more shaped by the strategic context than vice versa. The strategic history of the 1990s and 2000s shows contrasting dominant airpower stories, but those stories largely were not controlled or controllable by airpower itself.[4] Time and again in this text it has been necessary to insist upon a serious measure of contextualization. It is not possible to explain competently what airpower tried to do and to evaluate how well it did it, let alone what strategic difference airpower made to the course of history, unless the whole strategic context is comprehended. Through the 1970s and especially the 1980s, conventionally armed airpower slowly acquired the means to be so formidable that its guardians and prophets might have aspired to seek the leading operational role in regular warfare. It is true that the technological transformation of airpower from a distinctly industrial-age cudgel in the 1960s to an information-age, somewhat stealthy rapier today increasingly offered policy makers discriminate yet still effective military choices for coercive and brute-force strategies. But it is no less true to claim that the strategic context of the 1980s was not friendly to an operational view of airpower, save in practice as a junior partner to land power.[5]

No matter how potent kinetic airpower seemed to have become or promised to become, the strategic context frustrated ambition and vision. There was no convincing way one could craft a story that allowed friendly airpower a decisively coercive role without running into catastrophic nuclear events.[6] Moreover, to recall Edward Luttwak's insistence upon the ironic nature of strategy, the more potent NATO's conventional airpower was believed to be, the stronger the Soviets' motive to offset its putatively deadly effect with chemical and nuclear weapons.[7] All the while the dominant strategic context was one of conflict between mighty states and their rival coalitions for the highest of stakes. Hence, a plausible story for the feasibility or the relevance of conventional operational airpower was hard to develop, let alone sell to rightly skeptical politicians.

Accepting some risk of repetition from the previous chapter and the peril of oversimplification, it is useful to recap the main plot in the strategic history of airpower through the Cold War, even at the expense of appearing to neglect the full, rich variety of historical experience. What follows is a terse effort to identify and relate the principal character of airpower thought and behavior to its dominant strategic context, decade by decade.

1950s—Cold War with Hot, Limited War in Korea (1950–53); Preparation for General (Nuclear) War with Soviet Union

Airpower waged limited conventional war in Korea, but that experience was not regarded officially as an authoritative precedent for future warfare. Conventionally armed airpower was considered all but wholly in the context of warfare that would be decided by, at the least would be waged with, nuclear weapons.

1960s—Cold War with Hybrid Warfare in Vietnam

Vietnam neither had the character of limited warfare that largely civilian-authored strategic theory had anticipated in the 1950s, nor resembled the all-out struggle that had been the guiding light, the True North, for the USAF for nearly two decades. The practice of air-power in the 1960s was dominated by the unanticipated demands of the hybrid warfare of the conflict over Vietnam, a conflict for which the United States lacked suitably tailored doctrine and military posture.[8] The contest for South Vietnam saw US airpower seriously un-ready for a complex kind of prime time that was not expected. As ex-plained in the previous chapter, although US airpower was tactically impressive, unsurprisingly it was suboptimal for a mission in Vietnam for which it had not been designed. Moreover, the strategic potential of that airpower was fatally compromised and inhibited by its com-mitment to an endeavor that lacked political and strategic integrity.

1970s—Cold War Warmed by Mid-1960s; Deep Chill Returned

Airpower thought and behavior sank the Vietnam experience with little trace remaining, save negatively in the form of a determination best summarized in the words "never again." For many if not most Americans, Vietnam was categorized as their regrettable entry to the short list of history's greater strategic disasters. Vietnam was pro-moted promptly to the Hall of Fame of notorious misadventures, alongside Athens' Sicilian expedition (415–13 BC) and the predomi-nantly British (with Australia and New Zealand) calamity at Gallipoli (1915). Subsequently, both Iraq and, arguably, Afghanistan were to join the historical roll call of strategic dishonor. The airpower com-munity rallied and regrouped from Vietnam, refocused on the Euro-pean theater, and seriously addressed the question of how best it could assist the Army in defending NATO's central front by truly joint endeavor. The US (and British) Army discovered with perilously uncritical enthusiasm an operational level to warfare of which it ap-proved, not realizing fully that the nature and evolving character of airpower inherently is relatively permissive, even encouraging, of operational-level thinking. In retrospect it is reasonably clear to see that, inadvertently, when US land power began to think adventurously about the design and conduct of theater-deep operations in Europe for joint forces, it was likely to stir potentially unwelcome, long-suppressed, stifled, and mislaid operational ideas from the airpower community.

1980s—Cold War Reheated near Boiling Point, Sputtered, and Faded to Oblivion—To the General Surprise

Variants of deep operations were the flavor of the decade for wishful nonnuclear combat by land forces. A potent source of hope for dramatic improvement in NATO's ability to defend in Europe was reposed in the Assault Breaker program established in 1977 by the US Defense Advanced Research Projects Agency (DARPA). The technical key to the viability of the operational concept was to be the provision of

> aircraft equipped with a radar that could detect and track vehicular traffic deep in Eastern Europe from high above NATO territory. The aircraft would pass this targeting information to units that would destroy enemy forces with air-launched standoff weapons. The goal of Assault Breaker was to field a system capable of destroying two thousand vehicles operating between twenty and one hundred kilometers behind the front lines in a span of three hours.[9]

It should be needless to say that this ambitious idea caught the Soviets' attention.

In this context it was inevitable that some air-minded people would recover notions from the past that could challenge contemporary doctrine and plans for acceptably joint behavior. Land power's official adoption of the concept of an operational level of war in 1982 was added to, perhaps multiplied by, a basket of technological advances for airpower certain to enhance and possibly transform the lethality of strikes from the sky.[10] With benefit of hindsight one can see that the stage was set in the 1980s for a classic clash of military cultures and institutional interests between land and air.

If the US Army could teach itself to think operationally instead of only tactically, so also could the Air Force. It was in no small measure paradoxical and ironic that some genuine, if admittedly qualified, enthusiasm for a joint approach to strategic and military problems should stir thoughts that had notable implications unfriendly to a land-dominated jointness. In truth, there is no stable reality to the exact meaning of joint military behavior in the appropriate balance among geographically specialized efforts. A strategically and situationally specific intelligence is needed to determine what jointness and balance mean for each conflict, even for each phase of each conflict, should the warfare proceed in such a linear way. US Army doctrine in the 1980s could mislead the unwary, because AirLand Battle clearly was approached as land-air battle. But while the main text for airpower was to function as support for a ground war in Europe, technological progress was eroding the pragmatic, if not the extant, doctrinal basis for a relationship between unequal partners that favored land power. Many factors served as a brake upon airpower thought and contingency planning in the 1980s. Most notably one must cite a healthy, potent fear of rapid escalation to nuclear use; allied reluctance to endorse, let alone help pay for, a more adventurous operational-level (conventional) strategy in Europe; technological immaturity; some conceptual timidity by the air-minded, probably not unrelated to changes in the leadership cadre of the USAF as the bomber pilots were succeeded by the fighter pilots after Vietnam;[11] and fashionable as well as authoritative views that privileged a ground-heavy emphasis as the focus of joint warfare. But cometh the hour, eventually cometh the man. In this case the call of strategic history was answered by a lieutenant colonel in the USAF, John A. Warden III, a true intellectual successor to the theorist-prophets of the Air Corps Tactical School of the 1930s.

This speedy recapitulation is provided to ensure that understanding of the post–Cold War world is well enough situated within a chronological context. The intent is to claim a vital continuity to history in general and to airpower history in particular. If this discussion has a master proposition to advance, it is that strategic history has had a greater influence on airpower than airpower has had on strategic history. Recognition that this has been so, in decade after decade, is necessary if the airpower dimension to national and international security is to be presented accurately and plausibly to those who are not strongly predisposed to privilege airpower in their strategic judgment. Performance cannot be assessed fairly in isolation from the relevant specific historical terms of reference. For example, if the political narrative for military effort is seriously weak—as was the case with France in Indochina, and then in Algeria, and, albeit less so, for the United States in South Vietnam—it follows that the military effort must thereby be strategically disabled. This is a fundamental, eternal, and universal reality of strategic history. Whether or not one assesses the emergence and maturing of airpower to be a revolutionary development, it cannot alter the fact that war by definition is political behavior.

Weapon of Choice: Operational Airpower, 1991–99

It is only two decades since the Soviet Union retired from world politics, taking with it the Cold War into the void wherein yesterday's conflicts reside.[12] Those two decades, approximately a generation in common human accounting, were, as the saying goes, a game of two halves for airpower. In the 1990s and very early 2000s, the dominant story for airpower was more or less triumphalist. But in the 2000s, following initial swift success in the toppling of Saddam Hussein's appalling regime, the airpower story was a notably modest one, especially when compared with the optimism in the theory and doctrine that had been fashionable so recently. Almost abruptly, airpower was demoted from the (near-) all-purpose solution to a range of political and strategic challenges to being, at best, simply a necessary contributor to the messy, protracted, and frustrating joint and combined projects that were (post-victory!) Afghanistan and (post-victory?!) Iraq. Instead of rereading Douhet, Mitchell, or John Warden, America's military personnel were looking for inspiration to T. E. Lawrence (of Arabia),[13] to Field Marshal Sir Gerald Templar (of Malaya fame), and to David Galula (a French soldier-theorist of counterinsurgency).[14] Inevitably, the newly ground-centric and also culture-centric strategic focus of the 2000s encouraged some demotion of airpower's relative joint standing,[15] not to mention a detectable taste of imperial nostalgia, if not envy.

A significant sign of the times was the widely praised *Counterinsurgency Field Manual* (Army FM 3-24; Marine Corps Warfighting Publication 3-33.5), jointly published by the Army and Marines on 15 December 2006 in response to an accelerating pace of strategic disaster in Iraq and a troubling resurgence of Taliban activity in Afghanistan.[16] Prominent among the remarkable nonfeatures of this publication was the near absence of recognition, let alone sophisticated appreciation, of the multidimensional value of airpower. In a supposed deeply joint era, the new American bible for counterinsurgency dedicated only 10 of its 419 pages explicitly to the airpower contribution to the COIN enterprise. It would not be accurate or fair to observe that *culture* and *cultural* are "in" while *airpower* is "out," but the former terms are employed 88 and 90 times, respectively, whereas the latter, to be polite, is rather stealthy.[17]

Contrary to appearance, perhaps, the purpose of the above comments on FM 3.24 is not so much to advance the claim that airpower is slighted, though that would not be an unreasonable or implausible position to adopt. Rather, the point is to highlight the sharp contrast between the two decades of the 1990s and most of the 2000s. The strategic contexts of the two short periods differed markedly, and as a direct and unavoidable consequence so also did the character of the challenge to airpower. Perhaps more clearly than ever before, the contrasting strategic narratives for airpower in the 1990s and the 2000s expose mercilessly why and how Gresham's Law (which holds that bad money drives out good money) applies no less to airpower: bad airpower theory, doctrine, and practice drive out good.

Airpower theory in practice, as particular historical strategies in execution, allows for a wide range of potential utility depending upon the situation. But when theorists and doctrine writers adopt a teleological and strategically deterministic view of airpower, they confuse themselves and guarantee that their favored military tool must to some extent fail to deliver on what is promised to flow strategically from its employment. As this text has sought to argue time and again, the principal strategic problem with airpower has not been, and is not, its technological and tactical immaturity. Most technical instruments improve with time, education through operational experience, and effort—airpower certainly has done so no less than others; indeed, it has advanced more and more rapidly than most others. The conceptual error is one of fundamental foundational vision. The technical history of airpower has long, possibly forever, been confused with its strategic and political history. Because the former is literally essential to the latter, the two have been collapsed into each other, indeed fused. The plainest illustration of this phenomenon has been the fusion, and confusion, of tool and consequence evident in the concept of strategic airpower. My argument is not that some airpower is not strategic; rather, I insist that airpower of every character is strategic in its meaning. The mind-set that hinders comprehension is miseducated by the belief that the history of airpower can be likened to a journey toward perfection. This "perfection of airpower" is somewhat reminiscent of anthropologist and mythologist Joseph Campbell's powerful theory of the "hero's journey."[18] Through trial and tribulation, the hero—in this

case airpower—travels ever onward and upward toward full realization of his/its promise/destiny.

What is wrong with the airpower version of the hero's journey is
that the revered tool in question is not capable of reaching Jerusalem. More to the point, the fallacy lies in the belief that Jerusalem—
meaning essentially nonjoint, strategic decision achieved by airpower acting wholly independently of other forms of military
power—eventually will be reachable. The error is a fundamental one
of what can be termed category creep. Military means, no matter
how potent, are not synonymous with military ways, and still less are
they one and the same as political goals. There is some small exaggeration for the sake of clarity in the way that this argument is
phrased here. The root of the problem is that only rarely have airpower theorists, doctrine developers, and warriors allowed the logic
of strategy to command their endeavors. The result, time after time
over the course of an exciting, all-too-action-packed 100 years, has
been a persisting conceptual failure that has undermined understanding and, hence, the intelligent practice of airpower for strategic
effect. One suspects that the sheer wonder of airpower has much for
which to answer. So great has been that wonder that many of airpower's active advocates have had difficulty accepting, if they even
comprehended, the titanium logic that requires airpower to be subordinate to strategy as well as to the character of particular conflicts.
The relationships among war, strategy, and airpower may be complex, nuanced, and sometimes chaotic, but there is no excuse for
confusion as to the proper formal cascade of authority in the hierarchy. Not for the last time in these pages, it is appropriate to observe
that for airpower to achieve more, it has to claim less. This is not an
argument for modesty as a virtue. There are strategic contexts
wherein airpower should be the leading edge of the military power
threatened and, if need be, applied coercively or for victory by denial.[19] What matters is for the military instrument of grand strategy
to be fit for the situationally specific political purpose. Given that
that purpose can vary widely, so also will airpower's strategic contribution. Airpower does not fail when it is not the sole deliverer of
strategic decision, nor when it is only a supporting element, even a
relatively minor one.

The homily offered immediately above is all too relevant to the two
post–Cold War decades. Readers need to be warned that although
historical distance is no guarantee of balanced judgment, its absence

ipso facto must render many judgments inherently suspect. Attitudes toward airpower are not unconnected from the broader and almost certainly deeper attitudes toward the politically chosen strategic projects for which it is committed. The swelling tide of victory has a way of raising all contributing elements, almost regardless of their contestable imperfections. US airpower in general performed heroically and with great tactical skill over Korea and Vietnam. But the former imbroglio was a successful stalemate, while the latter has achieved iconic status as an ill-chosen venture. For different reasons, airpower could not secure strategic success akin to victory and certainly not a victor's peace in either historical case. The airpower portion of those conflicts, though tactically very important, simply was overwhelmed in relative significance by the negative effect derived largely from political and strategic factors quite beyond its purview.

By way of sharp contrast to Korea (1950–53) and Vietnam (1965–73), the conflicts in which US airpower was engaged actively in the 1990s and very early 2000s were ones that the United States and its allies would have had difficulty losing. As mentioned earlier in this chapter, it so happened that American airpower genuinely was transformed, to use Ben Lambeth's choice of words as well as a concept generally much favored in the late 1990s in the US defense community.[20] However, today it is less obvious that airpower's undoubted triumphs in that decade and shortly thereafter were attributable to its own recently enhanced lethality, as compared with the permissive circumstances of its employment. Bluntly put, in the first post–Cold War decade airpower was assigned tasks that it could do. The strategic story of the second post–Cold War decade would be very different; at least superficially it would seem so. In fact, when properly regarded, airpower was no less useful in the 2000s than it had been in the 1990s. What changed was the feasibility of achievement of the strategic effect necessary for overall success in the conflicts of the respective brief eras.

It is difficult to contextualize airpower strategically without appearing to wish to demote its relative significance. The importance of chronology for appreciation of the force of historical context is hard to exaggerate. Undoubtedly in a technical-tactical sense, quite plausibly in an operational one, but only contestably in a strategic sense, the 1990s recorded a flowering of airpower effectiveness. The new level of potency had been many years in the making—the USAF first employed a few precision-guided munitions (PGM) in 1967, for example—but cumulatively, the complex synergistic technical-tactical reality amounted to a kinetic lethality that unarguably was new. Moreover, the novelty of airpower that seemed able to hit its targets with precision came as a revelation to many people in 1990–91 who were underinformed, ignorant, skeptical, or frankly hostile. The precision with which US airpower eventually downed the vital Paul Doumer and Thanh Hoa bridges in North Vietnam on 10 and 12 May 1972 somehow was lost in the "noise" about that year and was not recognized widely among defense professionals as heralding a revolution in warfare from the air.[21]

Such is the unmatchable advantage of reading history backwards that in long retrospect it is easy to locate the roots of the dramatic improvement in the tactical effectiveness of airpower made evident in 1991 in the war against Iraq; they grew from a host of developments stretching back at least a quarter of a century. However, to those present in real time in 1990, airpower, even the apogée of advanced airpower in its contemporary American character, did not seem to many people around the world to have near-magical strategic value. Although America's military muscle overall certainly impressed, prior to the Gulf War of 1991 the country's recent actual military achievements were somewhat short of awe inspiring. It was bizarre. On the one hand, the Soviet Union definitely had lost the Cold War to America—though it was not clear beyond all reasonable argument whether Moscow collapsed more for internal reasons, as George F. Kennan had predicted as early as 1946, than as a consequence of external pressure for which Washington could claim major-league credit.[22] On the other hand, the America that had just won the Cold War had not demonstrated much contemporary military prowess. The undoubted victories against Cuba in and over Grenada in 1983 and the successful intervention in Panama in 1989 both invited only ironic congratulation. It is probably no exaggeration to claim that in the estimation of nonprofessional observers around the world, and even of many defense specialists, as of 1990 the American armed forces still resembled a gang that could not shoot straight. This reputation for incompetence, deserved or not, was the cumulative product of the perception of an American military power that had lost the war in Vietnam (even if it won its warfare, unquestionably it did not win the war), failed to stage a successful military rescue of the hostages from downtown Tehran in 1980 (recall "Desert One"), blundered to victory in Grenada, retreated in humiliation from Beirut (remember the Marine barracks truck bomb), missed Colonel Qaddaffi but killed his daughter,[23] and took down Manuel Noriega's narco regime in Panama.

The paradox was stark. The fearsome Soviet Union had been outlasted and outcompeted by a United States that literally had an unenviably fragile military strategic record of recent decades. The modesty of America's demonstrated military competence in the 1970s and 1980s set the political stage perfectly for a US military performance in the 1990s that appeared, and indeed was, awesome. Unfortunately, too much of the political and strategic shock and awe achieved by US military prowess from Gulf War I in 1991 to Gulf War II in 2003 was felt by Americans themselves. It is an ancient tale that connects hubris to nemesis as an inevitable and merited progress. More balanced, certainly more nuanced and context-attentive assessment, tells a rather different story. But there is little doubt that although America's military mass was recognized universally as was its broad and deep technological lead over every other polity, the tactical effectiveness of US conventional forces for operational and strategic advantage did not inspire exaggerated respect at the end of the Cold War. This was a seriously mistaken opinion, as the 1990s soon revealed. Moreover, it was an error to which the more competent analysts and leadership on the Soviet General Staff had not subscribed throughout the 1980s—quite the contrary, in fact.[24]

There was an essential unity to the US airpower master narrative of 1991–2003. This focused narrative both happened to be and often was intended to be dominant in the US conflict-warfare narrative as a whole. At least in the US strategic experience of the first post–Cold War decade, airpower plainly was either the leading or the sole edge of America's sword. There were good and plausible technical reasons why this should be so, but there were even better political ones. Some readers may need reminding that in a little more than 13 years, from 1991 to 2003 inclusively, US or US-led airpower was employed with significant force on no fewer than six notable occasions. Airpower also functioned independently in an air policing role for more than a decade, enforcing "no-fly zones" over Iraq and (after 1993) Bosnia. The tactical and operational details of these principal air campaigns of the period have been well attested in histories and do not pose great persisting uncertainties of interpretation. However, the strategic histories of those campaigns are indeed more than a little controversial.

The six episodes of air warfare, major and minor, were those directed against Iraq (Operation Desert Storm), 17 January–24 February 1991; Bosnian Serbs (Operation Deliberate Force), 30 August–14 September 1995; Iraq (Operation Desert Fox), 16–19 December 1998 and after through 1999; Serbia (Operation Allied Force), 24 March–7 June 1999; Afghanistan Taliban (Operation Enduring Freedom), 7 October–23 December 2001; and Iraq (Operation Iraqi Freedom), 19 March–1 May 2003. Afghanistan 2001 and Iraq 2003 and the "wars after the wars" are discussed in chapter 8. America's post–Cold War airpower obviously was regarded by the occupants of the White House in those years as a handy tool. As the master story of Soviet-American strategic relations had been deterrence, so the main plot-line after 1990 was coercion, closely challenged for pole position by denial (or brute force). It may be recalled that coercion is the concept or the strategy that refers to the actual infliction of punishment for persuasion; painful persuasion is another way to express the idea.

In the 1970s and through the 1980s, the strategic focus of US airpower development was preeminently and understandably upon the Soviet threat to NATO-Europe. As the technologies for ever more accurate target identification and nonnuclear weapon delivery evolved, so the prospective tactical prowess of NATO, especially US, kinetic airpower began to bear the promise to deliver what might well prove to be campaign-deciding, even war-deciding, strategic effect. Some influential Soviet officials were impressed by what they anticipated to be a cumulatively dramatic improvement in the effectiveness of US-led standoff fire effects. With hindsight it would seem that most of the vastly expensive modernization of Soviet land power in the 1970s and early 1980s and its doctrinal redirection was being more than offset by the new and rapidly accelerating lethality of US/NATO precision firepower. Soviet military modernization was fueled by petro-ruble accounts recently swollen as a consequence of the astronomical oil price rises produced by Middle Eastern conflict and tension.[25]

Fortunately we will never know, but it would seem that the enhancement of the lethal potential of US and some allied airpower could never be realized for its full deterrent, coercive, or denial benefit in a strategic context laden with nuclear menace. It was not plausible to argue that the Soviet Union would concede a conventional defeat or even a stalemate rather than escalate to chemical and nuclear use.[26] Furthermore, the more anxious the Soviets became about the lethality of US smart nonnuclear firepower, the more likely were they to attempt to preempt its effect with nuclear strikes. Admittedly, the prospects for deterrence in East-West relations might be enhanced as a consequence of the logic just outlined. But once one sidelines the rational if speculative argument of abstract strategic theory and introduces real human beings, interests, cultures, and the grammar of the dynamics of conflict, the dominant storyline becomes notably opaque. On balance, America and NATO's emerging ability in the 1980s, in theory, to cripple and defeat a Soviet land power offensive in Europe by conventional means alone most probably would have served to lower the nuclear threshold rather than to enable the successful conduct of a nonnuclear theater campaign.

However, the airpower-led revolution in military effectiveness that fortunately was not tried and tested in battle against the Soviet Union was more than ready enough to achieve decisive strategic effect in the 1990s against adversaries unable to deter, resist coercion, or ultimately avoid outright military defeat. By and large, the tactical and operational detail of the six aerial campaigns of this decade-plus are not controversial, as was noted above. Since the stories of these episodes have been well narrated and analyzed at those levels, this text will confine itself to the far more controversial area of strategy. It is tempting to say strategy and politics, because strategy can make no sense in a political void. Ways to employ military means must serve political ends, both those intended and, courtesy of the law of unintended consequences, also those not anticipated or even necessarily desired. Despite the grip of that steely logic, it is not the purpose of this study to examine the political wisdom or otherwise that emerges as policy for the guidance and direction of airpower among the military instruments. Of course, the grand political narrative is, and always has been, literally critical to the strategic utility of airpower. When airpower is ordered to wage the wrong war, no manner or degree of tactical and operational excellence is likely to enable it to deliver success for policy that is politically valuable. Indeed, tactical military competence most likely will dig the pit of strategic error ever deeper. Tactical success unsoundly directed translates strategically as unintended self-harm according to the cruelly ironic logic of strategy.[27] This all but self-evidently true comment does not disable, and certainly does not delegitimize, this study. All that I am claiming is that airpower and air warfare are not synonymous with war. The trouble is that a much-favored military instrument is always at risk of guilt by association with its political guidance. It need not be the case, but often it is true to judge that airpower—and land power and sea power—fails to deliver a strategic advantage that is not achievable because of political constraint on the scope for strategic gain.

Airpower in the 1990s and early 2000s at last effected a tolerable fusion of technically driven tactical and operational competence with the classical aspirations of air theorists for "victory through airpower." For the contextual reasons of the apparently nonpermissive character of actual wars and warfare, understandable and sensible fears of nuclear catastrophe, and continuing if diminishing technical-tactical immaturity, airpower through the Cold War decades remained a work still in progress. This condition amounted strategically to a promise long remaining unfulfilled. But in the 1990s, with the virtual retirement of the great nuclear menace as an active concern, airpower was liberated as a sword arm, arguably *the* sword arm, of the only superpower left standing. And as some expert commentators observed persuasively, strategically speaking, America quintessentially was an air power.[28] Writing in 1994, historian and strategist Eliot A. Cohen observed that

> reliance on air power has set the American way of war apart from all others for well over a century. . . . Only the United States . . . has engaged in a single-minded and successful quest for air superiority in every conflict it has fought since World War I. Air warfare remains distinctively American-high-tech, cheap in lives and (at least in theory) quick. To America's enemies—past, current and potential—it is the distinctively American form of military intimidation.[29]

Cohen's claim and argument carry serious weight for an enduring authority.

Conceptual Renaissance

Even before the political revolution of the Soviet imperial political implosion of 1989–91 that effectively removed much of the restraint on US freedom of strategic action, a few theorists of airpower relit the beacon for conceptual revival. The two most responsible for a revival of airpower theory were two USAF colonels, John Boyd and John A. Warden III. Both fighter pilots, the former is most famous as the parent of the super-theory come formula of the OODA loop (observe, orient, decide, act), the latter for authoring the five rings model of aerial bombardment. Boyd's strategic thinking was a grand extrapolation and reflection on his personal experiences as an F-86 Sabre pilot dogfighting with MiG-15s over Korea. Warden was responding to the apparent operational-level, certainly strategic, deficit in Air Force thought that he discerned in the 1980s. Both men have attracted first-rate intellectual biographies.[30]

There is substantial merit in both Boyd's and Warden's theories.[31] They emphasized the contribution of the intellect to warfare, and their thought could not help but encourage strategic and operational thinking, even if only for the purpose of resistance to their logic. Boyd played a key role in the revival of the American fighter arm, especially with respect to its competency in air-to-air combat. The air force that was built and trained largely for nuclear delivery in a short war with the Soviet Union was not exactly the air force that America needed to control the sky over North Vietnam. US airpower rediscovered the temporarily lost art of dogfighting and laid claim to a dominant future by acquiring the F-15 and, especially, the F-16. If the USAF of the 1940s, 1950s, and most of the 1960s had been run by a "bomber mafia," then that of the 1970s and after, in reaction to the reality bites of Vietnam, was to be dominated by a "fighter mafia."[32] The pendulum of relative dominant influence swings as historical strategic context shifts, as it always does.

Detailed critiques of Boyd and Warden are not hard to produce, but they lack high interest for this study. What matters here is recognition that these two colonels helped in a major way to reconnect airpower with its full operational and strategic potential. Both men obliged those attentive to them to ask deep and consequential questions of a strategic nature about airpower in particular, though Boyd's theory achieved, and suffered severely from, seriously contestable mission creep. It would be profoundly unfair to criticize Boyd and his OODA loop here for a single flaw, given that his cogitations grew in grandiosity to the level where they could compete for the award as the "mother of all super-briefings." Probably only Herman Kahn could have competed with the scope and depth of Boyd's master theory briefing.[33] By way of the tersest of summary judgments, Boyd transferred to every level of conflict a concept born out of the aerial dogfight of Sabre versus MiG. To be polite and succinct, this was a leap far too far, even though it was interesting and not without merit. The basic problem is that the OODA loop does not capture conceptually the key to victory for a country as it might arguably do for a fighter pilot engaged in aerial combat. The theory emphasizes the le-

thal merit of superiority in tempo, which is not transferable to strategy and politics, at least not without so many caveats as to risk it being compromised fatally. Also, the OODA loop is simply naïve in its
treatment of adversaries, their options, and their potential to influence the course of events. Interstate conflict is not akin to single combat in the sky. That said, Boyd's theorizing is admirable for its focus
on the mind of the enemy as the center of gravity to be disabled. This
is not quite synonymous with Clausewitz's identification of the enemy's will to resist as the target, but it is notably close.[34] Boyd sought
the spiritual, mental, or psychological disablement and even destruction of the adversary as an effective contestant rather than its physical
impairment. He stressed the potency of the ability to outthink and
prospectively so outmaneuver an enemy who would be disoriented,
confused, disabled, all but paralyzed, and, as a consequence, defeated.

While John Boyd was leading an intellectual and procurement insurgency against an airpower that recently had been caught danger-
ously undertrained and poorly equipped for air warfare, so Warden
led an insurgency against airpower that had ceased to think or plan to
behave as an air power true to its potential should. Somehow, some-
where, because seriatim modern airpower had focused on nuclear
war—and then by force majeure on air control, air interdiction, and
close air support—operational air war was missing from the action.
Warden authored a thesis in 1986–87 at the National Defense University that became a book which revived the dreams, hopes, and ambitions of the airpower theorists of the interwar years. Warden's theory
did differ markedly from the ideas of the ACTS and of the prewar
RAF, but more significantly, it was fundamentally the same story of
victory through airpower. In his 1989 book, *The Air Campaign: Planning for Combat*, Warden argues forcefully that airpower "can do it."
But the ACTS in the 1930s sought to defeat the enemy primarily by
physically damaging and destroying the key nodes, the bottlenecks,
in its "industrial web." RAF thought on bombardment tended to
identify civilian morale—via much damage and destruction, admittedly—as the real target.[35] Warden, and Boyd to some degree, sought
victory by disruption and paralysis. Biologically expressed, Warden
believed that kinetic airpower could disable an enemy by damaging
its nervous or control system rather than by cutting away its muscle
and draining its blood. The American airpower that John Warden
had very much in mind should be capable of an exactitude of precise
military achievement of which the ACTS in the 1930s could barely

dream, or so he believed, at least. Thinking organically of the enemy as a system in best 1930s style, Warden updated comprehensively the theories of the classic airpower theorists.[36] The US airpower that as early as April 1972 could drop the Thanh Hoa bridge with only five sorties employing laser-guided bombs, after failing utterly over three years previously with 873 sorties employing iron bombs, was ready by 1991 to do the heavy lifting for strategy. If Warden were to be believed and followed, airpower alone could secure all of the strategic effect that the grand anti-Iraqi coalition required.

Many critics of John Warden lose the plot and allow the more obvious weaknesses in his theory to obscure the merit in his work. His famous, infamous to some, model of targeting specified a notional abstract enemy as consisting of five rings from inside (bullseye) to outside proceeding thus by target categories: (1) leadership, (2) essential industry, (3) transportation and communications infrastructure, (4) civilian population (morale of), and (5) fielded military forces.[37] This was the core of the matter, though the exact domain of each category was subject to some flexibility in definition and applications. His theory is more than a little Jominian; it is highly prescriptive.[38] As much to the point, it is somewhat mechanistically prescriptive. Furthermore, he does appear to insist that his master targeting template can fit all enemies. Warden argued that airpower can wage operational-level air warfare that should have the result of controlling the enemy by paralyzing its ability to function strategically, if indeed it can function at all. The focus would be on the enemy's center of gravity, identified as its leadership and its ability to command and control.

It is not hard to criticize Warden. For example, one might well prefer to schematize the enemy as a target employing the geometry of the Venn diagram, with its suggestive overlapping inclusivities, rather than the classic dartboard of Warden's concentric circles. Also, the theory suggests that the strategic effects of aerial bombardment are calculable, contrary to historical experience and common sense.[39] It has to be noted that even if the logic of Warden's targeting-for-victory theory were sound, its relevance is always liable to be subverted lethally by lack of exact information about, and understanding of, the enemy. Moreover, real live enemies, no matter how accurately mapped and diagrammed, are always going to be adaptive systems enjoying considerable redundancies for the performance of vital functions. Despite these among many possible charges against Warden, the fact remains that he sounded a loud trumpet for a genuinely operational and strategic approach to airpower. It must be obvious, although I am less than persuaded that John Warden discovered the golden key to unlock airpower's potential, that nonetheless I am deeply impressed by his willingness and his ability to think ambitiously about the subject.

For a bold claim that admittedly risks overreaching, Warden's conceptual demarche on behalf of conventional airpower in the late 1980s was the first of its kind with logical merit to appear for more than 40 years. It was sophisticated in its focus upon leadership and command ability, and it was ever more plausible, given the revolutionary advances being achieved in C4ISTAR (command, control, communications, computers, intelligence, surveillance, target acquisition, and reconnaissance). Warden's book, briefings, and articles not only presented a genuinely operational-level view of airpower's contribution to strategic success, they also offered a grand narrative for kinetic airpower that carried the promise to deliver all of the effect for strategic success that the country would need. The details differed, of course, but Warden's message was the same as Douhet's, Mitchell's, Trenchard's, and the ACTS's: it was the claim for victory through unaided airpower. All too predictably, Warden and his five rings theory fell afoul of hostile competing interests as well as of sincerely held opposing views. Moreover, it has to be said that Warden's theory suffered, deservedly, as a result of its weaknesses and, less deservedly, as a consequence of the personality of its author. Not many prophet-geniuses in strategic history have themselves been wholly effective communicators; large egos and aggressive style tend to invite antagonism. But when all is said and done, John A. Warden III almost single-handedly kick-restarted serious theorizing about airpower considered operationally and strategically.

Warden's critics have tended to miss the point that his vision of airpower's utility in the main is plausible. He was right to insist that airpower can and should strive to deliver decisive operational, for strategic, effect. Indeed, he was right, albeit for the wrong reasons, in 1988 when he denounced Billy Mitchell's unwise 1916 distinction between tactical and strategic airpower.[40] When Warden's theory is considered in relation to the general theories of airpower and of strategy, much that is patently unsound about it falls away, leaving truly precious metal if not entirely pure gold. It is of great importance to the progress of this narrative to recognize that John Warden and John Boyd, considered together, bequeathed to the 1990s and the 2000s a theory of conventional kinetic airpower hugely more ambitious than was authoritative, or even operationally feasible, in previous decades. There was an essential correctness, at least to the path that those theorists lit, from which airpower's practitioners would prove both unable and unwilling to deviate very much, at least until the strategic context altered in the 2000s. The Cold War and its nuclear shadow had all but chained conventional airpower thought and behavior for the better part of 50 years. Boyd and especially Warden provided necessary intellectual stimuli for airpower to exploit the newfound opportunities opened up by the demise of the Cold War antagonism.

Now it is necessary to reengage with the strategic historical narrative, a duty that is met by providing brief strategic assessments of the principal episodes of airpower action in the 1990s and early 2000s. The story continues up to date in the next chapter, which treats the conflicts of the 2000s. Readers should be aware that these terse strategic overviews of recent and contemporary episodes are designed noticeably to contextualize the aerial dimension. I am convinced that airpower quite generally has not been approached and assessed properly. More to the point, airpower continues to escape sound understanding. In that regard I am gratified to record my agreement with William M. Arkin when he wrote,

> The task at hand then is to tell the story of an airpower-dominated campaign [Israel vs. Hezbollah, 12 July–14 August 2006], one that was deeply flawed in its design yet impressive in its efficiency, without being either pedantically fault-finding or apologetic about a modern instrument that is still little understood, even by its practitioners.[41]

It is commonplace to observe that we hurt most the ones we love. That maxim has applied all too often to the effort expended by defenders of, and advocates for, airpower. Time after time the case for airpower has suffered severe political damage that has had adverse strategic consequences as a direct result of friendly fire. This text tries to improve on that record.

Gulf War I: Iraq, 17 January–28 February 1991

An important maxim claims that the enemy too has a vote in war, but in 1991 Iraq proved to be one of history's rare exceptions to the rule. The coalition that the United States assembled for the purpose of ejecting Iraqi forces from Kuwait waged a war that it could lose only as a result of extraordinarily bad luck or incompetence, or both. The war was brief and conclusive in regard to the Iraqi temporary seizure of oil-superrich Kuwait, but the coalition's unarguably decisive military victory was not quite the strategically, let alone politically, decisive success that the United States and others both desired and anticipated with confidence. The familiar problem was that the outcome of the warfare, and indeed of the interstate war itself, could not dictate the desired political consequences. While in a vital sense war is violent politics, nonetheless it is not synonymous with politics. The 42-day war was a military triumph for the US-led coalition—of that there was no doubt.[42] However, in retrospect it is plausible to argue that Washington and its closer NATO partners expended so much political effort and capital in gathering the coalition in the run-up to the fighting that they had too little energy and political will leftover for the prudent exploitation of their well-merited victory. It is necessary to remember that in 1990–91 Iraq enjoyed a formidable military reputation. It had initiated, waged, survived, and at least did not lose an eight-year war with revolutionary Iran.[43] In addition to its enormous army numbering around 1.1 million men, which may have ranked fourth in the world for size (experts differ), its air force certainly enjoyed a global ranking of sixth, its well-integrated air defense system looked competent or better, and Saddam Hussein's regime maintained an elite private army in its Republican Guard divisions. In southwestern Iraq and Kuwait, Saddam had deployed approximately 600,000 troops. For its part, the coalition fielded nearly 550,000 troops and deployed close to 1,800 aircraft.

Just four large points will suffice to interpret the Gulf War of 1991 for this study. First, although it is highly plausible to argue that the coalition would have won this war no matter what strategy it had adopted, there is little doubt that the strategy that was adopted illustrated yet again the wisdom in Sun Tzu's advice to attack the enemy's strategy.[44] In a phrase popular in the United States in this period—and subsequently, since it has come around again in the late 2000s on the familiar conceptual carousel—the coalition chose to pursue a very effectively competitive strategy.[45] Saddam did not expect to have to fight, but if that proved erroneous, evidently he was confident that his army would impose attritional warfare such that the will of the mighty-looking enemy would bend and break. He was wrong. GEN Norman Schwarzkopf was able to wage so effective a war of maneuver, led and enabled by airpower, that Iraqi forces were unable to achieve the bloodletting that was required of them—save, alas, painfully with respect to their own casualties.

Second, the decisively successful maneuver effected by coalition ground forces, though impressive if somewhat obvious and incomplete, in truth was a walkover, actually a dash around, perhaps. The principal, though not sole, reason why the ground war was won so easily was coalition command and exploitation of the air. Coalition airpower achieved control of the air by fatally disabling Iraq's air defense system in the first 24 hours of the war. The subsequent 26 days of bombardment from the air prior to the launching of the ground offensive at 4 a.m. (local time) 23 February all but comprehensively destroyed, damaged, disabled, and demoralized the nominal Iraqi capability to resist. The better histories of the war agree on the decisive role played by airpower. For example, a much praised study claimed without equivocation that "the key to victory was complete mastery of the air."[46] Another historian has offered a like verdict that expresses a view that truly has not been seriously controversial ever since the dust and smoke settled in 1991. John Andreas Olsen advises persuasively that

> in assessing the speed and scale of the victory, it is important to grasp that coalition accomplishments were, in large measure, made possible by the comprehensive air offensive. The fighting on the ground unfolded without the fluctuating fortunes that normally mark major military campaigns because air operations, with more than 1,800 combat aircraft in action, roughly 110,000 flights recorded, and more than 90,000 tons of aerial ordnance delivered, had decided the fate of the battle well before the ground offensive began.[47]

Essential though it probably was to conduct a ground campaign, it is beyond argument that the heaviest lifting for overall strategic effect was done by airpower. Even had Saddam's army sought to conduct a war of maneuver, it would have been unable to do so. Iraq suffered an extreme variant of the disablement of its army that Germany also had suffered in North Africa in 1942–43 and then in France in 1944. The disabling effect of enemy air supremacy is manifested in both material and psychological damage; John Boyd was at least partially correct.[48] Employed against Iraq in 1991, coalition airpower did not quite win the war unaided, but assuredly its positive strategic effect decided who would win the war, and it enabled the warfare to be conducted in the style preferred.

Third, the air-led warfare waged by the coalition was, alas, consistent with both political success and failure. Operation Desert Storm was a political triumph in that it was a UN-blessed campaign triumphantly conducted by a multinational coalition to eject Iraqi forces from Kuwait as its core legitimizing objective. However, there was some confusion among broader objectives. Iraq's military power needed to be defeated and indeed reduced for the longer term. But should Iraq be too reduced strategically, the result would be a much undesired strategic elevation of revolutionary Iran in the regional balance of power. It was expected in Washington, London, and some other capitals that military humiliation and damage would trigger domestic revolts and probably a coup that would remove Saddam Hussein and possibly the Ba'ath Party from power. There were opportunistic sectional revolts in the North and the South, but both were suppressed savagely by a regime whose ability to coerce was not fatally compromised. For several reasons, good and less so, Schwarzkopf halted the warfare far short of the complete military disabling of the regime. Coalition airpower had not decapitated, probably one can say that it had not been able to decapitate, the regime in Baghdad, though it had damaged and harassed it severely. The Iraqi leadership was hindered by coalition airpower to the point of near ineffectiveness in its ability to conduct the war coherently, but it survived well enough, as subsequent events demonstrated clearly. Saddam could retreat, rally, regroup, reorganize, recover, and exact revenge on his domestic enemies, and the coalition proved unable or unwilling to prevent his doing so. Airpower performed magnificently. It disabled and all but paralyzed the regime's ability to command and approached the historically unprecedented goal of 50 percent disablement of enemy ground forces prior to initiation of the land campaign. But airpower could not magically cut through the political confusion caused by the genuine conundrum that impaired the coalition's political peacemaking behavior. The Gulf War of 1991, triumph though it certainly was for the coalition and especially for coalition airpower, reaffirmed the eternal lessons that excellent tactical performance guided by clearly focused strategy must be devalued when policy is not fit for the necessary purpose. The victory that airpower decided in 1991 was insufficient for the political story that the coalition really required; but to say that is, unimpressively, to be wise after the event.

Fourth, whatever the wisdom or lack thereof in the policy content to the political context for the Gulf War, there seemed to be little room for doubt that the actual coalition warfare revealed what to many observers were startlingly novel military capabilities. Though quite long heralded and even demonstrated on a minute scale against Manuel Noriega's Panama in 1989, the new prowess in precise and stealthy air warfare attracted maximum public and official attention. The debate took a few years to mature, but by mid-decade in the 1990s, strategic debate was well and truly underway on the merit in the proposition that an information-led air revolution in military affairs (RMA), keyed to the computer, was underway.[49] The great RMA debate actually had been long gestating, but the dazzling success of US-led airpower in 1991 provided most of the fuel necessary for speculative argument. With the formal demise of the Soviet Union on 25 December 1991, the United States and its ever more potent airpower looked to be fit to accomplish any purpose. A disabling trouble was, of course, that for the next decade the United States, though glorious in its suddenly solitary superpower status, lacked for an overriding major political purpose. Clear and present danger was mercifully absent for the first time since the 1930s. This happy condition was not quite so agreeable for the United States, indeed the Western extended defense community, because prudent defense planning is always hard to do in a condition of profound political uncertainty. Defense planners feed well on threats.[50]

The largely American RMA debate, which morphed into a debate marginally about transformation, was a distinctly astrategic, possibly even antistrategic, exercise. Though certainly well enough rooted both in the commonsense thesis that from time to time there are changes in the grammar of warfare that merit the label *revolutionary* and in the plausible promise of computer-led technological advances currently well under way, still the RMA theory was and largely remained significantly divorced from vital contextual considerations. Strategy-lite or strategy-absent military theory invites strategic and political disappointment, and so it was to prove. The American technology-led RMA, proclaimed by a host of military experts as being on the cusp of dispersing the fog of war, was to falter and fail strategically because it was not sufficiently grounded in an understanding either of war or of warfare. Michael Howard's justly famous considerations of width, depth, and context were all unduly neglected or at best employed inappropriately on the advocacy side of the RMA debate.[51]

Contrary to appearances, perhaps, the argument in the paragraph immediately above claims only that the subject of RMA was poorly handled, not that it was meaningless. I certainly do accept the proposition that revolutionary changes in military capability have been achieved over the course of the past quarter century. But as always should be the case, what is needful is an answer to the strategist's question "So what?" The US-led coalition was a war in 42 days in 1991 that indeed was decided by airpower. But that war would have been won even had coalition airpower not been so lethal. So airpower won the war that was waged, but it is not plausible to maintain that the war could not have been won had coalition airpower been much less potent than was the case. Strategic judgment as to the relative virtue of a military instrument has to be calibrated for the scale of the challenge. It is worth noting that the authors of the summary volume of the USAF's *Gulf War Air Power Survey (GWAPS)*, Thomas A. Keaney and Eliot A. Cohen, titled the work intriguingly, *Revolution in Warfare? Air Power in the Persian Gulf.* In a subsequent article published prominently in *Foreign Affairs*, Cohen or his editor omitted the question mark from his title, "A Revolution in Warfare."[52] At a conference held in the immediate wake of Desert Storm, Luttwak offered these appropriate judgments:

> The outcome of the air campaign against Iraq was more unexpected than it should have been. Seventy years of overpromising by air power advocates had left a deep residue of distrust in Washington's military culture. Because air power was thought to have failed in Indo-China in some very general sense and because it was not deemed to have been decisive in the Korean or the Second World War, many people believed that its role against Iraq would also be indecisive—with some of them expecting outright failure, as that term was variously defined. These negative expectations overlooked the profound implications of both the permanently *situational* character of air power and of its novel capabilities. In fairness, the air power advocates of the past also slighted the supremely situational character of air power in making claims for it independently of the context.[53] (emphasis in the original)

Bosnia, 30 August–14 September 1995, and Iraq, 16–19 December 1998 and through 1999

Airpower's triumphal procession through the 1990s registered ambiguous success in two significant episodes in the mid-to-late part of the decade. In the first case, when employed to coerce recalcitrant Bosnian Serbs in the summer of 1995, airpower seemed to deliver strategic decision for a tolerable political outcome. But in the second episode, when employed to coerce Iraq late in 1998, airpower was strategically useful more because of its standoff distancing nature rather than for reason of any particular anticipated strategic consequences. Both cases are instructive. They had in common a self-perceived Western political need for firm-looking action. In both instances airpower served its political purpose, though in the case of Iraq in 1998 the strategy looks today, as it did to many observers at the time, to have been ill designed, notwithstanding its obvious political utility. Admittedly, this is contestable. One must admit, albeit with serious misgivings, that there can be occasions when strategic utility is not to be sought reliably in any close relation to immediate military or even strategic consequences. For an extreme example, it is possible to derive net strategic benefit in a worthy cause from tactical military failure. One may cite the Spartan sacrifice at Thermopylae as a classic, indeed classical, example of this ironic truth of strategic history.

Acting as a muscular sword-arm for the United Nations Protection Force (UNPROFOR) in Bosnia in the summer of 1995, NATO undertook Operation Deliberate Force to coerce the Bosnian Serbs. In summary,

- NATO air units flew 3,535 sorties and dropped more than 1,100 bombs, losing only a single aircraft. As intended, collateral damage was minimal—Serb deaths numbered slightly more than two dozen. Precision munitions accounted for nearly three-quarters of those expended.[54]

- The purpose of the air campaign was to "inflict pain but not death," in the words with which UNPROFOR's French commander, Gen Bernard Janvier, expressed the strategic intention to coerce.[55]

The Bosnian Serbs were making a mockery of the UN's commitment to provide and police "safe areas" for Bosnia's Muslims and needed to be persuaded to halt or at least be much more restrained in their incursions and their violence toward both civilians and UNPROFOR units, as well as against armed Bosnian Muslims. The targets for the air campaign primarily comprised Serb heavy weapons (approximately 250 of them), initially those deployed in the hills around the besieged city of Sarajevo. Notwithstanding the statistical fact that Deliberate Force was the first air campaign wherein the ordnance overwhelmingly was delivered with navigational aids for true precision, the leading historian of the episode offers an illuminating contextual caveat. Robert C. Owen advises,

> Despite first impressions, however, precision weapons were not critical to the successful outcome of Deliberate Force. Indeed, under the specific circumstances of the conflict, the *fact* of the bombing was more important to Serb calculations than

its *means*. Serb resistance collapsed in the face of NATO's clear determination and ability to destroy key targets of military value.[56] (emphasis in the original)

Owen argues persuasively that while precision-guided weapons made it easier for NATO to decide to act, indeed reduced collateral damage and reduced the needed scale of air sorties, the coercive task could have been achieved with dumb bombs. Deliberate Force was not in its targeting a strategic air campaign as defined by orthodox theory and doctrine. But assuredly, it was potently strategic in its coercive effect upon the increasingly beleaguered Bosnian Serbs.[57] The focus of the campaign was distinctly military—close air support and battlefield interdiction—which was just the kind of strategic effect that the Serbs needed if they were to be coerced. The whole context for NATO air strikes included a resurgent Croatian military effort, increasing military competence on the part of Bosnia's Muslims, more-effective NATO military measures on the ground, and a waning of political (and more substantive) support from Belgrade and even Moscow. It would be a considerable exaggeration to claim that Deliberate Force alone delivered the Bosnian Serbs in an abruptly if ungraciously acquiescent mood and primed for political agreement. But it is plausible to argue that the air campaign was physically and psychologically important, and perhaps decisively so. Airpower had been employed successfully for coercion. By 13–14 September the Bosnian Serb leadership realized that it was now seriously overmatched militarily by its enemies. Those enemies seemed both able and now politically willing to accept the costs that would be entailed in reversing the Bosnian Serbs' bloody adventure in national assertion at the expense of other ethnicities. Airpower was employed successfully.

Whereas airpower unquestionably was used to productive strategic effect in 1995 over Bosnia, quite the reverse was the case with reference to the Desert Fox exercise of 16–19 December 1998, as well as the months of desultory aerial bombardment succeeding that brief episode.[58] If anything, Operation Desert Fox—a title which risks the charge of being a slander against the military genius of Field Marshal Erwin Rommel—can stand as an icon for the misuse of airpower. The short air campaign was far more a case of expressive violence than the execution of anything worthy of being called a strategy unless, of course, one is prepared to label hope a strategy. In the face of substantive and politically token insult to the United Nations and the United States and its allies over the issue of arms inspection relevant to prohibited so-called weapons of mass destruction (WMD), Washington and London decided that "something must be done"—the classic phrase that usually signals strategic impotence.

The several political contexts were not exactly permissive of bold coercive action on the US and British part. The usual suspects on the UN Security Council were eager to lift sanctions against Iraq. In addition, the American and British publics, and certainly the publics in other NATO countries, were not excited or apparently capable of being excited in the near term by the unmistakable evidence of Iraqi disdain for its formal, if not terribly solemn, international obligations. In such unpromising political circumstances—since "soft power" in all its forms was entirely irrelevant—the only options reduced to a choice between a humiliating tacit acquiescence or a strategically futile but somewhat honor-preserving exercise of force.[59] The force had to be delivered from the air because, self-evidently, there was no appetite anywhere in 1998–99 for another invasion of Iraq.

The four-day exercise in intended coercion in December 1998 was an exercise in strategic futility, as was the episodic but frequent bombardment that succeeded it through 1999. The Clinton administration seemed not to understand that strategy and tactics differ. US and British airpower was employed with great skill, and in safety at altitude (no casualties), against actual and suspected military facilities and especially air defense elements, but not in realistic quest of a strategically decisive purpose. The purpose, to topple Saddam Hussein, was appropriate enough, though this was far more an ambitious aspiration than a goal well matched to allied ways and means. The Desert Fox bombing most probably was intended to encourage, even trigger, a coup that would effect regime change in Baghdad. Political leadership facilities were targeted as were command and control facilities. Attacks on the barracks of the regime's praetorian guards, the Republican Guard and the Special Republican Guard, resulted in more than 1,000 fatalities.[60] The bombing may well have promoted local unhappiness with Saddam's misgovernance as well as the understandable annoyance with the bombers, but alas, such unhappiness was not translated into action for regime change, effective or ineffective. The fact appears to have been that Saddam and his henchmen essentially had coup-proofed their misrule by 1998. Most certainly Iraq was all but immune to political decapitation or to revolt as a consequence of the force that the United States was willing and able to apply at that time. Airpower was highly constrained by political considerations from targeting installations collocated with civilians or from taking risks with the lives of aircrew. Moreover, given that there was no prospect whatsoever of joint supporting or supported military force on the ground, it was hard to discern a functioning strategic brain on the US and British side. Washington appeared not to appreciate the danger that it was so misusing its world-premium airpower in an astrategic manner against Iraq in 1998–99 that, ironically, it was demonstrating lack of resolve rather than determination. In truth, the United States and Britain showed emphatically that they were not politically prepared to attempt decisive action. Exercise of a standoff power safely at altitude, employed with high precision and great restraint, sent exactly the wrong political and strategic message to Saddam Hussein. More important, though, was the likelihood that the United States foolishly was inviting some international devaluation of the respect in which it, and especially its fearsome air weapon, was held. And this might matter, should Washington need to be respected and feared. As it was, through 1999, "*after* Desert Fox, US and British warplanes unloaded nearly 2,000 missiles and precision guided bombs against several hundred targets scattered throughout Iraq" (emphasis in the original).[61] This may have provided good tactical exercise for American airpower—experience usually is useful—but it certainly was terrible strategy in aid of politically ill-judged policy. Belatedly, the Clinton administration effected a policy creep into the zone of regime change in Baghdad. All that was lacking was the political will and political context necessary for this sentiment to be of live relevance. For those conditions to be fulfilled, there needed to be a change in American leadership and a radical shift in American perception of its strategic environment.

The Balkans Again: Kosovo, 24 March–7 June 1999

To adapt for our purpose Jane Austen's opening words in *Pride and Prejudice*, "it is a truth universally acknowledged" that politics rules, often overrules, and certainly misrules the realm of airpower. It should be some consolation to air-minded persons to appreciate that their subjection to matters political is far from being a singular condition. Politics governs and misgoverns the entire military project; that is simply how it is as well as how it needs to be. It is ironic that the air warfare conducted against Serbia by NATO over the issue of governance in the Serbian province of Kosovo has to be judged both a victory for airpower and also a dreadful example of strategic, even astrategic, misconduct. Luttwak indeed wrote truly when he argued that strategy is paradoxical and ironic. In a way, the success of US-led NATO airpower in the coercion of Serbia over Kosovo in 1999 is especially impressive, given the ample reasons why it might have failed. As in high-diving competitions, the marking of strategic performance needs to be calibrated for degree of (largely structural) difficulty of the particular enterprise. It would have been a lesser strategic challenge had NATO been able to decide to inflict a decisive military defeat on Serbia in and about Kosovo. Instead, the decision to coerce Slobodan Milosevic was considerably harder. There is a dual problem attendant upon coercion by airpower. First, there is the general challenge posed by the fact that the intended coercee is at liberty to decline to be coerced. In short, Milosevic had to choose to cooperate and allow himself to be coerced. While the United States and its NATO allies largely could control how much hurt they would inflict on Serbia, they could not control reliably the Serbian political response. Second, airpower in action, unlike ground power taking territory in land warfare of a regular character, does not achieve readily measurable gains. Aerial bombardment imposes damage upon the enemy, but so what? This question inherently is difficult to answer with high confidence. Airpower itself cannot shift visible and tangible territorial control such that one can know how well one is faring strategically. By a wide margin, damage assessment and strategic assessment need not be the same.

The somewhat negative cast to this discussion thus far should not be permitted to mislead. It is a fact that US-led airpower achieved a justly famous, even unprecedented and hence historic, victory with its successful employment in the coercion of Serbia from 24 March to 7 June 1999. Though it suffers in its impact from the familiarity resulting from excessive repetition in quotation (much as does the force of Baldwin's 1934 over-quoted and unsound aphorism claiming that "the bomber will always get through"), there is no evading the necessity to quote British historian Sir John Keegan's apostate words in strategic praise of the performance of airpower over Kosovo.

> There are certain dates in the history of warfare that mark real turning points. Now there is a new turning point to fix on the calendar: June 3, 1999, when the capitulation of President Milosevic proved that a war can be won by air power alone. . . . The air forces have won a triumph, are entitled to every plaudit they will receive and look forward to enforcing a transformed status in the strategic community, one they have earned by their single-handed efforts.[62]

Keegan was somewhat correct; certainly he was more correct than were many among airpower's critics who sought, and of course identified, a wide mix of explanations for Milosevic's surrender that were alternatives to coercion by airpower. Existentially regarded, NATO's quarrel with Serbia unquestionably was prosecuted by the action of a single military means: airpower employed coercively. The evidence for Milosevic being coerced more by the fear of a NATO intervention with land forces than he was by the exercise of airpower is distinctly uncertain. What does need to be claimed in regard to Kosovo, as may yet be true with respect to Afghanistan a decade and more later, is that Serbia (and the Afghan Taliban?) lost the political contest of wills. The war about control of Kosovo revealed itself more accurately to be a war with the future of NATO as the primary perceived stake. The NATO allies discovered that they were far less committed to defeating Milosevic than they were to preserving the alliance. In one key strategic respect not entirely unlike Dowding's RAF Fighter Command in the summer of 1940, NATO in 1999 won against Milosevic's Serbia significantly as a consequence of the strength of its determination not to lose, or as much to the point, not to be seen to lose.[63]

By way of brief political background and context, the Kosovo crisis of 1999 had been brewing for years, because although it was a province of Yugoslavia and then of Serbia and had legendary iconic value pertaining painfully to Serbian national identity, by the 1990s its population was largely Albanian. Milosevic played upon Serbian ethno-religious hostility and anxieties regarding the Muslim Albanian Kosovars to undertake a process of ethnic cleansing, meaning forced expulsion of those unwanted by him in Kosovo (save as a valuable target for his regime to exploit for domestic political advantage). Serbian oppression, brutality, and even some atrocities worthy of the label accelerated and grew in scale through 1998. Violence by the Yugoslavian/Serbian army, as well as by Albanian Kosovars (the Kosovo Liberation Army, or KLA), produced a crisis situation. The international community, through the United Nations—though effectively by NATO, led in a humanitarian outrage by Britain's faith-driven prime minister, Tony Blair—decided that "something must be done," that ominously familiar astrategic demand.

Milosevic declined to be deterred from his efforts to expel the Albanian Kosovars and failed to restrain the violent thuggery of Serbian irregulars who were enjoying their cleansing efforts. As a result—reluctantly for the most part, belatedly, and in practical consequence half-heartedly—NATO proceeded to attempt to coerce Milosevic by aerial bombardment. Militarily this was the most that NATO could agree to do, while strategically and politically it was expected that even such a limited character of coercion easily would prove sufficient. Eventually NATO optimists were proved correct, but it transpired that Milosevic's Serbs were a tougher strategic foe than had been expected. The bombardment was anticipated by NATO to last only for three or four days, following which Milosevic, having taken some distinctly modest amount of pain, would be able to concede with a little honor still intact. But this agreeable script was not followed. The expected four-day war endured for a full 78 days instead. To risk understating the matter, Serbia's refusal to "cry uncle" proved deeply politically embarrassing to NATO, even humiliating, and it risked taking the edge and more off the reputation for reliable deadly effectiveness and persuasiveness that US airpower had garnered since Desert Storm in 1991.

Some readers may have noticed that this study has been careful not to refer to NATO's aerial endeavor over Kosovo as an air campaign. I am amply persuaded by Ben Lambeth's reasons for declining to accord it that dignity. Tellingly and conclusively, Lambeth finds that the air war in question did not meet the requirements specified by extant USAF doctrine for an air campaign. The then-contemporary official wording (as of 1997) defined an air campaign as "a connected series of operations conducted by air forces to achieve joint force objectives within a given time and area." In Lambeth's convincing judgment,

> By that standard [quoted immediately above], NATO's air war for Kosovo did not attain to the level of a campaign, as did the earlier Operations Desert Storm [1991] and Deliberate Force [1995]. Rather, it was a continuously evolving coercive operation featuring piecemeal attacks against unsystematically approved targets, not an integrated effort aimed from the outset at achieving predetermined and identifiable operational effects.[64]

Most NATO members could agree that something had to be done to try to arrest the accelerating pace of humanitarian disaster, not least because Kosovo was integral to the entire conflict in the Balkans in the 1990s. That conflict amounted to an interconnected and interdependent, overlapping series of wars of Yugoslavian succession. In practice, the main issue tended to be the question of a Greater, or Lesser, Serbia. Unfortunately NATO's tepid-to-medium enthusiasm for doing something to discipline Milosevic legally in his own country was not matched by a willingness to apply whatever force might prove necessary to ensure political compliance. As this section claimed at its outset, politics rules. It can be true to argue also that values rule, but such cases tend to be restricted to those wherein strategic success is expected to be achieved cheaply and, even then, preferably by the efforts of others.[65] In the case of Kosovo, as noted already, strategic success was anticipated to be a swift "slam dunk." Also, as has been claimed, the most potent value at stake for NATO countries over Kosovo was not the human rights of the Kosovars; rather was it the reputation and possibly the very future of the alliance itself. That was the reason why NATO dared not permit Milosevic to win.

Nonetheless, it must be granted that the air warfare waged by NATO was conducted so poorly that Milosevic was accorded more than the common measure of good future in war. I must hasten to claim that the reasons why NATO's largely American airpower was applied in strategically so air-unprofessional a manner had little to do with its own limitations. Airpower could only be as effective as circumstances permitted, and those circumstances were awesomely constraining. Since airpower is a military instrument of grand strategy that can have meaning only in political terms, it is not entirely appropriate to offer an assessment of this air war in a way that finds incompetence, if not quite villainy, in NATO policy. It is not unusual for air warfare to be constrained strategically, operationally, and tactically by explicitly political considerations. Moreover, those considerations frequently will offend against the professional military grammar of strategy, operations, and tactics. British and German political guidance for bombing strategy in 1939–40 (until September) was highly constrained (e.g., London was off limits to the Luftwaffe). Kosovo was frustrating for air professionals, but so had been Korea and Vietnam. Lambeth issued a heartfelt caveat on the often inappropriate employment of kinetic airpower for diplomatic effect when he wrote,

> Although it can be surgically precise when precision is called for, air power is, at bottom, a blunt instrument designed to break things and kill people in pursuit of clear and militarily achievable objectives. Not without reason have air warfare professionals repeatedly insisted since Vietnam that if all one wishes to do is "send a message," call Western Union.[66]

Lambeth is mainly right to register skepticism about the efficacy of collapsing airpower into diplomacy. Nonetheless, the existential realities of contemporary military operations with which airpower must cope only limit, they do not cancel, the authority of politics. The bottom-line judgment on NATO's air war over Kosovo is that it was good enough to play its essential part in generating the strategic effect necessary to bring Milosevic politically to heel. Airpower professionals have to come to terms with the enduring fact that their military instrument will always be constrained in its application by political guidance—or even, ironically, by its absence—as well as by the myriad other harassments that can inhibit performance. On balance, it is probably safe to claim that NATO waged as much warfare over Kosovo as effectively as the political context of the time permitted. Furthermore, for an ironic thought that will not please military professionals, it was only the curbing authority exercised by militarily unwise, certainly suboptimal, essentially political inhibitions that politically enabled the warfare to be waged at all. If this reasoning is sound—which I regret to have to claim that it is—it should follow logically that, in principle at least, the military arm of policy cannot object to politically charged rules of engagement. But—and it is a very substantial but— the professional military are obliged to tell policy makers the military truth as they understand it about the likely adverse strategic consequences of political guidance that will constrain military effectiveness. The making of strategy is a process of "unequal dialogue" in civil-military relations.[67] The war over Kosovo in 1999 may appear convincingly to have been a strategic episode more thoroughly political in its character than is usual among conflicts, but such would be an erroneous conclusion. War and its warfare, including its air warfare, are always political in nature and more or less politically shaped in the detail of their character.

The political outcome to the Kosovo crisis and conflict of 1999 speaks loudly to the effectiveness of kinetic airpower. That claim does not diminish the force of the argument advanced earlier that it was the strength of NATO members' interests in the future health of the alliance itself that was the motor driving airpower. However, that powerful engine also imposed limitations under which NATO airpower had to labor. The entire range of problems that coalesced to inhibit the strategic effectiveness of NATO's air war included a persistence of appalling weather over Serbia, complex terrain that rendered target identification a major challenge, initially a shortage of suitable aircraft, a poor target-planning process, interallied (19 countries) differences over targeting (i.e., strategy), American interservice differences over strategy, unempathetic media oversight, and poor political and military assumptions about the determination and competence of the Serbian enemy (wishful thinking). The Serbs in 1999 were not akin to the hapless and hopeless Iraqis of 1991 who had played to near perfection the role of operationally inert victims. It is a little difficult to conclude that the air war, which was the whole of the NATO warfare, was conducted as well as it could have been, given its contexts. That reluctant judgment is mandated by the wisdom granted by a relatively unforgiving hindsight. I admit that at the time my assessment was even less generous.

The critics of coercive airpower by and large were confounded by the Kosovo experience, notwithstanding the fact that NATO airpower proved largely ineffective in its efforts to damage the Serbian army in and about Kosovo. The aerial assault did gain in effectiveness when and where the KLA induced the Serbs to concentrate. This vital synergism between airpower and ground power seems to have been a revelation to some commentators, but actually it is a truly joint military narrative that is nearly as old as air warfare itself. Nonetheless, for those in need of this air-ground, or ground-air, epiphany, Kosovo provided a healthy if belated lesson.

As, if not more, important was the lesson that air-inflicted societal punishment can be strategically effective. It has become almost the accepted conventional wisdom to believe that Milosevic conceded after 78 days of aerial bombardment only because, at long last, he had good enough reason to anticipate a forthcoming NATO invasion on the ground. When added to, perhaps multiplied by, the potency of Milosevic's apparent loss of Russian support, one has enough of a compounded explanation of Serbian behavior to license demotion of the significance of airpower—so it appears to many commentators, at least. Although Milosevic may well have anticipated a regime-ending NATO invasion occurring eventually, such a judgment is highly speculative. Even if we choose to grant that view some respect, it is more relevant to recognize that Milosevic had nontrivial and more pressing reasons to fear for his political authority and, quite possibly, his life. The NATO bombing of economic and national communications infrastructure targets in Serbia triggered a distress and then a political dissatisfaction that had obvious implications for personal and regime survival.[68] The bombing of Serbian economic assets, although initially politically counterproductive, eventually achieved some of the strategic effect that classical strategic airpower theory had predicted. Serbia was coerced successfully, in good part, as a consequence of the effects of aerial bombardment.

On the one hand, the air war over Kosovo assuredly damaged the thesis that the coercive use of airpower never works—an argument undercalibrated for historical contextual fit.[69] On the other hand, Kosovo 1999 certainly did not demonstrate beyond plausible contention that coercion from the air should be regarded as an ever-trusty, as in all situations, military tool of grand strategy and policy. What NATO's air war in 1999 did reveal, yet again, were some persisting truths about war, warfare, strategy, and airpower.

The Kosovo experience demonstrated, one can say unsurprisingly, that (1) politics ruled such strategy as there was, which was not much, though it may be more accurate to observe that too many competing strategic ideas were allowed to shape targeting choices; (2) the enemy needs to be respected politically, strategically, and tactically; (3) physical, mental, political, and strategic geography continue to matter in detailed ways; and (4) specific contexts shape and all but determine what is and what is not strategically feasible. Given the constraints upon a militarily efficient and effective air war that harassed NATO's air effort, it is perhaps surprising that Serbia conceded. Such a view, potent though it is, must be offset by recognition of the strength of NATO's evidence of determination to persist strategically, albeit with only one steel fist.

Conclusion:
Airpower Transformed—but "So What?"

This chapter has discussed airpower, admittedly by and large American airpower, in the first post–Cold War decade, which plausibly saw its technical-tactical "transformation," as Lambeth argued forcefully in his major study published in 2000.[70] Moreover, the technical-tactical transformation of airpower's potency in the political and strategic context of a probably only temporary cessation of active great-power rivalry had notable political and strategic implications. Eliot Cohen judged as follows in 2001:

> After Operation Desert Storm, however, and despite the continuing skepticism of General Colin Powell, the extraordinarily influential chairman of the Joint Chiefs of Staff, civilian elites came to see air power as the ideal vehicle for deriving political utility from U.S. military dominance in a unipolar world. The apparent contribution of air power to the triumph over Iraq, and its subsequent applications—however inelegant—in Bosnia, Serbia, and Kosovo persuaded many that air weapons employed independently offered the ideal

tool for the sorts of military problems facing the United States in the 1990s, and the new century beyond. As a result, in the first decade of the post–Cold War era, air power became the weapon of choice for American statecraft.[71]

Cohen cited two key technological changes: "routinization of precision" achieved by kinetic airpower and its demonstrated "ability to employ weapons against an adversary without suffering losses, except very rarely and indeed almost by accident."[72] Some technical-tactical trends are significant. Cohen's "routinization" is a pardonable exaggeration given the trend toward ever greater reliance upon precision-guided munitions in the air ordnance delivered. To be specific, whereas the air campaign against Iraq was executed with only 9 percent PGMs, Serbia received an aerial bombardment consisting of 35 percent PGMs. In the 2000s the PGM percentage climbed to 57 percent for Operation Enduring Freedom (Afghanistan, 2001), while Operation Iraqi Freedom (2003) registered allied PGM use at 67 percent. The smart laser guidance and electro-optical enablers of the early 1970s had been joined by truly precise navigational assistance from mid-Earth orbit in the form of the NAVSTAR global positioning system (GPS) constellation of 24 satellites. Enemies could still hide successfully, as the Serbs demonstrated in 1999, but if they were located, they could be struck. The old airpower dream-come-aspiration of one sortie for one target (or more) had become a reliable tactical reality.

Airpower enjoyed a newfound reputation both for getting the strategic job done and for doing it with minimum involvement or seriously embarrassing loss of life, both friendly and other. In the strategic world after the Cold War, if not before, it became thoroughly orthodox, certainly politically correct, to claim that Western (politically, democratically owned) airpower was directed only against evil dictators and their hench-people and not against the enemy as a people or society. A logical corollary of this attractively liberal view was the somewhat less liberal, or technically legal, idea that individual evil enemy persons are highly appropriate, even necessary, targets. As a general rule in modern times, enemy leaders have been off-limits for attempts at assassination—murder(?)—even in time of war. But it should be recalled that John Warden's influential theory of strategic air war unambiguously specified enemy command, not excluding the commanders, as the bull's-eye in his five-ringed "dartboard" for aerial targeting.[73] One can seek to soften the story by talking about command and control facilities as targets, but the principal actor in those facilities will be the enemy's chief executive. Recalling earlier euphemisms, when the RAF bombed German "morale" and sought to do so in good part by "de-housing" the civilian (including foreign slave-labor) workforce, in practice it was attacking people, period.

There is scant room for doubt that a technological transformation of kinetic airpower matured rapidly through the 1990s. From a distinctly blunt though mighty instrument of strategy, advanced kinetic airpower both was and henceforth is required to be precise in execution and, broadly speaking, economical in the consequences of its use—certainly in any unintended and undesirable consequences. The satellite-enabled, now-global media of the very late 1990s and early 2000s expected airpower to damage and kill only as its political directors intended. The tactical revolution in airpower's precise kinetic effectiveness and ability to perform stealthily with little if any human loss—only facilities, material assets, things rather than people—was not seriously in doubt. The unexpected resilience to air attack of the Serbian army deployed in the field provided some food for sober thought on the subject of the dynamic competitive grammar of warfare. But still, a trend strongly in favor of airpower's tactical effectiveness seemed securely established, even though the recent evidence from Kosovo yielded caveats arguing for some restraint in exuberant claims for its potency.

The upward surge in airpower's relative popular ranking in the strategic historical narrative of the 1990s was plain to see. Less obvious was the political and strategic meaning for the future of the recent more and less arguable triumphs of airpower. A question in urgent need of answer, at least of attention, was the classic "So what?" of the strategist. Even if airpower's recent and contemporary record of tactical achievement for operational goals in the service of strategy executed for political purposes was indeed as impressive as seemed to be the case, what did that mean for the future? The reasons why airpower so often was the weapon of first choice in the 1990s certainly included a growing confidence in its tactical efficacy. However, another reason, scarcely of lesser significance, was that the very nature of airpower, as well as its attractive, newly more potent and precise lethality, seemed an admirable fit with the political context for the major strategic challenges of the decade. Was transformed, certainly transforming, airpower a military tool appropriate to play the lead in any and all strategic contexts?

To frame the key question thus is necessary, if only to refute the authority of assessments of airpower that are inappropriately exclusive in their focus on the kinetic. That said, as has been true of most decades in the short history of airpower, the first 10 years of the twenty-first century would pose challenges substantially discontinuous from those of the immediate past.

Notes

1. See two period pieces by Krauthammer, "Unipolar Moment" and "Unipolar Moment Revisited." For a thoughtful and controversial critique of the American response to the unanticipated opportunities that flowed from the Soviet demise, see two books by Bacevich: *American Empire* and *New American Militarism*. These works carry a little more attitude than is good for their scholarship, but nonetheless they are studies with weight.

2. Black, *Great Powers and the Quest for Hegemony*, provides helpful historical context, as does Grygiel, *Great Powers and Geopolitical Change*.

3. See Schelling and Halperin, *Strategy and Arms Control*, for the theory; and Gray, *House of Cards*, for its rough handling.

4. See Gray, *Another Bloody Century*, chaps. 2–3, on the importance of context and on technology. Useful studies expressing differing perspectives on technology and strategic history include Frederick Kagan, *Finding the Target*; Boot, *War Made New*; Mahnken, *Technology and the American Way of War since 1945*; and Harris, *America, Technology and Strategic Culture*.

5. See especially Winton, "Ambivalent Partnership." Also helpful are Mahnken, *Technology and the American Way of War*, chap. 4; Lock-Pullan, *US Intervention Policy and Army Innovation*; Tomes, *US Defense Strategy from Vietnam to Operation Iraqi Freedom*; and Kinross, *Clausewitz and America*, 98–102, 121–27.

6. The concept of conventional deterrence is attracting favorable official notice at this time of writing (2010), but with respect to Cold-War Europe it was excruciatingly strategically problematic, at least it should always have been so regarded. With irrefutable strategic logic in 1967, Brodie, *Escalation and the Nuclear Option*, explains why. For a contemporary late-Cold-War-era discussion (1983), see Mearsheimer, *Conventional Deterrence*.

7. Luttwak, *Strategy*.

8. *Hybrid warfare* is a term-of-art that has become fashionable in the 2000s. It is a contested concept that indicates an episode of warfare wherein irregular and regular features mix if not quite compound. The principal prophet for the interesting idea of hybrid warfare, Frank G. Hoffman, describes his conceptual offspring thus: "*Hybrid threats* can be defined as: 'any adversary that simultaneously and adaptively employs a fused mix of conventional weapons, irregular tactics, terrorism, and criminal behaviour in the battlespace to obtain their political objectives.' " Hoffman, "Hybrid Threats," 443. Hoffman's article, just quoted, was preceded by several less defensively aggressive analyses, for example, *Conflict in the 21st Century*, and "Hybrid Warfare and Challenges." The concept is by no means unsound, though it does risk rediscovering the obvious and familiar, and thereby distinguishing a category of conflicts that might better not be so singularized. Conceptually regarded, the

thesis that there are hybrid wars, threats, and strategies should prudently be regarded as a work still in progress.

9. Mahnken, *Technology and the American Way of War*, 130. Additional historical perspective is on offer in Creveld, Canby, and Brower, *Air Power and Maneuver Warfare*.

10. David Johnson, *Learning Large Lessons*, is of good value.

11. See Worden, "Rise of the Fighter Generals."

12. The question of whether the Soviet Union collapsed more from within than as a result of pressure from without is an issue that will forever be contested but remain beyond conclusive answer by historians. Since agreement still is lacking on whether imperial Rome more so fell than was pushed, it is improbable that the mystery of the Soviet eclipse will be resolved anytime soon. In common with the Roman analogy, it is permanently open season for theories of decline and fall. All purported explanations for the demise of the Soviet Union should be regarded as speculative.

13. Lawrence, *Seven Pillars of Wisdom*.

14. Galula, *Counterinsurgency Warfare*.

15. See Dunlap, *Shortchanging the Joint Fight?* The question mark is gratuitous. The leading negative analysis of the unduly cultural turn in American strategic thinking and would-be military practice is Porter, *Military Orientalism*.

16. US Army and Marine Corps, *Counterinsurgency Field Manual*. The Afghan adventure has yet to appear in history books worthy of the name, of course, but two impressive instant histories, perhaps opinionated analytical chronicles, of the US experience in Iraq in the 2000s are the books by journalist Thomas Ricks, *Fiasco* and *Gamble*. These are highly recommended. They are far from being the last word on the subject, but their immediacy provides some authoritative compensation for their lack of historical perspective.

17. I am grateful to Porter, *Military Orientalism*, 7, for this telling metric.

18. Campbell, *Hero with a Thousand Faces*.

19. I am not at all persuaded by the general proposition that coercion by kinetic airpower does not work. It follows that I am underimpressed by the evidence and argument in Pape, *Bombing to Win*. See Gray, *Understanding Airpower*, 35–41, for a terse raid on the theory that coercion from altitude always is foredoomed to fail.

20. Lambeth, *Transformation of American Air Power*. Also see Frederick Kagan, *Finding the Target*.

21. See Lambeth, *Transformation of American Air Power*, 39–41; and Wayne Thompson, "Operations over North Vietnam," 114–20.

22. Kennan, "Moscow Embassy Telegram No. 511."

23. Venkus, *Raid on Qaddafi*, is an informative memoir by a participant in Operation El Dorado Canyon of 14 April 1986. I do not assume that the official, albeit unacknowledged, operational intent was to assassinate Qadaffi.

24. Soviet military experts had a quality of respect for US military-technical prowess, actual and credible near-term potential, that few Western commentators shared. See Adamsky, "Through the Looking Glass." Also see Keaney and Cohen, *Revolution in Warfare?* 199–201; Krepinevich, *Military-Technical Revolution*, 5–7; and the formidable analysis in Odom's excellent study, *Collapse of the Soviet Military*.

25. This is a principal persuasive argument in Stuermer, *Putin and the Rise of Russia*.

26. See Heuser, "Warsaw Pact Military Doctrines in the 1970s and 1980s."

27. Here I am grateful to Luttwak and Coker—to the former for his insistence upon strategy's ironic nature (*Strategy*, xii); to the latter for alerting me to Karl Marx's useful discovery, probably rediscovery, of the phenomenon of unintended economic harm (*Ethics and War in the 21st Century*, 99). I have simply compounded their several insights into the high-caloric concept of ironic unintended self-harm, though I admit that it is probably gratuitous to label such unintended harm "ironic."

28. This is a modest expansion upon the judgment of John Warden, who has written that "airpower [as displayed in Iraq, 1991] became quintessentially an American form of war; it uses our advantages of mobility and high technology to overwhelm the enemy without spilling too much blood, especially American blood." Warden, "Employing Air Power in the Twenty-first Century," 61.

29. Cohen, "Mystique of U.S. Air Power," 120. Also see Gray, *Explorations in Strategy*, chap. 5, "United States as an Air Power."

30. The following are outstanding: on Boyd see Hammond, *Mind of War*; Coram, *Boyd*; Osinga, "On Boyd, bin Laden, and Fourth-Generation Warfare as String Theory"; and Osinga, *Science, Strategy and War*. On Warden see Mets, *Air Campaign*; and Olsen, *John Warden and the Renaissance of American Air Power*. And for two-for-one deals of high value, see Fadok, *John Boyd and John Warden* and "John Boyd and John Warden." All of these works are more than competent, but Olsen's empathetic though not uncritical biography truly is a gem.

31. Boyd, "Discourse on Winning and Losing"; Warden, *Air Campaign*, "Employing Air Power in the Twenty-First Century," and "Enemy as a System," inter alia itemized in Olsen, *John Warden and the Renaissance of American Air Power*, 333–34.

32. See Worden, "Rise of the Fighter Generals."

33. I was a beneficiary, or victim, of a Kahn super-briefing (potentially three days) on more than one occasion. Happily, or otherwise, I was spared the endurance test of the fully matured Boyd super-briefing.

34. Clausewitz, *On War*, 75.

35. See Meilinger, "Trenchard, Slessor, and Royal Air Force Doctrine before World War II"; Faber, "Interwar US Army Aviation and the Air Corps Tactical School"; and Tami Biddle, *Rhetoric and Reality in Air Warfare*, chaps. 2–3.

36. Warden, "Enemy as a System."

37. The five-ring thesis is laid out in Warden, "Employing Air Power in the Twenty-first Century," especially 64–65. Olsen, *John Warden and the Renaissance of American Air Power*, 255–56, offers sensible comments (see also 149).

38. Jomini, *Art of War*, is highly prescriptive. Shy, "Jomini," 183–84, captures brilliantly the overconfident, prescriptively mechanistic element in Jomini and the continuing appeal of this approach to American defense professionals.

39. Loo, "Decisive Battle, Victory and the Revolution in Military Affairs," raises pertinent issues.

40. Olsen, *John Warden and the Renaissance of American Air Power*, 124. Olsen quotes Warden from a 1988 paper as follows:

> We should not distinguish between tactical and strategic forces. The "tactical" fighter bombers of today are fully capable of attacking every enemy strategic ring—and should be used to do so whenever possible. Consider the Libyan operation [Operation El Dorado Canyon, 14–15 April 1986]: by any measure it was a strategic operation designed to af-

fect the state's high command, and it was certainly conducted over "strategic" distances. It serves us poorly to think of tactical air forces as being limited to "tactical" missions. The word itself tends to drive our thinking down to a very low level with very small objectives. Air Forces are big-picture weapons, which have war-winning capabilities.

Here Warden is correct in his denunciation of the tactical and strategic distinction, though it is a pity that he did not proceed to a more fundamental level of critique and, resorting to the wisdom of Clausewitz, insist that all airpower behavior is strategic in meaning, if tactical in action. See Clausewitz, *On War*, 158, for the definitive explanation of why this is so.

41. Arkin, *Divining Victory*, xiv.

42. Sources for airpower in Gulf War I are ample and first rate. Cohen tells most of the story in *Gulf War Air Power Survey*, while Olsen, *Strategic Air Power in Desert Storm*, offers valuable context to the airpower narrative and analysis. Much broader context still is offered in Freedman and Karsh, *Gulf Conflict, 1990–1991*. Additional perspectives include Pape, *Bombing to Win*, chap. 7; Lambeth, *Transformation of American Air Power*, chap. 4; David Johnson, *Learning Large Lessons*, chap. 3; and Olsen, "Operation Desert Storm, 1991." Shultz and Pfaltzgraff, *Future of Air Power in the Aftermath of the Gulf War*, published in 1992, captures the newly optimistic ethos of American airpower commentators post-Iraq.

43. See Cordesman and Wagner, *Lessons of Modern War*, vol. 2.

44. Sun Tzu, *Art of War*, 77.

45. By way of personal evidence for the fashionable status of the concept of competitive strategy at the time, see Gray, "U.S. Naval Power and Competitive Grand Strategy." Few, if any, strategic ideas are ever truly discarded. Defense establishments will hit the "delete" button on concepts that lose favor, but one can be sure that they will be recovered at some point in the not too distant future. They will then appear fresh and exciting to those who (re)discover them. This is not a cynical point. Most strategic concepts do have some merit, whether or not they are fashionable. It is a matter of suitability to context and skill in implementation.

46. Freedman and Karsh, *Gulf Conflict 1990–1991*, 302.

47. Olsen, "Operation Desert Storm, 1991," 177.

48. See Hammond, *Mind of War*. It should be redundant to say that in war one strives to influence the mind of the enemy were this obvious point not so frequently ignored. When the enemy is combat competitive with friendly forces in material respects, its fighting power will be decided by its—and our—will to overcome. This important dimension to the airpower effectiveness is highlighted appropriately in Lambert, *Psychology of Air Power*.

49. As a selection of sources amidst a library of possibilities, see Krepinevich, "Cavalry to Computer"; Owens, *Lifting the Fog of War*; Hundley, *Past Revolutions, Future Transformations*; Knox and Murray, *Dynamics of Military Revolution*; Gray, *Strategy for Chaos*; Benbow, *Magic Bullet?*; Frederick Kagan, *Finding the Target*; and Mahnken, *Technology and the American Way of War*.

50. Imlay and Toft, *Fog of Peace and War Planning*; and Gray, "Strategic Thoughts for Defense Planners."

51. Owens, *Lifting the Fog of War*, assumed iconic status, which plausibly it merited both for uncritical enthusiasts for RMA as well as for its critics. But note Howard,

Causes of Wars, 215–16; and Gray, "Technology as a Dynamic of Defence Transformation."

52. Keaney and Cohen, *Revolution in Warfare?*; and Cohen, "Revolution in Warfare."

53. Luttwak, "Air Power in US Military Strategy," 20.

54. Conversino, "Executing Deliberate Force," 168.

55. Ibid., 133.

56. Owen, "Operation Deliberate Force, 1995," 223.

57. Relevant studies include Gow, "Coercive Cadences"; Byman, Waxman, and Larson, *Air Power as a Coercive Instrument*; and Byman and Waxman, *Dynamics of Coercion*.

58. See Luttwak, "From Vietnam to Desert Fox"; Byman and Waxman, *Confronting Iraq*; Bacevich, "Neglected Trinity," 180–82; and Metz, *Iraq and the Evolution of American Strategy*, 68–70.

59. Unfortunately, Saddam Hussein would seem not to have read, or at least understood, Nye, *Paradox of American Power*, 8–11, on "soft power." Perhaps he was shaking so much with laughter that he could not keep the book open. Ultimately, he was to learn that America was not to be mocked indefinitely, and the laugh was on him. That said, it cannot plausibly be denied that Saddam did not mistake William Clinton for Theodore Roosevelt.

60. Byman and Waxman, *Dynamics of Coercion*, 93.

61. Bacevich, "Neglected Trinity," 180.

62. John Keegan quoted in McInnes, *Spectator-Sport War*, 106.

63. This point is advanced forcefully in the finest analysis of the air war available: Lambeth, *NATO's Air War for Kosovo*, 36, 236. Other perspectives that are helpful include Roberts, "NATO's 'Humanitarian War' over Kosovo"; Daalder and O'Hanlon, *Winning Ugly*; Lambeth, *Transformation of American Air Power*, chap. 6; Bacevich and Cohen, *War over Kosovo*; Cordesman, *Lessons and Non-Lessons of the Air and Missile Campaign in Kosovo*; Gentile, *How Effective Is Strategic Bombing?* 191–94; Ritchie, "Air Power Victorious?"; Clark, *Waging Modern War*; McInnes, *Spectator-Sport War*, chap. 5; Frederick Kagan, *Finding the Target*, 190–98; Lake, "Limits of Coercive Airpower"; and Tony Mason, "Operation Allied Force."

64. Lambeth, *NATO's Air War for Kosovo*, 20.

65. See Coker, *Ethics and War in the 21st Century*, who manages to be sophisticated without straying into an unhelpful cynicism.

66. Lambeth, *NATO's Air War for Kosovo*, 249.

67. See Cohen, *Supreme Command*, chap. 7; Murray and Grimsley, "Introduction: On Strategy"; and Gray, *Strategy Bridge*, 56–57.

68. See Lake, "Limits of Coercive Airpower," which selects domestic regime weakness as far more important than either the incredible NATO ground menace or the bombing. I suspect that the scholarly jury will always be out on this question. The causes of events typically are far more uncertain than their consequences.

69. Such a negative view pervades Pape, *Bombing to Win*.

70. Lambeth, *Transformation of American Air Power*. I am pleased to learn that he may revisit this contemporary classic in the light of the several exciting episodes that have lent color to the 2000s.

71. Cohen, "Kosovo and the New American Way of War," 53.

72. Ibid., 53–54.

73. In September 1990, Gen Michael Dugan was relieved as chief of staff of the USAF because he spoke too publicly and too explicitly about the threat that US airpower could and should pose to the Iraqi leadership. Dugan crossed a political line in explicitly advocating enemy decapitation, but in addition and perhaps of greater significance, his argument for airpower as the leading edge in warfare was interpreted by JCS chairman GEN Colin Powell as unduly short on team spirit. See Olsen, *John Warden and the Renaissance of American Air Power*, 196–99.

Chapter 8

Strategic History V:
Airpower after 9/11

The more carefully one reflects upon the course of strategic history, the more respectful is one likely to be of Edward N. Luttwak's claim that strategy in its nature is inalienably ironic.[1] The key reason is strategy's adversarial persona. Evidence of strategic advantage motivates adversaries to seek ways and means to neutralize its source. Or, as with al-Qaeda and its 9/11 atrocity, airpower is employed imaginatively to humiliate and hurt the United States, the world leader in the air. There was only apparent irony in the deadly emergence in the 2000s of a leading category of conflicts that seemed to devalue the relative strategic worth of airpower. To many commentators and scholars, the post–9/11 world appeared to pose challenges that demoted airpower as a player for national and international security. If the 1990s witnessed the strategic reality of airpower functioning ever more convincingly as the supported (by land power and sea power) rather than the supporting element in joint warfare, the 2000s have been widely regarded as registering some notable measure of retreat in airpower's relative significance—so a popular narrative argues. This chapter finds fatal fault with that narrative, but it does acknowledge that a major reason why such an argument has enjoyed traction is because airpower's strategic story has not been developed and explained soundly and persuasively. This has not been a matter merely of poor public relations; rather, the difficulty lies in the way in which some airpower advocates have set up their favored military instrument for an audit that was all but certain to judge it wanting. The "own goal" problem has been systemic in airpower history. This theme of self-inflicted damage has been a permanent feature of the airpower story. The true irony in airpower history is that aviation actually has been seriously undersold as a consequence of its being oversold. This familiar sad characteristic of airpower history was donated an unwelcome gravity assist in the 2000s by the eruption or explosion—one can hardly say merely the appearance—of what is widely believed to be a transformed security context.

Just when airpower seemed to be completing its transformation into a truly precision instrument, history staged an ambush by presenting a form of strategic challenge for which, either alone or as the leading edge in the joint project, it seemed to provide a less than decisive answer. At least, so the story can be written if the airpower narrative is miscast. By the beginning of the twenty-first century, it was incontestable that US airpower enjoyed and could enforce an air supremacy both over and distant from the battlefield such that no enemy ground force that could be located would be able to function effectively. Both the claim and the caveat are significant. Any military force visible on the ground could be defeated conclusively and beyond recovery by US airpower. The cumulative achievement in C4ISTAR in the 1990s enabled a lethality to kinetic, and increasingly standoff, airpower to the point where an air force supreme on the overhead flank would be dominant, or more, in air-land battle—as it long had been dominant, even supreme, in air-sea engagement.[2] Caveats are necessary, however. Ground forces tactically at liberty to disperse, who are clever at hiding in complex terrain and able to contest low altitudes with highly mobile, including man-portable air defense systems (MANPADS) would compel a loss-sensitive enemy to fly high, while themselves presenting only elusive targets to airpower. As the 2000s progressed, such a challenge to the strategic value of control of the air became less important for precision engagement, but it was a limiting factor of significance for airpower in some of its ground-supporting roles. Better-armed irregulars acquired the ability to make lower altitudes unduly hazardous for helicopters.

As the next section explains, the undoubted technical and tactical transformation of airpower, which Ben Lambeth explained and celebrated so well in his 2001 study, did not, indeed could not, itself carry transformative operational, let alone strategic, meaning.[3] The fundamental reason why airpower, especially US airpower, could not match its recent near perfection in technical-tactical achievement with a like operational and strategic success had little or nothing to do with airpower itself. At some risk of appearing to erect a straw target that can be destroyed with suspiciously consummate ease, I must indicate the basic error in believing that what one might term a "perfection of airpower" could, might, or perhaps even has the ability reliably to deliver favorable strategic decision when serving as the sole, or nearly sole, military agent.

There are two principal reasons why airpower must disappoint, no matter how near it is judged to be technical-tactical perfection. First, because war is a duel, enemies are motivated and, given time and resources, usually are able to find ways to offset military disadvantages. Leads tend not to last, and their operational and strategic merits vary from situation to situation and by context (e.g., political, geographical, military). To illustrate, an American supremacy in the air positively invites—actually, strategically mandates—asymmetric endeavors by America's enemies. Second, and really as a license for the first reason, war and warfare are highly complex enterprises. Just as airpower cannot intelligently be reduced solely to the status of a kinetically achieved influence—which means that targeting is not synonymous with air strategy, no matter what Douhet and a small but influential cohort of air theorists have claimed to the contrary[4]—so war and warfare cannot sensibly be reduced to air warfare. The sole major exception to this argument would be the truly desperate case wherein large-scale nuclear weapon employment would, admittedly, assert an unarguably strategically conclusive, if politically irrelevant, authority.

The airpower dimension to the grand strategic narrative of the 2000s seems to be diminished only when contrasted with what many air-minded persons anticipated at the millennium. In truth, the air story of "the age of terror" has been all that it could be. If airpower has somehow failed, that failure belongs far more to faulty theory and doctrine than to flaws in the military instrument. Misconceived missions and the wrong questions are guaranteed to produce disappointing operational performance and inappropriate answers. If one requires of airpower that it achieve the impossible, that it answer to questions that are wrongly framed, then in a sense it will fail. But such failure is really nothing of the kind. If the argument in this study has a true *Schwerpunckt*, a dominant focus of effort, it lies in the claim that context has to be allowed both to reign and to rule in understanding the meaning and significance of airpower. Recognition and application of the greater enduring truths about statecraft, war and warfare, and strategy located in a well-framed and empirically funded general theory (see chap. 2) are essential if one is to locate airpower properly in strategic history.

The decade of the 2000s can appear to have shown massive irony in the contrast between a newly achieved technical-tactical excellence in (US) airpower and a national and alliance strategic debility in the face of the challenges of the era. Contemporary standoff kinetic airpower is a strategist's dream of a military tool, but it is not the only tool in the toolbox, not even in the toolbox of airpower alone. The more often and the more vociferously air theorists assert the strategically decisive value of an ever-improving kinetic lethality, the more certain are they to orchestrate their own defeat in debate. To hazard a claim that no doubt some theorists will dislike intensely and resent, airpower advocacy that rests its argument overwhelmingly upon claims for a kinetic effectiveness truly amounts to an intellectual and political suicide note. Poor argument invites refutation by better argument. The position taken here is that the only sound argument capable of explaining the strategic importance of airpower is one that both defines its subject with due inclusivity and which treats it suitably in context. The end of the age of industrial mass warfare, though most probably not of major state-on-state warfare, has posed a strategic question that the faultily framed airpower argument criticized above cannot answer convincingly. If airpower as kinetic menace is a subordinate joint team player in conflicts where the enemy does not present itself in a regular and visible order of battle for evisceration from altitude, surely it must be yesterday's instrument of strategic decision—except that yesterday it lacked the technical-tactical lethal excellence to deliver on the promise of its more excited advocates. If, or when, the dominant airpower community obviously fails the test for strategic success that it sets itself, it can hardly complain when people from other communities point to airpower's weakness in performance. It is commonplace to criticize some air theory as, in effect, defining airpower as a single tool, a hammer, and all its jobs as being nails. But in reality, airpower is not akin to a single tool, a hammer, and assuredly most of its tasks bear no resemblance to nails. Thus it is that a distressing quality of often heated argument over airpower is so misconceived in its basic elements that intelligent debate and, it must be said, national security cannot fail to be impaired as an unavoidable consequence.

Airpower and the War on Terrorists

The messy and seriously unanticipated strategic history of the 2000s proved not so much a laboratory for testing the prowess of contemporary airpower, but rather more one for testing the authority of airpower's long-standing general theory. Regarded in retrospect, the novelty in airpower's technical-tactical potency in the 2000s was less impressive than the persistence of some key familiar verities. The transformation of the most modern airpower enabled by the substantially information-technology-fueled RMA in C4ISTAR was indeed both impressive and important. But it is undeniable that the global strategic history of 2000–2010 signally failed to record decisive strategic victories achieved either wholly or significantly by the application of airpower in its several forms. Self-evidently, whatever is meant by the plausible proposition that US (and Israeli) airpower was transformed cannot mean that it was transformed in its ability to deliver the strategic effect necessary to produce a favorable postwar political settlement. But paradoxically and ironically, this apparently pejorative judgment does not mean that airpower failed in the 2000s. To repeat a point registered earlier, if one poses the wrong questions, one will elicit answers that are irrelevant at worst and seriously misleading at best.

Given that perfection is not to be expected or required of human endeavor—save, arguably and potentially, lethally with respect to nuclear deterrence—and that friction, accident, and an inconveniently uncooperative enemy are apt to impair the scorecard of success, still airpower had a distinctly good decade in the 2000s. Airpower achieved what reasonably could be asked of it and perhaps even more than that. As a flat claim unencumbered by qualifying escape clauses, this text argues that in four wars or historically notable episodes of warfare from 2001 to 2008, airpower—(largely) US and Israeli—performed magnificently by any suitable standard. It is possibly ironic that this laudatory judgment can be registered with particular reference to four episodes of war that popularly are regarded as strategic failures or troublingly unstable "draws" at best. Accepting the risk of possible banality, it is useful not to shrink in strategic argument from recognizing the merit in the maxim that the impossible is impossible.[5] In 1940, Britain's Fighter Command won a significant military victory that had the most profound, albeit unpredictable, of strategic consequences for the whole course of the war. Air Chief Marshal Sir Hugh Dowding won the Battle of Britain by not losing it; he could not win the war as a whole. His generalship enabled his command to win all that it could win.[6] Similarly, US (or US-led) and Israeli airpower in the conflicts of the 2000s enabled all of which it was capable. The four episodes of most interest here—Afghanistan, 2001–present; Iraq, 2003–present; Second Lebanon, 2006; and Gaza, 2008 (with the arguable exception of Israel's Operation Cast Lead in December 2007–January 2008 in Gaza)—were none of them concluded as the belligerent dominant in the air anticipated or desired. Indeed, each of these conflicts comprises more or less unfinished strategic, but especially political, business both for the United States and for Israel.

The principal challenge to intelligent appreciation of airpower is the folly in seeking to examine it as though it were a stable material entity upon which reliable judgment can be pronounced. To clarify, if such is needed, airpower is both an abstraction and an ever-dynamic particular historical reality. Airpower in the abstract, explained in its general theory, cannot be tested in particular historical situations. Of course, a country's airpower may fail to deliver the strategic effect that is reasonably asked of it, while it is all but certain to fail to achieve what strategically should *not* be demanded. Context is sovereign, regardless of the technical-tactical potency of the military airpower instrument. To rephrase the argument, even a near perfection of kinetic airpower is able to deliver only that of which such precise lethality is capable. If effectively zero circular error probable (CEP) is achievable from altitude, the quality and quantity of the strategic effect of that remarkable prowess is hostage to an uncertain currency conversion rate. The recent conflicts in Afghanistan, Iraq, Lebanon, and Gaza have occurred in contexts about as tough for the relevance of mass industrial-age, let alone nuclear-war, metrics of success as one could imagine. Therefore, it is scarcely surprising that the transformation of airpower-as-firepower into a truly minuteman-like marksmanship could not reliably be cashed for conclusive strategic, let alone political, success. But it must be emphasized that to claim thus is to criticize neither airpower in general, in the abstract, nor necessarily even US-led or Israeli airpower of the 2000s. Conflict, war, warfare, and strategy in that decade comprised and engaged a great deal more than airpower.

Of course airpower occasionally was mishandled strategically, operationally, and tactically in these four episodes. Every military instrument always is commanded and performs somewhat short of what expectations of perfection specify. However, the relevant standard for sensible historical strategic judgment is not perfection; rather is it suitability and task adequacy. Although Israel came close to refuting the rule in the early days of its Second Lebanon War in July 2006, it is essential to recognize that modern states in recent times have waged joint warfare. In principle there could be a stand-alone air campaign that would constitute the entire military strategic narrative of a war, but such was not the case from 2001 to 2010. There is much that a strategic analysis can and should find to criticize in US (or US-led) and Israeli performance in the warfare of the 2000s, but that criticism cannot persuasively be laid at the door of airpower. If a war is misconceived or seriously mishandled overall, or both, then every military contributor to the more or less dire event is likely to fare ill in the total audit of the project. Strategic history is not sentimental and forgiving of good effort. For example, did the Wehrmacht do well and deserve high strategic praise for winning what it won? Or should it be condemned for its unarguable failure to win more than was strategically essential? This is a familiar strategic challenge for the scholar. Does one praise a belligerent who fights well but not well enough? A competent strategy should not attempt the impossible, but who can identify for certain the boundary of the possible, short of the honest, determined attempt? The scholar may be able to pin a silver medal on a gallant loser, but history is not usually so generous.

This book is not interested in passing judgment upon the wisdom or otherwise of American or Israeli policies and strategies in the 2000s, save only insofar as necessary to illuminate further the enduring nature, yet necessarily changing character, of airpower. The principal challenges to American and Israeli national security addressed by warfare in the 2000s were not ones that airpower alone could meet satisfactorily. To go further, those challenges were not open to fundamental resolution even by US-led or Israeli military power regarded holistically and jointly. If Afghanistan, Iraq, Lebanon, and Gaza can be likened metaphorically to strategic train wrecks, airpower had ample company in arguable failure. And the failure that may plausibly, though again arguably, be ascribed to those episodes obviously is assignable far more to the zone wherein politics (policy) and grand and military strategy meet than to that wherein strategy meets the operations that command tactics.

An important reason why I am reluctant to venture far into the perilous realm of strategic judgment on necessarily still-moving history is precisely because it is still moving. A book dedicated to the mission of understanding airpower cannot sensibly ignore recent, even truly contemporary, behavior. It is inevitable that scholarly standards must be severely stressed in such an exercise. Perspective is lacking on the 2000s, and since the irregular conflicts of this period are of a character that ensures protraction, instant judgment on a moving story has to be imprudent in its potential to mislead. Happily for this study, the continuities in and about airpower history are deemed here to be so much more significant than the discontinuities, that the ever-emerging details of airpower performance are at some discount in their value for our understanding. While it is certainly desirable to comprehend the dynamic reality of airpower today, such grip as one can secure on understanding real-time actuality is not liable to affect the reliability of one's total grasp of the subject. I write this firmly and assertively, with high confidence, but also with the humility appropriate to a willingness to be surprised and recognize a few exceptions to general rules. Theory in social science has a lower standard for success in the testing of its hypotheses than theory in the hard sciences.[7] The "laws" of social science are apt to be held to the most-not-all-cases standard.

It is perilous to attempt to draw lessons from an incomplete strategic narrative. That point granted, what follows is a deliberately brief, airpower-focused consideration of the strategic history of the 2000s. Readers are warned that strategic prediction usually is faulty. Rapid assessment of (near) contemporary history almost invariably comes in time to be judged as more or less unsound. Temporal perspective does matter.

A Decade of Terror

The political theater of violence that is terrorism is not at all new.[8] That said, there is no obvious historical precedent for a decade wherein the dominant, indeed the defining, security challenge for the substantially hegemonic world power was posed by terrorists. While the 2000s recorded some state-on-state warfare (e.g., Russia versus Georgia, the United States and NATO versus Taliban Afghanistan, and the United States, Britain, and other allies—but not NATO— versus Ba'athist Iraq), there is no question but that the terrorist menace was the threat flavor-of-the-period. Actually, the threat had many local flavors, which meant that what the George W. Bush administration chose on 20 September 2001 to term the "global war on terror" (which of course acronymed delightfully as GWOT) most probably was perilously misconceived, though perhaps over-conceived might be a better descriptor, if I may be pardoned for the neologism. It should hardly need saying that if the threat question is unsoundly reduced conceptually to the challenge posed by a single global terrorist danger, a Master Menace, the answer provided by would-be counterterrorists also is likely to be flawed—wrong question, wrong answer. This is not to deny that al-Qaeda was, and remains, a transcendentalist jihadist menace that had globally franchiseable elements.[9] Nonetheless, the whole course of the 2000s shows unmistakably that the truth in the global terror plot is more than offset by the error. Those sincere but mistaken people who once were convinced that nearly all the security trouble in the world was the direct or indirect product of a global, super-competent, communist conspiracy found an adequate conceptual replacement in al-Qaeda and the GWOT. Given that an important role of theory is to provide explanation that translates as a comforting intellectual order, the GWOT filled the awkward threat void of the 1990s.

The main reason why the GWOT was misconceived was because the terrorist threat was plural, not singular; it was indeed global, but it was not centrally so. It is always a serious mistake to fixate upon ways or means to the near exclusion of ends. The ways and the means in the classic strategy trio (ways, means, and ends) must be addressed and answered because they are manifested in dangers to one's security, but the fact remains that they are perils only because of the ends—the politics and policies—of would-be perpetrators. While one cannot wage war on an all but indefinable abstract effect, terror, one can combat terrorists and, in many cases, defeat their strategy and marginalize or even defeat their policies. None of these comments should be interpreted as meaning that I am confused about terrorism. Terrorists determined and able to do harm have to be stopped, by whatever weapons and means are effective—period.

To understand airpower in "the age of terror," it is first essential to attempt carefully to comprehend the context for its multidimensional application.[10] As this study has emphasized throughout, the strategic value of airpower relative to other military and nonmilitary policy instruments is highly situational. But what was the relevant situation(s) for airpower in the first decade of the twenty-first century? Official US (and British, it must be added) policy and rhetoric advanced the GWOT thesis, albeit not always in exactly those words. Whatever the minor variations in choice of language, there was no doubt that the dominant strategic policy concept of the Cold War, containment (that ambiguously was both policy and strategy), along with its close dependant enabler, deterrence, was replaced by the GWOT. The big test of the GWOT covered a host of counterterrorist (CT), counterinsurgency (COIN), and stabilization and development activities. At this juncture in the story, it is necessary to remind ourselves of what was probably the most important judgment delivered by Clausewitz for our education in On War: "The first, the supreme, the most far-reaching act of judgment that the statesman and commander have to make is to establish by that test [of fit with policy ends] the kind of war on which they are embarking; neither mistaking it for, nor trying to turn it into, something that is alien to its nature. This is the first of all strategic questions and the most comprehensive."[11]

The Cold War years may be characterized fairly as being dominated by a principal source of menace, while the 1990s were all but free of a major threat to help guide Western defense policy makers and planners. For its part the decade of the 2000s most truly was cluttered with several large political grievance–driven terrorist and insurgent threats that had some globalized manifestation. The agents for these threats claimed some religious authority for their purposes and deeds. The real past—as contrasted with the more or less legendary ones that our memories and, one must say, historians construct—was always complex yet essentially stable and even simple in its strategic nature. Things are ever thus. Perception of complexity tends to correlate closely with intimacy of knowledge and understanding. Those who know little about the past can be comfortable in their ignorant passing references to, for examples, "the Westphalian states system" or World War II. The former is a gross oversimplification that is arguably wrong, while the latter is such a big-picture compound of diverse conflicts that it can hardly help but mislead.[12]

The four conflicts in the 2000s of most interest to this study can be regarded as two distinct pairs that happen to share the same historical time zone, and that may well be an appropriate perspective to adopt. Whatever the many connections one can identify contestably as linking Afghanistan, Iraq, Lebanon, and Gaza (Palestine), there is no doubt that each had an airpower dimension with a character of high interest to this inquiry. By way of picture framing for the case-specific analyses that follow, it is useful, indeed it is necessary, to appreciate the contrast between the major contexts for airpower application of the Cold War decades and the 1990s and 2000s, especially the latter. Since commentators are unhappy when obliged to float adrift without anchor to a dominant paradigm in which they have confidence, let us compare and contrast the containment and the terror eras. In historical reality, which is to say the actual past, 1945–89 was complex and messy, but the master narrative was anything but. A global Soviet-authored-and-led menace was contained by the strategic effect of an essentially nuclear deterrence. The Soviet foe was cunning and unscrupulous, but it was also a regular state in key respects that fielded regular armed forces. The Soviet enemy had an address with targetable geographical coordinates, and existentially it appeared to fit well enough into the framework for explanation as a belligerent in terms of Clausewitz's secondary trinity of people, army and commander, and policy reasons. Furthermore, Thucydides' triptych of "fear, honor, and interest" obviously applied. The Soviet Union fought and was expected to fight wars much as would any modern state—in short, as our contemporary jargon puts it, symmetrically.

The previous paragraph knowingly oversimplifies to register an important point. Although airpower has been employed in all genres of warfare since the 1900s, its dominant strategic tasks, both in action and in peacetime preparation, have been geared to assist, to defeat, or to provide a viable alternative to other regular armed forces engaged in a regular style of combat. Accepting the nontrivial hazards of possibly posing alternatives with an exaggerated clarity, the principal conflicts of the 2000s had the following selected features:

- Expressive violence, especially in the inaugural airpower form on 9/11, that is rationally strategic even though it is partially transcendental in its meaning, though scarcely reasonable to most people.[13]

- Occurrence in difficult, complex, human, human-constructed, as well as most natural kinds of physical terrain.

- Combatants and noncombatants, "innocent" and otherwise, are intermingled and frequently indistinguishable; the enemy is hard to locate for targeting.

- Although all wars by definition are political phenomena, in warfare against nonstate but possibly state-sponsored and often only part-time combatants, generally it is exceptionally challenging to match military activity and metrically assessable achievement to advancement toward the desired political outcome.

- Warfare against irregular enemies who are obliged to fight in guerrilla style, usually including terror tactics, almost always is cumulatively attritional in character and therefore is protracted and apparently indecisive for long periods.[14]

- The global geography of most significance for the prosecution of the Cold War became as familiar as did each of the principals to one another (such familiarity did not guarantee true understanding, of course). The contexts of strategic focus in the post–

Cold War era and then the GWOT decade were as contrasting in degree of familiarity as they could be. From containment of the Eurasian Soviet heartland hegemony, with its geographical centers of potential strategic engagement in northern Europe and the high Arctic, the actual warfare of most interest to this text migrated to the Balkans, the Middle East, central Asia, the Caucasus, and the Horn of Africa, inter alia. None of the regions thus identified are political or physical geographies with which America, the leading air power, was at all familiar.

- The conflicts, wars, and warfare of the 2000s had a political character such that the matching violence primarily was of irregular kinds. The dominant strategic narrative for airpower examined in these pages overwhelmingly has reflected the paradigm of state-on-state, regular-combat-style warfare. The world's major air forces have been shaped overwhelmingly to meet the needs attendant upon regular forms of warfare. From time to time air forces have been obliged to address the challenges of irregular war, but the expertise and much of the equipment tailored to those particular tasks have tended to be fleeting capabilities and competencies.[15]

The items just listed need to be highlighted, but their strategic significance should not be exaggerated. It is necessary to remember that there is more of importance about politics, statecraft, conflict, war, warfare, and strategy that does not change than does. Although the new concept of, say, "hybrid" war arguably may have some merit, it is well to insist that the noun is more authoritative than the fashionable adjective. War is war, and it might sometimes be called *hybrid* if it is waged against a state-sponsored irregular force that is exceptionally well armed (e.g., Israel against Hezbollah in Lebanon).[16] It is a powerful truth that strategy, though essentially effected by tactics, is superior to them. It is an even more powerful truth that strategy both reigns and rules over conflict, war, and warfare of every character. The warfare episodes of the 2000s support this dictum with overwhelming empirical authority.

Afghanistan and Iraq, 2001–Present

Triggered politically by American anger as well as cool consideration of national security, the swiftly successful military campaign to take down Taliban Afghanistan (Operation Enduring Freedom, 7 October–23 December 2001) seemed for a brief while to demonstrate a new lethal way in warfare.[17] Alas, it was to be no accident, as Soviet spokesmen used to intone, that the US strategic experiences of Afghanistan and Iraq in the 2000s were to have so powerful a similarity at every level of effort and analysis. The two countries or states—to hazard some inadvertent misdirection with reference to Afghanistan—were hugely different, and yet the US-led strategic narratives of the wars there in the decade of the 2000s reveal a few plainly dominant and broadly common strategic features that merit exploitation as contributions to our understanding of airpower. By way of a necessary prefatory caveat, although lengthy historical perspective offers no guarantee of objectivity and balanced judgment, it is a certainty that the unavoidable absence of such perspective does ensure a fragility of assessment. That said, before examining some detail it is important not to lose the central plot that is our theme—the role(s) and relative significance of airpower in strategic history. What follows is a summary shortlist that hits the keys to understanding what happened and why in both Afghanistan and Iraq in the 2000s, with particular reference to the airpower narrative.

The linkages and independencies among the distinguishable levels of war were asserted in a wonderfully compounding sentence on the very first page of *On War*. "But in war more than in any other subject we must begin by looking at the nature of the whole; for here more than elsewhere the part and the whole must always be thought of together."[18] Alas, the US-led multinational coalitions of the willing that intervened in Afghanistan and Iraq lacked a viable political narrative as a vital enabler of strategic success.

Because the coalitions were bereft of credible and tolerably legitimate political stories for Kabul and Baghdad, they had inordinate difficulty locating strategies that could serve them well enough. Recall that the strategic function requires a purposeful, mutually enabling marriage among (political) ends, (strategic) ways, and (military and extramilitary) means. When the political ends are absent, unclear, or flatly contradictory, strategy worthy of the name is impossible, and one is reduced to an effort comprising tactics alone. This tacticization of strategy is inevitable when the strategy function cannot be performed because of the absence of identified, firm, and achievable political goals.

Military behavior is directed at the operational level for limited goals in ways and by tactical action that often, paradoxically, are militarily competent-to-exemplary, yet which must fail to contribute either sequentially or cumulatively to strategic success.[19] When a centrally directed "whole country" strategy is missing from the action, advantage in this locale and that one typically registers historically as only hollow victories that have no meaning beyond themselves.

Tactical military excellence is the product of a few universal and eternal qualities—leadership, morale/motivation, doctrine, training, equipment, and numbers, to cite but the leading items. However, because the context of every war is unique, tactical effectiveness is always a highly situationally specific story. Whereas policy and strategy can be shifted rapidly, the tactical competence of an armed force cannot. It takes time to generate the fighting power needed from troops suitably equipped, doctrinally well prepared, appropriately trained, and sufficient in numbers to do the jobs that policy, strategy, and operational art require. Even if soldiers in the field can function consistently for tactical success, that force-on-force superiority will be at a severe discount in its strategic effect if the higher levels of the whole enterprise are in poor condition.

Argument over whether airpower is more supported than supporting, or vice versa, sadly is probably as unavoidable as it is foolish. Rival tribal theorists for ground power and airpower are almost certain to mislead both themselves and the more credulous among their readers. The relative significance of the air contribution to the joint fight certainly has shifted from war to war, or it has and will among different kinds of terrain (and at sea). But in modern warfare, which is to say from late 1916 to the present, the combined-arms fight has always been joint.[20] The jointness has not always been fully recognized to be essential, and frequently it has not been practiced competently (e.g., French and British land-air performance in May–June 1940). Nonetheless, when there is a ground warfare dimension to a conflict, which is the usual condition, it is sensible to conceive of a greater or lesser degree of fusion of airpower and ground power. The tactical, operational, and strategic relations between the two cannot be stable, because the context for threat and action is ever dynamic and various. It is necessary to recognize the sovereignty of context yet again and the wholeness of the trinity that comprises the strategic function. It has to follow that assessment of airpower's performance in Afghanistan and Iraq must appreciate empathetically the almost overwhelming fact that the worth of behavior in and from altitude was thoroughly hostage to the quality of military and other performance on the ground. Furthermore, the whole military project in and bearing upon these two countries has been hostage to the wisdom, or otherwise, in the political direction given to strategy. One must seek to "join up the dots." This is a matter with decisive practical implications; it is not merely a fine scholarly point.[21]

The tactical story of airpower in Afghanistan and Iraq has been one of innovation in technology and procedures.[22] Unsurprisingly, 10 years of complex, even hybrid, warfare have tested ideas and equipment in a way that peacetime cannot. This is not to claim that military organizations with their all-but-tribal cultures and subcultures are uniformly able to learn from experience, either their own or others'. However, the painful warfare experiences of Afghanistan and Iraq eventually, albeit belatedly, did see the US Army perform admirably as a learning organization. I am not uncritical of what was learned, but the effort was strongly praiseworthy. The British Army was far slower to recognize that it needed both to learn new things and, as much, to recover lost learning from past eras.[23] Wherever one looks in the Afghan and Iraqi experiences, one finds technical-tactical competence and better typically shackled unfortunately to operational irrelevance because of the strategy deficit produced in good part by the political incompetence that has driven unwise policy. These are hard words, and they bear not at all upon the overall judgment that, by and large, the sharp end of US-led coalition fighting power was admirable indeed. So much so that one is struck by the familiar paradox that an excellent military machine was ill matched by a policy and strategy-making process—to fuse the two rather boldly—that demonstrated it was not fit for the political purpose it was given.

The strategic effect of tactical and operational airpower is thoroughly hostage to the integrity of the master military and grand strategies that it serves and no less to the soundness of the policy that provides the "ends," the political purpose of the whole endeavor. Notwithstanding the distinctiveness of the airpower experiences of Afghanistan and Iraq in the 2000s, the major, indeed the overriding, commonality is almost startling. In both cases the United States and its allies addressed the wrong question and therefore provided the wrong solution. It is not important for this text to argue the rights and wrongs of the decision to intervene in Afghanistan in 2001 and Iraq in 2003, but what is important and relevant to our airpower focus is the plain fundamental errors in strategy that flawed both projects. There is always room for improvement, and friction is a reality no matter how modern the military instrument, but the practical and operational narrative of airpower in the joint campaigns in the 2000s is overwhelmingly positive. With only minor exceptions, such as always happens with any military force, US-led airpower did all that it could be expected to do and probably more. In summary, supported by small numbers of largely, but not only, American special operations forces performing a significant measure of the target-cueing role on the ground, US airpower, primarily sea-based (obviously the US lacked air bases on land close to Afghanistan in 2001), enabled local Northern Alliance Afghan forces to defeat the Taliban. In the judicious words of campaign historian Ben Lambeth,

> in addition [to the UAV], a new concept of offensive air employment against enemy ground forces was successfully tested in Enduring Freedom [Afghanistan, 2001]. Although often mistakenly equated with close air support (CAS), it was, in fact, something fundamentally new by way of air power application that entailed direct air attacks against fielded enemy forces who were *not* in direct contact with friendly troops.[24] (emphasis in the original)

Lambeth broadly is correct, though there were some distinctly imperfect historical precedents for such target cueing by a ground element. Also, he offered these wise words:

> Granted, one must take care not to overgeneralize from Operation Enduring Freedom. Much like Desert Storm, Deliberate Force, and Allied Force before it, the war was, at bottom, a one-sided application of space-enabled air power to produce a desired outcome, one in which the enemy really never had a chance to counter allied offensive operations. Taliban air defenses, with so few weapons of any reliability, were all but nonexistent.[25]

The "kill chain was shorter than ever," to employ the unlovely concept, because of technological and, no less, organizational improvements in the early 2000s over the 1990s.[26] It must also be said that US airpower over Afghanistan in 2001 was not harassed and hindered by a severely dysfunctional allied target planning process and chain of command. However, notwithstanding the excellence of SOF-identified and GPS-directed joint direct attack munitions (JDAM) and other munitions delivered by a multi-altitude taxi rank of aerial fire support, there was only so much that airpower could achieve. The triadic new American way of war that effectively fused US (and a few allied) SOF, (largely) US airpower, and Afghan allied ground forces accomplished what would have been difficult to fail in doing: it took down the Taliban regime in impressively short order. There were very few American boots on the ground, and the dominant US war aim seemed to have been achieved.

The near-absence of an American (and other US-allied) footprint in Afghanistan in 2001 could not be repeated against the notably more-robust-looking state of Saddam Hussein's Iraq in 2003. However, the American (and British) invasion in spring 2003, an enterprise launched in the satisfactory, not to say triumphal, afterglow of apparent victory in Afghanistan, was as light on the ground as it could be for the purpose of taking down the regime. Secretary of Defense Donald H. Rumsfeld appeared to be vindicated. Two decades and more into the lengthy process of military transformation via an IT-led RMA indeed had produced an American military instrument that could march "up country" with a dominant, fairly bold style of maneuver that was critically enabled by air and cyber assault.[27] US and British ground power would have made short work of the Iraqi army and the regime's more political military formations in any event, but the record of the campaign shows quite clearly that US airpower and cyber power fatally disrupted and disabled any prospect of Iraq putting up a cohesive defense.[28] It is worth noting that Iraqi forces were deployed and commanded in all respects more with a view to the security of the regime against a domestic military or paramilitary coup than with regard to defense against invasion.

There was no doubt that in 2001 and in 2003 the United States, with some allied assistance, conclusively and impressively defeated the Afghan state of the Taliban and the Ba'athist regime in Baghdad. Unfortunately, the peace that followed each successful brief war deteriorated more (Iraq) or less (Afghanistan) rapidly into a condition of complex irregular warfare. US-led airpower was neither responsible for such deterioration, nor could it arrest the slide into bloody chaos. The problems of and in Afghanistan after 2001, and of and in Iraq after the swift victory in regular-style conventional warfare in the spring of 2003, could not be answered by US-led military power, let alone by US airpower as a dominant element employed more and less jointly. It is easy to be misunderstood when one registers a claim such as that just uttered. The military part of the US political-strategy projects in Afghanistan and Iraq were and are vital, but the political contexts in those countries have determined noticeably the practicable bounds for military achievement.

Tactical excellence cannot substitute for strategic incompetence, and the United States could hardly help but be strategically incompetent because its political and military leaders did not grasp with an adequate understanding the true character of the strategic challenges either in Afghanistan or in Iraq. The fundamental problem in Afghanistan was, and remains, the fact that it has never been and is not a modern state. This deceptively simple, though surely obvious, fact means that the US-led military intervention, which recorded serious mission creep from standoff aerial coercion and close air support (CAS), through CT, to COIN, grossly misread the character of the challenge. American CT and COIN doctrine, even in its much improved post-2006 FM 3-24 variant, fails to grip the implications of the reality that Afghanistan is not and has never been a functioning centralized modern state. No matter how correctly some approximation to what is believed to be best practice in CT and COIN is conducted by America and some—too few—Afghan allies, the enterprise is all but certain to fail because it is conducted on behalf of a near fiction that is, or should be, the state and society of Afghanistan. The political and social-cultural contexts of the warfare in Afghanistan are not likely to be permissive of US-led, or much assisted, CT and COIN efforts. It should be needless to say that the airpower narrative, virtually no matter how high its impressively varied tactical competence, is powerless to shift what appears to be a structure for failure. When politicians and strategists require their military agents to do the impossible, those agents will duly fail to deliver.

It is ironic that the airpower story in Afghanistan, both for the brief 2001 campaign and as a pervasive enabler of the mission creeping since then, has been as first-rate as ultimately it was futile. The Afghan experience in the 2000s emphatically does not show that airpower is a much lesser military element as compared and contrasted with the boots on the ground to which it should be thoroughly subordinate. Airpower, both kinetic (CAS, interdiction, independent strikes) and in varied other forms (e.g., for logistics, tactical and operational mobility, reconnaissance, command and control, medevac, security at all levels), is a literally essential, pervasive enabler of, as well as executive agent for, CT, COIN, and the stabilization and humanitarian tasks inalienable from irregular conflicts. The strategic value of airpower in the irregular conflicts of the 2000s has been decided far more by the structural character of the conflicts in Afghanistan and Iraq than by particular US technical, tactical, and operational choices.

The strategic, perhaps astrategic, story arc of the US-led intervention in Iraq launched in March 2003 is unsurprisingly similar to the sad Afghan case analyzed immediately above. The reasons are not hard to locate; they can be summarized as same (American) people, same ideas, same military instrument, and same time-space. Characteristically, Lambeth hits the target again:

> Operations Enduring Freedom [2001] and Iraqi Freedom [2003], in marked contrast, [to the distinctively different personalities in command in each campaign in the 1990s] differed from the earlier US conflicts of the 1990s in that they took place in such close temporal proximity to one another that each was conducted by the same principal players, from the White House and Pentagon in Washington through CENTCOM headquarters in Tampa to the CAOC [combined air operations center] in Saudi Arabia and even, in many cases, at the shooter level in all three services.[29]

Interestingly, given the wisdom of some little hindsight-foresight, Lambeth states unexceptionally that "if there was ever to be any opportunity in principle for 'lessons learned' from one experience to be applied to a second, one would think that Operation Iraqi Freedom would have presented precisely such an opportunity."[30] Sad to say, although the military agents of intervention indeed had learned much from the tactical and even operational errors committed in Afghanistan in the fall of 2001, they had not learned the strategic and political lessons that pertained most critically to the prospects for project success.

The United States had learned, or relearned, in Afghanistan that local allies had local agendas, so that distinctively American objectives could be pursued effectively only by American forces. In retrospect, that lesson, though true, may be less strategically consequential than one might suppose. If one does not grasp the complicated social and political realities of a country and its military implications for security, even competently conducted CT and COIN will disappoint. By the same token, although it is valid to assert that a tolerable level of security in Afghanistan can be achieved only by the Afghans themselves, sensible appreciation of this less than dazzling epiphany does not in any way guarantee that the Afghans will be capable of playing their necessary part in the US-oriented security script.

It will be obvious that this discussion chooses to subordinate the technical-tactical and even operational narratives of airpower in

Afghanistan and Iraq to the all-important strategic and political contexts. Both cases of military intervention are still ongoing, though the Iraqi venture is running out of political patience and toleration of the time needed, both in Iraq and in the United States. Whether or not the American-led strategic experiences in Afghanistan and Iraq will be judged in retrospect to have been successful must depend both upon consequences that are yet to be evident and upon the politically authoritative definition of success. The "warfare after the war" in Afghanistan that emerged slowly from mid-decade onward was a reflection of basic Afghan realities that the swift victory over the Taliban in regular-style battle had scarcely touched. By 2009, it was recognized that the strategic mission was both CT and COIN and that the fuel for the terrorism, insurgency, and criminal violence was economic, political, and ideological (probably only to a modest degree).[31] Airpower in all its forms was more than merely helpfully enabling, but it could neither build nor rebuild a centralized functioning state in Afghanistan that enjoyed a sufficient political legitimacy in the eyes of a majority of very socially diverse Afghans. Nation creation is a high-risk, long-term endeavor; it is a natural and contingent process, not one that can be engineered and made to happen by a short burst of political will, especially if that will is a foreign one.

As the United States mistook victory over the Taliban in late 2001 for a lasting political peace in Afghanistan, so it repeated the error in Iraq in the spring of 2003. Quite nicely fused with the other military instruments, airpower paralyzed and demoralized the Ba'athist power of regular resistance. Indeed, the job was done superbly. Unfortunately, the destruction of Saddam's state was not the core of the strategic challenge. Wars are waged not for the sake of military victory, but rather for the political and other rewards of such. Predictably, though perhaps surprisingly not officially predicted in Washington, the consequence of US military victory was chaos. Ironically this was in good part a result of the manner in which it was swiftly achieved. Whereas Afghanistan had never enjoyed a centralized functioning state with legitimate authority, the state of Iraq was blown away or sent home by an American (and British) force light in its footprint and replaced by nothing much that could or did work.[32] In the collapsing, then collapsed, security context of Iraq, airpower performed nobly as a tactical enabler. It could not turn the insecurity condition around or even really help to do so, pending the emergence of a workable political solution that could be advanced strategically. Bereft of strategic guidance directed by political goals, tactical behavior is only that, tactical. Tacticians bereft of a strategic story arc are condemned merely to "mow the grass," as the Israelis like to put it.[33]

It would be difficult to exaggerate the importance of the point that in war after war, airpower is as necessary as it is insufficient. And to make that claim is not to criticize airpower. To risk undue emphasis of what should be obvious, airpower no more failed in Afghanistan and Iraq than did land power, sea power, space power, or cyber power. The critical challenge was political and strategic to the degree, as is historically familiar, that technical-tactical and even operational achievement cannot deliver the success that the country believes it needs, rightly or wrongly. The technological, tactical, and doctrinal narratives of the 2000s are overshadowed and dominated by politics and strategy.

Second Lebanon and Gaza

The Israeli strategic experience with airpower is of particular interest here because, paradoxically, it has features similar to the American while the context is about as different as it could be. The two national narratives are massively distinctive yet almost eerily similar in a few vital respects. The fundamental reason why this short section qualifies for inclusion here is because the Israeli strategic experience with airpower is the same subject generically as the US experience with airpower, and the single general theory of airpower embraces both.

It does not strain credibility to claim that for both the United States and Israel, airpower long has been the most consistently favored asymmetrical source of strategic advantage.[34] This claim easily is defensible for the United States from late 1943 onward, and it is highly plausible for the Israel Defense Forces (IDF) arguably from the mid-1950s and unarguably from the 1960s onward. This is not to discount the combined-arms fighting power of Israeli ground forces, but it is to emphasize the strategic significance of the air superiority or air dominance earned and exploited by the Israeli Air Force (IAF). That strategic significance typically, though not quite always, was a truly great enabler of combined-arms success on the ground. When the IAF did not own the sky over the terrestrial battlespace, as painfully was the case in the opening phase of the Yom Kippur War, Israel's army found itself in desperate straits.

Time after time Israeli strategic performance in war was punished for the sin of underestimating the enemy. In 1973, Soviet mobile air defense weapons provided to Egypt denied the IAF the ability to operate effectively at low altitude over the Sinai approach to the Suez Canal, while in 2006 Iranian-provided mobile SAMs again rendered low-altitude IAF flight somewhat hazardous. Israel may not have learned that "winning ugly," while certainly preferable to "losing ugly," can appear credibly to some important audiences as losing. This text argues that Israel, strictly viewed, was strategically successful in 2006 and 2008, but the undoubted fact that this is a controversial claim is significant. As this study keeps insisting, to understand airpower, its strengths, and its limitations and to assess its relative strategic value, the assay needs to be pervasively contextual. For the purpose of this study, we are not so much interested in judging the sense or otherwise in Israeli strategic behavior overall as we are in understanding the strategic narrative of Israeli airpower in the campaigns of 2006 and 2008. To that end one cannot address the airpower story, as it were, self-referentially. The threat and use of airpower must be considered in its place and in relation to the statecraft that it should serve and the war plan(s) it is commanded to help implement. And the whole endeavor must be considered in the strategic framework generically of ends, ways, and means.

Airpower as tactical effectiveness for anticipated—rightly or wrongly—strategic effectiveness cannot substitute for missing statecraft. And it must be said, even statecraft a great deal more skillful than was demonstrated by Israel in 2006 and 2008 is apt to be thwarted by motives for hostility that are deep, wide, and effectively permanent. (Nothing in politics truly is forever, but some inter- and intrasocietal animosities are close to being beyond reconciliation.) Thucydides captures the nub of the matter with his identification of "fear, honor, and interest" as the wellsprings of enmity. It follows that although the IAF could forcefully delete some hearts and minds from the adversary's order of battle, and for deterrent effect it might be able to reach out usefully and touch a rational cost-benefit calculus, it could not achieve the political peace that Israel desires and needs. This inability does not translate as strategic failure, provided one cannot demonstrate plausibly that the IAF defeats itself politically as a consequence of the ways and means to which it resorts in effective pursuit of advantage.

There is probably some merit in the argument that the IAF of the mid 2000s was unhealthily overimpressed by the speculative proposition that airpower alone might be able to deliver strategic victory against its more (Hezbollah in Lebanon) and much less (Hamas in Gaza) hybrid enemies. An influential study written in 1998 concluded, "Large-scale ground operations against guerrilla forces resulting in heavy losses and political damage would be avoided if operational doctrine and conception of counter-guerrilla air warfare were formulated. Offensive air campaign is the very soul of the war against a guerrilla movement."[35]

The Second Lebanon War of 12 July–14 August 2006 might be judged to have revealed a failure of airpower. The Israeli military effort was restricted to air strikes until 19 July, at which juncture IDF ground forces invaded Lebanon. While a case can be made that the neo-Wardenesque airpower optimism that was a significant mood of the "strategic moment" at the turn of the millennium and beyond—from Kosovo in 1999, through Kabul in 2001, and on to Baghdad in 2003—found significant favor in Israel also, other explanations for Israeli performance in 2006 press for recognition. Specifically, against Hezbollah in 2006, the IDF first attempted an aerial coercion strategy alone that did not succeed well enough.[36] The strategic challenge faced by the IDF required the classic synergistic blend of military skills that comprise best (or just good) practice in the modern style of combined-arms warfare.

For once this discussion must risk breaking the golden rule of contextual authority not to clutter the argument with political and other considerations that are not strictly germane. Airpower cannot be a solution to Israel's security and hence political problems with its Arab neighbors. But just because a military instrument cannot achieve everything, it does not follow that it has to be either irrelevant or harmful. For reasons of no concern to this analysis, in 2006 and 2008 Israel had pressing military problems with, respectively, Hezbollah and Hamas. With Iranian backing (subsequently admitted on Iranian television on 7 October 2007 by Hezbollah leader Sayyed Nassan Nasrallah), on 12 July 2006 Hezbollah terrorists crossed the border into Israel, ambushed an Israeli patrol, and took two Israeli soldiers as prisoners/hostages. Although this Hezbollah provocation served as the trigger for the 34-day war, it is essential to appreciate that wars historically do not erupt from nothing and nowhere. Israeli intelligence was fully aware of the Iranian arming of Hezbollah, and, of course, Israel had occupied a strip of southern Lebanon from 1982 (the First Lebanon War) until its complete final withdrawal on 23 May 2000. What occurred in the summer of 2006 was not expected by either side: Hezbollah staged what was intended to be an incident but triggered a short, intense war. Israel was ready for action in the limited standard sense that it had prepared alternative war/campaign plans, both ground-centric and autonomous air. A heady combination of certain people in office, and therefore command; the intellectual strategic fashion of the "moment," favoring precise kinetic airpower; the extant orientation of the Israeli Army, which was still in counter-Intifada mode; and a laudable concern to minimize casualties sufficed to produce the decision to respond with airpower alone.[37] What ensued was a highly successful counterforce campaign targeting Hezbollah's missile firepower. The air campaign succeeded in wreaking huge damage as intended. For example, as one careful American analyst records, the IAF hit "59 of Hezbollah's permanent rocket launchers in a '34-minute' operation" on 13 July.[38] The same author, William M. Arkin, also claimed, with lesser authority, that "the 'failure' of airpower in the 2006 Israeli-Hezbollah war was not that it promised too much or that it did not deliver. It was instead a grand strategic failure in the application of force against terrorism."[39] Arkin reads plausibly, but his judgment is not thoroughly persuasive.

It is true that Israel fought poorly in 2006. It is true also that Israel lost the contemporary and subsequent running battle of the political narrative.[40] An IDF reshaped to defeat the second and largely extramilitary intifada and its adjunct suicide bombers lacked some of the critical skills in combined arms for which once it had been justly famous.[41] The ground forces that some in the IDF were surprised to discover were needed to identify and flush out the better-concealed of Hezbollah's ready shorter-range missile arsenal were by no means fully fit for that purpose. And as usual in strategic history, an important reason why the Israeli army could not succeed as in wars of yore was because its enemy in 2006 unexpectedly was tactically, operationally, strategically, and politically competent. Hezbollah was not quite the enemy from hell, the Huns reincarnated, but for Israel in that year it was certainly a much more worthy enemy than had been anticipated (Hezbollah was not the Wehrmacht at its peak, but in 2006 it fought its style of hybrid regular and irregular warfare rather better than the Israelis conducted their counterhybrid operations). The IDF subsequently acknowledged its deficiencies by reverting in its training to emphasize the classic combined-arms fighting competencies that were noticeably missing from the action in 2006. The airpower dimension to 2006 is hard to misunderstand, though many commentators have succeeded in such an endeavor against the odds. The story should be familiar by this late stage in our inquiry. By way of summary, Israeli airpower (1) destroyed or disabled a substantial fraction of the Hezbollah missile arsenal that intelligence could locate, (2) was unable totally to suppress missile strikes across the frontier (approximately 4,000 largely 120 mm Katyusha rockets were fired during the 34-day war), and (3) inflicted great military damage on Hezbollah, both when striking independently and also when operating in joint, combined-arms supporting and supported mode. But there is no doubt that the political-moral narrative of the war in the eyes of the globalized media was not dominated by the realities of Hezbollah provocation and atrocities. Rather were the master stories those of presumably helpless Arab victims being bombarded throughout much of Lebanon by ruthlessly applied Israeli firepower safely delivered bully-fashion from altitude. It is perhaps doubly ironic that although, on the one hand, Israel lost the war politically, Hezbollah was indeed taught a painful lesson that it heeded, despite its assertion of success. Hezbollah provocations in Galilee ceased. But despite the military shock of the unexpected large-scale Israeli response in July 2006, Hezbollah plausibly could proclaim a "Divine Victory" to many audiences around the world because it had succeeded in not losing to the fearsome Israeli military machine.

The political and strategic fault line from Hezbollah in Lebanon in 2006 to Gaza in January 2008 is plain to see. In both cases the IDF was not seeking some variant of total victory. The mission was the limited one of demotivating Hezbollah and Hamas from undertaking hostile acts against Israelis in Israel. With some good reason Israelis believed that although the military story in Lebanon in 2006 ultimately was satisfactory, nonetheless they had suffered a truly damaging blow to their strategic reputation. Hezbollah had been hurt and, as became clear over time, also successfully coerced. But the IAF had not been able to destroy or deter rocket launchers in large and rather steady numbers during the short war. Also, the IDF on a whole, especially the ground forces, plainly were proved not to be fully fit for maneuverist combined-arms warfare, their erstwhile forte. Most damaging of all, Hezbollah appeared, though genuinely bloodied, heroically victorious because it was still standing after intense combat with the local superpower.

The Israeli campaign against Hamas in Gaza from 27 December 2008 to 17 January 2009 was provoked by the preceding campaign of unaimed rocket and mortar fire from Gaza across the border into Israel. The Palestinian militant organization Hamas—Iranian backed, though not wholly sponsored, à la Shiite Hezbollah in Lebanon—had achieved control in Gaza in 2006 and subsequently engaged in protracted irregular warfare with largely random standoff rocket and mortar attacks against Israeli civilians. Whatever the political and moral rights and wrongs of the conflict between Hamas and its electorate in Gaza and the state of Israel, the latter could not tolerate the assault it was under by late December 2008. Approximately 60 rockets and mortar shells hit Israel from Gaza on 24 December 2008 alone. The consequence, inevitably, was a campaign to restore security that had to achieve effective suppression of the terroristic military threat and inflict potent punishment for a coercive effect to discourage further menace, for a while at least. The result was Operation Cast Lead, wherein between 27 December 2008 and 17 January 2009, the IDF proved effective both in its operationally independent targeting of Hamas weaponry and command targets (27 December 2008–2 January 2009) and in its CAS role for combined-arms fighting in an urban environment.[42] Looking to the future, as one must in warfare, since the activity is all about its strategic and political consequences— the varieties of peace, or nonwar, that follow—the IDF needed both to damage Hamas and, as already noted, coercively demotivate it from its terroristic harassment, as well as restore the reputation for effectiveness that Israel believed it had lost in Lebanon in 2006. It is fair to say that the IDF succeeded well enough on all counts, though a noteworthy caveat must be registered.

Even as the IAF and the IDF in general somewhat restored their damaged prestige by their apparent success in Gaza, the manner in which they did this against the character of enemy they faced caused some political self-harm that was not completely avoidable. The employment of airpower in the twenty-first century, which is to say in a world permanently blessed with the near-ubiquitous presence of a globalized media, cannot avoid scoring some own goals. When the enemy is a nonstate belligerent, is somewhat civilian, deliberately deploys around and fights close to "innocents," and obviously is more than a little materially disadvantaged—though this matter needs nuanced treatment—the air power looks like a bully, the irregular or hybrid fighter the hapless and hopeless victim. Similarly, for contemporary-conflict standoff, firepower can only be as precise as its cueing and other targeting intelligence allows. Even that claim is unduly flattering, because no application of military force, indeed no human activity, will be entirely accident and error free. As Clausewitz insisted, friction happens, and we should add, even when the CEP effectively is zero.

The true problem is not imperfect technology or flawed people, though those are ever with us. Rather the basic problem is the behavior itself that we compound as the portmanteau concept of war. For reasons that are plainly not rational, kinetic airpower often is presented as more brutal and inhumane than the close fight on the ground. Airpower theorists who are career air persons may be excused having some genuine difficulty viewing their beloved military instrument in the same way as much of the world populated overwhelming by non-air-professional persons. Clean, precise action conducted surgically through and from the "wild blue yonder" is one point of view. Another is machine war waged from a distance by morally indifferent warrior-technicians. The media's unfortunate habit of referring to American, British, or Israeli military aircraft as "war planes" carries a pejorative conceptual adjectival menace that is not helpful for balanced understanding. The cases just discussed highlight this structural problem. Israeli ground and air actions in Operation Cast Lead, for example, may have caused close to 1,400 "civilian" casualties. When fighting in the close proximity of a hostile urban populace, it is no easy matter to know who is an innocent civilian bystander or who is a full- or part-time combatant.[43] If a belligerent today has an advantage in the air, that strategic fact can be more than a little offset by the difficulty avoiding damage to the political story consequential to the occasional errors that attend firepower from altitude. Of course, intelligently regarded, the problem is war and warfare, not airpower uniquely, but since when did intelligence rule authoritatively in human affairs? Airpower has suffered much unjust censure in its history. From deliberate city-burning in World War II to the striking of a wedding party in Afghanistan, warfare is hell, as it has always been. Often the public support that enables policy action employing airpower either is ignorant or chooses to be ignorant of the inherently brutal reality of warfare. There have been paradox and irony in a history of airpower that has recorded sincere determination to make war less bloody an enterprise, yet which often appears to have been frustrated in practice. Airpower theorists can and should insist that the villain is humanity itself, not one of its military agencies, but such argument will not convince those who believe in the miracle of war without violence or pain.

Conclusion: Continuity in Change in the Big Picture

It would be satisfying to be able to claim that the airpower narrative in modern strategic history has a story arc. However, on reflection such a proposition would risk inadvertently concealing major truths as a price to be paid for recognizing and celebrating some obvious but relatively lesser ones. The history of airpower is a story of all but incredible technological advance. Regarded in isolation, it is quite a stretch to identify the Wright brothers' Flyer as a member of the same technical and functional species as an F-22 Raptor or a B-2 Spirit, able stealthily to dispense 60 JDAMs to specific addresses. The historian is appropriately impressed by the uniqueness of each stage in the technological development of airpower, by its tactical prowess and hence operational potential and possible strategic meaning at every individual juncture and in each historical context. That historian, though, may miss the continuities because of the undoubted important changes. The general theory of strategy, as well as the general theories of war and of statecraft, enforce an essential unity to the airpower narrative. Nonetheless, one must be careful not to overshoot on the key point that asserts the unity of airpower experience. To explain, the strategic significance of airpower, though not unrestricted—there are some inherent limitations to the relative utility of flying machines—certainly is affected by its technical performance (speed, range, height, payload, and so forth). But regardless of its technical accomplishment as its character alters, airpower cannot transcend its nature. It is in the nature, the very DNA of airpower, to be an agent of politics-as-policy and to function for strategic effect in greater or lesser duels with the military agents of rival belligerents. Airpower is what it is, which means it is flying platforms for the purpose of generating strategic utility. Airpower is not war, it is not strategy, and it is not even, or at least hardly ever, the whole of warfare. Air war could occur, but generally speaking, the reality is aerial warfare within a war.

The battle of Britain comprised the first and only strictly (protracted) air battle between two air forces, but it was conducted in a much broader context that yielded its meaning. Reading history backwards, Germany ultimately was defeated for strategic reasons connected vitally and quite logically to the consequences of Dowding's victory in the summer of 1940. But that marvelous and well-merited success itself could only decide how the stage was set for acts which might or might not follow. With crystal clarity Dowding understood that he had not won the war; his was a defensive victory for airpower, and that alone cannot deliver the enemy dead or cap in hand.

It is tempting to argue that the airpower shown to be so lethal in the 1990s and early 2000s re-registered itself, as it were, as a change in species from the airpower that theretofore had always struggled to work around (with numbers, courage, and skill) its own technical and therefore tactical frailties. Such temptation must be resisted because airpower's inherent contextuality denies it the ability to change species. To illustrate, the IAF cannot become so technically and tactically proficient that in and by effect it would become or wholly substitute for Israeli policy and strategy. An ideal airpower, to hypothesize to make the point, could only be technically and tactically ideal as a servant of policy and strategy that one can be certain would fall some way short of perfection. And even if friendly political, strategic, and military performance were exemplary, there is always the nagging possibility that an enemy might prove yet more exemplary or perhaps just plain lucky.

It is striking that the undoubted technical and tactical multi-dimensional value of airpower in the 2000s somehow has not enabled the world's leading air powers (the United States, with Britain and Israel as worthy junior members of the top flyers' club) to cash such excellence to better strategic effect. The compound reason for this is not hard to identify, provided one has learned how to think about airpower in the appropriate way, which is to say in context. Many readers must have been struck, as have I, by the contrast between the apparent military potency of aircraft captured on film and the tedious, messy, and invariably bloody, complicated reality of conflict, war, and warfare as a whole. To date, at least, although airpower certainly has transcended the bounds of terrestrial Earth, it has not transcended the authority of the contexts of war and strategy that give it meaning. Far from diminishing the weight of airpower in the grand strategic historical narrative, this full recognition of the lore, even law, of context enables us to understand it sensibly and frame debate about it in ways compatible with its nature. Now it is time to turn from the somewhat contestable record of airpower's century of deeds to the general theory that, permissively on interpretation, has governed the now-extensive practice.

Notes

1. See Luttwak, *Strategy*, xii; and Gray, *Strategy Bridge*, 34–35 (inspired by Luttwak).

2. See the careful analysis in David Johnson, *Learning Large Lessons*. The longstanding trend in the ground-air balance in favor of the latter with reference to many contexts of land warfare can be traced reliably in the following studies covering the whole airpower era: Slessor, *Air Power and Armies*; Hallion, *Strike from the Sky*; Creveld, Canby, and Brower, *Air Power and Maneuver Warfare*; Frederick Kagan, *Finding the Target*; and Mahnken, *Technology and the American Way of War since 1945*.

3. Lambeth, *Transformation of American Air Power*.

4. Douhet, *Command of the Air*, 50. He defined targeting as "aerial strategy."

5. I defend this important maxim in my book, *Fighting Talk*, 86–89.

6. In truth, Dowding constructed the weapon system that his battlespace commander, Park, wielded to an effective deadly conclusion in 1940. See the discussion in chap. 5 herein; and Bungay, *Most Dangerous Enemy*.

7. See Chiabotti, "Deeper Shade of Blue," 74.

8. Asprey, *War in the Shadows*, and Laqueur, *Guerrilla Warfare*, offer helpful historical perspective.

9. Superior treatment can be found in Akbar, *Shade of Swords*; Kelsay, *Arguing the Just War in Islam*; Sookhdeo, *Global Jihad*; and Reilly, *Closing of the Muslim Mind*.

10. Two wide-ranging studies provide considerable historical depth: Corum and Johnson, *Airpower in Small Wars*; and Hayward, *Air Power, Insurgency and the "War on Terror."*

11. Clausewitz, *On War*, 88–89.

12. On Westphalia see the potently revisionist Osiander, "Sovereignty, International Relations, and the Westphalian Myth," while for those to whom Osiander is a little too exciting, see Croxton and Parker, "A Swift and Sure Peace." I explain my point about the complexity of World War II in my *War, Peace and International Relations*, 126–29, on "The Structure of the War."

13. Some commentators make the mistake of contrasting expressive behavior with instrumental, strategically rational behavior. While expressive violence is violence perpetuated to make a statement, it is not nihilistically astrategic. Violence effected to make a point may not be designed to contribute cumulatively in a linear way to the course of events, but it can be designed, and may well serve, to advance a cause strategically.

14. On types of strategy, see Gray, *Strategy Bridge*, 65–70.

15. See Peterson, Reinhardt, and Conger, *Symposium on the Role of Airpower in Counterinsurgency and Unconventional Warfare*; Towle, *Pilots and Rebels*; Corum and Johnson, *Airpower in Small Wars*; Vick et al., *Air Power in the New Counterinsur-*

gency Era; Hayward, *Air Power, Insurgency and the "War on Terror"*; and Read, "Airpower in COIN."

16. See Hoffman, *Conflict in the 21st Century*.

17. See Boot, "New American Way of War." Lambeth, *Air Power against Terror*, provides a reliable operational history and analysis.

18. Clausewitz, *On War*, 75.

19. See Wylie, *Military Strategy*, chap. 2.

20. See Bailey, *First World War and the Birth of the Modern Style of Warfare*.

21. I endeavor to emphasize the importance of the connections that should make a whole enterprise out of the political ends, the strategic way (plans), and the tactical means that comprise the strategic function in my *Strategy Bridge*, chap. 6.

22. The airpower dimension to the US and later the NATO intervention in Afghanistan is discussed most usefully in Lambeth, *Air Power against Terror*. Also see Lambeth, "Operation Enduring Freedom, 2001," which is a convenient excerpt from the book just cited. Johnson, *Learning Large Lessons*, chap. 5, also should be consulted, as should Stephen Biddle, *Afghanistan and the Future of Warfare*. It is interesting to look back to the Soviet airpower experience in Afghanistan in the 1980s, as does Withington, "Night of the Flying Hooligans"; for a view from the other side, see Yousaf and Adkin, *Afghanistan—The Bear Trap*, especially chap. 11. A very short list of studies of particular value on the Iraqi project that began a new phase with the invasion on 20–21 March 2003 includes the following: Murray and Scales, *Iraq War*; Gordon and Trainor, *Cobra II*; Johnson, *Learning Large Lessons*, chap. 6; Mahnken and Keaney, *War in Iraq*; Metz, *Iraq and the Evolution of American Strategy*. Also, one should not neglect the two powerful books by Ricks, *Fiasco* and *Gamble*, that make one uneasy because they are investigative journalism presented as contemporary history—the former can have too much attitude, while the latter must be so short of perspective that it is an oxymoron.

23. Nagl, *Learning to Eat Soup with a Knife*, 2005, is an important if over-praised period piece. Nagl was a significant contributor to the US Army and Marine Corps, *Counterinsurgency Field Manual*.

24. Lambeth, *Air Power against Terror*, 341.

25. Ibid., 359.

26. Ibid., 365. The words quoted are admirably graphic and accurate, yet have the potential to upset hypocritical and squeamish domestic publics in NATO countries who do not like to be reminded that what is happening in Afghanistan is warfare.

27. Inspired by Xenophon's *Anabasis*, which is a little odd given the radical difference in the military challenges of the two historical cases. The triumphal mood of 2003 was captured all too well in West and Smith, *March Up*. As a matter of historical fact, the successful and heroic retreat of the 1st Marine Division from the Chosin Reservoir in North Korea in December 1950 would have a vastly better claim on Xenophon's march "up country" as a precedent than did the advance to Baghdad in 2003.

28. The airpower dimension to the campaign is not undersold in Andres, "Deep Attack against Iraq."

29. Lambeth, *Air Power against Terror*, 367–68.

30. Ibid., 368.

31. The title "strategic theorist of the decade of the 2000s," if it is not too soon to designate such, probably should be conferred upon the Australian soldier-theorist

David Kilcullen. It is uncertain whether the near cult status of his writings merits the respect in which they are held—only time and arguably, perhaps unjustly, the outcomes in Iraq and Afghanistan will tell. The Kilcullen canon now includes the following: "Countering Global Insurgency"; "Counter-Insurgency Redux"; *Accidental Guerrilla*; and for a user's manual, *Counterinsurgency*.

32. See Ricks, *Fiasco*, and Chandrasekaran, *Imperial Life in the Emerald City*, for the appalling story.

33. Johnson, *Military Capabilities for Hybrid War*, 2.

34. See two books by Creveld, *Sword and the Olive* and *Moshe Dayan*. For more exclusive focus on Israeli airpower, see Mason, "Airpower as a National Instrument"; Gordon, "Air Superiority in the Israel-Arab Wars, 1967–1982"; Arkin, *Divining Victory*; Kreps, "Air Power's Role in Asymmetrical Operations"; Brun, "Second Lebanon War"; and Brun, "Israeli Air Power."

35. Gordon, *Vulture and the Snake*, 34. Parton, "Air Power's Illusion?" is a tough critique.

36. See Arkin, *Divining Victory*, for an excellent narrative of the war, especially Appendix B, "Chronology," 165–242.

37. See Johnson, *Military Capabilities for Hybrid War*.

38. Arkin, *Divining Victory*, 171.

39. Ibid., 157.

40. I admit to succumbing to fashion and employing the concept of the strategic narrative. Narratives are defined convincingly by Lawrence Freedman as "compelling story lines which can explain events convincingly and from which inferences can be drawn. . . . Narratives are designed or nurtured with the intention of structuring the responses of others to developing events." *Transformation of Strategic Affairs*, 22.

41. See Biddle and Friedman, *2006 Lebanon Campaign and the Future of Warfare*, for a careful analysis. For a frank and critical expert Israeli appraisal, see Siboni, "Military Campaign in Lebanon." Siboni should also be read on the subject of the desirability of Israel redefining what it means by victory: see his timely and incisive article, "War and Victory."

42. See Johnson, *Military Capabilities for Hybrid War*, 6–7.

43. Rupert Smith highlights this contextually structural challenge in his book, *Utility of Force*, where he focuses on the problem of trying to fight effectively when the situation is one of "war amongst the people." He regards this situation as "a new era of conflict—in fact a new paradigm," which I think is an exaggeration. However, today's instant globalized media coverage of military behavior certainly is new and poses dilemmas for soldiers who frequently do not wage war against other combatants ("soldiers"?) on terrain empty of civilians (by any reasonable definition).

Chapter 9

Airpower Theory

Airpower theory has suffered from two persisting lethal defects. First, it has been both logically unsound and empirically fragile, or worse. The second of these enduring problems has been more than marginally the result of the first. Confusing and unintentionally misleading language and argument understandably have had profound difficulty explaining events and behavior. It is my thesis that although there will always be scope for differing judgments on specific issues, the meaning of airpower yesterday, today, and tomorrow is neither mysterious nor is it, at least nor should it be, particularly controversial. The century-plus of airpower history to date can tell us all we need to know to understand this kind of power. To borrow and adapt from Antulio J. Echevarria's persuasive judgment on Clausewitz, the strategic narrative of airpower is complete yet unfinished.[1] By that I mean that although the character of contemporary airpower is always changing and every situation wherein airpower is applied is unique, the whole subject can be revealed convincingly in a general theory. To avoid any possibility of misunderstanding, I am claiming that the theory of airpower presented in this chapter is able to cover the subject completely. The whole nature of airpower can be explained now, even though the technical and tactical stories are ever shifting. I must add hastily that I am not claiming that this offering is or should be the final take on explaining airpower. That task, which is the role of airpower's general theory, can always be done in different ways, including some that may constitute improvements on what is offered here. The validity of the general theory of airpower—unlike airpower strategies, operations, and tactics—is not hostage to particular technical or other judgments. Whatever the marvels of technology in the years to come, they will not change the nature or the strategic narrative of airpower in national security. At least, they will not do so provided that narrative is explained competently.

Theory is explanation—at its core, that is all—but in the case of airpower, it is explanation with attitude. While certainly it strives to identify truth, the pervasive and driving motive behind theory-making is the search for truth with practical value. Airpower theory is founded upon the empirical evidence of somewhat arguable historical experience, and its primary function is to assist those who must execute airpower in the future. Some practical-minded air persons have been known to have difficulty understanding why theory matters. To them the "serious stuff" is the science and engineering that keeps them at altitude, and the pleasure and professional satisfaction is in "doing it." Such people are not much inclined to waste their time thinking about *why* one is doing it. I am not unsympathetic to such a worldview, but nonetheless, it is necessary to insist that airpower must be understood if it is to be done usefully and not irrelevantly as an end in itself.

With respect to theory itself, a warrior-scholar at the School of Advanced Air and Space Studies, Harold L. Winton, has made a constructive suggestion. He advises that theory should accomplish five basic missions: define the field of study, categorize the field's constituent parts, explain how the parts relate to one another, connect the field of study to other human endeavors, and anticipate how changes in the future will affect the field of study.[2] This is excellent advice. The challenge is to do it for airpower in such a manner that it can serve as a complete, if forever unfinished, general theory that is both broad enough to cover all the relevant phenomena yet sufficiently specific to avoid banality. Readers should bear in mind Professor Winton's wise counsel when they audit the merit in the airpower theory laid out in this chapter.

History tends to be light on theory, while social science is apt to be light on the history that is the only accessible source of empirical evidence for theory. Laboratory experimentation is not available for testing candidate hypotheses for airpower theory, though some conflict episodes were treated effectively as laboratory tests—the airpower dimension to the Spanish Civil War of 1936–39, for an example.[3] Reading history backwards, one often can characterize a battle or campaign as a rehearsal with malice for much larger events that followed. The aerial narrative to the Battle of France in 1940 springs to mind, especially the distinctive air battle over the evacuation of the BEF from Dunkirk in late May and early June. In that battle the Luftwaffe met RAF Fighter Command seriously for the first time, though under conditions wherein neither side could function close to optimally. Context tends to be sovereign over inherent capability, which is why it is perilous to draw large lessons from what amounts to strongly exclusive historical evidence. Not only should one resist the temptation to celebrate the particular believed lessons of a recent clash of arms as eternal truths about airpower, also one should not do so for the apparent evidence that can be drawn convincingly from a whole decade or two of airpower experience. This is one reason why the argument here has taken the entire period of heavier-than-air flight as its historical domain. The other reason is that I believe airpower can and should be regarded most usefully as having a single nature whose character is ever changing and changeable. Of course, airpower theory is written today in a distinctively contemporary form. And all theorists of airpower, no matter how sincere their intent to be general in probing the subject and encompassing all relevant historical experience, cannot avoid being uniquely acculturated persons with attitudes and opinions fairly specific in time, place, and concerns to their own historical context.

It can be difficult to walk a steady path between undue engagement with the issues of the day and a lofty philosophizing so abstract that it is ethereal and, to be blunt, uselessly banal. There is probably some merit in asserting that if, or when, airpower theory is found useful as a conceptual tool for the advancement of a contentious argument for an issue of today, it has in fact been either faultily drafted or misused. Airpower theory educates for action; it does not provide the ammunition.

Even when explanation for understanding is pitched at the exalted level of a general theory, claimed to be universally and eternally true, it is advisable to be less than fully reverential. What follows here is not suggested as comprising candidate nuggets of revealed truth for an "airperson's creed." This is not a "credo"; it is only an explanation of airpower to provide the necessary understanding. Airpower theory is not religion/faith, philosophy, doctrine (except with regard to its value for education), legend, or myth.[4] But it is a serious attempt to provide sufficiently reliable (i.e., most-cases) truth about airpower, a truth that is admittedly only social (soft) scientific and not physical (hard) scientific, that rests upon history and logic.

Readers will notice that the theory addresses many issue areas that seemingly are never settled conclusively or, even when apparently settled in one conflict, reappear yet again unsettled in the next. The reason is that there are large questions that must be framed as such—as ever-open questions in theory that must be resolved in every specific historical episode to fit the character of that conflict. These are big questions that are really conditions more than issues—the proper relations among land power, sea power, and airpower, to cite an obvious example.

Beautiful theory is elegant in its simple economy of words and items and parsimonious in its itemization as it presents a brilliant, tautly packaged, minimalist story that contains and suggests everything knowable about a subject. My draft of the general theory of airpower, alas, fails the tests just cited. It is wordy, though I am hopeful not gratuitously prolix, and it is granular. While the whole edifice is a unified conception, a single building, it does contain many, probably far too many, rooms. $E=mc^2$ this is not. I have discovered that simple formulae purporting to explain airpower are simply wrong. To rephrase that claim hastily, they are insufficiently correct, with the inevitable consequence that they are certain to mislead the unwary.

In the interests of clarity, accuracy, and practical utility, airpower theory is presented here in the form of many dicta. Each item is a dictum, meaning simply, a formal pronouncement. A *dictum* is a considered, seriously evidenced, and even claimed authoritative statement; the term is chosen because it carries less baggage than does *principle* or *law*. A dictum is much more serious than an opinion, but it carries neither the weight of a principle nor the asserted true authority of a law. Each dictum is distinctive, but many overlap with others. This is deliberate and desirable, because the overriding purposes of the exercise, as noted already, are clarity, accuracy, and utility, and for those it is essential that connections be specified. Many potentially combinable dicta are separated here so that significant nuance is not sacrificed. The peril is the risk of a terse and therefore elegantly PowerPoint-able airpower theory that would be tersely and elegantly simplistic and therefore wrong.

The theory here is as complete as usefully I can make it, for now. But it is work that can never be finished and, for certain, the dicta chosen can be amended by addition, deletion, or combination ad infinitum. And lest modesty was too much to the fore above, it should be understood that although the dicta are not claimed to be principles or laws, they are advanced as candidates that should be regarded and treated as permanently valid statements.

Before exposing this study's preference in airpower theory to critical view, it is only just and fair to acknowledge the massive contributions to our understanding of airpower drafted by other theorists. Much was said earlier about the classic theorists. However one judges the quality of their thought, there is every reason to recognize that a study such as this present one could only be built on the back of their efforts to explain airpower. We are all Clausewitzians because it is not possible to think about war and strategy today without employing the Prussian's concepts, whether or not we agree with them. Similarly, airpower theorizing today is performed in the company of Douhet,

Trenchard, Mitchell, and Warden, inter alia. Moving to the present day, the content and form of my theory of airpower is heavily indebted to two distinguished American Air Force historian-theorists, Phillip Meilinger and Richard P. Hallion, for whom I have high respect. Each has drafted his own elegant 10-item short list of potent "propositions" on airpower (Meilinger) and "attributes" of airpower (Hallion). I will not claim arrogantly that those propositions and attributes are wrong, but I must flag the fact that I have some serious disagreements or reservations about them. With reference to Meilinger's 10 propositions, I agree with four, half agree with a further three, and disagree with another three. My audit of Hallion's attributes registers agreement with five, half agreement with three, and disagreement with two. These items of agreement, half agreement, and disagreement now are listed and tersely annotated below. Rather than provide a detailed critique, my full views on the individual topics are exposed where appropriate in the dicta presented below. It is probably sensible not to view Meilinger's 10 propositions and Hallion's 10 attributes so much as rivals to my 27 dicta; rather the three should be regarded as different explanations of the same subject. By analogy, three artists will paint a common topic in three distinctive but, one would hope, still recognizable ways.

It is encouraging to note that Hallion has described Meilinger's 10 propositions only as "an important beginning." He himself proceeded to offer what he describes as "airpower attributes that are of particular importance."

The reason for preceding my version of theory by noting where I have significant differences with such eminent theorists as Meilinger and Hallion is that their theorizing has a provenance in ideas that, arguably, have been harmful. Poor theory does damage in the real world of behavior, because organizations and people are moved to action by ideas. My mission to present airpower theory does not launch from time zero. Airpower theory today comprises more than a century of good, bad, and sometimes correct but often misleading propositions and maxims. This richly populated, if not always richly endowed, intellectual inheritance for theorizing today cannot be ignored where it is weak, or worse. As Clausewitz insists, theory has to sort things out and distinguish the weeds from the flowers.[5] What follows is overwhelmingly constructive in form and wholly constructive by intent, but occasionally it has to be destructive of poor ideas that do not explain airpower persuasively.

Meilinger's 10 propositions regarding airpower[6]

1. "Whoever controls the air generally controls the ground."

   Half agree—this is misleading because it ignores contextuality.

2. "Airpower is an inherently strategic force."

   Disagree—this is conceptually wrong *and* seriously misleading in its practical implications.

3. "Airpower is primarily an offensive weapon."

   Disagree—this is much too restrictive an understanding.

4. "In essence, airpower is targeting, targeting is intelligence, and intelligence is analyzing the effects of air operations."

   Disagree—again this is a restrictive approach that risks a serious short-changing of the airpower story.

5. "Airpower produces physical and psychological shock by dominating the fourth dimension—time."

   Half agree—this is often true in an obvious sense, but it fails to answer satisfactorily the strategist's most vital question, "So what?"

6. "Airpower can conduct parallel operations at all levels of war, simultaneously."

   Half agree—this is obviously true, despite its implied basic conceptual error, yet again the "So what?" question points to some contestable contextuality.

7. "Precision air weapons have redefined the meaning of mass."

   Agree—this is incontestable and of great importance.

8. "Airpower's unique characteristics necessitate that it be centrally controlled by airmen."

   Agree—this claim should be obsolescent, but it is not—non-air persons are not really to be trusted with command over most uses of airpower.

9. "Technology and airpower are integrally and synergistically related."

   Agree—this is true, but does not imply that airpower is about technology, which it is not—it is about the strategic effect it should generate on behalf of policy.

10. "Airpower includes not only military assets, but [also] an aerospace industry and commercial aviation."

    Agree—this is less true than it used to be, given some of the specialized needs of distinctively military aviation, but nonetheless it is still a valid point.

Hallion's 10 attributes of airpower[7]

1. "Airpower today, and for the foreseeable future, possesses some innate synergistic qualities and advantages that have matured over a half century of development and refinement"—airpower has the "virtues" of speed, range, flexibility, precision, and lethality.

   Half agree—these are indeed attributes of airpower, but the strategic value of their virtue is dependent upon contexts of war and warfare—it is not an absolute.

2. "The time compression inherent to airpower."

   Agree—this can be important, but sometimes it is not—enemies may be able to deny you advantage in the fourth dimension if they can protract hostilities.

3. "Only airpower has the ability to bring strategic and other high-value targets an enemy holds most dear under rapid attack in simultaneous or near-simultaneous fashion."

   Half agree—this is true as it is intended to be read but it suffers from the serious error of believing that there are "strategic" targets, and it ignores the contextual dependency of strategic relevance.

4. "Fulfillment of this parallel, simultaneous attribute [attribute 3 above] of airpower requires information mastery of such magnitude as to constitute a fourth attribute itself."

   Half agree—indeed information is a key requirement, and airpower helps mightily to provide it, but the enemy has a vote in the realm of information denial, and the contexts of war and warfare limit the uses to which information can be put.

5. "Thus a fifth aspect of modern airpower is that airpower is really air and space power."

   Disagree—space power is not an attribute of airpower; it is different, albeit now essential.

6. "A sixth attribute of airpower is its duality, for both combat and humanitarian purposes."

   Agree—this is correct, but it does not sit entirely comfortably as an attribute, because it is a competence shared with sea power and land power—which is not to deny the virtue of speed of response by air.

7. "A seventh attribute of airpower is its dominance over other forms of warfare. Today and for the foreseeable future, it is no longer possible to state with any certainty that surface forces are the primary instruments whereby a nation secures victory in war."

   Disagree—the second sentence more than modestly contradicts the first. The second claim is persuasive but has forfeited victory by the obvious overstatement in the first.

8. "Historically, airpower works best when it is projected by a genuine air force."

   Agree—this is sufficiently true as to warrant it being treated as "the rule," certainly the default choice—niche exceptions should be recognized as such.

9. "In the airpower era, loss of air superiority equates to loss of the ability to exercise national prerogatives."

   Agree—by and large this is true, but it is unduly reductionist in that it plainly implies air superiority enables strategically.

10. "My tenth attribute of airpower is its inherently dynamic character and dependency upon high technology."

    Agree—this is correct, but the unique measure of technological dependency bears the risk of undue devotion to machines and their performance and too little attention to what the machines are needed to enable or accomplish, strategically regarded.

Airpower Theory in 27 Dicta: A Granular Approach

The theory of airpower is presented in the form of 27 dicta. Each dictum (D) is stated as tersely as is compatible with clarity and utility and is augmented by the necessary explanation and illustration. The list below provides a convenient check on dicta subjects.

Airpower theory dicta subjects

1. The general theory of strategy and airpower theory
2. Education for practice
3. Theory and doctrine
4. Definition
5. Aircraft, air forces, and the Air Force
6. Dedicated Air Force
7. Warfare, geography, jointness
8. Attributes
9. Strengths and limitations
10. Strategic value
11. Control of the air
12. Strategic commons
13. Control of air, land, and sea contrasted
14. Unity of air and airpower
15. Strategic effect
16. Strategic value

17. Airpower supporting and supported
18. Strategic and operational perspectives
19. Offensive and defensive instrument
20. Single historical narrative, single theory
21. Targeting
22. A revolutionary instrument
23. Parallel operations
24. Aerial bombardment
25. Technology
26. Space power and cyber power
27. Air forces differ

D1: Airpower theory is subordinate to the general theory of strategy.

Airpower theory is not an alternative to general strategic theory—the latter is not discretionary; it is always authoritative. No matter how revolutionary airpower is or appears to be in its nature, character, and consequences, it has not, will not, and indeed cannot revolutionize the nature of strategy, war, or statecraft. But it certainly can and plainly has led to changes in the character of warfare that warrant the adjective *revolutionary*. The general theory of airpower is a specific application of strategy's general theory to the air environment. The technological, tactical, and operational details and the strategies of warfare must vary among the distinctive geographical domains, but there is only a single template for strategy; conceptually it organizes every domain.

D2: Airpower theory helps educate airpower strategists; it is theory for practice.

Just as the general theory of strategy has as its primary function the education of strategists who are charged with devising actual, historically unique strategies, so airpower theory serves above all else so to educate air strategists that they are able to meet their distinctive challenges competently. Fighting power most essentially is the compounded product of three principal elements: material, intellectual/conceptual, and moral. Airpower theory alone cannot deliver superior airpower, but it can help ensure that the air agent of policy is employed in ways that are strategically intelligent. Though general in nature, airpower theory often points the way to the kinds of solutions that may work in addressing the practical challenges of the day. It is worth noting that a leading German airpower historian, Horst Boog, highlights the lack of a formal education in strategy as a significant weakness of the Luftwaffe.[8]

D3: Airpower theory educates those who write airpower doctrine and serves as a filter against dangerous viruses.

Theory is not doctrine. The purpose of theory is to educate, while that of doctrine is to instruct in a more or less mandatory, discretionary way. Doctrine, meaning that which is taught authoritatively as believed best current practice, is an ever moving story, and the pressures of the present can be so insistent that it is essential for the doctrine-writing process to be impregnated with the structural perspective of a *longue durée* provided by airpower theory. In reality, airpower theory and airpower doctrine overlap as their focus ascends from the tactical through the operational to the strategic. Because of the key roles played by individuals and their creativity, or lack thereof, and the uniqueness of strategic challenges, consideration of the use of airpower above the tactical level calls for judgment that is creatively strategic. Where that is so, plainly one has left the high utility zone for any meaning of doctrine that leans toward mandatory instruction rather than discretionary guidance as advice.

D4: Airpower is the ability to do something strategically useful in the air.

Both parts of the compound concept of airpower are somewhat problematic. This is the main reason why a consensus on authoritative definition has been hard to attract over the course of airpower's first century. *Air* is problematic because it can be held to include capabilities of many kinds that are able to contest aerial passage (e.g., ground-based air defenses) and machines that fly aerodynamically and otherwise (some kinds of missiles). *Power* is problematic because it can refer to capabilities—both military "teeth" and their ground (space and cyber) support of all varieties to demonstrated or credibly potential performance in action—or to some relative metric (e.g., US versus Chinese airpower). Experience in historical assessment as well as common sense should advise us that the all-too-popular comparative listing of airpower that simply cites aircraft numbers is always likely to mislead and frequently to mislead massively (e.g., the Luftwaffe was very much a shop window air force; it was not permitted to divert resources to the spare-parts inventory that drives serviceability for operational readiness). Any definition of airpower that proceeds in detail much beyond the adapted Billy Mitchell formula favored here as D2 immediately is in peril of passing the conceptual "culminating point of victory."[9] It is a general rule that less is more in a definition, provided the few words chosen convey the most essential meaning unambiguously. Rephrased, any ambiguity that is tolerated should be deliberate and on balance cost effective.

D5: Airpower is aircraft and air forces, not only the Air Force.

There is an unanswerable case for an organizationally and legally independent Air Force (see D6), but this fact does not detract from the authority of D5. In the logic, if not quite the letter or the spirit, of Mitchell again, it should be obvious that the nature of airpower is not directive over issues pertaining to color of uniform. Of course, there are highly important questions with immense practical military, strategic, and political significance relating to a security community's choices for airpower ownership and control. For just one example, I believe that World War II most probably would have been lost had the RAF not been independent of the British Army. It is close to inconceivable that the RAF Fighter Command of 1940 could have been created and directed (air generalship) effectively had it or its hypothetical equivalent been a part of the army.[10] However, it is a general truth that a country's airpower should be understood inclusively, not exclusively, and it should be assayed for everything strategically useful that flies. Often in historical practice it has mattered significantly which color uniform is in the cockpit, but that sometimes regrettable reality cannot negate the importance of appreciating airpower as inclusively as possible. There will always be some grounds to argue about such academic issues as when is an aircraft an aircraft rather than something else and exactly where does the aerial domain meet Earth-orbital space? These questions can be answered clearly and even rather arbitrarily, and that is usually good enough for sensible people who should not demand an absolute and incontrovertible truth that even geophysics may be unable to provide.

D6: Airpower requires a dedicated air force, though not all airpower needs to be air force.

Although there is an essential unity to a community's security problems and certainly to any episode of warfare, there is both a distinctive grammar to the preparation for and conduct of warfare in the air and a unique strategic perspective derived from an aerial focus. Similar judgments pertain to the land, sea, space, and cyber domains.[11] In some of its roles airpower rightly is to be regarded as forms of land power or sea power that happen to fly. But the authority of that judgment is limited by implications of the geophysical unity of the air domain as well as by potential opportunity costs. Airpower can be and sometimes needs to be flying firepower, ambulances, and trucks functioning as an integral component in the land power combined-arms team. Moreover, it is absolutely necessary that the requirements for direct and indirect airpower support for land power and sea power be provided in ways and with means that reflect the respective realities and needs of land and sea warfare. That said, in addition and sometimes even instead, there can be an advantageous principally air-oriented character to warfare as a whole, as well as specifically in its aerial tactical and operational detail, that soldiers and sailors are not likely to identify or grasp fully. Broad national security problems, as well as particular challenges, need to be addressed by defense professionals educated in the nature of airpower and its contemporary character. Airpower as land power and airpower as sea power are not adequate as intellectual centers of gravity for determining how best to develop and employ airpower. The unarguable and therefore rather banal fact that all conflict ultimately must have terrestrial reference because man can live only upon the land simply loses the strategic plot. It invites the strategist's most classic question, "So what?"

D7: Warfare is joint, but physical geography is not—the air domain is different.

There can be no reasonable dispute over the necessity for military jointness and even the strong desirability of some integration beyond jointness. Nonetheless, the logic of warfare cannot command a fully matching logic of geography. There is a different grammar, though not ultimately strategic logic, to military effort in each of the five unique environments. Armies, navies, air forces, space forces, and cyber forces all have the same nature strategically, but they also have thoroughly different natures because of the specific physical conditions in which they must function. Air forces are different from armies in almost all respects save for their ultimate purpose in war, which is to influence the will of the enemy by the strategic effect of their several more or less well-joined and integrated but certainly complementary behaviors. Armed forces necessarily specialized for each geographical domain do different things differently. It is not impossible, but it is improbable, that a lifetime of professional focus upon warfare on land or at sea will prepare a person as competently to understand how airpower can be employed most effectively as would a lifelong commitment to airpower.

It is well to recall the old advice against correcting so well for one kind of error that one promotes a yet worse kind. To explain, every armed service dedicated to a single geography, or at least not confused about its primary domain of concern, is virtually preprogrammed to err in exaggerating the relative strategic value of its particular domain. Air forces, both independent and especially those still politically aspirant to be so, have been more guilty than the other services of extravagant claims for strategic primacy. However, this undeniable and regrettable historical fact in no way weakens the argument that it is essential for the aerial dimension to national security to be considered by the people and organization who by education, training, and experience should understand it best. The plain record of some poor, actually if inadvertently self-harming, airpower theory is no justification at all for a country gratuitously denying itself the net benefits of superior airpower understanding. Evidence of faulty airpower theory demonstrates the need for better airpower theory, not the advisability of jettisoning the enterprise.

D8: Airpower in its very nature has fundamental, enduring, though variable attributes that individually are unique, especially when compounded synergistically for performance.

It is commonplace for airpower theorists, and especially for official Air Force doctrinal publications, to itemize the fundamental "core characteristics" of airpower. This is of little value to air professionals who know it intuitively by education, by osmosis, and by experience; however, it is vitally important that the non-air professionals, who constitute a substantial majority in the defense community as well as in society at large, be educated as to the nature of airpower. That nature cannot be grasped securely unless its enduring attributes are appreciated. It is probably true that the very familiarity of these attributes tends to work against their being understood fully in their strategic implications. It is important to note that there are two lists of advertised attributes, or claimed core characteristics, on sale in the strategic marketplace for ideas, but only one is to be trusted fully; the other is best disregarded. The reliable list of airpower characteristics itemizes strictly enduring physical features: speed, reach, height, and as a consequence, ubiquity, agility, and concentration. So says Britain's RAF plausibly, indeed unarguably.[12] In its most basic doctrine manual the RAF proceeds honestly to balance its argument by recognizing, admirably, that airpower has some variably important and enduring limitations: impermanent presence, limited payload, fragility, cost, dependence on bases, and some vulnerability to the weather. The second, unreliable list of airpower's alleged attributes shifts fatally between essential geophysical truths and arguable and unnecessary strategic assertions. Specifically, for example, Hallion identifies the following as airpower's attributes: height, reach/range, speed, mobility, payload, precision, flexibility, and lethality,[13] whereas the RAF was safely physical in its argument. Hallion registers claims that, at best, are potently misleading and certainly are implausible to most non-air professionals. Airpower is not uniquely precise in what it can do, and neither is it characteristically lethal in clear and sharp distinction to land power and sea power, let alone to space and cyber power. Thus does an important and valid argument become infected by a virus of judgment that it does not need. There is no disagreement that contemporary airpower can be precise and deadly, but that does not mean that precision and lethality are unique and eternal attributes of airpower.

D9: Airpower has persisting characteristic strengths and limitations.

It is plausible to argue that airpower has enduring, indeed characteristic, both strengths and limitations. Moreover, it is compelling to maintain that its strengths have grown much stronger over the course of its century-plus of existence, while its no less characteristic limitations have been addressed so that they have become ever less limiting. I am grateful to Phillip Meilinger for that twin-barreled insight, and I find it well supported by the evidence of historical experience.[14] That granted, the fact remains that airpower does have characteristic strengths and limitations that derive far more from its very nature than they do from context. The contexts within which airpower must operate are highly variable, but what follows applies to all cases, albeit with differing potency. A useful way to translate airpower's rather abstract generic strengths and weaknesses into more meaningful strategic ones is to organize a four-way split of categories in answer to the basic question of strategic utility. I choose to ask (1) What uniquely can airpower do? (2) What can airpower do well? (3) What does airpower tend to do poorly? and (4) What is airpower unable to do? Opinions are certain to differ over some of the detail, but what follows should command a near consensus.

The details just provided are more evident in some cases than others; as always, context reigns and rules. It need hardly be said that some of the enduring features listed, though still authoritative, have altered almost beyond technical-tactical recognition over the years. Most obviously perhaps in the category "What does airpower tend to

Characteristic strengths and weaknesses of airpower

What uniquely can airpower do?

- Directly assault physical centers of gravity regardless of their location, attack the enemy inside to outside from his center to his periphery
- Project force rapidly and globally
- Observe "over the hill" from altitude (admittedly, this is not unique; it is a capability shared with space power)
- Transport people, modest levels of equipment, and supplies rapidly and globally
- Insert and sustain small isolated expeditions, raids, and even garrisons

What can airpower do well?

- Protect friendly land and sea forces and other assets from enemy airpower
- Deter and be the decisive strategic agent for high-level and mid-level regular and conventional conflicts
- Compensate effectively for (some) deficiencies in friendly land and sea forces
- Deny or seriously impede enemy access to particular land and sea areas
- Deny enemy ability to seize, hold, and exploit objectives

What does airpower tend to do poorly?

- "Occupy" to control territory from the air alone
- Send clear diplomatic messages
- Close with and grip the enemy continuously
- Apply heavy and potentially decisive pressure for conclusive strategic effect in (largely) irregular conflicts
- Discriminate with thorough reliability between friend and foe, guilty and innocent

What is airpower unable to do?

- Cost-effectively transport very heavy or bulky cargo
- Seize and hold contested territorial objectives
- Accept, process, and police an enemy's surrender

do poorly?" state-of-the-art airpower today is vastly more capable of discrimination in targeting than used to be the case. However, this technical-tactical fact is substantially offset by the reality that today the political, legal, social-cultural, and strategic contexts for the use of kinetic airpower typically are far less permissive than in the past. Readers are invited to amend the detail in my four categories or even the categories themselves as they find most persuasive. It is important to note that this four-way split on strategic utility must be employed only within the framework of the whole of airpower theory and the general theory of strategy. The latter, in particular, is essential because the details in the "split" must function in reality in the duel of conflict and in the face of friction.

D10: The strategic value of airpower is situational but is rarely zero.

The relative strategic worth of airpower varies widely with types of conflict and geographical setting. All warfare is joint, just as all strategy is a part of grand strategy. Airpower is both enabler and enabled, supporter and supported; exactly how much of each depends upon the ever different contexts for its employment. There is no general truth beyond the sense in the wording chosen for this 10th dictum. On the one hand it is possible, indeed necessary, to decide the relative weight that each geographically specialized military agent should be able to bring to a particular conflict. But usually it will be the case that the outcome was secured by virtue of a total strategic effect that was the product of truly joint team effort. There is no reason in principle why airpower alone cannot deliver decisive strategic success, but the conditions permissive of such a victory are rare indeed. Usually the damage and pain inflicted from the air is strategically decisive only because it enables friendly ground power to seize, hold, and exploit. Damage and pain that is not connected credibly to hostile action of a close and personal kind on the ground tends to be easier to bear than direct terrestrial engagement. Some death from altitude is less conclusive than is physical presence for occupation. As J. C. Wylie argues, it is "the man on the scene with the gun" who is in control.[15] Nonetheless, Wylie's powerful dictum should not be applied indiscriminately. There are conflicts wherein a state does not wish and may not need to occupy an enemy on the ground that has been coerced successfully. Any general maxim or dictum that claims to capture the relative strategic value of airpower is either fraudulent or simply erroneous. Circumstances determine what airpower can contribute, which is not to deny that the quantity and quality of the contribution and its share of the total strategic effect that friendly forces generate are ever variable with net skill and determination. Context in the sense of historical opportunity is not everything. Opportunity has to be exploited, and that can never be guaranteed.

D11: Control of the air is the fundamental enabler for all of airpower's many contributions to strategic effect.

Control of the air allows friendly airpower to be all that it can be, to achieve all that it can achieve strategically in particular situations. One may choose to distinguish among the imperious Douhetian concept of command of the air, the scarcely less prideful idea of air supremacy, and the ever popular notion of air superiority. The core idea, with an obvious maritime provenance, is that friendly aircraft can fly when, where, and how they choose while enemy aircraft cannot, at least not reliably.[16] One is not referring necessarily to an absolute and impermeable air blockade of the enemy but rather to a situation wherein the enemy can have almost no confidence in the ability of its surviving aircraft to execute any mission of strategic importance. It always matters to be strategically sovereign in the sky, but just how much it matters must depend upon the character of the conflict and the potency of airpower in the context of the course of events. States that achieve and exploit control of the air tend to win regular conventional wars, particularly when the principal terrestrial referents are relatively open (i.e., not too much complex and difficult mountainous, triple-canopied, or urban terrain). The critical point is that although airpower can indeed make strategic history, it is always what might be considered a dependent strategic variable, not an independent one. As a general rule there are practical limits to what airpower can achieve strategically, no matter how preclusive its control of the air or how excellent it is technically, tactically, and even operationally. Airpower is a wonderful, multiuse, strategic tool, but it is not the only such tool that grand strategy needs. Very occasionally that will not be true, and airpower all but unaided will serve up decisive strategic success. The Berlin airlift of 1948–49 unarguably was just such an exception to the rule; NATO's air war against Serbia over Kosovo in 1999 contestably was another; while RAF Fighter Command's strategic victory in 1940, again somewhat arguably, registered a conclusive success for (defensive) airpower alone (though it was only a campaign victory, not victory in the war as a whole, no matter that it happened to enable most that followed to a satisfactory outcome). There is never any room to question the importance of controlling the air, but there is usually a great deal of room for questioning just what quantity of favorable strategic effect such control enables and delivers. When airpower professionals insist upon the necessity for achieving control of the air, as they should, they must be ready to answer the strategist's question: "So what" does control mean for us, and for the enemy, in likely strategic consequences?

D12: Superior airpower enables control of vital strategic "commons."

The air and the sea cannot be fortified against undesired intruders, but they can be blockaded meaningfully. Mahan referred to the high seas as the world's "wide common," then the only physical medium for global communications.[17] Today the global commons have four geographical and virtual geographical domains: sea, air, space, and cyberspace.[18] Air superiority is always only partial, because of the nature of the aircraft instrument. But that granted, an air force able to control who flies reliably to achieve useful strategic effect and who does not is close to a literally essential enabler of all terrestrial military operations. When hostile airpower is at liberty to fly where, when, and even how it will, readily visible military effort on the earth's surface becomes either difficult or impracticable. As airpower has developed technically and tactically, so control of the airspace over the terrestrial battlespace has become ever more likely to enable victory on land and sea. The seas and the air cannot be employed at sovereign discretion if enemies rule the sky. This was not always unarguably so, but since 1940–41 this argument has acquired ever greater military authority. It is well to remember that even a magnificent and unchallengeable quality of control of the great global commons of the sea and the sky suffices only to enable the dominant airpower to engage terrestrially where it wishes; it does not guarantee strategic success. Most conflicts require military effort on the ground. Control of the air common is a priceless strategic advantage, but not all advantages can be cashed for a politically meaningful victory. There is a sense in which orbital space and cyberspace qualify even more comprehensively than the air as a global common and certainly far more completely than the sea. However, on balance it is wise not to risk conflating air and space, let alone spicing up the already heady brew with cyberspace as well (see D26). D12 has quite enough importance and authority; it does not need to make imperial claims that co-opt the orbital and cyber domains as additions to its own. Moreover, it is essential that understanding of the vital roles of access enablement and denial that airpower plays in the air should not be imperiled by a shotgun brigading with the other domains. In the latter case, none of the domains of air, space, and cyber is likely to be approached properly on its own terms.

D13: Control of the air is either essential or highly desirable but differs qualitatively from control on the ground.

All that looks alike, reads alike, and sounds alike nonetheless may be unalike. For example, *control* in English carries the meaning of enforced and enforceable will. In French, by contrast, *contrôle* generally means only supervision of behavior. It is a matter of degree, but the matter is significant. French usage refers to a relatively light hand on the activity of interest, English usage to a hand that is willing and able to be as heavy as required. If it is elementary to appreciate that different languages employ the same word somewhat differently, it is rather less so to recognize the distinctions in meaning among control as in sea control, control on land, and control of the air. This is not the minor matter that it might appear, because frequently the question of what airpower might accomplish more or less unaided has been a live strategic issue. To a soldier, the control of territory has a robust meaning, and for it to be claimed credibly, the enemy truly must be *hors de combat,* or at least resting well out of sight. More to the point, control of the ground means control of the relevant people's behavior, which should mean that the war, perhaps the conflict, is over (if only for a while and in its recent character). For air professionals to claim control of their geographical domain need not carry the implication that the terrestrially bound humans that are their enemies will be ready to "cry uncle" and sign the grand surrender document. The successful soldier can look the surviving enemy in the eye and pose the choice between "surrender or die." Airpower by its nature cannot be that up close and very personal. This is not a criticism; it is just a fact of strategic geography. When airpower theorists write quite properly about control of the air and, with excellent reason, extol its virtues, they should never forget that they are sharing usage of *control* with other communities. The worldviews of our military tribes differ and find expression in distinctive military cultures and subcultures. The same key words may carry significant differences of meaning among the land, sea, air, space, and cyber domains. Control is an important example of one such concept.

D14: The air is one and so is airpower.

This belief was among the sounder thoughts of Marshal of the RAF Lord Trenchard. Regarded as a law of strategic nature, this dictum is all too easy to abuse. However, when regarded as open to some discretion in practical applicability, it contains a large kernel of essential truth. There is a geophysical unity to the sky that is in sharp contrast with the land and stands in some distinction from the condition of the sea(s). In practice as opposed to theory, of course, airpower is not truly a unity, just as some parts of the sky are more friendly than others. Nonetheless, D14 claims persuasively that for basically geophysical reasons, it is sensible to think about the sky as a single strategic domain and about airpower, friendly and other, as a unitary force. By its nature airpower is manifested in highly mobile machines that are able to concentrate and disperse rapidly over great distances and therefore with a reach orders of magnitude more rewarding to military direction than land power or sea power. This is not really a matter fit for debate; it is simply a material, tactical, and strategic reality consequential upon geography. To operate at altitude, aircraft must have the performance qualities that lend them persuasively to unified command. Some truths, no matter how unarguable at core, lend themselves to abuse in unwise practical application. D14 does not claim that all friendly airpower, of whatever character, ought to be commanded and controlled centrally. But this dictum does insist without equivocation that the essential unity and distinctiveness of the aerial domain and the nature of aircraft imply that airpower should be employed in ways that exploit its nature rather than contradict it. There is a danger that non-air-minded military people will fail to use airpower as it should best be used. Also, there is the risk that air persons will demonstrate an unduly parochial concern for air-specific matters at the cost of some neglect of the challenges facing their joint allies on land and sea. The sensible way to interpret this dictum is to say that the geography of air warfare and the necessary nature and evolving character of airpower demand that a centralizing approach to the air be the default wisdom. Particular cases will demand and require some dispersion and variety in airpower commitment, but those need to be recognized as tolerated exceptions to the rule of unity. Air strategy should be indivisible.

D15: Airpower has strategic effect, but it is not inherently strategic.

Some logical and empirical fallacies are so well entrenched that they are probably beyond reach by reason. Alas, such may well be the case with the long-standing and notably authoritative claims by some airpower theorists that (a) airpower inherently and uniquely is a strategic instrument and/or (b) some airpower is strategic and some is not (i.e., allegedly tactical). These twin beliefs have approximated major items of faith in air communities; therefore, I am all too aware that I may appear to be denying beliefs and usage that far transcend the ordinary realm of opinion and customs. With malice toward none, deep respect for some, and empathy for their historical circumstances, still it must be said that airpower theorists and practitioners have misused the concept of strategy for nearly a century. Inadvertently this has been to the detriment of their cause and to the interests that they have striven to advance for the national security. To avoid needless confusion, the logic of dictum 15 is the following:

- Strategic effect is the compounded product of all the behavior (military and other) that shapes the course and outcome of a conflict.

- In its military dimension, the course of a war is shaped and progressed by the net effect of friendly and enemy behavior.

- Again in its military dimension, which is to say in warfare, all behaviors by all military agents and agencies ultimately have some strategic effect. The logic of this argument was expressed thus by Clausewitz: "But in war, as in life generally, all parts of a whole are interconnected and thus the effects produced, however small their cause, must influence all subsequent military operations and modify their final outcome to some degree, however slight. In the same way, every means must influence even the slightest purpose."[19]

- It is appropriate to think of war as having tactical, operational, strategic, and political levels, but those "levels" should not be reified inappropriately. All military behavior is tactical in the doing. Approached collectively on a large scale, the tactical has operational meaning, while the large-scale tactical as operational-level behavior is consequential fuel in greater or lesser (a net positive or net negative) amount for the political outcome.

The view that some airpower is uniquely strategic both short-changes allegedly nonstrategic and therefore presumably much lesser airpower and relegates land power, sea power, and now space and cyber power to the second, nonstrategic division of military instruments. The fundamental conceptual error is the proposition that because airpower in one form is able to reach and strike an enemy's center(s) of gravity directly, without first defeating its army and navy, it is therefore inherently strategic. The reasoning is not entirely implausible. In theory, at least, it is possible for airpower alone to coerce an enemy's political leadership. But this speculative possibility does not suffice to render airpower strategic. The reason is because the strategic effect is decided by the target, not by the attacking airpower. To have a very great, even strategically decisive effect, does not miraculously change one's nature from the tactical to the strategic. It should be needless to explain that definitions are discretionary and can neither be true nor false. There is a sense in which "strategic" can be whatever I choose so to label. But the tactical/strategic distinction coined by Mitchell was truly a misfortune for his cause. The principal damage to understanding inadvertently caused by the distinction is, ironically, that the strategic badge can hardly help but discourage strategic planning and thought worthy of the title. After all, if some or all of my airpower is by definition (of operational mission and performance characteristics, especially range and therefore reach) inherently strategic, there is little necessity to think beyond what it might do to what might be the consequences of what it does. The tactical, operational, and strategic thus all are compounded, fused, at the price of the neglect of strategy.

D16: All airpower has strategic value in every kind of conflict.

Airpower universally and ubiquitously is strategically useful. There is an air narrative integral to every conflict, actual or anticipated, and potential. The rather foolish arguments that have persisted over the years with respect to airpower's strategic value relative to land power in particular have tended to obscure the more significant reality of airpower's true pervasiveness. Modern military operations of any character must have a joint, indeed an integral, air dimension. When ground forces are tasked with the heaviest of heavy lifting missions, as currently in Afghanistan, the "boots on the ground" still are enabled to perform their tasks by airpower in its several forms. To illustrate, airpower provides an air bridge for mobility both to and within Afghanistan, provides and supports all C4ISTAR functions, delivers essential medevac services, and both manned and unmanned—but not unpiloted—provides agile precise firepower. Regardless of who is in command and how one might assay the relative weight of air and ground forces, the permanent reality is that all military effort in all warfare today (and tomorrow) contains an indispensable and more or less diverse air component. This was an arguable truth from the 1910s, but it has been an axiomatic truth since the 1930s at the latest. The challenge is not in recognizing the merit in D16; that is hardly a stretch. Rather the challenge is to give the sense in this claim its practical due. It is an enduring problem to plan and conduct operations so that each geographically specialized military instrument contributes all of which it is capable in the specific context of the day.

D17: Airpower both supports and is supported by land power and sea power (and space power and cyber power).

The relationship between land power (perhaps better expressed as ground power) and airpower has shifted over the years, as the latter has become an ever more reliably lethal tactical instrument.[20] A superior, even supreme, airpower was a decisive advantage for the Western allies in World War II, provided the ground forces were fit to exploit the opportunities that airpower gave them. As those ground forces cashed the tokens earned by airpower, so the latter in turn could provide yet more critically enabling assistance. Airpower enabled ground power to take and hold territory, and the territory thus seized and defended could be exploited to provide hasty airfields, which enabled . . . and so on. It was a cycle of mutually reinforcing success between land and air. To expand the story, sea, land, and air each performed to enable the others. As the title to a famous US Marine Corps memoir put it, there was a "jungle road to Tokyo."[21] But the Marines' jungle road comprised islands connected by maritime and air bridges and seized at the point of combat contact with vital assistance from the airpower of all the armed services. Recall the significance of the seizure, holding, and use made of Henderson Field on Guadalcanal in 1942, while the controversial assault on Peleliu was prompted by MacArthur's fears about Japanese use of the airfields on the small island. It is appropriate to claim that today superior airpower rules the ground battlespace in open terrain. This means that locatable enemy ground forces should be reliably defeatable by a state-of-the-art airpower that enjoys control of the air. For contemporary airpower to defeat enemy ground forces, it may be necessary for friendly ground power so to menace the enemy that it is obliged to maneuver, mass, and reveal itself—as notably did not happen in Kosovo in 1999. Airpower and ground power render each other more lethal. Air menace can induce enemy ground forces so far to disperse and hide that they are unable to function effectively against massed friendly ground power. Ground menace, in turn, can be so threatening that enemy ground power has no option other than to concentrate and probably move and thereby expose itself to try and avoid destruction in land battle. Such preparation for effective conduct of ground combat must yield targets that a first-class airpower could hardly fail to destroy or paralyze. One must add the caveats that warfare is complex and that it is truly a duel. Friendly airpower that should offer the potency for favorable strategic decision might be greatly weakened in practice by, for examples, enemy ground-based air defenses and political, legal, and social-cultural constraints on targeting.

D18: By its nature airpower encourages operational and strategic perspectives, a fact with mixed consequences for good and ill.

I am uncomfortable introducing an admittedly rather jarring, apparently exhortatory note into this dictum. D18 is logically safe, as one might say. The inherent mobility of the aircraft that quintessentially comprise airpower encourages a breadth of view that can be constructive or otherwise. Although the sharp end of war is always absorbingly tactical and horribly personal, it is persuasive to argue, with Wylie, that the worldviews of soldiers, sailors, and airmen tend characteristically to differ.[22] Every person fighting or in support contributes cumulatively if minutely to total strategic effect, but it is easier to see the bigger picture, read the whole script, from the vantage point of 20,000 feet unimpaired by terrain than from the ground at eye level or from the bottom of a muddy, leech-infested ditch or even from a ship able to see to the horizon. It can be claimed that airpower theorists should be all but uniquely able to think strategically, such being a gift from their military specialty. Unfortunately, to date the merit in this assertion has been more than offset by its measure of error. The mobility, and hence range, reach, and temporal compression, enabled by airpower ought to encourage a somewhat matching width, breadth, and generously contextualized view of the strategic world. However, the historical record reveals that airpower theorists and practitioners have fallen into the "tacticization" trap.[23] Instead of exploiting their high vantage to adopt a truly strategic big-picture view, they have been seduced into confusing their mobile and wide-ranging instrument with strategy itself. If one is permitted to define *strategic* as meaning long-range and as pertaining to menacing an enemy's nonmilitary center(s) of gravity, then it is understandable that one would assert one's uniquely strategic character. It has to follow that if one authorizes a Strategic Air Command, perhaps more inclusively a Strategic Command, one is saying by unmistakable exclusion that all else among one's forces in some vital way is not strategic. The nonsense in this should be obvious. Strategic theorists do not rule the world, but they have to honor the memory of Clausewitz and call conceptual folly what it is.

D19: Airpower is not inherently an offensive instrument; rather it has both offensive and defensive value.

The belief that airpower inherently is an offensive military instrument can be dated with certainty to 1916, when it was pronounced by Gen Hugh Trenchard of the British Army's Royal Flying Corps as though it were a law of nature. If airpower has a First Law, a Prime Directive, then plausibly it has been the maxim that it is inalienably offensive. The problem with this now classical maxim—dictum is too weak a descriptor—notwithstanding the longevity of its impeccable genealogy, is that it is incorrect. What is correct is to argue that airpower is a weapon that has had an ever increasing potential to be employed offensively for high strategic effect. Once one leaves the comfort zone of a faith-based airpower credo and instead reasons strategically, the fallacy in the classic assertion becomes obvious. Offensive and defensive are determined by intent and situation, not by science and engineering. Any weapon or military support system of any kind can be employed either for offense or for defense or for both. The key question is definitional; what is the decision rule that discriminates? Do the qualities of the weapon (or other) system provide the answer, or should one look to the purpose for which it is used? America's global striking power, its expeditionary ability to project military force worldwide, is obviously operationally and tactically offensive in character. But its policy and strategy preeminently have been and remain politically and strategically defensive. It is not air forces that are, or even can be, offensive; rather is it the political choices as policy that direct strategy to find the ways in operational designs and to command tactical behavior to realize those choices as goals.

An air force ultimately is an offensive or defensive instrument according to who owns it and what that owner wishes to do with it. Strategic theory advises that while defense is the stronger form of warfare, offense is the more effective. Because of the vastness of the sky, the mobility and reach of aircraft, and their inherent relative fragility, it is understandable why most theorists and practitioners have endorsed the offensive maxim as a deep and sincere belief. Alas, the plausibility and the frequent success of airpower on the tactical offensive cannot remove the error in the belief and the peril that attends it. When airpower is held to be inherently offensive, it is easy to believe that it should always be employed in a tactically offensive manner—after all, such allegedly is the true grammar commanded by its nature. Whether offensive or defensive (effected from several means, air and ground based), the stronger is always a matter of exact historical context, not of general wisdom. Greatly better-resourced air forces have tended to be able to defeat, or at least fight their way through, the various kinds of air defense assets deployed by less-resourced foes. But even that claim needs qualification. RAF Fighter Command won a great defensive air battle in 1940 with only adequate, not overwhelming, resources. Belief that airpower properly used must be used offensively is a dangerous conviction unless one is a careful and competent theorist-practitioner. Trenchard's relentlessly offensive doctrine resulted in almost needlessly high RFC casualties in World War I. Moreover, his doctrinal legacy spurred RAF Fighter Command to celebrate its 1940 victory by indulging in large-scale offensive fighter sweeps over occupied France in 1941, with painful results. In France at the time, the Germans owned the ground upon which many RAF airmen were obliged to descend, and they staged an unpleasant combat surprise with the appearance of the highly capable new Fw 190 fighter.

There is a time, place, and occasion for the offensive employment of airpower, but it is a serious error to believe that the agile nature and reach of airpower require that it must be employed for offensive purposes. Operational offense married to tactical defense can be the most lethal of combinations for the enemy. By way of historical illustration, consider an operationally offensive bomber campaign wherein the bomber "stream" or "waves" actually are bait to entice or oblige the enemy air force to do battle and hopefully die. This was the story of 1940 when the Germans employed this operational offense/tactical defense stratagem, and it failed them; also it was the story of the Anglo-American Combined Bomber Offensive of 1943–45 when—eventually—it was successful. To strike a personal note, I have had some experience in the arms control field of grappling with the proposition that there are inherently offensive, or contrasted with defensive, weapons, and that some "strategic" weapons are inherently stabilizing and some are inherently destabilizing. Readers are advised that such distinctions are in practice nonsense, despite their episodic but alas recurring political popularity.

D20: The history of airpower is a single strategic narrative, and a single general theory has authority over all of it—past, present, and future.

It can be difficult to appreciate fully the true unity of the airpower experience. It is not hard to discern the continuities that bind together Giulio Douhet and John Warden. However, the technical and tactical distance between the world's first purpose-built military aircraft flown by the Wright brothers in 1908 and, say, the F-22 Raptor of today is so large that the airpower story can hardly help but threaten to burst out of conceptual bounds that appear inappropriate.[24] It can seem plausible to argue that changes in quantities mean changes in quality also. In other words, when the technical-tactical details of aircraft performance shift radically, as they have cumulatively over many decades, it is surely reasonable to suppose that the airpower instrument needs a new, indeed probably several new, theory(ies) to explain it. This is a fallacy. It is a glorious merit of the general theory of strategy that it can cope with all cases and conditions at all times, and the like claim holds good, certainly good enough, for airpower. The key point simply is that airpower has an enduring character but an ever variable nature. Historically specific strategies for the employment of airpower cannot evade the authority of the former, but they need always to be crafted for particular circumstances. Lest the point remain obscure, no matter how technically sophisticated airpower becomes, no matter how tactically effective it is, and no matter how dominant a position it assumes vis-à-vis land power and sea power, it can only ever be a military instrument of strategy in the service of political objectives. Airpower cannot serve itself strategically; it is unable to transcend and substitute for policy.

D21: Strategy for airpower is not all about targeting—Douhet was wrong.

It is in the nature of ground power, and even sea power, to have strategic effect by loitering with attitude in a neighborhood. Airpower has an improving ability to loiter, as it were, to occupy terrain by overlook from the overhead flank. Nonetheless, airpower has usually contributed to strategic effect not simply by "being there," by hovering with implicit menace, but rather by doing something. And the core of that something for many decades has been the delivery of firepower to the ground. To risk oversimplification, to an air person who naturally believes that his most favored military instrument inherently is an offensive and strategic tool of policy, the world of the enemy is akin to a bombing range or even to a dartboard. It would be a calumny to claim that the elemental equation of targeting = (air) strategy captures anything close to the full strategic historical narrative of airpower. But the belief that air strategy is mainly about targeting has a classical authority in provenance traceable to the great Italian at his clearest and endorsed by generations of air theorists since the 1920s. The problem is not that it is an error to focus on targeting; indeed how could it be? Given that the dropping and firing of ordnance is how some aircraft fight, of course targeting is of high importance. The problem is not with targeting. Rather is the error in confusing targeting with its effect(s) and in conflating those effects with the whole narrative of warfare and of war itself. To be crystal clear, I must assert in the most unambiguous manner of which I am capable, that targeting is important. The challenge, though, is to contextualize targeting from altitude. A significant cost in falsely equating targeting strategy with the whole strategy for a war is that the "whole house" of airpower, not only the kinetic, will be shortchanged in appreciation. Airpower may well be judged the decisive enabler of overall victory in a war, but rarely will it be able to deliver that success by conclusive strategic virtue of its own unaided kinetic effort directed by a brilliant, or even just a good enough, targeting strategy. This is not an issue of giving credit and assigning campaign medals. Typically, a country's war effort requires that its airpower be all that it can be, and perhaps then some. An airpower whose equipment, doctrine, and training heavily favor firepower over logistical mobility, intelligence gathering, medical evacuation, and so forth unintentionally is likely to impose damaging opportunity costs on its political owners. All airpower is strategic. For a major contemporary example, helicopters, too, "do strategy," whether they are fire platforms or flying troop carriers.

D22: Airpower has revolutionized tactics, operations, and strategies but not the nature of strategy, war, or warfare.

Some people have difficulty coping with the existential dualism of the radical, even revolutionary, change that airpower has effected along with the continuities in the subjects that airpower addresses. The nature of strategy, of warfare in the execution of strategy, and of war itself, has not been altered by the birth and maturing of airpower. But having said that, also one must say that airpower, the third dimension of warfare (the fourth is time), has transformed the conduct of war strategically, operationally, and tactically. The point in need of emphasis is that airpower is a revolutionary military instrument that gradually but irresistibly has changed the manner in which war is waged at every level. It is not an exaggeration to talk of the air revolution.

D23: Airpower is uniquely capable of waging geographically parallel operations of war, but this valuable ability does not necessarily confer decisive strategic advantage.

By its nature, airpower (land or sea based) can reach and therefore touch enemy assets at any distance. Kinetically at least, this quality is not shared with land power or sea power, with the notable recent exceptions of the ability of the latter two to project force by and as airpower or to conduct long-range bombardment with missiles. If one believes that to reach an enemy is to be able to deter it by threat, coerce it through pain, or disable and destroy it by brute force, then kinetic airpower must be the magic potion that cures all strategic maladies.

Unfortunately, perhaps, this is not so. Polities are not always deterrable; they may decline to be coerced, and even when heavily physically damaged, they may elect to soldier on and hope for a change in strategic fortune. That said, airpower is a uniquely agile and flexible military tool able to menace or strike at enemies on, approaching, or far distant from the terrain or sea space of close terrestrial engagement. Airpower often generates more strategic effect by harassing or destroying enemy assets at locations distant from the land battlespace than it does, or could, by close air support or battlefield interdiction. However, wisdom in that regard is highly contextual. When, between which belligerents, and where are we discussing? The tactical lethality of airpower in parallel strike operations has advanced radically in recent decades, even very recent years. If the technical-tactical achievement of such lethality is indeed the golden key to sufficient strategic effect for victory, then one would be talking about kinetic airpower as the emerging, probably the finished article. It would be the fully emerged complete solution to many and perhaps most strategic challenges wherein the need for force is a high priority. But airpower, no matter how competent in the conduct of parallel operations of war, is not axiomatically able to be strategically decisive in conflicts. Nevertheless, on occasions, a leading air power is able to craft a feasible strategy for a particular war that depends critically and convincingly on the achievement of lethality from altitude. Then, truly, the natural attributes of airpower, in dominant manifestation, should be the leading military edge that decides who wins or even that wins itself with little if any assistance from land or sea forces.

D24: Aerial bombardment "works," though not necessarily as the sole military instrument that decides a war's outcome.

Since the 1920s, airpower theory has been presented by its leading, certainly it noisiest, authors as having at its core what has been known as "strategic" bombing. To strike at the center(s) of gravity of an enemy far behind the lines on land and distant from the domain contested by naval power was held to be the unique and uniquely strategically effective contribution of airpower. This item of advocacy and faith came to be equated with the whole of airpower theory. The theory had little time or space for the character of airpower that supported armies and fleets directly or indirectly. Moreover, airpower theory was not exactly eloquent on the merits in potential achievements in performance of duties other than long-range bombardment. On one of his better days, and in less Trenchardian mode, Mitchell could be quite sensible. After all, he did bequeath us the timeless and persuasive definition of *airpower* as anything useful that flies, strictly "the ability to do something in the air."[25] Of course, if one decrees as doctrine that the only strategically useful duty of airpower is long-range bombardment, then one is in deep trouble with empirical evidence. It was not, is not, and will not be true. But because long-range (also known as "strategic") bombing cannot sensibly be regarded as the sole important mission for airpower, most emphatically it does not follow that it is unimportant or that it is always doomed to fail. If approached intelligently, aerial bombardment is likely to disappoint only if unreasonable expectations are held for its accomplishments. Long-range bombing has been strategically useful in all periods in airpower's short history. What was attempted was not always tactically wise; hence, operational and strategic ambitions were frustrated. The result was that many brave aircrew died as innocent servants of faulty doctrine and ill-conceived plans. Nonetheless, long-range aerial bombardment always had some, and on occasions major (albeit nonmeasurable), positive strategic effect.

The point in need of clearest registration is that aerial bombing as a threat to deter, inflict damage and pain to coerce, and paralyze or destroy "works" to provide strategic advantage.[26] It should not be expected to decide by its own unassisted kinetic effort who will win a conflict. It is understandable in the historical context of the 1920s and 1930s why classical airpower theorists tended to embrace this heroic claim for the unique strategic value of their instrument. However, they were ill-advised to do so. Then there was some excuse derived from institutional political circumstances for their extravagant strategic claims for long-range aerial bombardment, but no like explanation is plausible today. The early excessive strategic ambition was the product largely of immaturity: political, technological and military, and conceptual. In recent years the echoes of that ambition are attributable jointly to an understandable overexcitement at the believed value in the new lethality achievable with unprecedented precision and to a poor grasp of the general theory of strategy.

Bombardment can be important in warfare, but typically, neither the outcome of warfare nor a whole war project of which warfare is the defining part is reducible strategically to the consequences of bombing. This is an enduring fact, not a contestable argument. And the proposition that an ever-improving airpower is closing in on achieving true fusion with strategy and war is simply wrong.

D25: The high relative (to land power) degree of technology dependency inherent in airpower poses characteristic dangers as well as provides characteristic advantages.

The technical performance qualities of machines have always been literally vital to airpower to a much greater degree than generally is true for land power or even for sea power. This fundamental physical fact can encourage, and historically has encouraged, an affection for technical performance at the expense of paying due attention to the tactical, operational, strategic, and political purposes of the flying machines.[27] Even at the tactical and operational levels, where technical performance is vital—for example, speed, range, height, rate of climb, payload, "stealthiness," and so forth—there can be a weight of focus on airpower characteristics that tends to absorb creative energy that would be better devoted to combat skills and their sensible exploitation by air generalship.[28] Competence in the cockpit does not necessarily equate to competence that is competitive in combat. And a technologically impressive air order of battle is likely to be wasted if air strategists as commanders are not ready to perform for the purpose of employing technically excellent air assets usefully. A relatively high technological focus by air forces is inevitable, necessary, and desirable. But the balance is wrong if that focus translates in practice into an air force that bears some resemblance to a costly and exclusive combination flying club and science and engineering society at the expense of what should be the dominant features of a fighting force. It is not inevitable that air forces must err in this way, but the theory of airpower should alert air persons to the inalienable danger. The risks of undue fascination with the material tools are far weightier for air forces than for armies, though not necessarily for navies. With this dictum, airpower theory serves a warning, not an unavoidable indictment.

D26: Airpower, space power, and cyber power are strongly complementary, but they are not essentially a unity.

It can seem unjust to dedicatedly air-minded people that just as their most favored and even beloved air instrument unquestionably came of age in all senses, it was challenged in the rankings of relative modernity. Ballistic and (unmanned and unpiloted) cruise missiles, atomic and hydrogen weapons, and then orbiting space systems were followed closely by a galloping emergence of computer-based cyber power. Despite being the last word in modernity for futurists in the 1920s and 1930s through the Cold War decades, airpower's former status as the leading material icon of the present and future has been successfully threatened by more recent and therefore yet more modern technologies.[29] Different security communities with fairly distinctive dominant strategic and military cultures regarded the new technologies in some characteristic ways in strategic theory, policy, doctrine, organization, strategies, and tactics. For example, the Soviet Union almost naturally absorbed long-range ballistic missiles into its vast artillery park, while the United States, equally naturally, added long-range, land-based ballistic missiles to the order of battle of its Strategic Air Command.[30] Whereas land power and sea power have had centuries and more to find ways in which to function effectively for joint purposes, airpower, as the newly arrived and still growing third partner in the joint party or to the joint marriage, had to muscle in and demonstrate its utility (when it was allowed to leave the bench and play in more than minor roles).

The historically rather brief and unstable triad of land power, sea power, and airpower now has become an even more unstable quintet with the arrival of an immature space power and yet more teenage (at best) cyber power. The need for intelligent interdomainal relations plainly is pressing, even though the technological and tactical stories are shifting at a pace that outruns confidence in analysis. One must add that whereas there are literally millennia of experience with land power and sea power in action—singly as well as more and less jointly—and there is slightly more than a century of record for airpower performance, combative space power and cyber power are seriously untried, perhaps undertried, in war and warfare. The feature of immaturity is particularly important to the question of military organization because the plausible case can be advanced that it is most appropriate for space and cyber assets to be housed bureaucratically under the wing—no irony intended—of preexisting military structures until they mature and are better understood. That position is reasonable and may even be correct, but on balance most probably it is imprudent. The undeniable and critically serious fact that contemporary land power, sea power, and airpower today are vitally dependent upon complementary space power and cyber power would seem to indicate the wisdom in postponing, even just resisting, the undoubted ambitions of the new Billy Mitchells of space and cyber to own their own military domains. After all, for the dual reasons of technical immaturity and pervasive joint dependencies, surely it is sensible organizationally to fuse space and cyber with land, sea, and air; not encourage, let alone authorize and thereby celebrate, fission.

The practical logic of extensive historical experience suggests to this theorist that the same reasons why Trenchard and Mitchell insisted upon a legally and politically separate air service should be judged strategically compelling for space power and cyber power. The core of the logic lies in geophysics. The five geographical domains of warfare are physically different, a fact that commands unique tactics, operations, and strategies (though not strategy, singular). It is only sensible that a country's airpower should be developed and employed by an organization dedicated to its understanding and most skilled in its employment. Of course, the variety of tasks in that employment suggests the merit in permitting land power and sea power to provide some airpower highly specialized for their unique needs. However, airpower is far too important a national strategic and military asset to be entrusted, in the main, to any organization other than an air service whose principal concern is the health of the country's military air assets. Soldiers and sailors certainly care about airpower, but they care even more about their troops on land and their ships at sea and therefore, reasonably enough, about what airpower can do specifically for them. By extension it is understandable that soldiers, sailors, and especially air persons care very deeply indeed and appropriately about the quality of service that they receive from space power and cyber power. But these are not the right people to be entrusted with ensuring that national space power and cyber power will be all that it could usefully strategically be and become. The fact that space power and cyber power today need to be integral to terrestrial warfare should be no less self-evident than the needed fact of genuinely joint, and sometimes more, airpower on the national strategic team. An organization dedicated to space power and to cyber power is likely to advance understanding and capability, not least for joint effectiveness, more rapidly than an arrangement whereby space and cyber concerns are not the primary foci of loyalty and concern.

I am not advocating any particular organizational structure nor criticizing extant policy. But the theory of airpower claims persuasively that it is best protected and developed, indeed only safely so, by an organization devoted to that duty as its prime directive (in service of the nation, naturally). That logic holds for space power and now probably for cyber power also. One notes that air forces have adjusted to changing times, first in the 1950s by asserting dominion over a geophysically amazing hybrid domain of "aerospace," while much more recently, leading air forces (certainly the USAF and the RAF) have come to favor a complementary co-option in the formula of "air and space." The latter is a large intellectual improvement over the former, though there are reasons to doubt whether it is improvement enough. It is probably safe to claim as a certainty that the "air and space" formula expresses a transitional phase of air force adjustment to technological and strategic change.

D27: One character of air force(s) does not suit all countries in all circumstances.

There is a single theory of airpower, but the shape and size of a particular country's air force are highly variable. Not only does individual context suggest uniquely tailored strategic needs, but also each belligerent air power is both enabled and constrained in its acquisition of air force by its unique attributes. Bizarrely perhaps, it is enlightening to adapt Karl Marx's famous fundamental socialist principle of distributive justice, "from each according to his abilities, to each according to his needs," for our purpose here. Translated, each polity develops or otherwise obtains the airpower that its unique circumstances require, at least insofar as its assets (or attributes) allow. This is an idealized formula, borrowed both from Marx and from Alfred Thayer Mahan. The point of this twin-focused final dictum is to insist upon the individuality of a particular country's airpower needs in the context of the enablers and constraints that permit those identified to be realized in practice. Many strategic needs identified by many countries and for much of the time are less than perfectly matched with operationally ready capabilities. The strategy function of ends, ways, and means is logically impeccable, and its recognition is essential for discipline in behavior, but it is an ideal that frequently is not realized in state practice. Because the character of airpower at all times offers some alternative to those buying an air force, there is always fuel for argument over the wisdom in the choices made. What must be appreciated is the base argument advanced in D26 that a state has both a particular set of strategic needs—which will vary over time and in different strategic contexts, even at the same time—and a particular more or less constrained ability to purchase what it decides it needs and then employ it optimally. Mahan identified six "principal conditions affecting the sea power of nations":

1. geographical position;

2. physical conformation, including, as connected therewith, natural production and climate;

3. extent of territory;

4. number of population;

5. character of the people; and

6. character of the government, including therein the national institutions.[31]

If we add to Mahan as just quoted a further, less contestable thought by Marx, the theory of airpower is usefully enriched. Specifically, in "The Eighteenth Brumaire of Louis Napoleon," he advised, "Men make their own history, but they do not make it as they just please; they do not make it under circumstances chosen by themselves, but under circumstances directly encouraged, given and transmitted from the past. The tradition of all the dead generations weighs like a nightmare on the brain of the living."[32]

Countries cannot necessarily buy the airpower that they need in good enough time for when they need it. A careful comparative study of historical cases of airpower failure concluded that such failure was rarely the product of some shortfall in performance "on the day," but rather is more plausibly attributable to long-term structural weaknesses in defense preparation.[33] As noted already, British air generalship was good enough in 1940; certainly it was better than the Germans'. But the RAF's decisive advantage in that critical year had been earned by virtue of 23 years of serious systemic preparation. Polities that seek to improvise effective airpower to meet unanticipated strategic needs are apt to fail. An air force competitive for the demands that may well be made of it always requires years and ideally benefits from decades of preparation. Moreover, it is necessary to remember that an air force fit for the fight and to support the fight, whatever that means in context, is not synonymous with such ingredients of airpower as tax revenue, science and engineering industry, or even military organization and equipment handling skills. To fly well is one thing; to fly well in combat, at least in aid of combat, is something else that requires focus on the dueling aspect of all warfare. The history of air warfare reveals that the best pilots have not always been the most effective fighting pilots. Flying skills and killing skills are not synonymous, valuable though the former is for the latter. For a similar thought applied on a larger scale, although airpower can only be grown from much money and advanced science and technology, still it has to be created, sustained, and prudently modernized. It is not sufficient for a polity to be wealthy for it to be secure; indeed wealth may well fuel insecurity. Money, knowledge, and material must be committed years in advance to produce airpower. It is in the nature of airpower that it has to be a long-term project. Even in the much less complex and development- and productionwise speedier days of the 1930s, airpower did not lend itself to quick fixes. Britain's RAF Fighter Command had no modern fighter aircraft for 18 months in 1937–38—mercifully, only a temporary shortfall but one that could have proven nationally and internationally fatal. Actual airpower varies with strategic need as translated into capability and with the assets of countries available and chosen to be applied to meet the need identified.

While both history and logic argue for the importance of an independent air force, it cannot be denied that the USAF and British RAF are by no means the only institutional models that have proven effective.[34] States with defense budgets far smaller than the American or even the British can be attracted to the economies attendant upon assignment of a country's airpower to a single umbrella air force. Alternatively, there are countries that are comfortable subordinating all kinds of airpower to their army and navy. Such control by land and sea power is fundamentally unsound, but it is prudent to recognize the fact of strategic exceptions to the rule of the general necessity for air to be independent or at least considerably autonomous. D27 should be treated as a reinforcement of D6. That dictum in principle endorsed, perhaps condoned, distribution of a state's airpower among several air forces (corps, components, or elements). However, empathetically it asserted the virtues of a dedicated air force. What is essential is that a state's airpower should be developed, commanded, and controlled by the military professionals who best comprehend how it can be employed effectively. Institutional forms and command arrangements that weaken the relative influence of air-minded professionals over airpower's quantity, quality, or tasking inherently are undesirable. This is not a challenge to, rather is it a challenge for, "jointery."

Conclusion: Theory Rules!

The evidence of historical experience is in for airpower theory. As strategic history continues to roll, new episodes in unique contexts fuel more debate over many aspects of airpower. Air strategy, airpower in strategy, choices among technologies, airpower generalship and performance, and so forth—there is no end to the stimuli for debate. However, more than a century of extensive and intensive experience with airpower provides ample—indeed probably redundant because repetitive, albeit confirming—evidence on the basis of which to construct general theory. There is no need to wait on events, anticipate further technological change, or test more hypotheses. The century-plus from 1903, more realistically 1908, to the present can tell all that we need to know for us to make sufficient strategic sense of airpower. Some readers may well prefer to shape that theory somewhat differently than presented here. However, it should be the case that no matter how they choose to package the explanation, the content of their airpower theory ought to approximate that provided in this chapter. Accepting the controversial character of a few of my dicta, I am probably being too optimistic in that conditional aspiration. Nonetheless, I do not believe that my interpretation of airpower in theory differs significantly from what most other theorists have said or at least from what they were trying to say.

In a few major elements the theory of airpower offered here may appear heretical to those who sincerely have been content to adhere to some classic items of faith that I judge, respectfully but firmly, to be unsound. Anyone writing airpower theory today has a great deal of rewriting to do, because some large conceptual weeds have been allowed to prosper in airpower's intellectual garden. Longevity of ideas, even if not especially poor ideas, confers an authority of its own. To adapt what Marx so aptly wrote, the poor ideas of dead generations of airpower theorists can weigh heavily indeed.

Airpower theory should be permitted to educate only in how to approach the actual challenges of ever changing airpower. The theory ought not to be raided for its direct value as added authority in aid of some eminently contestable preference today. If airpower's general theory is deployed to do battle on the issue of the day, it is near certain that it will be abused, misused, and, as a result, suffer some loss of authority. Airpower theory can guide us only in how to think, not in what to think. It yields words as concepts that have explanatory power about essential matters and how and why they interact. But concepts require application; they should not themselves be commanded to serve in debate over discrete historical strategic choices.

In common with land power, sea power, space power, and cyber power, airpower should be developed and employed in ways that merit description as strategic. If airpower is not built or used in a manner worthy of the label *strategic*, then its own will pay a price for that strategic deficit. Airpower is a strategic instrument in that it is a servant of politics and policy, as are land power and the others. When airpower simply is used to do what it can do because it happens to be available, only undeserved good fortune or compensating strategic incompetence on the part of the enemy will rescue the project in question from failure.

Carl Builder, in his strongly worded meditation on the contemporary ills of the USAF as he saw them, *The Icarus Syndrome*, argued that air professionals had lost their way because they had fallen too much in love with their machines as ends in themselves. They had lost interest in, and appreciation of, the airpower theory that made strategic sense of those machines. Whether or not his judgment on the USAF at the close of the Cold War was fair and plausible, in one major respect at least, his argument had the potential to do harm. To be all that it can be, *ceteris paribus* (e.g., willing taxpayers, prudent politicians, and competent scientists, engineers, and industrial managers), airpower is not simply in need of its theory. Rather does airpower require explanation by the right enough identification and explanation of that theory. And the theory can be discovered only by disciplined strategic reasoning and on the basis of empirical evidence. Whether and how airpower theory is understood and permitted to educate for airpower practice is ever uncertain, but such concerns do not absolve theorists from their duty.

Notes

1. Echevarria, *Clausewitz and Contemporary War*, 7.
2. Winton, "Imperfect Jewel," 2–3.
3. See Corum, *"Luftwaffe* and Lessons Learned in the Spanish Civil War."
4. I am indebted to Holley, "Reflections on the Search for Airpower Theory."
5. Clausewitz, *On War*, 578.
6. Meilinger, "Ten Propositions Regarding Airpower."
7. Hallion, "Future of Airpower," 381–99.
8. Boog, "Higher Command and Leadership in the Luftwaffe, 1935–1945."

9. Clausewitz, *On War*, 566.

10. Bungay, *Most Dangerous Enemy*, makes what I believe to be a definitive and conclusive case for the independence of the RAF.

11. Builder, *Masks of War*, chap. 5, and Wylie, *Military Strategy*, chap. 5, are both distinguished analyses of service cultures and strategic perjuries that have lasting merit.

12. Royal Air Force, *British Air and Space Power Doctrine*, 16–17.

13. Hallion, "Future of Airpower," 382–83. Hallion's itemization was borrowed from Air Force Manual (AFM) 1-1, *Basic Aerospace Doctrine of the United States Air Force* (1992). For a check on progress, see AFDD-1, *Air Force Basic Doctrine* (2003), especially 27–33.

14. Meilinger's presentation to the 6th annual conference of the Fisher Institute for Air and Space Strategic Studies, Herzliyah, Israel, 10–11 May 2010.

15. Wylie, *Military Strategy*, 72.

16. See Corbett, *Some Principles of Maritime Strategy*, part 2, chap. 1.

17. Mahan, *Influence of Sea Power upon History*, 25.

18. Posen, "Command of the Commons," is instructive.

19. Clausewitz, *On War*, 75.

20. Johnson, *Learning Large Lessons*, is outstanding.

21. Eichelberger, *Our Jungle Road to Tokyo*.

22. Wylie, *Military Strategy*, chap. 5.

23. See Handel, *Masters of War*, 353–60.

24. Hallion, "Air and Space Power," 372.

25. Mitchell, *Winged Defense*, xii, 3–4.

26. This claim flatly contradicts Pape, *Bombing to Win*, 314; though see his later assessment in "True Worth of Air Power."

27. Builder, *Icarus Syndrome*, is a minor classic fueled by recognition of this malady.

28. See Bungay, *Most Dangerous Enemy*, 379, where he argues that "the Germans were out-generaled" in 1940 in the battle of Britain.

29. See Corum, "Airpower Thought in Continental Europe between the Wars"; Palmer, "Peasants into Pilots"; and Overy, *Morbid Age*, chap. 5, for the dark side of the modernity brought by scientific progress. Also, Tami Biddle notices that among Anglo-American airpower theorists in the 1930s "there was . . . too great a readiness to focus on the future without rigorously considering the past." She proceeds expansively to claim that "this is an endemic problem in air forces, which develop their institutional identity around claims to see and understand the future more clearly than other services do." *Rhetoric and Reality in Air Warfare*, 291–92.

30. The USAF waged political battle energetically but in vain to save its follow-on (to the B–52) manned bomber, the Mach-3 B-70, from cancellation in favor of the ICBM. See Roman, "Strategic Bombers over the Missile Horizon, 1957–1963."

31. Mahan, *Influence of Sea Power upon History*, 29.

32. Marx, "Eighteenth Brumaire of Louis Napoleon," 247.

33. Higham and Harris, *Why Air Forces Fail*, 355.

34. Nikiforidis, "Comparative Analysis of the Prospects for Air Power," identifies, contrasts, and evaluates the historical strategic performance of different models of airpower organization. See also Lambeth, *Air Operations in Israel's War*.

Chapter 10

Per Ardua ad Astra

The length and complexity of the airpower narrative told here demand terse summative interpretation. To that end, this conclusion seeks to encapsulate the airpower story in just eight broad points.

First, 1903–present has been the airpower century-plus. Alone, certainly, airpower has not defined the period strategically, but its influence on the course of history has been so great that to label it a revolutionary instrument is not an exaggeration. Indeed, it is defensible to argue that among the revolutions in military affairs more and less contestably carried through since 1900, that effected by airpower has been the most significant. But the world today has become so familiar with flight that airpower has lost some of the glamour and excitement that it possessed in the early decades of the twentieth century. Familiarity breeds lack of appreciation.

Second, leading on directly from the first point, the commercial and strategic history of airpower is a triumphant one. Airpower is one of history's most impressive success stories. Everyone wants some of it. Billy Mitchell's apparently loose and undisciplined definition of airpower as "the ability to do something in the air" captures exactly the spirit of the air achievement. There is a ubiquity to the utility of airpower in its many characters that seems banal only because today it is so well appreciated that it is taken for granted. Although I have amended Mitchell's definition so that it reads, "the ability to do something strategically useful in the air," I admit that less may be more in favor of his austere if apparently casual formula. Airpower is apt to underimpress when its actual achievements obviously fall short of some excessive claims for it. Airpower advocates have had the self-harming proclivity to sacrifice both an arguable "A" grade and undoubtedly a "B+" mark in implausible demands for an "A+." Airpower as a stakeholder interest in the structure and provision of modern state power has needed to fight its corner against competing demands for scarce national resources. And again, naturally, airpower has had to demonstrate what it could do in the teeth of domestic skepticism and some hostility, both sincere and

---

The title of this chapter is the motto of the RAF and a number of other Commonwealth air forces. It was officially adopted by the Royal Flying Corps in 1912. The Latin is not quite right, but literally it is taken to mean "through struggles to the stars."

self-interestedly expedient. However, the airpower story was in scant need of embellishment. To the contrary, greater modesty in explicit promises would have yielded more respect and subsequent political support as a due reward. This is written with all the Olympian authority of the historical and strategic understanding gained from hindsight, that most helpful of advantages. Nonetheless, I confess to some sadness over the paradox that the balanced and realistic airpower strategic story from 1917–18 onwards was quite wonderful enough without the claims for military primacy that were as implausible at the time as they were speculative. Had airpower theory been properly formulated in the early years, much subsequent strategically idle and unhelpful debate might have been avoided. Admittedly, today it is a little late to try and reset the clock—the best one can do is try.

Third, it is a mighty truth about airpower that context rules. However, it would be a serious mistake to assign all authority to this important and true claim. On the one hand, context both prejudices and enables the strategic influence of airpower. But context not only "is"; in addition, it is what air-minded people are able to make of it. Airpower is not a puppet behaving in an utterly prechoreographed manner. There are not many strategic contexts where it is entirely self-evident exactly who should do how much of what among land, sea, and air elements. Despite the loose conceptual image that licenses reference to strategic and operational doctrine, in reality there cannot be doctrine, meaning best practice for particular large-scale operations, let alone for choice of strategy, because each historical circumstance approached at those levels is more or less unique. Strategists educated by strategic theory have to be creative in deciding how best to employ the airpower available to the distinctive context at issue. This is not to diminish respect for the discipline imposed by those features of context that genuinely do constrain real-time discretion. But it is to insist that strategically educated air strategists will always be able to be more or less helpful to the whole war project; they will not be consigned by an iron rule of context to a particular quality and weight of strategic contribution to the variably joint endeavor. There is no law of strategy that commands a fixed place in the batting order. But the relative strategic value of airpower—and land power and sea power—is determined by context, though for another repetition for emphasis, in practice context is what one can make of it.

Fourth, it is asking too much to require and expect soldiers and sailors, and now space warriors and cybernauts also, to understand airpower properly, but it is a necessity that air professionals should understand their own military instrument strategically. To be blunt, if airmen do not understand and cannot explain airpower, no one else can be trusted to step into the intellectual void. Today, and most probably for many years to come, airpower is and will remain a massive potential source of potentially asymmetrical advantage to the United States and its close allies. It follows necessarily that just as America's rivals and enemies are motivated to design and effect ideas and capabilities to negate that US advantage, so America should be motivated to make of its airpower, defined inclusively following the Mitchell formula, all that it can be strategically. If that logic has appeal, then it is essential to recognize and act on the recognition that airpower theory is the necessary basis for understanding what contemporary and future airpower can and ought to bring to the country's security challenges. In addition, there is vital need to recognize that the theory of airpower is intelligible only when it is appreciated conceptually and applied in practice in actual strategies as a specific case or domain of the general theory of strategy. Strategic theory may not seem as difficult to grasp as rocket science, but that is probably a misapprehension. In common with rocket science, or should one say aeronautics in this context, strategy is more difficult to do than it is to understand. But without conceptual grip on sound dicta, precepts, or principles (as preferred) for airpower, one needlessly is flying strategically blind.

Fifth, because of the political variety of wars and conflicts, there has been and will be no conclusive tactical-technical resolution to the strategic question of whether airpower is more the supporting than the supported military instrument. Generic and rather abstract debate on this subject is not unlike the Christological debate in the Church in the fifth century. There is no final truth to be discovered. Theologian-strategists will debate the true nature of the airpower–land power relationship, but common sense, if not necessarily scholarship, will tell one that circumstances suggest and case-by-case trial and error will demonstrate what the relationship needs to be in the particular conflict in question. One might think that the "transformation of American air power," in Lambeth's potent phrase, would have settled the matter in favor of altitude.[1] However, we humans are land animals and only land animals, and our struggles for power, faith, and wealth typically, though not necessarily—as by law, lore, or nature—require close terrestrial engagement. War is hugely complex, while even warfare is sufficiently complex as not to lend itself to satisfactory resolution by air action alone and unsupported (except by airpower's own dedicated infrastructure, which must include extradomainal contributions from the orbital and cyber communities, even if maritime assistance is not required). Intelligent adults reasoning strategically should appreciate that the long-running and unfortunately still live supporting/supported antagonism is a strategic nonsense. The necessarily domain-specialized military forces need each other.

Canine-like precedence argument is a strategic absurdity at a generic level, because each historical situation is somewhat distinctive. This is not to deny the political reality of interservice rivalries or the genuineness of the stakes for people, careers, budgets, and relative institutional standing. But it is to decry this kind of competition, save only when it is constructive. Strategic debate over the relative weight of contributions by land power, sea power, and airpower is by no means foolish, given the kind of discretion that usually is available to a well-resourced military machine like the American. The argument ceases to be constructive when it reflects conceptual faith born of institutional interests. After a century-plus of outstanding strategic achievement, defenders of what can fairly be termed the airpower interest ought to be beyond need of reassurance that their nation still loves airpower sufficiently. Airpower is strategically essential. The argument for airpower's strategic value has long passed its culminating point of victory. The time has come to realize that the airpower interest for national and international security has won. Of course it is true that the struggle for budget share is always alive, and as a consequence, the warriors for the right (or right enough) dare not relax, let alone sleep. However, regardless of the practical necessity for airpower budgets to be protected, still it would be healthy were air professionals to be more confident in their hard-earned success. There will always be wolves, old ones and young ones, threatening the airpower sledge, to borrow a metaphor, and they have to be treated with the seriousness that they merit.

Sixth, the whole strategic narrative of airpower history should be permitted to instruct with regard to the importance of a fundamental question: Where does airpower come from? This study has emphasized that the strategic demand for airpower is generated, at root, by

the political responses of security communities to actual or anticipated dangers. Strategically viewed, airpower has been, is, and long
will remain a rich source of military answers to strategic questions.
But it is important to flag the key importance of "preparations for
war," as Clausewitz put it with admirable directness.[2] In common
with the great Prussian, I have not wished to risk diverting readers'
attention from strategic matters that have as their center of gravity
the use or threat of use of airpower. However, I am aware that in my
endeavor to be sufficiently disciplined as not to lose the strategic plot,
inadvertently I may have seemed to be dismissive of all the activities
and resources that are necessary to produce airpower capabilities and
sustain them in combat. With Clausewitz, I have chosen to focus on
"fighting."[3] To use the familiar metaphor, the emphasis has been as
swordplay and not on sword making and repair. Belatedly, it is essential to recognize that the entire history of airpower demonstrates the
validity of the general rule that the airpower capability expressed in
machines and organizations, as well as in combat prowess, cannot be
improvised. Lead-times have lengthened with the advancing complexity of technology, but nonetheless, airpower has always been a
relatively long-haul project. It is generated by national wealth; by an
advanced basis of science, technology, and industrial skills and capacity; and by a workforce competent to produce what the technolo-
gists and engineers invent and design. Airpower is not and never has
been all about frontline, operationally ready, and serviceable aircraft.
Rather, any competent audit of a country's airpower and analysis of
the reasons why it performed well or otherwise in combat must take
full account of these aspects of the subject: the size of the aircraft park
of reserve machines and engines; the rate of aircraft production; the
size of the pool of trained, operationally ready aircrew and the rate
at which the training establishment is processing new aircrew; the
quality and duration of flying and air combat training; and the scale
and efficiency of the aircraft repair and maintenance organization.
And then one has to assess the quality of staff work of all kinds that
supports performance in the air: intelligence, personnel management, and so forth—the list can be little short of encyclopedic. My
intention here is not to attempt to cite exhaustively all of the varied
assets that have to be marshaled and directed to produce this wonderful product of airpower. It is my purpose to alert readers to the
fact that the focus of this text on strategic performance was chosen
deliberately as the plot of the study. The neglect of the equivalent of

the sword maker's science and art was intended for reasons both of manuscript length and concern lest the clarity of the strategic story might be hazarded as a result.

Readers may have noticed that, save in passing, the analysis has devoted scant attention to the crucial matter of basing.[4] Regardless of one's beliefs about the relative strategic value of airpower in this war or in that, aircraft have always had to be based on land or on carriers at sea. Airpower is the product of terrestrial resources, it must operate from terrestrial bases, and it must have strategic meaning for the course of history on land. These near banalities should not be forgotten amidst the excitement of the aerial narrative. I have mentioned aircraft production because although quality of machine and person usually is key in aerial warfare, when quantity is too low, quality of strategic performance will descend in a deadly spiral. This was the story of the Luftwaffe from 1943 to 1945.[5] When airpower is too small in size to be competitive against a worthy enemy, it is likely to decline at a rate that precludes recovery. Germany's problems with inadequate airpower in the second half of World War II were substantially the result of production goals set early in the conflict at too low a level.

Seventh, airpower certainly is about technology, but it is not all about it. Similarly, airpower is about flying, but that is not all it is about. The most skillful pilots have not always been the ones most successful in combat. To fly prettily may be desirable, but war after war has revealed that personality rather than the highest of technical competence is key to being a killer in the cockpit. This is not to suggest that aircraft handling is unimportant. The whole history of manned flight has demonstrated that air forces suffer more or less serious attrition due to accidents caused primarily by pilot (or navigator) error, often in the context of bad weather, quite aside from combat losses attributable to enemy action. At times, the flying accident loss rate has been chronic. In the two world wars of the twentieth century, rightly fearful and very young men have been placed in sole charge of extremely powerful machines that in many cases they had barely mastered technically before they were expected to fly in combat. When air forces have little choice other than to truncate flying hours in training and are unable to afford the time necessary for a prudent transition period in operational training in units before commitment to combat, the result will be the kind of losses suffered by the British RFC in 1917–18 and the Luftwaffe in 1944–45. Of course, airpower is about science as technology, technology as engineering, and engineering as machines that can perform as desired when controlled by technically competent aircrew, especially pilots. However, the very centrality and essentiality of technology to airpower can have the effect of being so fascinating, not to say entertaining, to air persons that the strategic utility of the air instrument is an understudied and therefore somewhat neglected subject. Aircraft, flying, and even air fighting are not existentially useful. "Doing it" is not necessarily doing something that generates the strategic effect required. Airpower is in need of air generalship, whether seriously jointly influenced or not. "Bombs away with Curtis LeMay!" conveys a suitable spirit for airpower on the offensive, but it should not be forgotten that General LeMay the air strategist tore up the extant operational concept for the bombing of Japan when he discovered by painful experience that high-altitude precision bombardment, as per ACTS-, USAAC-, and USAAF-preferred doctrine, was wrong for the conditions over Japan in the summer of 1945.[6] The effectiveness of airpower is highly dependent upon the quality of (variably joint) air strategy that directs it, and that quality rests upon the quality of strategic education absorbed, understood, and applied by air strategists.

Eighth and finally, it is useful to confront some leading generic criticisms of airpower by way of what one might call a targeted sanity check on much that has gone before in this study. Brief general comment is appropriate on these sweeping charges against contemporary and prospective future airpower: (1) insupportable high cost, (2) irrelevance to control of people (on the ground), (3) immorality of collateral damage from aerial bombardment, (4) strategic misuse by credulous politicians, and (5) yesterday's weapon.

Regarding cost, all of the armed services are expensive. If the sticker shock for an F-35 appalls, try the cost of soldiers deployed to Afghanistan. While there is no case for aircraft that are more expensive than they need to be or that have much cheaper, strategically adequate substitutes, there is an unanswerable case for aircraft whose cost is amply justifiable in relation to their strategic value.[7] One cannot debate cost intelligently absent prudent assessment of the value of the anticipated effectiveness as well as the strength of the strategic need. Saving money is a simple matter; saving it in a strategically prudent manner often is not. Any weapon unlikely to perform as required is likely to be a waste of money.

Next, by its very nature airpower is more or less distant from the ground whereon people live. This spatial separation is both an advantage and a disadvantage. There is much that airpower can do to enable the ground element of joint operations to succeed. But for those tasks that require friendly forces to be continuously up close and personal to people—enemy, allies, and the undecided—one needs soldiers present. Sensibly understood, airpower does not aspire to perform all strategic missions unaided in all forms of warfare.

Of course collateral damage is regrettable, but it need be neither immoral nor illegal, provided both that the rules of engagement reflect closely the constraints required by the laws of war and that those rules are followed. Inevitably, accidents do happen. Friction and chance flourish in warfare. Perspective is necessary because in recent years collateral damage more often has been the result of ground warfare than of bombardment from the air.

The next criticism holds that contemporary airpower, with its all-but-immaculate precision, can be so attractive an only slightly strategic option that its availability seduces credulous politicians into being too ready to draw and fire the aerial gun. This may be true, but it has no more logical, practical, or moral merit than would advise to prohibit any other activity that is attractive when used properly but which might be abused by ignorant or malicious people. Automobiles can be deadly weapons, while many popular sports provide ample opportunity for participants to damage both themselves and others. The sensible answer to this generic criticism is to say that we should elect only politicians whom we trust to use military force carefully and strategically.

The final broad criticism is the apparently deadly claim that airpower is "yesterday's weapon," the horse cavalry of the early twenty-first century. The intelligent answer to this more than marginally unintelligent charge is to say that (1) airpower takes such a variety of forms and serves so many essential purposes that categorical obsolescence on the path to being obsolete is literally an absurd prospect; (2) the flexibility and agility that manned and piloted aircraft provide cannot be duplicated in unmanned, let alone autonomous, unpiloted platforms; (3) airpower, as always, will adopt, adapt to, and exploit new technological opportunities and will reshape itself to suit different strategic circumstances; and (4) the emerging technologies that appear to challenge some or all of the future of airpower, for example those of orbital space systems and cyber systems, are much more likely to enhance airpower through their co-option than they are to replace it. Some of the critique that bottom lines as "airpower is obsolescent" is fundamentally unsound because it rests upon an unduly exclusive understanding of what constitutes airpower. Also, there is a widespread underappreciation of the prudent limits of flexible performance by technically autonomous vehicles; unprogrammed human eyeballs and a human moral as well as strategic compass on the spot can be critically important. Plainly there are several major issue areas here: manned versus unmanned, piloted versus unpiloted (autonomous), and the long-running important subject of ground-based as opposed to airborne systems (e.g., artillery versus close air support). It is the sincere belief of this strategic theorist that airpower in all its wonderful variants is not about to pass away after the fashion of the horse cavalry that it replaced. Some of what manned and piloted airpower traditionally has performed will be conducted by unmanned and in a few, a very few, cases even unpiloted vehicles. But the process of adaptation to new and emerging technologies and strategic opportunities will be continuous. No convincing case has yet been made to suggest that the time is fast approaching for a wake to be ordered for airpower.

The most recent obituary for airpower in the literature has been written by Israeli military historian Martin van Creveld.[8] In *The Age of Airpower* (2011), he offers a wealth of historical detail, much of it interesting, in attempted support of a characteristically exciting argument about disappointment, decline, and now, allegedly, fall. Unfortunately, his attitude and thesis tend to drive his historical judgment, with the result that the airpower narrative is systematically misassessed and therefore misunderstood.

The grand strategic historical narrative of airpower is complete in the record to date, but it is seriously unfinished. Airpower is still in the process of becoming something different in character, though not in nature. I considered deploying the phrase "the airpower era" in the title to this study, but I rejected the idea because it carried the implication that airpower defined a period that had a clear beginning—which is true—and a distinct end—which is not true and is unlikely to be true on any timeline of much interest today. It has been my high ambition to help reset the clock on the understanding of airpower. This immodest mission has been pursued with the immense and invaluable assistance of the theorists of airpower who preceded me. To them, whether I agree or disagree with their reasoning, I am deeply grateful.

Notes

1. Lambeth, *Transformation of American Air Power.*
2. Clausewitz, *On War*, 131.
3. Ibid., 127–32.
4. For an airpower focus to the persisting basing challenge to strategists, see Wohlstetter, *Selection and Use of Strategic Air Bases*; for a study in historical breadth, depth, and context it would be difficult to improve on Harkavy, *Strategic Basing and Great Powers, 1200–2000.*
5. A grim narrative of the attritional demise of airpower is particularly well told in Murray, *Luftwaffe.*
6. See Werrell, *Blankets of Fire*; Kozak, *LeMay*, chaps. 7–9; and Tillman, *Whirlwind.*
7. For a critical blast try the broadside in Cordesman and Wagner, *America's Self-Destroying Airpower.*
8. Creveld, *Age of Airpower.* See also his "Rise and Fall of Air Power." It is sadly ironic that van Creveld, a gifted historian, can know so much about airpower, past and present, yet advance an argument so likely to mislead.

Bibliography

Abella, Alex. *Soldiers of Reason: The RAND Corporation and the Rise of the American Empire.* Orlando, FL: Harcourt, 2008.

Adamsky, Dima P. "Through the Looking Glass: The Soviet Military-Technical Revolution and the American Revolution in Military Affairs." *Journal of Strategic Studies* 31, no. 2 (April 2008): 257–94.

Air Ministry (UK). *The Rise and Fall of the German Air Force, 1933–1945.* 1948. Reprint, Poole, UK: Arms and Armour Press, 1983.

Akbar, M. J. *The Shade of Swords: Jihad and the Conflict between Islam and Christianity.* London: Routledge, 2002.

Andres, Richard B. "Deep Attack against Iraq: Precision Weapons, Cyber Attack, and the Future of War." In *Military Operations in Iraq*, edited by Thomas Mahnken and Thomas Keaney. London: Routledge, 2007.

Ardrey, Robert. *The Territorial Imperative: A Personal Enquiry into the Animal Origins of Property and Nations.* New York: Athenaeum, 1966.

Arkin, William M. *Divining Victory: Airpower in the 2006 Israel-Hezbollah War.* Maxwell AFB, AL: Air University Press, August 2007.

Asprey, Robert B. *War in the Shadows: The Classic History of Guerrilla Warfare from Ancient Persia to the Present.* Rev. ed. Boston: Little, Brown and Co., 1994.

Bacevich, Andrew J. *American Empire: The Realities and Consequences of US Diplomacy.* Cambridge, MA: Harvard University Press, 2002.

———. "Neglected Trinity: Kosovo and the Crisis in US Civil-Military Relations." In *War over Kosovo: Politics and Strategy in a Global Age*, edited by Bacevich and Eliot A. Cohen, 155–88.

———. *The New American Militarism: How Americans Are Seduced by War.* Oxford: Oxford University Press, 2005.

Bacevich, Andrew J., and Eliot A. Cohen, eds. *War over Kosovo: Politics and Strategy in a Global Age.* New York: Columbia University Press, 2001.

Bailey, Johnathan B. A. *The First World War and the Birth of the Modern Style of Warfare.* Occasional Paper 22. Camberley, UK: Staff College, Strategic and Combat Studies Institute, 1996.

Ball, Desmond, and Jeffrey Richelson, eds. *Strategic Nuclear Targeting*. Ithaca, NY: Cornell University Press, 1986.

Ball, Desmond, and Robert Toth. "Revising the SIOP: Taking War-Fighting to Dangerous Extremes." *International Security* 14, no. 4 (Spring 1990): 65–92.

Baram, Abdul Karim. *Technology in Warfare: The Electronic Dimension*. Abu Dhabi: Emirates Center for Strategic Studies and Research, 2008.

Barnett, Correlli. *Engage the Enemy More Closely: The Royal Navy in the Second World War*. New York: W. W. Norton, 1991.

Barnhart, Michael A. *Japan Prepares for Total War: The Search for Economic Security, 1919–1941*. Ithaca, NY: Cornell University Press, 1987.

Beard, Edmund. *Developing the ICBM: A Study in Bureaucratic Politics*. New York: Columbia University Press, 1976.

Bellamy, Chris. *Absolute War: Soviet Russia in the Second World War*. London: Macmillan, 2007.

Benbow, Tim. *The Magic Bullet? Understanding the Revolution in Military Affairs*. London: Brassey's, 2004.

Bethel, Scott A., Aaron Prupas, Tomislav Z. Ruby, and Michael V. Smith. "Developing Air Force Strategists: Change Culture, Reverse Careerism." *Joint Force Quarterly* 58 (3rd quarter 2010): 82–88.

Betts, Richard K. *Nuclear Blackmail and Nuclear Balance*. Washington, DC: Brookings Institution, 1987.

———. *Soldiers, Statesmen, and Cold War Crises*. Cambridge, MA: Harvard University Press, 1977.

Beyerchen, Alan. "From Radio to Radar: Interwar Military Adaptation to Technological Change in Germany, the United Kingdom, and the United States." In Murray and Millett, *Military Innovation in the Interwar Period*, 265–99.

Bialer, Uri. *The Shadow of the Bomber: The Fear of Air Attack and British Politics, 1932–1939*. London: Royal Historical Society, 1980.

Biddle, Stephen. *Afghanistan and the Future of Warfare: Implications for Army and Defense Policy*. Carlisle, PA: US Army War College, Strategic Studies Institute, November 2002.

Biddle, Stephen, and Jeffrey A. Friedman. *The 2006 Lebanon Campaign and the Future of Warfare: Implications for Army and Defense Policy*. Carlisle, PA: US Army War College, Strategic Studies Institute, September 2008.

Biddle, Tami Davis. *Rhetoric and Reality in Air Warfare: The Evolution of British and American Ideas about Strategic Bombing, 1914–1945.* Princeton, NJ: Princeton University Press, 2002.

Black, Jeremy. *Great Powers and the Quest for Hegemony: The World Order since 1500.* Abington, UK: Routledge, 2008.

Boog, Horst, ed. *The Conduct of the Air War in the Second World War: An International Comparison.* Oxford: Berg Publishers, 1992.

———. "Higher Command and Leadership in the Luftwaffe, 1935–1945." In Wells, *Air Power,* 111–38.

Boog, Horst, et al. *Germany and the Second World War,* vol. 4: *The Attack on the Soviet Union.* Oxford: Clarendon Press, 1998.

———, *Germany and the Second World War,* vol. 6: *The Global War.* Oxford: Clarendon Press, 2001.

Boog, Horst, Gerhard Krebs, and Detlof Vogel. *Germany and the Second World War,* vol. 7: *The Strategic Air War in Europe and the War in the West and East Asia, 1943–1944/5.* Oxford: Clarendon Press, 2006.

Boot, Max. "The New American Way of War." *Foreign Affairs* 82, no.4 (July/August 2003): 41–58.

———. *War Made New: Technology, Warfare, and the Course of History, 1500 to Today.* New York: Gotham Books, 2006.

Borgiasz, William S. *The Strategic Air Command: Evolution and Consolidation of Nuclear Forces, 1945–1955.* Westport, CT: Praeger Publishers, 1996.

Borowski, Harry R. *A Hollow Threat: Strategic Air Power and Containment before Korea.* Westport, CT: Greenwood Press, 1982.

Boyd, John R. "A Discourse on Winning and Losing." Unpublished briefing, August 1987.

Bratton, Patrick C. "A Coherent Theory of Coercion? The Writings of Robert Pape." *Comparative Strategy* 22, no. 4 (October–November 1993): 355–72.

Brodie, Bernard. *Escalation and the Nuclear Option.* Princeton, NJ: Princeton University Press, 1966.

———. *Strategy in the Missile Age.* Princeton, NJ: Princeton University Press, 1959.

———. *War and Politics.* New York: Macmillan, 1973.

Brown, Louis. *Technical and Military Imperatives: A Radar History of World War II.* New York: Taylor and Francis, 1999.

Brun, Itai. "Israeli Air Power." In *Global Air Power,* edited by John Andreas Olsen. Washington, DC: Potomac Books, 2011.

———. "The Second Lebanon War." In Olsen, *A History of Air Warfare*, 297–324.

Buckley, John. *Air Power in the Age of Total War*. London: UCL Press, 1999.

Budiansky, Stephen. *Air Power: From Kitty Hawk to Gulf War II: A History of the People, Ideas and Machines that Transformed War in the Century of Flight*. London: Penguin Books, 2004.

Budieri, Robert. *The Invention that Changed the World: The Story of Radar from War to Peace*. London: Abacus, 1996.

Builder, Carl H. *The Icarus Syndrome: The Rule of Air Power Theory in the Evolution and Fate of the US Air Force*. New Brunswick, NJ: Transaction Publishers, 1994.

———. *The Masks of War: American Military Styles in Strategy and Analysis*. Baltimore: Johns Hopkins University Press, 1989.

Bungay, Stephen. *The Most Dangerous Enemy: A History of the Battle of Britain*. London: Aurum Press, 2000.

Burleigh, Michael. *Moral Combat: A History of World War II*. London: Harper Press, 2010.

Byman, Daniel L., and Matthew C. Waxman. *Confronting Iraq: US Policy and the Use of Force since the Gulf War*. Santa Monica, CA: RAND, 2000.

———. *The Dynamics of Coercion: American Foreign Policy and the Limits of Military Might*. Cambridge, UK: Cambridge University Press, 2002.

Byman, Daniel L., Matthew C. Waxman, and Eric Larson. *Air Power as a Coercive Instrument*. Santa Monica, CA: RAND, 1999.

Campbell, Joseph. *The Hero with a Thousand Faces*. Princeton, NJ: Princeton University Press, 1969.

Chandrasekaran, Rajir. *Imperial Life in the Emerald City: Inside Iraq's Green Zone*. London: Bloomsbury, 2008.

Chiabotti, Stephen D. "A Deeper Shade of Blue: The School of Advanced Air and Space Studies." *Joint Force Quarterly* 49 (2nd quarter 2008): 73–76.

Chickering, Roger. "Total War: The Use and Abuse of a Concept." In *Anticipating Total War: The German and American Experiences, 1871–1914*, edited by Manfred Boemeke, Roger Chickering, and Stig Förster, 13–28. Cambridge, UK: Cambridge University Press, 1999.

Chickering, Roger, and Stig Förster, eds. *The Shadows of Total War*. Cambridge, UK: Cambridge University Press, 2003.

Citino, Robert M. *The German Way of War: From the Thirty Years' War to the Third Reich.* Lawrence: University Press of Kansas, 2005.

Clark, Wesley K. *Waging Modern War: Bosnia, Kosovo, and the Future of Combat.* New York: Public Affairs, 2001.

Clausewitz, Carl von. *On War.* Edited and translated by Michael Howard and Peter Paret. Princeton, NJ: Princeton University Press, 1976.

Clodfelter, Mark. "Aiming to Break Will: America's World War II Bombing of German Morale and Its Ramifications." *Journal of Strategic Studies* 33, no. 3 (June 2010): 401–35.

———. *The Limits of Air Power: The American Bombing of North Vietnam.* New York: Free Press, 1989.

———. "Molding Airpower Convictions: Development and Legacy of William Mitchell's Strategic Thought." In Meilinger, *Paths of Heaven*, 79–114.

Cohen, Eliot A. *Gulf War Air Power Survey* (5 vols.) and *Summary Report.* Washington, DC: US Government Printing Office, 1993.

———. "Kosovo and the New American Way of War." In *War over Kosovo: Politics and Strategy in a Global Age*, edited by Andrew J. Bacevich and Cohen, 38–62. New York: Columbia University Press, 2001.

———. "The Mystique of U.S. Air Power." *Foreign Affairs* 73, no. 1 (January/February 1994): 109–24.

———. "A Revolution in Warfare." *Foreign Affairs* 75, no. 2 (March/April 1996): 37–54.

———. *Supreme Command: Soldiers, Statesmen, and Leadership in Wartime.* New York: Free Press, 2002.

Coker, Christopher. *Ethics and War in the 21st Century.* Abington, UK: Routledge, 2008.

Connelly, Owen. *Blundering to Glory: Napoleon's Military Campaigns.* Wilmington, DE: Scholarly Resources Books, 1987.

Conversino, Mark J. "Executing Deliberate Force, 30 August–14 September 1995." In Owen, *Deliberate Force*, 131–75.

Cooper, Matthew. *The German Air Force, 1922–1945: An Anatomy of Failure.* London: Jane's, 1981.

Coram, Robert. *Boyd: The Fighter Pilot Who Changed the Art of War.* Boston: Little, Brown and Co., 2002.

Corbett, Julian S. *Some Principles of Maritime Strategy.* 1911. Reprint, Annapolis, MD: Naval Institute Press, 1988.

Cordesman, Anthony H. *The Lessons and Non-Lessons of the Air and Missile Campaign in Kosovo.* Westport, CT: Praeger Publishers, 2001.

Cordesman, Anthony H, and Abraham R. Wagner. *The Lessons of Modern War,* vol. 2: *The Iran-Iraq War.* Boulder, CO: Westview Press, 1990.

———. "America's Self-Destroying Airpower: Becoming Your Own Peer Threat." Updated working draft. Washington, DC: Center for Strategic and International Studies, 9 February 2009.

Cornish, Paul. *British Military Planning for the Defence of Germany, 1945–50.* Basingstoke, UK: Macmillan Press, 1996.

Corum, James R. "Airpower Thought in Continental Europe between the Wars." In Meilinger, *Paths of Heaven,* 151–81.

———. "Defeat of the Luftwaffe, 1935–1945." In *Why Air Forces Fail: The Anatomy of Defeat,* edited by Robin Higham and Stephen G. Harris, 203–26. Lexington: University Press of Kentucky, 2006.

———. *Luftwaffe: Creating the Operational Air War, 1918–1940.* Lawrence: University Press of Kansas, 1997.

———. "The *Luftwaffe* and Lessons Learned in the Spanish Civil War." In *Air Power History: Turning Points from Kitty Hawk to Kosovo,* edited by Sebastian Cox and Peter Gray, 66–89. London: Frank Cass, 2002.

———. *The Roots of Blitzkrieg: Hans von Seeckt and German Military Reform.* Lawrence: University Press of Kansas, 1992.

Corum, James R., and Wray R. Johnson. *Airpower in Small Wars: Fighting Insurgents and Terrorists.* Lawrence: University Press of Kansas, 2003.

Cox, Sebastian, and Peter Gray, eds. *Air Power History: Turning Points from Kitty Hawk to Kosovo.* London: Frank Cass, 2002.

Craig, Campbell, and Sergey Radchenko. *The Atomic Bomb and the Origins of the Cold War.* New Haven, CT: Yale University Press, 2008.

Crane, Conrad C. *American Airpower Strategy in Korea, 1950–1953.* Lawrence: University Press of Kansas, 2000.

———. *Bombs, Cities, and Civilians: American Airpower Strategy in World War II.* Lawrence: University Press of Kansas, 1993.

Craven, Wesley Frank, and James Lea Cate, eds. *The Army Air Forces in World War II.* 7 vols. Chicago: University of Chicago Press, 1948–1958.

Creveld, Martin van. *The Age of Air Power*. New York: Public Affairs Press, 2011.

———. *Fighting Power: German and U.S. Army Performance, 1939–1945*. Westport, CT: Greenwood Press, 1982.

———. *Moshe Dayan*. London: Weidenfeld and Nicolson, 2004.

———. "The Rise and Fall of Air Power." In Olsen, *A History of Air Warfare*, 351–70.

———. *The Sword and the Olive: A Critical History of the Israeli Defense Force*. New York: Public Affairs, 2002.

Creveld, Martin van, Steven L. Canby, and Kenneth S. Brower. *Air Power and Maneuver Warfare*. Maxwell AFB, AL: Air University Press, July 1994.

Croxton, Derek, and Geoffrey Parker. " 'A Swift and Sure Peace': The Congress of Westphalia, 1643–1648." In *Making Peace: Rulers, States, and the Aftermath of War*, edited by Williamson Murray and Jim Lacey. New York: Cambridge University Press, 2009.

Daalder, Ivo, and Michael O'Hanlon. *Winning Ugly: NATO's War to Save Kosovo*. Washington, DC: Brookings Institution Press, 2000.

Davidson, Phillip B. *Vietnam at War: The History: 1946–1975*. New York: Oxford University Press, 1988.

Davis, Richard G. *Bombing the European Axis Powers: A Historical Digest of the Combined Bomber Offensive, 1939–1945*. Maxwell AFB, AL: Air University Press, April 2006.

———. *Carl A. Spaatz and the Air War in Europe*. Washington, DC: Smithsonian Institution Press, 1993.

Doubler, Michael D. *Closing with the Enemy: How GIs Fought the War in Europe, 1944–1945*. Lawrence: University Press of Kansas, 1994.

Douhet, Giulio. *The Command of the Air*. 1921, 1927. Reprint, New York: Arno Press, 1972.

Dunlap, Charles J. *Shortchanging the Joint Fight?: An Airman's Assessment of FM 3-24 and the Case for Developing Truly Joint COIN Doctrine*. Maxwell AFB, AL: Air University Press, 2007.

Echevarria, Antulio J., II. *Challenging Transformation's Clichés*. Carlisle, PA: US Army War College, Strategic Studies Institute, December 2006.

———. *Clausewitz and Contemporary War*. Oxford: Oxford University Press, 2007.

———. *Imagining Future War: The West's Technological Revolution and Visions of Wars to Come, 1880–1914*. Westport, CT: Praeger Security International, 2007.

Eichelberger, Robert L. *Our Jungle Road to Tokyo*. New York: Viking, 1950.

Emme, Eugene M., ed. *The Impact of Air Power: National Security and World Politics*. Princeton, NJ: D. Van Nostrand, 1959.

Esdaile, Charles J. "De-Constructing the French Wars: Napoleon as Anti-Strategist." *Journal of Strategic Studies* 31, no. 4 (August 2008): 515–52.

Evans, David C., and Mark R. Peattie. *Kaigun: Strategy, Tactics, and Technology in the Imperial Japanese Navy, 1887–1941*. Annapolis, MD: Naval Institute Press, 1997.

Faber, Peter R. "Interwar US Army Aviation and the Air Corps Tactical School: Incubators of American Airpower." In Meilinger, *Paths of Heaven*, 183–38.

Fadok, David S. *John Boyd and John Warden: Air Power's Quest for Strategic Paralysis*. Maxwell AFB, AL: Air University Press, February 1995.

———. "John Boyd and John Warden: Airpower's Quest for Strategic Paralysis." In Meilinger, *Paths of Heaven*, 357–98.

Ferris, John. "Achieving Air Ascendancy: Challenge and Response in British Strategic Air Defence, 1915–1940." In Cox and Gray, *Air Power History*, 21–50.

———. "'Airbandit': C3I and Strategic Air Defence during the First Battle of Britain, 1915–18." In *Strategy and Intelligence: British Policy during the First World War*, edited by Michael Dockrill and David French, 23–66. London: Hambledon Press, 1996.

———. "The Air Force Brats' View of History: Recent Writing and the Royal Air Force, 1918–1960." *International History Review* 20, no. 1 (March 1998): 118–43.

———. "Catching the Wave: The RAF Pursues a RMA, 1918–39." In *The Fog of Peace and War Planning: Military and Strategic Planning under Uncertainty*, edited by Talbot C. Imlay and Monica Duffy Toft, 159–78. Abington, UK: Routledge, 2006.

———. "Fighter Defence before Fighter Command: The Rise of Strategic Air Defence in Great Britain, 1917–1934." *Journal of Military History* 63, no. 4 (October 1999): 845–84.

———. *Men, Money and Diplomacy: The Evolution of British Strategic Policy, 1919–1926*. Ithaca, NY: Cornell University Press, 1989.

———. "The Theory of a 'French Air Menace': Anglo–French Relations and the British Home Defence Air Force Programmes of 1921–25." *Journal of Strategic Studies* 10, no. 1 (March 1987): 62–83.

Finney, Robert T. *History of the Air Corps Tactical School, 1920–1940.* Washington, DC: Center for Air Force History, 1992.

Frankland, Noble. *The Bombing Offensive against Germany: Outlines and Perspectives.* London: Faber and Faber, 1965.

Freedman, Lawrence. *The Evolution of Nuclear Strategy.* 3rd ed. Basingstoke, UK: Palgrave Macmillan, 2003.

———, ed. *Strategic Coercion: Concepts and Cases.* Oxford: Oxford University Press, 1998.

———. *The Transformation of Strategic Affairs.* Adelphi Paper 318. London: International Institute for Strategic Studies, 2006.

Freedman, Lawrence, and Efraim Karsh. *The Gulf Conflict, 1990–1991: Diplomacy and War in the New World Order.* Princeton, NJ: Princeton University Press, 1993.

French, David. *The British Way in Warfare: 1688–2000.* London: Unwin Hyman, 1990.

Frieser, Karl-Heinz. *The Blitzkrieg Legend: The 1940 Campaign in the West.* Annapolis, MD: Naval Institute Press, 2005.

Futrell, Robert F. *The United States Air Force in Korea, 1950–1953.* Rev. ed. Washington, DC: US Government Printing Office, 1983.

Gaddis, John Lewis. *The Long Peace: Inquiries into the History of the Cold War.* Oxford: Oxford University Press, 1987.

———. "On Starting All Over Again: A Naive Approach to the Study of the Cold War." In *Reviewing the Cold War: Approaches, Interpretations, Theory*, edited by Odd Arne Westad, 27–42. London: Frank Cass, 2000.

Galula, David. *Counterinsurgency Warfare: Theory and Practice.* 1964. Reprint, Westport, CT: Praeger Security International, 2006.

Galvin, John R. *Air Assault: The Development of Airmobile Warfare.* New York: Hawthorne Books, 1969.

Garrett, Stephen A. *Ethics and Airpower in World War II: The British Bombing of German Cities.* New York: St. Martin's Press, 1997.

Gat, Azar. *Fascist and Liberal Visions of War: Fuller, Liddell Hart, Douhet, and Other Modernists.* Oxford: Clarendon Press, 1998.

Gates, David. *Sky Wars: A History of Military Aerospace Power.* London: Reaktion Books, 2003.

Gentile, Gian P. *How Effective Is Strategic Bombing? Lessons Learned from World War II to Kosovo.* New York: New York University Press, 2001.

———. "A Strategy of Tactics: Population-centric COIN and the Army." *Parameters* 39, no. 3 (Autumn 2009): 5–17.

Glatthaar, Joseph T. *General Lee's Army: From Victory to Collapse.* New York: Free Press, 2008.

Gooch, John. "Airpower: Theory and Practice." *Journal of Strategic Studies* 18, no. 1 (March 1995).

Gooderson, Ian. *Air Power at the Battlefront: Allied Close Air Support in Europe, 1943–45.* London: Frank Cass, 1998.

Gordon, Michael R., and Bernard E. Trainor. *Cobra II: The Inside Story of the Invasion and Occupation of Iraq.* New York: Pantheon Books, 2006.

———. *The Generals' War: The Inside Story of the Conflict in the Gulf.* Boston: Little, Brown and Co., 1995.

Gordon, Shmuel L. "Air Superiority in the Israel-Arab Wars, 1967–1982." In Olsen, *A History of Air Warfare,* 127–55.

———. "The Vulture and the Snake: Counter-Guerrilla Air Warfare: The War in Southern Lebanon." *Mideast Security and Policy Studies* 39. Ramat Gan, Israel: Bar-Ilan University, Begin-Sadat Center for Strategic Studies, July 1998.

Gorman, G. Scott. *Endgame in the Pacific: Complexity, Strategy, and the B–29.* Maxwell AFB, AL: Air University Press, February 2000.

Gow, James. "Coercive Cadences: The Yugoslav War of Dissolution." In Freedman, *Strategic Coercion,* 276–96.

Grattan, Robert F. *The Origins of Air War: The Development of Military Air Strategy in World War I.* London: I. B. Tauris, 2009.

Gray, Colin S. *The Airpower Advantage in Future Warfare: The Need for Strategy.* Research Paper 2007-2. Maxwell AFB, AL: Air Force Research Institute, Air University Press, December 2007.

———. *Another Bloody Century: Future Warfare.* London: Weidenfeld and Nicolson, 2005.

———. "The Defence Policy of the Eisenhower Administrations, 1953–1961." DPhil dissertation, University of Oxford, 1970.

———. *Explorations in Strategy.* Westport, CT: Greenwood Publishing, 1996.

———. *Fighting Talk: Forty Maxims on War, Peace, and Strategy.* Westport, CT: Praeger Security International, 2007.

———. *The Future of Land-Based Missile Forces,* Adelphi Paper 140. London: International Institute for Strategic Studies, Winter 1977.

———. "Harry S. Truman and the Forming of American Grand Strategy in the Cold War." In *Grand Strategy: Nations and Militaries,* edited by Williamson Murray, Richard Hart Sinnreich, and Jim Lacey. Cambridge, UK: Cambridge University Press, 2010.

————. *House of Cards: Why Arms Control Must Fail*. Ithaca, NY: Cornell University Press, 1992.

————. "Mission Improbable, Fear, Culture, and Interest: Peacemaking, 1943–1949." In *The Making of Peace: Rules, States, and the Aftermath of War*, edited by Williamson Murray and Jim Lacey. Cambridge, UK: Cambridge University Press, 2009.

————. *Modern Strategy*. Oxford: Oxford University Press, 1999.

————. "Moral Advantage, Strategic Advantage?" *Journal of Strategic Studies* 33, no. 3 (June 2010): 333–65.

————. *The MX ICBM and National Security*. New York: Praeger Publishers, 1981.

————. *National Security Dilemmas: Challenges and Opportunities*. Washington, DC: Potomac Books, 2009.

————. "Nuclear Strategy: The Case for a Theory of Victory." *International Security* 4, no. 1 (Summer 1979): 54–87.

————. *Nuclear Strategy and National Style*. Lanham, MD: Hamilton Press, 1986.

————. *Schools for Strategy: Teaching Strategy for 21st Century Conflict*. Carlisle, PA: US Army War College, Strategic Studies Institute, November 2009.

————. *The Second Nuclear Age*. Boulder, CO: Lynne Rienner Publishers, 1999.

————. *Strategic Studies and Public Policy: The American Experience*. Lexington: University Press of Kentucky, 1982.

————. "Strategic Thoughts for Defence Planners." *Survival* 52, no. 3 (June–July 2010): 159–78.

————. *The Strategy Bridge: Theory for Practice*. Oxford: Oxford University, 2010.

————. *Strategy for Chaos: Revolutions in Military Affairs and the Evidence of History*. London: Frank Cass, 2002.

————. "Targeting Problems for Central War." In *Strategic Nuclear Targeting*, edited by Desmond Ball and Jeffrey Richelson, 171–93. Ithaca, NY: Cornell University Press, 1985.

————. "Technology as a Dynamic of Defence Transformation." *Defence Studies* 6, no. 1 (March 2006): 26–51.

————. *Understanding Airpower: Bonfire of the Fallacies*. Research Paper 2009-3. Maxwell AFB, AL: Air Force Research Institute, March 2009.

————. "U.S. Naval Power and Competitive Grand Strategy." *International Defense Review*, no. 3 (1990): 255–58.

———. *War, Peace and International Relations*. Abington, UK: Routledge, 2007.

———. *War, Peace, and Victory: Strategy and Statecraft for the Next Century*. New York: Simon and Schuster, 1990.

Gray, Colin S., and Roger W. Barnett. *Seapower and Strategy*. Annapolis, MD: Naval Institute Press, 1989.

Grayling, A. C. *Among the Dead Cities: Was the Allied Bombing of Civilians in WWII a Necessity or a Crime?* London: Bloomsbury, 2006.

Grygiel, Jakub J. *Great Powers and Geopolitical Change*. Baltimore: Johns Hopkins University Press, 2006.

Hall, R. Cargill, ed. *Case Studies in Strategic Bombardment*. Washington, DC: Government Printing Office, 1998.

Hallion, Richard P. "Air and Space Power: Climbing and Accelerating." In Olsen, *A History of Air Warfare*, 371–93.

———. "The Future of Airpower." In *The War in the Air, 1914–1994*, edited by Alan Stephens, 377–413. Maxwell AFB, AL: Air University Press, January 2001.

———. *Rise of the Fighter Aircraft, 1914–1918*. Baltimore: Nautical and Aviation Publishing Company of America, 1984.

———. *Storm over Iraq: Air Power in the Gulf War*. Washington, DC: Smithsonian Institution Press, 1992.

———. *Strike from the Sky: The History of Battlefield Air Attack, 1911–1945*. Washington, DC: Smithsonian Institution Press, 1989.

Halperin, Morton H. *Limited War in the Nuclear Age*. New York: Wiley, 1963.

Hammond, Grant T. *The Mind of War: John Boyd and American Security*. Washington, DC: Smithsonian Institution Press, 2001.

Handel, Michael I. *Masters of War: Classical Strategic Thought*. 3rd ed. London: Frank Cass, 2001.

Hansell, Haywood S., Jr. *The Air Plan That Defeated Hitler*. New York: Arno Press, 1980.

Hanson, Victor Davis, ed. *Makers of Ancient Strategy: From the Persian Wars to the Fall of Rome*. Princeton, NJ: Princeton University Press, 2010.

Harkavy, Robert E. *Strategic Basing and the Great Powers, 1200–2000*. Abington, UK: Routledge, 2007.

Harman, Christopher C. *"Are We Beasts?" Churchill and the Moral Question of World War II "Area Bombing."* Newport Paper 1. Newport, RI: Center for Naval Warfare Studies, Naval War College, December 1991.

Harris, Brice F. *America, Technology and Strategic Culture: A Clause-witzian Assessment*. Abington, UK: Routledge, 2009.

Hastings, Max. *Armageddon: The Battle for Germany, 1944–45*. London: Macmillan, 2004.

———. *Bomber Command*. New York: Dial Press, 1979.

———. *Finest Years: Churchill as Warlord, 1940–45*. London: Harper Press, 2009.

———. *Nemesis: The Battle for Japan, 1944–45*. London: Harper Press, 2007.

Hayward, Joel S. A. *Air Power, Insurgency and the "War on Terror."* Cranwell, UK: Royal Air Force Centre for Air Power Studies, 2009.

———. *Stopped at Stalingrad: The Luftwaffe and Hitler's Defeat in the East*. Lawrence: University Press of Kansas, 1998.

Head, William P. *War from above the Clouds: B–52 Operations during the Second Indochina War and the Effects of the Air War on Theory and Doctrine*. Fairchild Paper. Maxwell AFB, AL: Air University Press, July 2002.

Henrick, Richard P. *Crimson Tide*. New York: Avon Books, 1995.

Heuser, Beatrice. "Warsaw Pact Military Doctrines in the 1970s and 1980s: Findings in the East German Archives." *Comparative Strategy* 12, no. 4 (October 1993): 437–57.

Higham, Robin, and Stephen J. Harris, eds. *Why Air Forces Fail: The Anatomy of Defeat*. Lexington: University Press of Kentucky, 2006.

Hobkirk, Michael D. *Land, Sea or Air? Military Priorities, Historical Choices*. London: Macmillan, 1972.

Hoffman, Frank G. *Conflict in the 21st Century: The Rise of Hybrid Wars*. Arlington, VA: Potomac Institute for Policy Studies, December 2007.

———. "Hybrid Threats: Neither Omnipotent nor Unbeatable." *Orbis* 54, no. 3 (Summer 2010): 441–55.

———. "Hybrid Warfare and Challenges." *Joint Force Quarterly* 52, no. 1 (1st quarter 2009): 34–39.

Holland, James. *Fortress Malta: An Island under Siege, 1940–1943*. London: Orion Books, 2003.

Holley, I. B. "Reflections on the Search for Airpower Theory." In Meilinger, *Paths of Heaven*, 579–99.

Hooton, E. R. *Eagle in Flames: The Fall of the Luftwaffe*. London: Brockhampton Press, 1999.

———. *Phoenix Triumphant: The Rise and Rise of the Luftwaffe*. London: Arms and Armour Press, 1994.

———. *War over the Trenches: Air Power and the Western Front, 1916–1918.* Hersham, UK: Ian Allan, 2010.

Howard, Michael. *The Causes of Wars and Other Essays.* London: Counterpoint, 1983.

———. *The Continental Commitment: The Dilemma of British Defence Policy in the Era of the Two World Wars.* London: Temple Smith, 1972.

———. "Total War: Some Concluding Reflections." In *A World at Total War: Global Conflict and the Politics of Destruction, 1937–1945,* edited by Roger Chickering, Stig Förster, and Bernd Greiner, 375–83. Cambridge, UK: Cambridge University Press, 2005.

Hughes, Thomas Alexander. *Overlord: General Pete Quesada and the Triumph of Tactical Air Power in World War II.* New York: Free Press, 1995.

Hughes, Wayne P., Jr. "The Strategy-Tactics Relationship." In *Seapower and Strategy,* edited by Colin S. Gray and Roger W. Barnett, 47–73. Annapolis, MD: Naval Institute Press, 1989.

Hundley, Richard O. *Past Revolutions, Future Transformations: What Can the History of Revolutions in Military Affairs Tell Us about Transforming the US Military?* Santa Monica, CA: RAND, 1999.

Imlay, Talbot. "Total War." *Journal of Strategic Studies* 30, no. 3 (June 2007): 547–70.

Imlay, Talbot, and Monica Toft. *The Fog of Peace and War Planning: Military and Strategic Planning under Uncertainty.* New York: Routledge, 2006.

Iriye, Akira. *The Origins of the Second World War in Asia and the Pacific.* London: Longman, 1987.

Irving, David. *The Rise and Fall of the Luftwaffe: The Life of Luftwaffe Marshal Erhard Milch.* London: Weidenfeld and Nicolson, 1973.

Jacobs, W. A. "The British Strategic Air Offensive against Germany in World War II." In *Case Studies in Strategic Bombardment,* edited by R. Cargill Hall, 91–182. Washington, DC: Government Printing Office, 1998.

Johnson, David E. *Fast Tanks and Heavy Bombers: Innovation in the U.S. Army, 1917–1945.* Ithaca, NY: Cornell University Press, 1998.

———. *Learning Large Lessons: The Evolving Roles of Ground Power and Air Power in the Post–Cold War Era.* MG–405–AF. Santa Monica, CA: RAND, 2006.

———. *Military Capabilities for Hybrid War: Insights from the Israel Defense Forces in Lebanon and Gaza.* Santa Monica, CA: RAND, 2010.

Johnson, Jeannie L., Kerry M. Kartchner, and Jeffrey A. Larsen, eds. *Strategic Culture and Weapons of Mass Destruction: Culturally Based Insights into Comparative National Security Policymaking.* New York: Palgrave Macmillan, 2009.

Jomini, Antoine Henri de. *The Art of War.* 1838. Reprint, London: Greenhill Books, 1992.

Jones, David Martin, and M. L. R. Smith. "Grammar but No Logic: Technique Is Not Enough—A Response to Nagl and Burton." *Journal of Strategic Studies* 33, no. 3 (June 2010): 437–46.

———. "Whose Hearts and Whose Minds? The Curious Case of Global Counter-Insurgency." *Journal of Strategic Studies* 33, no. 1 (February 2010): 81–121.

Kagan, Donald. *On the Origins of War and the Preservation of Peace.* New York: Doubleday, 1995.

Kagan, Frederick W. *Finding the Target: The Transformation of American Military Policy.* New York: Encounter Books, 2006.

Kahn, Herman. *Thinking about the Unthinkable.* New York: Horizon Press, 1962.

Kaiser, David. *American Tragedy: Kennedy, Johnson, and the Origins of the Vietnam War.* Cambridge, MA: Belknap Press of Harvard University Press, 2000.

Karnow, Stanley. *Vietnam: A History.* New York: Viking Press, 1983.

Keaney, Thomas A., and Eliot A. Cohen. *Revolution in Warfare? Air Power in the Persian Gulf.* Annapolis, MD: Naval Institute Press, 1995.

Keegan, John. *A History of Warfare.* London: Hutchinson, 1993.

Kelly, Justin, and Mike Brennan. *Alien: How Operational Art Devoured Strategy.* Carlisle, PA: US Army War College, Strategic Studies Institute, September 2009.

Kelsay, John. *Arguing the Just War in Islam.* Cambridge, MA: Harvard University Press, 2007.

Kennan, George F. "Moscow Embassy Telegram No. 511, 'The Long Telegram,' February 22, 1946." In *Containment: Documents on American Policy and Strategy, 1945–1950,* edited by Thomas H. Etzold and John Lewis Gaddis, 50–63. New York: Columbia University Press, 1978.

Kennett, Lee. *The First Air War, 1914–1918.* New York: Free Press, 1991.

Kilcullen, David J. *The Accidental Guerilla: Fighting Small Wars in the Midst of a Big One*. London: C. Hurst, 2009.

——. "Countering Global Insurgency." *Journal of Strategic Studies* 28, no. 4 (August 2005): 597–617.

——. *Counterinsurgency*. London: C. Hurst, 2010.

——. "Counter-Insurgency Redux." *Survival* 48, no. 4 (Winter 2006/07): 111–30.

Kinross, Stuart. *Clausewitz and America: Strategic Thought and Practice from Vietnam to Iraq*. Abington, UK: Routledge, 2008.

Kissinger, Henry. *Diplomacy*. New York: Simon and Schuster, 1994.

Kitchen, Martin. *Rommel's Desert War: Waging World War II in North Africa*. Cambridge, UK: Cambridge University Press, 2009.

Knox, MacGregor, and Williamson Murray, eds. *The Dynamics of Military Revolution, 1300–2050*. Cambridge, UK: Cambridge University Press, 2001.

Kolenda, Christopher. *Leadership: The Warrior's Art*. Carlisle, PA: Army War College Foundation Press, 2001.

Kozak, Warren. *LeMay: The Life and Wars of General Curtis LeMay*. Washington, DC: Regency Publishing, 2009.

Krauthammer, Charles. "The Unipolar Moment." *Foreign Affairs* 70, no. 1 (Winter 1990/91): 23–33.

——. "The Unipolar Moment Revisited." *National Interest* 70 (Winter 2002/03): 5–17.

Krepinevich, Andrew F., Jr. *The Army and Vietnam*. Baltimore: Johns Hopkins University Press, 1986.

——. "Cavalry to Computer: The Pattern of Military Revolutions." *National Interest* 37 (Fall 1994): 30–42.

——. *The Military-Technical Revolution: A Preliminary Assessment*. 1992. Reprint, Washington, DC: Center for Strategic and Budgetary Assessments, 2002.

——. *7 Deadly Scenarios: A Military Futurist Explores War in the 21st Century*. New York: Bantam Books, 2009.

Kreps, Sarah E. "Air Power's Role in Asymmetric Operations: The Case of the Second Lebanon War." In *Air Power, Insurgency and the "War on Terror,"* edited by Joel Hayward, 141–55. Cranwell, UK: Royal Air Force College, RAF Centre for Air Power Studies, 2009.

Lake, Daniel R. "The Limits of Coercive Airpower: NATO's 'Victory' in Kosovo Revisited." *International Security* 34, no. 1 (Summer 2009): 83–112.

Lambert, A. P. N. *The Psychology of Air Power*. RUSI Whitehall Paper Series. London: Royal United Services Institute for Defence Studies, 1995.

Lambeth, Benjamin S. *Air Operations in Israel's War against Hezbollah*. Santa Monica, CA: RAND, 2011.

———. *Air Power against Terror: America's Conduct of Operation Enduring Freedom*. Santa Monica, CA: RAND, 2005.

———. *NATO's Air War for Kosovo: A Strategic and Operational Assessment*. Santa Monica, CA: RAND, 2001.

———. *The Transformation of American Air Power*. Ithaca, NY: Cornell University Press, 2000.

Laqueur, Walter W. *Guerrilla Warfare: A Historical and Critical Guide*. New Brunswick, NJ: Transaction, 1998.

Lavalle, A. J. C., ed. *Airpower and the 1972 Spring Invasion*. USAF Southeast Asia Monograph Series, vol. 2, monograph 3. Washington, DC: Government Printing Office, 1976.

Lawrence, T. E. *Seven Pillars of Wisdom: A Triumph*. New York: Anchor Books, 1991.

Levine, Alan J. *The Strategic Bombing of Germany, 1940–1945*. Westport, CT: Praeger Publishers, 1992.

Lewis, Cecil. *Sagittarius Rising*. 1936. Reprint, London: Penguin Books, 1977.

Libicki, Martin C. *Conquest in Cyberspace: National Security and Information Warfare*. Cambridge, UK: Cambridge University Press, 2007.

———. *Cyberdeterrence and Cyberwar*. Santa Monica, CA: RAND, 2009.

Lind, Michael. *Vietnam: The Necessary War: A Reinterpretation of America's Most Disastrous Military Conflict*. New York: Free Press, 1999.

Lock-Pullan, Richard. *US Intervention Policy and Army Innovation: From Vietnam to Iraq*. Abington, UK: Routledge, 2006.

Lonsdale, David J. *Clausewitzian Future: The Nature of War in the Information Age*. Abington, UK: Routledge, 2004.

Loo, Bernard Fook Weng. "Decisive Battle, Victory and the Revolution in Military Affairs." *Journal of Strategic Studies* 32, no. 2 (April 2009): 189–211.

Luck, Christopher J. "The Smuts Report: Interpreting and Misinterpreting the Promise of Airpower." Master's thesis, School of Advanced Air and Space Studies, Air University, Maxwell AFB, AL, April 2007.

Luttwak, Edward N. "Air Power in US Military Strategy." In *The Future of Air Power in the Aftermath of the Gulf War*, edited by Richard H. Shultz Jr. and Robert L. Pfaltzgraft Jr., 17–38. Maxwell AFB, AL: Air University Press, July 1992.

———. "From Vietnam to Desert Fox: Civil-Military Relations in Modern Democracies." *Survival* 41, no. 1 (Spring 1999): 99–112.

———. *Strategy: The Logic of War and Peace*. Rev. ed. Cambridge, MA: Harvard University Press, 2001.

MacIsaac, David. "Voices from the Central Blue: The Air Power Theorists." In Paret, *Makers of Modern Strategy*, 624–47.

MacKenzie, Donald. *Inventing Accuracy: A Historical Sociology of Nuclear Missile Guidance*. Cambridge, MA: MIT Press, 1993.

Mahan, Alfred Thayer. *The Influence of Sea Power upon History, 1660–1783*. 1890. Reprint, London: Methuen, 1965.

Mahnken, Thomas G. *Technology and the American Way of War since 1945*. New York: Columbia University Press, 2008.

———. *Uncovering Ways of War: US Intelligence and Foreign Military Innovation, 1918–1941*. Ithaca, NY: Cornell University Press, 2002.

Mahnken, Thomas G., and Thomas A. Keaney, eds. *War in Iraq: Planning and Execution*. London: Routledge, 2007.

Mansoor, Peter R. *The GI Offensive in Europe: The Triumph of American Infantry Divisions, 1941–1945*. Lawrence: University Press of Kansas, 1999.

Marcella, Gabriel, ed. *Teaching Strategy: Challenge and Response*. Carlisle, PA: US Army War College, Strategic Studies Institute, March 2010.

Mark, Eduard. *Aerial Interdiction in Three Wars*. Washington, DC: Government Printing Office, 1994.

Marshall, Andrew W., J. J. Martin, and Henry S. Rowen, eds. *On Not Confusing Ourselves: Essays on National Security Strategy in Honor of Albert and Roberta Wohlstetter*. Boulder, CO: Westview Press, 1991.

Marx, Karl. "The Eighteenth Brumaire of Louis Napoleon." 1852. In Marx and Friedrich Engels, *Selected Works in Two Volumes*, vol. 1. Moscow: Foreign Languages Publishing House, 1962.

Mason, R. A. "The British Dimension." In Wells, *Air Power*, 7–18.

Mason, Robert. *Chickenhawk*. London: Penguin Books, 1983.

Mason, Tony. "Airpower as a National Instrument: The Arab–Israeli Wars." In *The War in the Air, 1914–1994*, edited by Alan Stephens, 191–219. Maxwell AFB, AL: Air University Press, January 2001.

———. "Operation Allied Force, 1999." In Olsen, *A History of Air Warfare*, 225–52.

Mawdsley, Evan. *Thunder in the East: The Nazi–Soviet War, 1941–1945*. London: Hodder and Arnold, 2005.

McFarland, Stephen L. *America's Pursuit of Precision Bombing, 1910–1945*. Washington, DC: Smithsonian Institution Press, 1995.

McFarland, Stephen L., and Wesley Phillips Newton. *To Command the Sky: The Battle for Air Superiority over Germany, 1942–1944*. Washington, DC: Smithsonian Institution Press, 1991.

McInnes, Colin. *Spectator-Sport War: The West and Contemporary Conflict*. Boulder, CO: Lynne Rienner Publishers, 2002.

McMaster, H. R. *Dereliction of Duty: Lyndon Johnson, Robert McNamara, the Joint Chiefs of Staff, and the Lies That Led to Vietnam*. New York: HarperCollins, 1997.

Mearsheimer, John J. *Conventional Deterrence*. Ithaca, NY: Cornell University Press, 1983.

———. *The Tragedy of Great Power Politics*. New York: W. W. Norton, 2001.

Meilinger, Phillip S. *Airwar: Theory and Practice*. London: Frank Cass, 2003.

———. "Giulio Douhet and the Origins of Airpower Theory." In Meilinger, *Paths of Heaven*, 1–40.

———. "John C. Slessor and the Genesis of Air Interdiction." In Meilinger, *Airwar*, 64–74.

———, ed. *The Paths of Heaven: The Evolution of Airpower Theory*. Maxwell AFB, AL: Air University Press, 1997.

———. "Ten Propositions Regarding Airpower." *Air and Space Power Journal—Chronicles Online Journal*, n.d., http://www.airpower. au.af.mil/airchronicles/cc/meil.html.

———. "Trenchard, Slessor, and Royal Air Force Doctrine before World War II." In Meilinger, *Paths of Heaven*, 41–78.

Mets, David R. *The Air Campaign: John Warden and the Classical Airpower Theorists*. Maxwell AFB, AL: Air University Press, December 1998.

Metz, Steven. *Iraq and the Evolution of American Strategy*. Washington, DC: Potomac Books, 2008.

Middlebrook, Martin, and Chris Everitt. *The Bomber Command War Diaries: An Operational Reference Book, 1939–1945*. London: Viking, 1985.

Mierzejewski, Alfred C. *The Collapse of the German War Economy, 1944–1945: Allied Air Power and the German National Railway*. Chapel Hill: University of North Carolina Press, 1988.

Miller, Donald L. *Eighth Air Force: The American Bomber Crews in Britain*. London: Aurum Press, 2008.

Miller, Edward S. *War Plan Orange: The US Strategy to Defeat Japan, 1897–1945*. Annapolis, MD: Naval Institute Press, 1991.

Millett, Allan R. "Assault from the Sea: The Development of Amphibious Warfare between the Wars—The American, British, and Japanese Experiences." In Murray and Millett, *Military Innovation in the Interwar Period*, 50–95.

Millett, Allan R., and Williamson Murray, eds. *Military Effectiveness*. Vol. 3, *The Interwar Period*. Boston: Allen and Unwin, 1988.

Mitchell, William. *Winged Defense: The Development and Possibilities of Modern Air Power—Economic and Military*. 1925. Reprint, New York: Dover Publications, 1988.

Momyer, William. *Air Power in Three Wars*. Washington, DC: Government Printing Office, 1978.

Morgan, Patrick. *Deterrence: A Conceptual Enquiry*. Beverly Hills, CA: Sage Publications, 1977.

Morrow, John H., Jr. *The Great War in the Air: Military Aviation from 1909 to 1921*. Washington, DC: Smithsonian Institution Press, 1993.

Moyar, Mark. *Triumph Forsaken: The Vietnam War, 1954–1965*. Cambridge, UK: Cambridge University Press, 2006.

Muller, Richard. "Close Air Support." In Murray and Millett, *Military Innovation in the Interwar Period*.

———. *The German Air War in Russia*. Baltimore: Nautical and Aviation Publishing Company of America, 1992.

Murray, Williamson. *German Military Effectiveness*. Baltimore: Nautical and Aviation Publishing Company of America, 1992.

———. *Luftwaffe*. Baltimore: Nautical and Aviation Publishing Company of America, 1985.

———. "May 1940: Contingency and Fragility of the German RMA." In Knox and Murray, *Dynamics of Military Revolution*, 154–74.

———. "Strategic Bombing: The British, American, and German Experiences." In Murray and Millett, *Military Innovation in the Interwar Period*, 96–143.

———. "Thinking about Revolutions in Military Affairs." *Joint Force Quarterly* 16 (Summer 1997): 69–76.

———. *War in the Air War, 1914–45*. London: Cassell, 1999.

Murray, Williamson, and Allan R. Millett, eds. *Calculations: Net Assessment and the Coming of World War II*. New York: Free Press, 1992.

———. *Military Innovation in the Interwar Period*. Cambridge, UK: Cambridge University Press, 1996.

———. *A War to Be Won: Fighting the Second World War*. Cambridge, MA: Belknap Press of Harvard University Press, 2000.

Murray, Williamson, and Mark Grimsley. "Introduction: On Strategy." In *The Making of Strategy: Rulers, States, and War*, edited by Murray, MacGregor Knox, and Alvin Bernstein, 1–23. Cambridge, UK: Cambridge University Press, 1994.

Murray, Williamson, and Richard Hart Sinnreich, eds. *The Past as Prologue: The Importance of History to the Military Profession*. Cambridge, UK: Cambridge University Press, 2006.

Murray, Williamson, and Robert H. Scales Jr. *The Iraq War: A Military History*. Cambridge, MA: Belknap Press of Harvard University Press, 2003.

Nagl, John A. *Learning to Eat Soup with a Knife: Counterinsurgency Lessons from Malaya and Vietnam*. Chicago: University of Chicago Press, 2005.

Nagl, John A., and Brian M. Burton. "Thinking Globally and Acting Locally: Counterinsurgency Lessons from Modern Wars—A Reply to Jones and Smith." *Journal of Strategic Studies* 33, no. 1 (February 2010): 123–38.

Nalty, Bernard C. *The War against Trucks: Aerial Interdiction in Southern Laos, 1968–1972*. Washington, DC: Government Printing Office, 2005.

Newton, Paul, Paul Colley, and Andrew Sharpe. "Reclaiming the Art of British Strategic Thinking." *RUSI Journal* 155, no. 1 (February/March 2010): 44–50.

Nikiforidis, Charalampos. "A Comparative Analysis of the Prospects for Air Power and Air Forces, 1907–2010." Master's thesis, University of Reading (UK), 2010.

Norris, R. S., and H. M. Kristensen. "Global Nuclear Stockpiles, 1945–2010." *Bulletin of the Atomic Scientists* 66 (2010): 77–83.

Nye, Joseph S., Jr. *The Paradox of American Power: Why the World's Only Superpower Can't Go It Alone.* Oxford: Oxford University Press, 2002.

Oberg, Jim. *Space Power Theory.* Washington, DC: Government Printing Office, 1999.

Odom, William E. *The Collapse of the Soviet Military.* New Haven, CT: Yale University Press, 1998.

Olsen, John Andreas, ed. *Global Air Power.* Washington, DC: Potomac Books, 2011.

———. *A History of Air Warfare.* Washington, DC: Potomac Books, 2010.

———. *John Warden and the Renaissance of American Air Power.* Washington, DC: Potomac Books, 2007.

———. "Operation Desert Storm, 1991." In Olsen, *A History of Air Warfare,* 177–200.

———. *Strategic Air Power in Desert Storm.* London: Frank Cass, 2003.

Omissi, David. *The Royal Air Force, Air Power and Colonial Control, 1919–1939.* Manchester, UK: Manchester University Press, 1990.

Orange, Vincent. *Dowding of Fighter Command: Victor of the Battle of Britain.* London: Grub Street, 2008.

———. "Getting Together." In *Airpower and Ground Armies: Essays on the Evolution of Anglo-American Air Doctrine, 1940–1943,* edited by Daniel Mortensen, 1–29. Maxwell AFB, AL: Air University Press, 1998.

———. *Slessor: Bomber Champion: The Life of Marshal of the Royal Air Force Sir John Slessor, GCB, DSO, MC.* London: Grub Street, 2006.

Osgood, Robert E. *Limited War: The Challenge to American Strategy.* Chicago: University of Chicago Press, 1957.

———. *Limited War Revisited.* Boulder, CO: Westview Press, 1979.

Osiander, Andreas. "Sovereignty, International Relations, and the Westphalian Myth." *International Organization* 55, no. 2 (2001): 251–87.

Osinga, Frans P. B. "On Boyd, bin Laden, and Fourth-Generation Warfare as String Theory." In *On New Wars,* edited by John Andreas Olsen, 168–97. Oslo: Norwegian Institute for Defence Studies, April 2007.

———. *Science, Strategy and War: The Strategic Theory of John Boyd.* Abington: Routledge, 2007.

Overy, Richard J. "Air Power and the Origins of Deterrence Theory before 1939." In *Strategic Studies: A Reader*, edited by Thomas G. Mahnken and Joseph A. Maiolo, 135–55. Abington, UK: Routledge, 2008.

———. "Air Power in the Second World War: Historical Themes and Theories." In Boog, *Conduct of the Air War in the Second World War*, 7–28.

———. *The Air War, 1939–1945*. New York: Stein and Day, 1985.

———. "The Air War in Europe, 1939–1945." In Olsen, *A History of Air Warfare*, 27–52.

———. *The Battle of Britain: Myth and Reality*. London: Penguin Books, 2010.

———. *The Morbid Age: Britain and the Crisis of Civilization*. London: Penguin Books, 2010.

———. *Russia's War*. London: Allen Lane, 1997.

———. *Why the Allies Won*. London: Jonathan Cape, 1995.

———. "World War II: The Bombing of Germany." In *The War in the Air, 1914–1994*, edited by Alan Stephens, 107–41. Maxwell AFB, AL: Air University Press, January 2001.

Owen, Robert C. *Deliberate Force: A Case Study in Effective Air Campaigning*. Maxwell AFB, AL: Air University Press, January 2000.

———. "Operation Deliberate Force, 1995." In Olsen, *A History of Air Warfare*, 201–24.

Owens, William A. *Lifting the Fog of War*. New York: Farrow, Straus and Giroux, 2000.

Palmer, Scott W. "Peasants into Pilots: Soviet Air-Mindedness as an Ideology of Dominance." *Technology and Culture* 41, no. 1 (January 2000): 1–26.

Pape, Robert A. *Bombing to Win: Air Power and Coercion*. Ithaca, NY: Cornell University Press, 1996.

———. "The True Worth of Air Power." *Foreign Affairs* 83, no. 2 (March/April 2004): 116–30.

Paret, Peter. *Makers of Modern Strategy: From Machiavelli to the Nuclear Age*. Princeton, NJ: Princeton University Press, 1996.

Paris, Michael. *Winged Warfare: The Literature and Theory of Aerial Warfare in Britain, 1859–1917*. Manchester, UK: Manchester University Press, 1992.

Park, W. Hays. "'Precision' and 'Area' Bombing: Who Did Which, and When?" *Journal of Strategic Studies* 18, no. 1, special issue (March 1995): 145–74.

Parry, J. H. *The Discovery of the Sea*. Berkeley: University of California Press, 1981.

Parton, Neville. "Air Power's Illusion? Israel's 2006 Campaign in the Lebanon." *British Army Review* 143 (Autumn 2007): 41–47.

Peterson, A. H., G. C. Reinhardt, and E. E. Conger. *Symposium on the Role of Airpower in Counterinsurgency and Unconventional Warfare: A Brief Summary of Viewpoints*. Santa Monica, CA: RAND, March 1964.

Philips, Catherine. "Countdown to Disarmament." *Times* (London), 4 May 2010.

Pierce, Terry C. *Warfighting and Disruptive Technologies*. London: Frank Cass, 2004.

Podvig, Pavel, ed. *Russian Strategic Nuclear Forces*. Cambridge, MA: MIT Press, 2004.

Porter, Patrick. *Military Orientalism: Eastern War through Western Eyes*. London: C. Hurst, 2009.

Posen, Barry R. "Command of the Commons: The Military Foundation of US Hegemony." *International Security* 28, no. 1 (Summer 2003): 5–46.

Prados, John. *Vietnam: The History of an Unwinnable War, 1945–1975*. Lawrence: University Press of Kansas, 2009.

Price, Alfred. *The Last Year of the Luftwaffe, May 1944 to May 1945*. London: Arms and Armour Press, 1993.

Probert, Henry. *Bomber Harris, His Life and Times: The Biography of Marshal of the Royal Air Force Sir Arthur Harris, the Wartime Chief of Bomber Command*. London: Greenhill Books, 2001.

Quade, E. S. *Analysis for Military Decisions: The RAND Lectures on Systems Analysis*. Chicago: Rand McNally, 1964.

———. "The Selection and Use of Strategic Air Bases: A Case History." In *Analysis for Military Decisions*, 24–63.

Read, Derek. "Airpower in COIN: Can Airpower Make a Significant Contribution to Counter-Insurgency?" *Defence Studies* 10, nos. 1–2 (March–June 2010): 126–51.

Record, Jeffrey. *The Wrong War: Why We Lost in Vietnam*. Annapolis, MD: Naval Institute Press, 1998.

Reilly, Robert R. *The Closing of the Muslim Mind: How Intellectual Suicide Created the Modern Islamist Crisis*. Wilmington, DE: ISI Books, 2010.

Reynolds, Clark G. *The Fast Carriers: The Forging of an Air Navy*. New York: Robert E. Krieger Publishing Company, 1978.

Ricks, Thomas E. *Fiasco: The American Military Adventure in Iraq.* New York: Penguin Press, 2006.

———. *The Gamble: General Petraeus and the Untold Story of the American Surge in Iraq.* London: Allen Lane, 2009.

Rip, Michael Russell, and James M. Hasik. *The Precision Revolution: GPS and the Future of Aerial Warfare.* Annapolis, MD: Naval Institute Press, 2002.

Ritchie, Sebastian. "Air Power Victorious? Britain and NATO Strategy during the Kosovo Conflict." In *Air Power History: Turning Points from Kitty Hawk to Kosovo*, edited by Sebastian Cox and Peter Gray, 318–29. London: Frank Cass, 2002.

Roberts, Adam. "NATO's 'Humanitarian War' over Kosovo." *Survival* 41, no. 3 (Autumn 1999): 102–23.

Robinson, Derek. *Invasion, 1940: The Truth about the Battle of Britain and What Stopped Hitler.* London: Robinson, 2006.

Roman, Peter J. "Strategic Bombers over the Missile Horizon, 1957–1963." *Journal of Strategic Studies* 18, no. 1 (March 1995): 198–236.

Rosen, Stephen P. "Vietnam and the American Theory of Limited War." *International Security* 7, no. 2 (Autumn 1982): 83–113.

Rosenberg, David Alan. "The Origins of Overkill: Nuclear Weapons and American Strategy, 1945–1960." *International Security* 7, no. 4 (Spring 1983): 3–71.

———. "A Smoking Radiating Ruin at the End of Two Hours: Documents of American Plans for Nuclear War with the Soviet Union, 1954–1955." *International Security* 6, no. 3 (Winter 1981/82): 3–38.

Ross, Steven T. *American War Plans, 1945–1950.* London: Frank Cass, 1996.

Royal Air Force. *British Air and Space Power Doctrine.* AP3000. 4th ed. London: Air Staff, Ministry of Defence, 2009.

Schaffer, Ronald. *Wings of Judgment: American Bombing in World War II.* Oxford: Oxford University Press, 1985.

Schelling, Thomas C. *Arms and Influence.* New Haven, CT: Yale University Press, 1966.

Schelling, Thomas C., and Morton H. Halperin. *Strategy and Arms Control.* New York: Twentieth Century Fund, 1961.

Schmidtchen, David. *The Rise of the Strategic Private: Technology, Control and Change in a Network Enabled Military.* Duntroon, Australia: Land Warfare Studies Centre, 2006.

Schreiber, Gerhard, Bernd Stegemann, and Detlef Vogel. *Germany and the Second World War*: vol. 3, *The Mediterranean, South-east Europe, and North Africa, 1939–1941*. Oxford: Clarendon Press, 1995.

Schwartz, Stephen I., ed. *Atomic Audit: The Costs and Consequences of US Nuclear Weapons since 1940*. Washington, DC: Brookings Institution Press, 1998.

Sherry, Michael S. *The Rise of American Air Power: The Creation of Armageddon*. New Haven, CT: Yale University Press, 1987.

Shultz, Richard H., Jr., and Robert L. Pfaltzgraff Jr., eds. *The Future of Air Power in the Aftermath of the Gulf War*. Maxwell AFB, AL: Air University Press, July 1992.

Shy, John. "Jomini." In Paret, *Makers of Modern Strategy*, 143–85.

Siboni, Gabriel. "The Military Campaign in Lebanon." In *The Second Lebanon War: Strategic Perspectives*, edited by Shlomo Brom and Meir Elvan, 61–76. Tel Aviv: Institute for National Security Studies, 2007.

———. "War and Victory." *Military and Strategic Affairs* 1, no. 3 (December 2009): 39–49.

Slessor, John C. *Air Power and Armies*. Oxford: Oxford University Press, 1936.

Smith, John T. *The Linebacker Raids: The Bombing of North Vietnam, 1972*. London: Arms and Armour Press, 1998.

———. *Rolling Thunder: The American Strategic Bombing Campaign against North Vietnam, 1964–68*. Walton on Thames, UK: Air Research Publications, 1994.

Smith, Malcolm. *British Air Strategy between the Wars*. Oxford: Clarendon Press, 1984.

Smith, Michael V. "Ten Propositions Regarding Spacepower." Master's thesis, School of Advanced Airpower Studies, Air University, Maxwell AFB, AL, June 2001.

Smith, Rupert. *The Utility of Force: The Art of War in the Modern World*. London: Allen Lane, 2005.

Smuts, Jan Christian. " 'Magna Carta' of British Air Power." In Emme, *Impact of Air Power*, 33–37.

Sondhaus, Lawrence. *Strategic Culture and Ways of War*. Abington: Routledge, 2006.

Sookhdeo, Patrick. *Global Jihad: The Future in the Face of Militant Islam*. McLean, VA: Isaac Publishing, 2007.

Sorley, Lewis. *A Better War: The Unexamined Victories and Final Tragedy of America's Last Years in Vietnam*. New York: Harcourt Brace, 1999.

Spector, Ronald H. *Eagle against the Sun: The American War with Japan*. New York: Free Press, 1985.

Stanton, Shelby. *The 1st Cav in Vietnam: Anatomy of a Division*. Novato, CA: Presidio Press, 1999.

Stephens, Alan. "The Air War in Korea, 1950–1953." In Olsen, *A History of Air Warfare*, 85–106.

Stewart, James T. *Airpower: The Decisive Force in Korea*. Princeton, NJ: D. Van Nostrand, 1957.

Strassler, Robert B., ed. *The Landmark Thucydides: A Comprehensive Guide to "The Peloponnesian War."* Revised translation of Richard Crawley. New York: Free Press, 1996.

Stuermer, Michael. *Putin and the Rise of Russia*. London: Phoenix Paperback, 2009.

Sun Tzu, *The Art of War*. Translated by Samuel B. Griffith. Oxford: Clarendon Press, 1963.

Thompson, James Clay. *Rolling Thunder: Understanding Policy and Program Failure*. Chapel Hill: University of North Carolina Press, 1980.

Thompson, Wayne. "Operations over North Vietnam, 1965–1973." In Olsen, *A History of Air Warfare*, 107–26.

———. *To Hanoi and Back: The US Air Force and North Vietnam, 1966–1973*. Washington, DC: Smithsonian Institution Press, 2000.

Thucydides. *The History of the Peloponnesian War*. London: Penguin Books, 1954, 1972.

Till, Geoffrey. "Adopting the Aircraft Carrier: The British, American, and Japanese Case Studies." In Murray and Millett, *Military Innovation in the Interwar Period*, 191–226.

Tillman, Barrett. *LeMay*. New York: Palgrave Macmillan, 2007.

———. *Whirlwind: The Air War against Japan, 1942–1945*. New York: Simon and Schuster, 2010.

Tomes, Robert R. *US Defense Strategy from Vietnam to Operation Iraqi Freedom: Military Innovation and the New American Way of War, 1973–2003*. Abington, UK: Routledge, 2007.

Tooze, Adam. *The Wages of Destruction: The Making and Breaking of the Nazi Economy*. London: Allen Lane, 2006.

Towle, Philip Anthony. *Pilots and Rebels: The Use of Aircraft in Unconventional Warfare, 1918–1988*. London: Brassey's UK, 1989.

Trenchard, Hugh M. "Air Power and National Security." In Emme, *Impact of Air Power.*

Underwood, Jeffery S. *The Wings of Democracy: The Influence of Air Power on the Roosevelt Administration, 1933–1941.* College Station: Texas A&M University Press, 1991.

US Air Force. Air Force Doctrine Document 1. *Air Force Basic Doctrine,* 17 November 2003.

———. Air Force Manual 1-1. *Basic Aerospace Doctrine of the United States Air Force,* 2 vols., March 1992.

US Army and US Marine Corps. Field Manual 3-24 and Marine Corps Warfighting Publication 3-33.5. *Counterinsurgency.* Chicago: University of Chicago Press, 2007.

US House Armed Services Committee, Subcommittee on Oversight and Investigations. *Another Crossroads? Professional Military Education Two Decades after the Goldwater-Nichols Act and the Skelton Panel,* Report, Committee Print 111-4, April 2010.

US Strategic Bombing Survey (USSB). *Summary Reports (European War) (Pacific War)* [30 September 1945]. Maxwell AFB, AL: Air University, October 1987.

Venkus, Robert E. *Raid on Qaddafi.* New York: St. Martin's Press, 1992.

Vick, Alan J., et al. *Air Power in the New Counterinsurgency Era: The Strategic Importance of USAF Advisory and Assistance Missions.* Santa Monica, CA: RAND, 2006.

Waller, Douglas. *A Question of Loyalty.* New York: Harper Perennial, 2004.

Walton, C. Dale. *The Myth of Inevitable US Defeat in Vietnam.* London: Frank Cass, 2002.

Warden, John. *The Air Campaign: Planning for Combat.* Washington, DC: Pergamon-Brassey's, 1989.

———. "Employing Air Power in the Twenty-first Century." In Shultz and Pfaltzgraff, *Future of Air Power in the Aftermath of the Gulf War,* 57–82.

———. "The Enemy as a System." *Airpower Journal* 9, no. 1 (Spring 1995): 40–45.

Watts, Barry D. *Clausewitzian Friction and Future War.* McNair Paper 68. Rev. ed. Washington, DC: Institute for National Strategic Studies, National Defense University, 2004.

———. *The Foundations of US Air Doctrine: The Problem of Friction in War.* Maxwell AFB, AL: Air University Press, December 1984.

Webster, Charles, and Noble Frankland. *History of the Second World War: The Strategic Air Offensive against Germany, 1939–1945.* 4 vols. London: Her Majesty's Stationery Office, 1961.

Weigert, Hans W. *Generals and Geographers.* New York: Oxford University Press, 1942.

Wells, Mark K., ed. *Air Power: Promise and Reality.* Chicago: Imprint Publications, 2000.

Werrell, Kenneth P. *Blankets of Fire: US Bombers over Japan during World War II.* Washington, DC: Smithsonian Institution Press, 1996.

West, Bing, and Ray L. Smith. *The March Up: Taking Baghdad with the 1st Marine Division.* New York: Bantam Books, 2003.

Whiting, Kenneth R. "Soviet Air Power in World War II." In Wells, *Air Power,* 85–110.

Wiest, Andrew, ed. *Rolling Thunder in a Gentle Land: The Vietnam War Revisited.* Oxford: Osprey Publishing, 2006.

Winton, Harold R. "An Ambivalent Partnership: US Army and Air Force Perspectives on Air-Ground Operations." In Meilinger, *Paths of Heaven,* 399–441.

———. "An Imperfect Jewel: Military Theory and the Military Profession." Paper presented at the Annual Conference of the Society of Military History, Bethesda, MD, 22 May 2004.

Winton, Harold R., and David R. Mets, eds. *The Challenge of Change: Military Institutions and New Realities, 1918–1941.* Lincoln: University of Nebraska Press, 2000.

Withington, Thomas. "Night of the Flying Hooligans: Soviet Army Aviation and Air Force Operations during the War in Afghanistan, 1979–1989." In *Air Power, Insurgency and the War on Terror,* edited by Joel Hayward, 125–40. Cranwell, UK: RAF College, Centre for Air Power Studies, 2009.

Wohlstetter, A. J., et al. *Protecting U.S. Power to Strike Back in the 1950s and 1960s.* Santa Monica, CA: RAND, April 1956.

———. *Selection and Use of Strategic Air Bases.* Santa Monica, CA: RAND, April 1954.

Woodruff, Mark W. *Unheralded Victory: Who Won the Vietnam War?* London: HarperCollins Publishers, 1999.

Worden, Roy Michael. "The Rise of the Fighter Generals: The Vietnam Era and the Problem of Air Force Leadership (1945–1982)." PhD dissertation, Duke University, 1993.

Wylie, J. C. *Military Strategy: A General Theory of Power Control*. Annapolis, MD: Naval Institute Press, 1989.

Yarger, Harry R. *Strategy and the National Security Professional: Strategic Thinking in the 21st Century*. Westport, CT: Praeger Security International, 2009.

Yousaf, Mohammad, and Mark Adkin. *Afghanistan—The Bear Trap: The Defeat of a Superpower*. Barnsley, UK: Leo Cooper, 2001.

Zabecki, David T. *Steel Wind: Colonel Georg Bruchmüller and the Birth of Modern Artillery*. Westport, CT: Praeger Publishers, 1994.

Zaloga, Steven J. *The Kremlin's Nuclear Sword: The Rise and Fall of Russia's Strategic Nuclear Force, 1945–2000*. Washington, DC: Smithsonian Institution Press, 2002.

Zimmerman, David. *Britain's Shield: Radar and the Defeat of the Luftwaffe*. Stroud: Sutton Publishing, 2001.

Index

Airpower for Strategic Effect

Air University Press Team

Chief Editor
Jerry L. Gantt

Copy Editors
Sherry C. Terrell
Andrew Thayer

*Cover Art, Book Design,
and Illustrations*
Daniel Armstrong

*Composition and
Prepress Production*
Vivian D. O'Neal

Print Preparation and Distribution
Diane Clark